p ᵛ Sputnik
  1
  3 G.ᵒJ r's
  7 Torrance
 11 Guilford
12/13 Conclusions from literature review
 17 infreq. R's later
 19 Dentler & Mackler
 26 WK sample
29ff Tests ᵒ procedure
47f Tables 7,8,9 — intercorrels of IQ, C etc
 55 T. 16
 62 Nice quote

Modes
of Thinking
in Young Children

Modes
of Thinking
in Young Children

A Study of the
Creativity-Intelligence
Distinction

MICHAEL A. WALLACH and NATHAN KOGAN

Duke
University

Educational
Testing Service

HOLT, RINEHART AND WINSTON, INC.
New York · Chicago · San Francisco · Toronto · London

➥ Preface

It is a strange commentary on professional specialization that academic psychology and educational research have gone their separate ways for many decades. Although persons located within each of these professional domains have long been interested in questions of learning and thinking in children, it is only recently that serious attempts have been made to set up communication across the border between these domains. Indeed, both sides of the border have been strongly fortified toward keeping out intruders from the foreign discipline, and it is no exaggeration to say that the major attitude prevailing in each camp has been one of suspicion toward the other. To the academic psychologists, those engaged in educational research have appeared to be interested only in applied goals concerning pupil selection or concerning relative efficacy of teaching methods, with little attention to the general theoretical issue of how children come to obtain and organize knowledge. To the educational psychologists, those working within an academic environment have seemed to be little concerned with the real-life classroom setting and overly concerned with performance in what might well be artificially narrow situations of dubious generality.

The cleavage between these two professional groups should prove a ripe area for study by a sociologist of knowledge, in that, viewed from a substantive perspective, the separation is patently irrational. Educators have to be concerned with psychological processes as such if they ever expect to develop appropriate bases for choosing applied goals; academic psychologists have to be concerned with the learning and teaching situation as it exists in the classroom if they ever expect their theorizing about cognition to possess a meaningful range of applicability. The extent to which historical rather than substantive considerations have nourished the separation provides alarming documentation for the influence of historical fashions upon scientific behavior. That the situation can be otherwise is indicated by, for example, the professional arrangements in the Soviet Union, where the field of "pedagogical psychology" tends to include all investigations of children's learning, problem-solving, and thinking, and where the typical laboratory is the classroom.

It was partly in response to Sputnik, of course, that the relationships between the two fields of academic psychology and education began to change in this country. Ironically, therefore, it required the impetus of another historical consideration to goad the two fields toward the establishment of diplomatic relations. Partly also, however, intrinsic factors within psychology have in recent years been exerting pressures toward increased direct contact with the educational scene. One of these factors is the striking series of researches undertaken by Piaget and his collaborators in Geneva, where the study of children's thinking dealt with matters whose implications for educational practice were so clear that they could not be ignored. For example, it became evident that, before a certain age, the young child did not possess the concept that a number of objects remains invariant despite changes in their perceived arrangements. It was obvious that attempts to teach children in school about number operations before they possessed an appropriate conceptualization of the nature of number would necessarily come to grief and possibly even exert a deleterious effect upon the child's later attitude toward and understanding of mathematics. Another intrinsic factor has been the liberalization that has taken place within the psychology of learning. From an era of overly specific theorizing based largely upon experiments with rats, learning theorists have moved to a growing concern with the performance of humans and especially of children in all phases of the acquisition, transformation, retention, and use of knowledge. Yet a third intrinsic factor has been the greatly increased concern in academic psychology with social and motivational processes. Inevitably, this concern has forced psychologists to take a closer look at the rich complexity of human activity in its real-life setting, and to seek to capture more aspects of this complexity than hitherto in their attempts at systematic study.

Thus, various factors—extrinsic and intrinsic—have acted in recent years to bring academic psychology and the educational setting closer together. From this matrix of factors has arisen the present-day concern with creativity. It is not without some ambivalence that one approaches this topic, for the almost magical quality of the term's current popularity makes difficult the maintenance of perspective and objectivity. Indeed, our feeling upon studying much of the literature dealing with creativity was that the claims tended to exceed the achievements. The first chapter of this book will address itself to this point in some detail. The enthusiasm with which the cry for more creativity was taken up across the land seemed, in our estimation, to have the unfortunate effect of blurring certain critical issues, such as the analysis of the social psychological context within which evaluation of creative potential was to take place. There seemed to occur a too ready assimilation of creativity assessment to the general framework of intelligence testing, without sufficient consideration of whether the context of critical self-evaluation present in the case of traditional intelligence assessment would do justice to attempts to fathom the psychological nature of creativity. Here was a case where the educational framework of aptitude and achievement testing seemed to have induced a blind spot, which it was possible to understand by approaching the area from the standpoint of academic psychology in general and of social psychology in particular. We shall have more to say about this, too, in the chapter that follows, as well as in later chapters.

The present book took form as it became clear to us that the structure of our inquiry into modes of thinking in children did not lend itself to disjointed presentation as a series of research papers scattered among the professional journals. The work proceeded as a kind of bootstraps operation, wherein the outcome of the early phases determined the nature of the later phases. It is not inappropriate to compare the present research endeavor to the unraveling of a mystery story. We were just as eager as the reader of a detective story to discover clues as we proceeded and a final interpretative solution that would be maximally congruent with the evidence. Hopefully, however, the present enterprise differs from a mystery in being more real than fictive in its content. The basic objective was to characterize groups of children in terms of thinking styles that seemed to possess a sufficient degree of pervasiveness in the children's cognitive behavior, and then to study the correlates of these modes of thinking in other significant aspects of the children's lives: their general observable behavior in school and play settings, their ways of categorizing and conceptualizing the world, their esthetic sensitivities, and their affective and motivational dispositions. While the investigation was guided by general hypotheses, we could not know at the beginning exactly where we would arrive at the end. The present terminus is in fact not a stopping-point but a way-station in the study of thinking as it occurs in the midst of the social and affective life of the child. If the present volume stimulates others to join us in seeking answers to the various further questions that it raises, then our hopes will be fulfilled.

In some respects, the form of the work that we carried out can be traced to Henry A. Murray, beginning in the 1930s at the Harvard Psychological Clinic, where intensive studies of a sample of individuals over a period of time were undertaken with a diversity of techniques. Our effort has been directed at preserving something of the depth afforded by this approach, while at the same time enlarging the sample under study and gaining thereby the possibility of achieving greater refinement in assessment instruments. We were exposed to Murray's approach in our graduate student days at Harvard, where we also encountered and took inspiration from Jerome S. Bruner's efforts to bring the psychological study of cognitive processes into greater contact with education.

The research reported herein was supported in part through the Cooperative Research Program of the Office of Education, United States Department of Health, Education, and Welfare. It is a pleasure to acknowledge our indebtedness for this support, and our thanks in particular to Francis A. J. Ianni and Alice Y. Scates of the Office of Education for their encouragement. Paula M. Cohen and Eleanor F. Howland served as research assistants in the collection and analysis of data for the present study. Their high competence and devotion contributed very significantly to the undertaking, and they deserve a special note of thanks. Computational work was carried out at the Duke University Computing Laboratory, which is supported in part by a grant from the National Science Foundation. For their aid at the Computing Laboratory we are grateful to Nancy Bumann, Ruth Dowling, Thomas M. Gallie, Ames Schroeder, and Gretchen Snowden. Theodore R. Sarbin, Harold Schlosberg, and Renato Tagiuri provided us with stimulus materials which they had developed, and we wish to thank them for this aid. We are grateful to Dr. Tagiuri and to the Springer Publishing Company, Inc., for permission to reproduce the materials that appear in Figure 3. They derive from page 178 of "Movement as a cue in person perception," by Renato Tagiuri, in *Perspectives in personality research,* edited by H. P. David and J. C. Brengelmann; New York: Springer, 1960. We are grateful to Dr. Sarbin for permission to reproduce the materials that appear in Figure 4. The administrative personnel and the teachers at the schools where the research was carried out were extremely helpful in facilitating the study, and we are indebted for their aid. Thanks are particularly due Frank W. Etter, Walter P. Gleason, Chester Towne, Richard Wallace, and Alan M. White. For secretarial assistance in various stages of the work we are grateful to Ellen Anderson, Gerri Asbury, Judy Edquist, Jeanette Jeffords, Amby Peach, Janice Schramm, and particularly to Mary Ward, who typed the final manuscript with consummate care.

There are many individuals with whom one or another aspect of the present work was discussed, and we are grateful for the aid and criticism which they provided. Among those whom we wish to thank are Donald K. Adams, Irving E. Alexander, John C. Altrocchi, C. Alan Boneau, Lloyd J. Borstelmann, Jack W. Brehm, Roger B. Burt, Robert C. Carson, Norman Frederiksen, Harold Gulliksen, Edward E. Jones, Irwin Kremen, Martin Lakin, Salvatore R. Maddi, Samuel Messick, Harold Schiffman, Rodney Skager, and Karl Zener. Particular thanks are due Peter M. Bentler and William C. Ward, who provided extensive and illuminating discussion of various aspects of the manuscript. For their understanding and forbearance, our wives, Lise and Edith, also deserve our gratitude.

M. A. W.
Durham, North Carolina

N. K.
Princeton, New Jersey

August 1965

➤➤➤ *Contents*

Preface v

1. CREATIVITY AND INTELLIGENCE AS MODES OF THINKING *1*

2. CREATIVITY AND INTELLIGENCE: THE EVIDENCE OF THE PRESENT STUDY *25*

3. BEHAVIOR IN THE SCHOOL ENVIRONMENT *66*

4. CATEGORIZING AND CONCEPTUALIZING *95*

5. SENSITIVITY TO PHYSIOGNOMIC PROPERTIES *143*

6. THE ROLE OF ANXIETY AND DEFENSIVENESS *189*

7. STUDIES OF INDIVIDUAL CHILDREN *253*

8. CONCLUSIONS *286*

   Appendix: Sequence of Work with Each Class 333

   References 335

   Index of Names 349

   Index of Subjects 353

1 ≪≪←

Creativity and Intelligence as Modes of Thinking

For some time, interest has been growing concerning the possible limitations of the concept of intelligence in understanding individual differences in cognitive functioning. The term "creativity," it has been suggested, represents an aspect of thinking which is as important to assess in its own right as is intelligence. One can point, indeed, to an increasing popularity of "creativity" as a desired goal espoused by the culture at large, in circles that extend from educational to business institutions. Yet the empirical warrant for distinguishing a new concept that would be appropriately labeled "creativity" from the concept of general intelligence, turns out, upon inspection of the evidence, to be far from clear.

The aim of the research reported in this book is twofold. First, we wished to determine whether solid evidence could be found that would support the validity of a distinction between intelligence and creativity as modes of cognitive activity. Second, if a distinction between these concepts could be given acceptable empirical support, we wished to investigate the possible psychological correlates of individual differences in creativity and intelligence when variations along these two dimensions were considered jointly. The purpose of this first chapter will be to demonstrate that previous research on the present topic forces one to leave open the question of whether intelligence and creativity can be more accurately described as sharing a common psychological domain or as referring to relatively distinct psychological functions. In the second chapter we present the research with children that we conducted on this issue. Then, in subsequent chapters, we turn to our investigations of psychological correlates, presenting evidence drawn from directly observed behavior in school and play settings, conceptual processes, sensitivity to the physiognomic properties of visual stimuli, personality as studied through self description and fantasy, and clinical case reports.

We do not, in this chapter, plan to review the literature on creativity. This task already has been carried out in such sources as Stein and Heinze (1960), Getzels and Jackson (1962), Barron (1963), Taylor and Barron (1963), Golann (1963), and Taylor (1964). Rather, we shall direct our attention to a detailed consideration of those research efforts that bear most directly upon the elucidation of relationships between the concepts of intelligence and creativity. Two major questions emerge in this connection: the question of dimensionality within the creativity domain, and the question of task context. These are operational issues—issues concerning what is measured and in what manner. They are inextricably bound up with the problem of how to conceive of creativity as a psychological ability.

THE QUESTION OF DIMENSIONALITY WITHIN THE CREATIVITY DOMAIN

Is there a unified dimension of individual differences that discriminates cognitive behavior appropriately labeled as more or less creative? To ask this question is to inquire whether something akin to Spearman's G exists within the area of creativity. The concept of G refers to the fact that traditional indices of intelligence, whether verbal or quantitative in nature, intercorrelate to a substantial extent. G refers to that which they have in common, and constitutes in fact the referent of the term "intelligence" when it is used in the sense of a person's possessing a greater or lesser degree of general intelligence, or a higher or lower intelligence quotient. It is recognized by all, of course, that G does not constitute the entire story in the intelligence domain. Thus, evidence for specific abilities exists also (Thurstone, 1938). But the fact that different intellectual abilities are appreciably intercorrelated does suggest the existence of some common domain of individual variation, and it is the fact of such intercorrelation that justifies assigning a single label, such as "intelligence," to this domain.

Does anything like this concept of G exist in the area of creativity? To talk about "creativity *and* intelligence," as if the two terms refer to concepts at the same level of abstraction, is to assert just this. It is, furthermore, to assert that these two concepts define dimensions of individual differences that vary independently of each other, or that are at most only minimally related to each other. And, indeed, these very assertions have characterized most of the work that has been conducted on the topic of creativity. Yet the evidence for such assertions does not appear, on examination, to be convincing. Let us consider examples of the types of findings that have been reported.

Perhaps the most widely publicized recent research in this area is the volume *Creativity and Intelligence* by Getzels and Jackson (1962). These authors worked with five procedures labeled "creativity tests," and considered the performance of a large sample of students (class range, sixth grade through senior year of high school) on these and on one or another IQ measure. With 292 boys and 241 girls under consideration, all five of the creativity tests were significantly ($p < .05$) correlated with IQ for the boys, and four out of the five creativity tests were significantly ($p < .05$) correlated with IQ in the case of the girls. Two of those five correlations for the boys were not only significant but substantial (.38 and .37); analogously, for the girls, two of those five correlations were substantial as well as significant (.39 and .37). As a first point, then, one can question the degree to which the tests of creativity are independent of general intelligence.

Consider next the relationships *among* the creativity tests themselves. Inspection reveals that the five tests in question virtually are no more strongly correlated with one another than they are with intelligence, and that this is true for both sexes. Thus, the average correlation for boys is .26 between the creativity tests and IQ, and is .28 among the creativity tests themselves. For girls, the average correlation is .27 between the creativity tests and IQ, while it is .32 among the creativity tests themselves. Thus, if one wishes to argue from these data that a modicum of commonality underlies the creativity tests, then one must admit that almost the same degree of commonality also extends to the intelligence measure, so that no evidence is found for conceiving of a psychological dimension of creativity as existing apart from general intelligence. If, on the other hand, one wishes to propose from these data that the creativity indices possess much variance that is distinct from differences in general intelligence, then one must admit that these creativity tests are in just about the same degree independent of one another, so that no evidence exists for conceiving of a single, unified dimension that would be appropriately labeled creativity after the manner of the concept of general intelligence or G.

Given the evidence just described, it is quite illegitimate for Getzels and Jackson to proceed to sum the five creativity measures into a combined score for particular individuals, as if these measures possessed something in common that was distinct from what they also shared in common with general intelligence. At this juncture, then, one cannot avoid the conclusion that there is something wrong with a conceptual analysis of the creativity domain which results in the proposal that the five tests utilized by Getzels and Jackson are all indices of a common psychological concept, creativity, and that this is a concept distinct from that of general intelligence. What were the natures of the "creativity tests" under study here? They were quite varied in apparent psychological attributes. They concerned the ability to make up mathematical problems from given sets of numerical information, the ability to compose appropriate endings for fables, the ability to detect hidden geometric figures within more complex patterns, the ability to think up varied definitions for given stimulus words, and the ability to think up uses for a given object. Our examination of the Getzels and Jackson data indicates, then, that what these "creativity tests" have in *common* is the fact that they co-vary with individual differences in general intelligence, an inference far different from the one which Getzels and Jackson draw.

Thorndike's (1963) study of the Getzels and Jackson data leads him to the same conclusion as we have just described. In considering IQ and the five creativity measures, he writes, "It is of some interest to extract a first factor from this table of correlations and compare the factor loadings of the several tests. . . . the factor loadings are all fairly modest and the loading for the conventional intelligence test falls about midway among the 'creativity' tests" (1963, pp. 47–48).[1] That is to say, no warrant exists in these data for designating a psychological attribute of creativity distinct from general intelligence.

We turn next to other sets of recently reported data that lead us again to the same conclusion. A study by Cline, Richards, and Needham (1963) utilized California Mental Maturity IQ scores as the index of general intelligence, and explored seven "creativity" measures ranging across the same order of diversity as those used by Getzels and Jackson. Included, for example, were such tasks as the providing of synonyms for a given word; specifying uses for a common object; detecting hidden figures within more complex geometric forms; and solving "matchstick problems" in which the subject is given a drawing showing matches arranged in triangles, with the request that he remove a given number of matches in such a manner that a certain number of triangles remain. The subjects were 79 male and 40 female high school students. Inspection of the correlations indicates that six of the seven creativity measures were significantly ($p < .05$) correlated with IQ for the boys, and four of the seven were significantly ($p < .05$) correlated with IQ in the case of the girls. Five of the seven correlations for the males were substantial

---

[1] The same conclusion also emerges from a recent factor analysis of the Getzels and Jackson data by Marsh (1964).

as well as significant (.43, .40, .40, .39, .37), and this also was true of four of the seven correlations for the females (.41, .41, .38, .35). Once again, then, a goodly degree of relationship exists between general intelligence and the creativity measures.

Let us now, in a fashion parallel to our procedure with the Getzels-Jackson data, compare the magnitudes of relationships between the creativity tests and intelligence with the magnitudes of relationships among the creativity tests themselves. For boys, the average correlation is .35 between the creativity tests and the intelligence index, while it is .21 among the various creativity tests. In the case of the girls, the average correlation between the creativity tests and IQ is .33, while the average correlation among the creativity tests themselves is .24. If anything, then, we find from these data that the creativity tests are more strongly correlated with intelligence than they are with each other, and that this is the case for both sexes. Once again, in contrast with the point of view developed by Cline, Richards, and Needham, we find here no warrant for talking about "creativity *and* intelligence," as if the two terms were parallel and bore reference to equally pervasive and independent psychological realities. The "creativity tests" possess nothing in common beyond what they also share with the intelligence measure.

An earlier study by Cline, Richards, and Abe (1962) yielded results that are strikingly parallel to the ones just considered. Again, intelligence was assessed from California Mental Maturity Inventory IQ scores, the same seven creativity measures indicated above were utilized, and the subjects were high school students. The sample under study consisted of 95 males and 66 females. For the boys, all seven of the creativity measures were significantly ($p < .05$) correlated with IQ; for the girls, five out of the seven were correlated with IQ at the .05 level or better. Three of the seven correlations in the case of each sex were substantial as well as significant (.47, .40, and .39 for the boys; .46, .43, and .42 for the girls). Again, then, we find a sizable degree of relationship between the creativity measures and intelligence.

Consider now for these data the relative strengths of relationships between the creativity measures and intelligence on the one hand, and among the creativity measures on the other. The average correlation between the creativity indices and the intelligence measure was .35 for the males, .32 for the females. In contrast, the average correlation among the creativity indices themselves was .21 for the males, and .22 for the females. Once more we find a battery of "creativity" tests related more strongly to a standard intelligence index than they are related to one another.

Flescher (1963), taking the Getzels and Jackson research as his starting point, devised a group of procedures and measures that were assumed to tap the creativity domain. These included the number of different word associations given in response to each of various stimulus words; the making of drawings which, in response to a particular task requirement, deviated from the typical; the number of infrequent uses suggested in response to the request to think of uses for each of various familiar objects; the cleverness of plot titles devised for a given story plot; and the uniqueness of a composition that the child was asked to write about himself as he might be twenty-five years from now. In passing we might note such issues as the problem of scoring reliability for the judgments of cleverness regarding the plot titles and for the judgments concerning the written compositions. No descriptions of scoring methods nor information as to reliability of scoring were provided. These matters aside, however, we consider again the question of the dimensionality of these creativity procedures. This time we find that the creativity instruments are in fact independent of an intelligence measure. For the seven creativity measures used, the average correlation with IQ scores derived from the California Test of Mental Maturity was .04 for a sample of 110 sixth-graders with the two sexes combined. The general independence of the creativity indices from intelligence hence seems to be suggested from these data. The next question, therefore, must be whether the creativity indices themselves define a common dimension.

We turn, then, to the correlations among the seven creativity indices themselves. The average of the 21 correlations is .11. Thus, the average relationship among the creativity assessors is about the same as the average relationship between the creativity assessors and intelligence. In both cases, relationships are very low indeed. Neither .04 nor .11 is a statistically significant correlation for a sample of 110. Further, the one creativity measure which is most strongly intercorrelated with the others is that concerning the uniqueness of the child's written composition, and this turns out also to be the one creativity measure which is significantly correlated with general intelligence in the positive direction. But the clearest basic point is that the creativity measures as a battery possess very scanty intercorrelations indeed. There is no single underlying dimension that unifies these "creativity" measures, then, analogous to and independent of the *G* concept of general intelligence. Under these circumstances, we once again must question the practice of summing the individual's standard scores on the various measures of creativity to yield an over-all creativity index. Flescher computes such a sum and assigns it to each child as a "creativity" score. Such a procedure implies that the components being summed are comparable to one another in their psychological meaning, but we have seen that this is not the case for Flescher's seven creativity indicators. The result is that high composite scores can be earned in a myriad of psychologically different ways.

In the light of this problem, one is not overly surprised to learn that "creativity," defined in terms of the composite index just described, turns out essentially to be unrelated to anything else explored in Flescher's study. Regarding the creativity instruments in his battery, Flescher himself is led to conclude: "Different subtests were totally independent measures of different things. Apparently, certain divergent-thinking tasks are also widely divergent from each other. The absence of common characteristics in the assortment of scales may serve to explain the inconsistent findings on creativity among different investigators, and is one plausible reason for the nonsignificant findings of the present endeavor" (p. 265). As we have found to be the case before, the evidence of this study once again fails to suggest the existence of a pervasive basic dimension shared in common by the creativity assessment devices, comparable to and separable from a general intelligence dimension.

Further sources of evidence on the question of dimensionality within the creativity domain lead us in a similar direction. We shall consider the studies of two groups of researchers, the first under the direction of Torrance, the second under the direction of Guilford. Both groups once again imply the viewpoint that "creativity" and "intelligence" are terms that appropriately label unified but different psychological dimensions of comparable generality. Consider first the work of the Torrance group. Typical references are Torrance (1960; 1962), Torrance and Gowan (1963), and Yamamoto (1964a; 1964b; 1964c). A battery of tests has been developed over the years, with the objective of assessing behaviors assumed to vary in degree of creativity. Such tasks include drawing pictures that elaborate in as original a manner as possible upon some given visual element, such as circles; glueing a geometric form on a sheet of paper and using the form as part of a picture or object that is then to be completed by drawing; devising and then trying to answer questions concerning various pictures that are displayed; proposing the most clever and unusual ways one can think of for changing a given product, such as a toy dog, so that it will be more fun to play with; proposing improvements for common objects such as a bicycle; and thinking of unusual uses for a suggested object. The first two procedures are examples of visual or nonverbal indices, the remaining procedures are examples of verbal measures. Torrance and Gowan (1963) report, however, "There are low correlations between verbal and non-verbal creative abilities and they appear largely independent" (p. 3). Already, then, we find a distinction being made between two kinds of "creativity"—verbal and visual—which are found to be largely independent of each other.

We may compare this situation with the relationship between traditional verbal and performance indices of intelligence, as represented, for example, in the Wechsler Intelligence Scale for Children (Wechsler,

1949). The correlation between the sum of five verbal subtests and the sum of five performance subtests is .60 for a sample of 100 boys and 100 girls age 7½; .68 for 100 boys and 100 girls age 10½; and .56 for 100 boys and 100 girls age 13½. Thus, verbal and performance indices of intelligence are found to be substantially related. In contrast, the Torrance group reports that verbal and performance indices of "creativity" are largely independent. Here is evidence, then, to the effect that the creativity domain as defined by the Torrance group does not possess the kind of generality characteristic of the intelligence domain. In the light of such information, it becomes a rather serious distortion for the Torrance group continually to treat "creativity" as if it were the same *type* of psychological concept as "intelligence." On the evidence they describe, the creativity concept already breaks down into two relatively independent forms, one visual, the other verbal.

In view of these findings, we may well question whether the Torrance group's indices of visual and verbal creativity would have more in common with each other than the variance they also share with general intelligence. But to call them both indices of a single concept, "creative thinking," is to imply just this.

Consider next the issue of relations between intelligence and the creativity indices developed by the Torrance group. A number of studies have been concerned with this question (for example, Torrance, 1960; Yamamoto, 1964a; 1964b; 1964c). On the whole, the relationships obtained have been in the positive direction and of moderate degree. For example, in a high school population of 272, Yamamoto (1964a) obtained a correlation of .30 ($p < .01$) between IQ and an index of creativity. In another examination of these same data (Yamamoto, 1964c), high school students ranking within the upper and the lower 20 percent on the creativity index score were compared in terms of IQ. The 54 high creativity students had a mean IQ of 125.56, while the 54 low creativity students exhibited a mean IQ of 114.74. The difference in IQ between these two groups is significant beyond the .001 level by a *t* test. These two IQ means fall on either side of the mean IQ of 118.32 for the total sample of 272.

The "creativity index" used has varied for different studies, consisting in each case of a composite score based on the results of two or more different procedures. In the majority of these studies, the intelligence measure utilized has been an IQ score, a variable from which age differences have been partialled out. Age differences have not, in turn, been partialled out from the creativity scores. The effect of relating the creativity and intelligence measures under these conditions, if there is a reasonably extensive age range, is to underestimate the degree of relationship between them. This is the case since age has been partialled out of one variable but not the other. The evidence in question, then, cannot be said to convince one of the relative independence of "creativity" and "intelligence."

No data have been presented by the Torrance group that would permit one to evaluate whether and to what extent the various creativity procedures they utilize intercorrelate more strongly with one another than the degree of their separate correlations with general intelligence. However, the creativity instruments used by the Torrance group seem to possess about the same degree of diversity as those employed in the Getzels-Jackson, Cline-Richards-Needham, Cline-Richards-Abe, and Flescher studies, where the creativity procedures correlated to about the same degree with general intelligence as they correlated among themselves, or actually correlated more strongly with general intelligence than they correlated among themselves. From the direction of this evidence, therefore, we have to wonder whether the correlational situation would not be rather similar in the case of the Torrance group's materials.

For many years Guilford and his co-workers have been concerned with the creativity domain (see, for example, Guilford, 1956; 1959a; 1959b; 1959c; 1963). We turn now to a consideration of this work's import for the question of the present section. The Guilford group has tended to draw a broad distinction between a class of intellectual operations labeled "divergent thinking," and more conventional forms of intellectual operations. As Guilford (1959a) puts it, "In divergent thinking operations we think in different directions, sometimes searching, sometimes seeking variety" (p. 470). Among the more conventional kinds of intellectual operations, major attention has been focused on what are called "cognitive abilities." These refer to such matters as verbal comprehension—recognition of the meanings of words or ideas; classification ability—recognition of classes of word meanings or ideas; sensitivity to conceptual relations—recognition of relations between ideas or between meanings of words; and general reasoning—recognition of interrelations among more molar cognitive components. Discussing standard intelligence tests, Guilford has commented as follows: "Recently I indulged in some armchair analysis of the 140 tests in the latest Stanford revision of the Binet scale, from which comes the impression that, in spite of the great surface variety of the tests, there is an overwhelming weighting with tests of cognitive abilities . . ." (1963, p. 36).

The mode of interpretation adopted by the Guilford group in discussing their research suggests that the intellective functions represented by the term "divergent thinking" form a relatively distinct group which stand apart from those denoted by the classical concept of general intelligence. In the latter domain, we already know that the evidence for high internal consistency among various measures is very strong: for example, as we noted earlier, the verbal and the performance subtest totals of the Wechsler Intelligence Scale for Children are substantially correlated. At issue has been the question of whether a comparable degree of internal consistency could be isolated in the case of procedures designed to assess creativity, and, as we have seen, the evidence considered thus far has been quite discouraging in this regard. The Guilford group means to denote the general area of creativity with its divergent thinking label.[2] We must consider, therefore, the types of procedures utilized in assessing divergent thinking, the degree of their internal consistency, and the degree of their independence from indicators of conventional intelligence.

The first point that becomes apparent in viewing the divergent thinking procedures of the Guilford group is that these correspond to a sizable degree in type and diversity with the contents of the batteries of creativity tests used in the studies we have considered thus far. One type of test may concern the ability to produce words beginning with a given letter; another, to specify uses for a common object; another, to solve matchstick problems; a fourth, to think of titles for a given short story plot, the titles then being scored as clever or not clever; still another, to write punch lines for given cartoons. The evidence that we have reviewed indicated relatively weak intercorrelations among procedures embracing this degree of diversity, or correlations that, when stronger among these kinds of procedures, were approximately as strong or were stronger between these procedures and indicators of general intelligence.

To approach the same issues in connection with the Guilford group's work, we may consider some analyses carried out by Thorndike (1963) of typical examples of the Guilford group's research. Thorndike begins by raising the problem with which we have been dealing: ''When we use any term to designate an attribute of an individual, be it abstract intelligence, sociability, or creativity, the distinct label implies that there exists a set of behaviors of the individual that can be grouped together because they exhibit a common quality. Furthermore, if the label is a useful one, the set of behaviors that it designates can be differentiated from the sets designated by other labels. . . . We may appropriately ask how well the attribute 'creativity' meets these joint criteria of designating a reasonably extensive set of behaviors which (1) have some degree

---

[2] While all tasks placed in the "divergent thinking" rubric are assumed to reflect creativity, an occasional procedure not placed within that rubric also has been discussed by Guilford in connection with creativity. The clearest examples of the latter are the tasks considered to assess "sensitivity to problems," defined in terms of the ability to perceive problems or difficulties that might arise in connection with one or another matter—for example, with a particular appliance. It nevertheless is appropriate to say that Guilford tends to consider the terms "divergent thinking" and "creativity" as reasonably co-extensive.

of coherence and (2) can be distinguished from other sets of behaviors''
(pp. 44–45). In exploring the Guilford group's data, Thorndike has taken
the two tests with the strongest loadings on a given factor as representative of that factor, and has classified the factors in question as referring
to divergent thinking or to the conventional area of general intelligence.
The classification adheres to the general analysis of divergent thinking
and conventional intellectual abilities provided by the Guilford group
(see, for example, Guilford, 1959a; 1959b; 1959c; 1963). Thorndike then
computes the average correlation among tests representing the conventional intelligence domain, the average correlation among tests representing divergent thinking, and the average correlation between these
two sets of tests; much the same type of analysis as we have applied to
other studies considered in this chapter.

In the first of two sets of materials analyzed by Thorndike in this
way, Guilford and Christensen (1956) found three factors in the general
intelligence domain, labeled ''verbal comprehension,'' ''general reasoning,'' and ''eduction-verbal correlation.'' They found five factors, in
turn, considered to lie within the divergent thinking domain, labeled
''originality,'' ''expressional fluency,'' ''ideational fluency,'' ''word
fluency,'' and ''associational fluency.'' With the two highest-loading
tests taken to represent each factor, Thorndike reports that the average
correlation among the six general intelligence indicators was .43, while
the average correlation among the ten divergent thinking assessors was
.27. The average of the 60 correlations between the general intelligence
and the divergent thinking tests, in turn, was .24. These relative magnitudes suggest that most of what the divergent thinking measures have in
common is the variance they also share with the measures of general
intelligence.

Indeed, Thorndike points out that the word fluency and associational
fluency tests, assumed to be divergent thinking indicators, actually were
a bit more highly correlated with the conventional intelligence measures
than with the remaining divergent thinking measures. This observation
tempts us to raise briefly here a point to which we shall return at length
later. In elaborating on the nature of the fluency factors in his conception of divergent thinking, Guilford (1963; 1959c) defines fluency as
pertaining to the ''rapid generation,'' or generation within a limited
period of time, of various kinds of units. Rapidity or speed of production is part of his characterization of the creativity domain, and
indeed is inextricably connected with it by virtue of the fact that the
various assessment devices in question are timed; a feature not unique,
incidentally, to the work of the Guilford group. Let us begin here to pose
the question of whether such a feature is appropriate to an assessment
device attempting to tap creativity as this may exist apart from general

intelligence. Such a feature seems not to fit one's intuitions concerning the type of situation within which creativity may manifest itself most naturally. More systematic attention will be given to this matter below.

A set of materials gathered by Wilson, Guilford, Christensen, and Lewis (1954) also has been subjected to the same kind of analysis by Thorndike. In this set of data the Guilford group found six factors of the general intelligence variety, and eight factors considered representative of the divergent thinking domain. The general intelligence factors were labeled "verbal," "numerical," "perceptual," "visualizing," "reasoning," and "closure." The divergent thinking factors, in turn, were labeled "word fluency," "associational fluency," "ideational fluency," "originality," "adaptive flexibility," "spontaneous flexibility," "redefinition," and "sensitivity to problems."[3] Again taking the two highest-loading tests to represent each factor, Thorndike finds that the average correlation among the twelve general intelligence measures was .23; the average correlation among the sixteen divergent thinking indicators was .14; and the average of the 192 correlations between the general intelligence and the divergent thinking measures was .12. Here, then, we have a picture similar to the one just described for the first set of data. The general intelligence procedures are more highly related among themselves than the divergent thinking procedures, and the divergent thinking procedures are almost as strongly related to the general intelligence indicators as the divergent thinking procedures are related among themselves. Again, most of what unites the divergent thinking measures is the variance they have in common with the indicators of general intelligence.

It should be emphasized that in making the above computations, the factor labels quoted are those provided by the Guilford group, and the assignment of particular factor labels to the "divergent thinking" category follows from the analysis of divergent thinking abilities and creativity given on various occasions by Guilford (for example, 1959a; 1959b; 1959c). The present considerations suggest little warrant for conceptualizing a general cognitive dimension of creativity that is like the concept of general intelligence but exists apart from the latter.

In this section we have passed in review a considerable amount of evidence gathered by researchers concerned with the measurement of creativity. Our analysis of this evidence has pointed to the same general conclusion in all the instances considered. The measures that have been construed as indicators of creativity are not indicators of some single psychological dimension parallel to and distinct from the dimension of

---

[3] While "sensitivity to problems" is called an evaluative rather than a divergent thinking ability by Guilford, he considers it to be part of the creativity domain (for example, Guilford, 1963). See footnote 2.

general intelligence defined by conventional intelligence test indices. On the basis of this evidence, then, there is questionable warrant for proposing the very conceptualization which most researchers have proposed: that creativity is not intelligence, and that individual differences in creativity possess the same degree of psychological pervasiveness as individual differences in general intelligence. This is a rather discouraging conclusion to have to draw. Two paths lie open to us at this point. One is to assert that no substantial cognitive dimension of individual differences exists in the creativity area which is independent of differences in general intelligence. Were this to have been our inference, the present research endeavor might have ended right here. The other path available to us, however, is to wonder if the measurement approach taken to the creativity domain in the studies we have reviewed is necessarily the correct one. It may be that too diffuse a set of operations has been placed in the creativity category, and that what is needed at this point is a new attempt at conceptual analysis on which to base measurement procedures. This second path was the one we chose to follow.

AN ASSOCIATIVE CONCEPTION OF CREATIVITY

If the kinds of procedures considered thus far under the heading of "creativity" are too varied to define a cohesive dimension that is substantially independent of general intelligence, what psychological processes might be the appropriate ones on which to concentrate? As Mednick (1962) has noted, the introspections of highly creative persons seem to agree in pointing toward a particular arena of inquiry. Thus, for example, Einstein talks about the necessity for "combinatory play" and "associative play" concerning ideas and images (Ghiselin, 1952, p. 43). Poincaré refers to the situation during which he achieved an important mathematical insight as involving ideas that "rose in crowds" and collided against one another (Ghiselin, 1952, p. 36). Dryden describes the production of ". . . a confus'd Mass of Thoughts, tumbling over one another in the Dark" (Ghiselin, 1952, p. 80). Mozart refers to occasions upon which his ". . . ideas flow best and most abundantly" (Ghiselin, 1952, p. 44). We find Housman talking about springs of ideas that bubble up. "I say bubble up, because, so far as I could make out, the source of the suggestions thus proffered to the brain was an abyss which I have already had occasion to mention, the pit of the stomach" (Ghiselin, 1952, p. 91). Continually one finds creative people in the arts and letters preoccupied with the generation or production of cognitive units when they concern themselves with their own creativity. We find Thomas Wolfe saying ". . . I wrote and wrote and could not give up writing," when he is describing the work that eventually became *Of Time and the*

River (Ghiselin, 1952, p. 194). No more poignant a demonstration of this preoccupation exists than the fear of a writer, poet, or composer that he has gone dry, that he is no longer capable of this process of generating. "But what if," John Hyde Preston asks Gertrude Stein, "when you tried to write, you felt stopped, suffocated, and no words came and if they came at all they were wooden and without meaning? What if you had the feeling you could never write another word?" (Ghiselin, 1952, p. 160). From considerations such as these, Mednick (1962) proceeds to define creative thinking as ". . . the forming of associative elements into new combinations which either meet specified requirements or are in some way useful" (p. 221).

Now, it is possible, through the imposition of task constraints, so to structure a situation that only associations which are appropriate—which meet certain requirements—are given. For example, the individual may be asked to generate ways in which an object can be used, or ways in which different objects are similar, or instances that share some given attribute. In such situations, the person's associational behavior possesses a general orientation toward some given requirement that guides the nature of his responses. Under such conditions, where appropriateness of associations is assured, two variables should reflect individual differences in creativity as presently defined: the total number of associations of which a person is capable, and the relative uniqueness that his associations possess. This is not to assert that these variables necessarily would be independent of each other; rather, it is quite possible that more frequent associations will occur earlier and more unique associations later in a sequence, so that individuals who are able to produce a larger number of associations also should be able to produce a greater number of unique ones. This point will be taken up again below. We are suggesting, then, that if we arrange a situation in such a manner that only appropriate associations are provided by the individual, greater creativity should be indicated by the ability to produce more associations and to produce more that are unique.

It may be noted that while we begin with the same general associative conception of creativity as does Mednick, our operationalization follows a different approach from his. Mednick's procedure was to develop an assessment device, the "Remote Associates Test," in which a single verbal term had to be provided by the subject as an associative bridge to unite three given words. Only one word would constitute the correct answer to a given problem. For example, "cheese" would be the correct response to the triad, "rat," "blue," and "cottage." The quantity measured in this procedure, then, is number of test problems correctly answered. This approach seemed to us to be less desirable on two counts than the one that we have outlined. First of all, it conformed more to Guilford's conception of convergent thinking than to his general definition of divergent thinking. In convergent thinking, according to Guilford, there is a single right answer or best answer, while in divergent thinking there is not. Second, the approach seemed somewhat artificial in the sense that the experimenter placed himself in the omniscient position of knowing the single correct answer already. Thus, no subject could ever produce something creative from the experimenter's point of view. In other words, the experimenter chose to define the creative *product* before the fact, and then assessed whether or not the subject could attain it. The *process* of creating, on the other hand, which would seem to refer to the generation or production of associations, remained relatively hidden from view. At this early stage of inquiry, it did not seem appropriate to us to have to infer process from product. It seemed advisable, rather, to view in as direct a manner as we could the behavior that was concerned with the creative process. These considerations, then, led us to observe the number of associational responses that a person could generate under various circumstances, and the uniqueness of these responses.

It is interesting to consider that the cognitive units in question must be *capable* of production or generation if there is to be any hope of their being produced. That is, they must exist in some kind of stored form in the first place; were they not part of the individual's behavioral repertoire, they could not be generated under any circumstances. Thus, if we assess a person's capacity to generate cognitive elements, one factor influencing his performance as a ceiling or upper bound is the extensiveness of his repertoire. This consideration will make all the more impressive any demonstration that creativity, conceived of in the terms that we have been discussing, is relatively independent of the conventional dimension of general intelligence. One might have thought at first blush that a heavy contributor to this latter dimension would be individual differences in the capacity to store cognitive elements.

The present conception of creativity suggests the following kind of contrast between two gradients of associative response strength. Consider a hierarchy of possible responses to a stimulus word, with more conventional, stereotyped associates higher in the hierarchy and more unique associates lower in the hierarchy. The associates in this hierarchy may show sharp differences in relative availability: the stereotyped responses may be highly available and the more unique responses relatively unavailable. On the other hand, the associates in this hierarchy may show only moderate differences in relative availability: the stereotyped responses may be less available than in the first case, and the unique responses more available than in the first case. For both types of gradients, the stereotyped responses possess greater strength than the

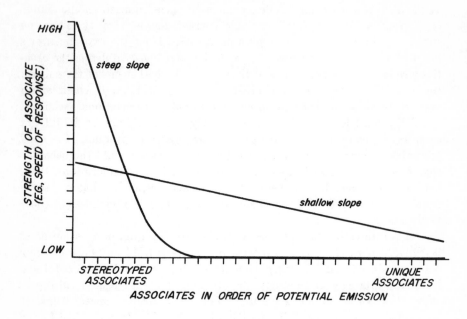

FIGURE 1. *Two hypothetical gradients of associative strength for the responses to a stimulus word.*

unique ones; but the former gradient has a sharp slope, while the latter gradient has a shallow slope. Figure 1 illustrates the proposed difference.

This gradient contrast, one which has been proposed by Mednick (1962), links high creativity with a shallow slope, low creativity with a sharp slope. The gradient of shallow slope defines a repertoire containing a larger number of cognitive elements; it is more extensive. The gradient of sharp slope defines a repertoire containing a smaller number of cognitive elements. The latter type of gradient, which we assume to describe the person low in creativity, implies maximum alacrity in producing stereotyped responses.

A person operating under the shallow gradient will most likely offer stereotyped associates to begin with, just as the person operating under the sharp gradient. But while the sharp-gradient individual will stop when the stereotyped associates have been exhausted, the shallow-gradient person will continue responding with increasingly unique associates. So also, the relatively greater associative strength for stereotyped responses under the sharp gradient implies that the sharp-gradient individual should give stereotyped responses at a faster rate (latency is one measure of strength) than the shallow-gradient individual. On the other hand, while unique responses possess greater associative strength under the shallow than under the sharp gradient, their absolute level of associative strength is lower than that of stereotyped responses even under the shallow gradient. Thus, while they will be given not at all under the steep gradient, their rate of production nevertheless will be relatively slow under the shallow gradient.

One may well ask why the curves shown in Figure 1 do not intersect the ordinate at the same point. Why should the response strength for stereotyped associates be greater in the case of low than of high creative individuals? Results reported by Houston and Mednick (1963) suggest that stereotyped associates may actually have aversive properties for those high in creativity. Such results reinforce the hypothetical curves illustrated in Figure 1.

When we consider the implications of this model of associative gradients for the behavior that one would expect to observe, two points deserve emphasis. First, responses of greater stereotypy are likely to come earlier in the sequential emission of a series of associates; responses of greater uniqueness, if they come at all, are likely to come later. This is the case whether the shallow or steep type of slope is under consideration. The implication, one which we noted earlier, is that the total number of associates a person is capable of generating, and the relative uniqueness of his associates, should be correlated variables. The individual who can produce a greater number of associates also will be the individual who can produce a greater number of unique ones. It will be possible to test this matter in various procedures reported in the next chapter. Notice that if responses of greater stereotypy are likely to come early in a sequence even in the case of creative persons, then it will not be possible to detect these persons if insufficient time is permitted for the more unique responses to emerge. An atmosphere of short time limits for the performance of given tasks thus would hardly be an appropriate one in which to attempt to measure creativity.

A second point that emerges from the model leads us in a related direction. Under the steep gradient, associations of high stereotypy are produced at a very rapid rate, and then the ability to produce falls off abruptly. If only a short time period exists during which production of associates is measured, the person with a steep gradient may look like an outstanding performer. His burst of facility may well carry him up to the point at which time is called. He may, in fact, look much superior to his peer with a shallow gradient, whose rate of producing stereotyped associates is lower. Turning to associations of low stereotypy, we note that, if they are generated at all, their rate of production will be considerably lower than the rate at which persons with steep gradients produce high stereotypy responses. Thus, in order really to discover how able a person is at the production of unique associates, it is necessary to allow the person a great deal of time. In fact, it may well be desirable to allow the person as much time as he wants. Associates should emerge at a slow but steady pace over a long time period for the shallow-gradient person, extending far into time during which the steep-gradient person is producing nothing. Again, we note how a situation of short time limits acts to sabotage attempts to measure creativity. Indeed, the above considerations suggest that the imposition of relatively short time limits may well leave the steep-gradient individual appearing superior in performance to the shallow-gradient person. For any possible superiority of the shallow-gradient over the steep-gradient individual to emerge, temporal freedom will be required.

Some data from work by Bousfield and Sedgewick (1944) are relevant to the associative gradients that have been proposed. They indeed found what the nature of these gradients implies: an inverse correlation between the total number of associations produced and the rate of producing them. The larger the number generated, the lower the rate of production. In the Bousfield and Sedgewick study, the subject was asked to generate as many items as he could within a specified category, such as animals. Such findings again emphasize the importance of permitting the individual ample time if we are to discover how many associates he is capable of generating. Another study relevant to these gradients, by Christensen, Guilford, and Wilson (1957), reported that later responses in time are more unusual and remote than earlier responses.

The model we have considered, then, suggests that if we wish to assess a person's capability with respect to number of associates and uniqueness of associates, the procedural context must provide for temporal flexibility. The introspections of highly creative individuals with which we began this section also lead us toward another point concerning procedural context. Recall Einstein's use of the terms "combinatory play" and "associative play"; Poincaré's detached witnessing of ideas rising in crowds; Housman's viewing of ideas that "bubble up." There is a modicum of distance and freedom from evaluation implied in these observations; a suggestion that the associative processes possess some degree of functional autonomy from the observer, rather than being entirely under his control. Critical faculties, censors, are to some extent stilled, when generation of cognitive elements is to be encouraged. The vectors that orient a person toward the selecting of a single correct answer are replaced by a nondirective carte blanche attitude that provides a license for production of a more free kind. Thomas Wolfe had to feel the freedom of expression that permitted him to generate many times over the number of words that eventually would find their way into print.

Rugg (1963), in his consideration of autobiographical accounts provided by scientists and artists, and in his consideration of Eastern religion, reports analogous material. In presenting his conception of the conditions for creativity, he uses such terms as "relaxed" and "permissive" to characterize the attitude he deems necessary for creative insights. Rugg feels that such an attitude possesses a kinship with the state of "letting things happen" described by the Taoists.

What these observations suggest is the presence of what might be described as an attitude of playfulness rather than evaluation when generation of associative material is to be maximized. Something akin to a diminution in the awareness or sense of self as actor seems to be involved. Thus, Rogers (1963) has recently remarked: "In the person who is functioning well, awareness tends to be reflexive, rather than the sharp spotlight of focused attention. Perhaps it is more accurate to say that in such a person awareness is simply a reflection of something of the flow of the organism at that moment. It is only when the functioning is disrupted that a sharply self-conscious awareness arises" (p. 17).

We may ask what type of context will foster the attitude that has been described. In general, one needs a situation that will induce the individual to give up the feeling that he is under examination or test, with its implication that what he does will reflect upon his self-worth. What we have in mind has been conceptualized in terms of the distinction between task-centered and ego-centered orientations (Asch, 1952, pp. 302–312). One context that our culture makes available for the definition of situations that are to be evaluation-free, concerns play and other activities engaged in for their intrinsic enjoyment. A situation closer to that context than to the context of a test or an examination hence would seem to be necessary if we are to assess adequately a person's ability to generate many associations and to generate many that are unique. Recent findings by Dentler and Mackler (1964) provide a suggestive demonstration of this point. When a test of unusual uses was administered under relaxed conditions, resultant creativity scores were significantly higher than when the same test was administered under any of several evaluational conditions.

We have noted that the kinds of procedures called for in the study of creativity as conceived above must involve the presentation of some specifications or requirements which the associations must fulfill. Immediately there comes to mind a possible contrast between two modes of presentation for such requirements: verbal (or conceptual) and visual. It has been thought for some time that persons show stylistic differences in regard to preference for dealing with words vs. sensory qualities. It would seem desirable, then, to sample both of these modes of presentation in our measurement endeavors. Mednick (1962), indeed, has suggested that there may be substantial differences in a person's associational productivity, depending upon whether the given task is cast in verbal or visual terms, or in conceptual or perceptual terms. Some people, he notes, are "verbalizers"; others are "visualizers." Hence he expects that the former should thrive when the mode of task presentation is verbal; the latter, when it is visual.

One may question, however, whether this is what we would anticipate if we start from the hypothesis that creativity, defined in terms of the present associational conception, refers to a dimension of individual differences that is as unitary and cohesive as that of general intelligence. Differentiation between verbal and visual skills is, after all, recognized in the field of intelligence testing, as reflected in, for example, the verbal vs. the nonverbal subtests in the Wechsler intelligence scales. The common variance defining the concept of general intelligence or G, on the other hand, is variance that cuts across this verbal vs. visual distinction. This common variance describes, among other things, the fact of the substantial degree of correlation that is found between verbal and visual types of intelligence-assessment instruments. If a creativity dimension exists that is analogous in its degree of internal coherence and pervasiveness to the dimension of general intelligence, then ought we not to expect that it too would cut across the contrast between verbal and visual forms of tasks? Ought we not to expect that, on the average, persons who produce many associates, and many that are unique, under task requirements of a verbal nature, also should do so when the task requirements are of a visual nature? It is clear that we would have more powerful evidence of a unitary dimension if this were so. If, in turn, it were not the case, then the analogy to a general intelligence G concept in the creativity domain already would be questionable. Recall that we raised this issue in considering the Torrance group's report of relative independence between verbal and visual forms of the procedures which they used as creativity assessors.

THE QUESTION OF TASK CONTEXT

Our discussion of an associative conception of creativity suggested two features that should be present in a procedure intended to assess individual differences in that dimension: freedom from time pressure and a gamelike rather than examination or test setting. In closing this chapter, let us return to the studies considered earlier and explore the extent to which these features are to be found.

Three generalizations can be made when we consider the situational context present for the various "creativity" procedures in the studies reviewed earlier in this chapter. First, the authors invariably refer to their procedures as "tests"; second, these procedures are group-administered to large numbers of students in a classroom setting; third, these procedures are timed and the time limits are relatively brief, or temporal constraint is implied through the use of the group administration arrangement. In short, the features of temporal freedom and a nontest context, which our analysis suggests are important if something akin to creativity is to be assessed, are conspicuous by their absence. Before exploring the causes and consequences of the states of affairs just mentioned, let us note the evidence for asserting that they prevail. We return first to the Getzels and Jackson (1962) research.

Throughout their book, Getzels and Jackson use the label "creativity tests" to describe their measuring instruments for assessing creativity. The instruments were printed in the form of examination-type booklets, were administered to a class of students in exactly the fashion to which they were quite accustomed in connection with the taking of academic examinations, and put a premium upon writing facility in that, by virtue of the group administration nature of the situation, a student's "answers" to the "questions" were to be written down by him in the test booklet. The procedures either had a set time limit or the examiner waited until the subjects seemed to be finished. We would submit that the latter circumstances nevertheless generate an atmosphere of time pressure when a student, working on a procedure that quite obviously concerns intellective functioning, is surrounded by the other members of his class and knows that the examiner is waiting until the class finishes a given instrument before proceeding to the next task. Such circumstances produce a rather strong coercion to finish up, along with feelings of inadequacy, if the individual sees that he is taking longer than the majority of his peers.

The time allowances mentioned by Getzels and Jackson in connection with the five procedures they utilized as measures of "creativity" all were relatively brief. That temporal coercion was present in the minds of the experimenters even when no official time limit was stated to the students, seems to be suggested by such evidence as the following. In describing one of their procedures, Getzels and Jackson write, "Subjects required approximately 30 minutes to complete the test, although no time limit was set in the instructions" (p. 206). Yet in another part of their description of the very same procedure, they write, "For each paragraph the student is to use the information given to make up as many mathematical problems as he can within the time limit" (p. 205). Our society's ethos of time pressure thus was working its effect on the experimenters, and it would be surprising indeed if a group-administration testing session identical in form to an academic examination were not sufficient to instill the same sense of time pressure in the students.

In the studies by Cline, Richards, and Needham (1963) and by Cline, Richards, and Abe (1962) we again find the instruments used in connection with creativity described as "creativity tests." These in- struments, assembled into a "battery," were group-administered to the students in a manner indistinguishable from that of academic examina- tions. Flescher's (1963) investigation, in similar fashion, involved the group administration of creativity "tests" in an academic examination context. The group administration was carried out by school authorities. Explicit or implicit temporal constraints again were present in these various studies.

Turning to the work of the Torrance group, we not only find the label "Tests of Creative Thinking," and group administration in class- room settings by teachers, but we also find the added evaluative stress of being *requested* by the teacher to be as original as possible in one's answers to the "tests": to provide the most clever, the most interesting, the most exciting answers that one can think of (see, for example, Tor- rance, 1962). For a teacher to instruct her class to be as clever as possible in answering the items of a test which then is group administered to the students in the fashion of an academic examination, is to leave the student virtually no alternative but to feel that he is under test and that conse- quential evaluations of him are being made by the school authorities. Once again, time limits of explicit or implicit kinds also are present in the Torrance group's assessment situations.

Consider briefly, finally, the research of Guilford and his associates. The story is the same. Guilford's attitude may be glimpsed in such a quotation as, "Until such time as measures of creative aspects of aptitudes can be included in aptitude batteries . . ." (1963, p. 38). There is the presumption that a testing context, with its evaluative implications, is perfectly appropriate for the study of creativity. The accepted re- search model is to think in terms of including tests of "creativity" among tests of other aspects of intellective functioning. Invariably the measurement undertakings carried out by Guilford and his co-workers concerning creativity involve the group administration of "tests," and most of these contain relatively short time limits. As we noted earlier, speed constitutes part of Guilford's conception of creativity. He defines ideational fluency as ". . . the rapid generation of units of verbal or semantic information" (1963, p. 33), and as ". . . the ability to produce ideas to fulfill certain requirements in limited time" (1959c, p. 146). He defines associational fluency as ". . . the rapid generation of semantic units to fulfill a relationship" (1963, p. 33), and writes that associational fluency ". . . is indicated best in a test that requires the examinee to

produce as many synonyms as he can for a given word in limited time''
(1959c, p. 145). Appropriate tests for expressional fluency, he writes,
assess ''. . . the need for rapid juxtaposition of words to meet the requirements of sentence structure'' (1959c, p. 146). As we noted earlier,
these three forms of fluency are among the characteristics included by
Guilford in his approach to creativity. In general, then, the Guilford
view of creativity tends to put a premium on rapid performance, and
assumes that it is appropriate to let the subject construe the creativity
assessment devices as tests or examinations not unlike those which he
is accustomed to encountering in his academic work.

If the associational conception of creativity outlined earlier provides
a relevant focus, then we can conclude not only that the studies we have
considered included too heterogeneous an array of procedures in their
attempts to operationalize the creativity concept, but also that they surrounded their procedures with two contextual features not maximally
appropriate for exploring individual differences in creativity: explicit
or implicit time limits and a test atmosphere. In reviewing studies of the
kinds noted, one tends to get the impression that the questions of context
treated in this section have hardly ever received explicit consideration.
It seems, on the whole, to be taken for granted that creativity, if it is to
be systematically studied, should be approached in essentially the same
framework as intelligence testing.

Such an assumption constitutes, of course, the path of least resistance empirically. It is considerably easier and more economical to
administer assessment procedures to a large group of students in a classroom than to work with these students individually. Group administration, in turn, then tends to necessitate the imposition of some degree of
temporal uniformity, implicit if not explicit. It is easier, further, to
permit the student to maintain his strongly held attitude that he is
undergoing a test or examination, than to make a serious endeavor to
change that attitude. The assumption in question—that creativity should
be approached within the framework of intelligence tests—also is the
one that is most in harmony with the tradition within which the testing
movement arose in the United States. This tradition has been mainly
concerned with test content, and only minimally concerned with the
social psychology of the testing situation. The evaluation of competence
through tests and examinations is so much the norm in American society
that it is quite difficult, and especially so for persons in the testing tradition, to focus upon the possible effects exercised by the evaluative
context as such.

Our conclusions at this point, then, are as follows. The evidence we
have reviewed points to the discouraging inference that procedures designed to assess creativity have in fact not revealed a dimension of in-

dividual differences that, on the one hand, is cohesive and unitary, and, on the other, is relatively distinct from general intelligence. Further exploration is necessary, however, because we find that the creativity label has been assigned to a host of quite varied procedures, including many, therefore, for which it may not really be relevant. It may be the case that creativity most appropriately refers to the ability to generate or produce, within some criterion of relevance, many cognitive associates, and many that are unique. Such a definition takes us away from a number of the procedures that have been given the title of creativity assessment devices. We also find that the creativity label has been assigned to procedures whose context of administration involves some kind of explicit or implicit temporal constraint, and a test or examination atmosphere with its strong implication of evaluation. It may be the case that creativity, on the other hand, if it is to reveal itself most clearly, requires a frame of reference which is relatively free from the coercion of time limits and relatively free from the stress of knowing that one's behavior is under close evaluation.

It is these considerations that led us to undertake the research reported in the next chapter.

2 ⋘

Creativity and Intelligence: The Evidence of the Present Study

In this chapter we shall describe our research concerning the measurement of and relationships between creativity and intelligence in children. Given the considerations raised in the previous chapter, four major goals stood before us in this work. First, we needed to develop and/or adapt procedures that would assess generation and uniqueness of associates in accordance with the associational conception of creativity we have outlined, and that would cover a reasonable range of substantive content, such as verbal and visual forms of presentation. Second, we hoped to be able to demonstrate that productivity and uniqueness measures would be correlated within each such procedure, and that all the procedures would be intercorrelated quite strongly in terms of both measures. Third, it was necessary for us to assess the conventional area of general intelligence with measurement techniques oriented toward skills in verbal, numerical, performance, and academic subject-matter areas. We hoped to be able to demonstrate a high degree of intercorrelation among these various indices. Our fourth objective, in turn, was to determine whether minimal interrelationships can be shown to exist between creativity measures on the one hand and general intelligence indices on the other.

If these four goals could be attained, we would be in a position to assert that there exists a unified, pervasive dimension of cognitive activity which is properly characterizable as creativity, standing relatively independent of another pervasive cognitive dimension which is properly characterizable as general intelligence.

PROCEDURE

The Sample and the Setting

We chose to carry out our work with children in the fifth grade of elementary school, and hence approximately ten to eleven years of age. It also was our decision to focus upon children whose socio-economic status level placed them in the middle-class category.

The choice of children rather than adults as the subjects of our study was premised upon the following consideration. Our evidence would be all the stronger if a distinct dimension of creativity differences could be located at an age when the adult's degree of differentiation of cognitive skills from one another has not yet been achieved. The fifth grade level, in turn, was chosen on the ground that the general age of ten or eleven was sufficiently advanced for the children to possess the requisite verbal skills for dealing with the instructional context in which our procedures had to be cast, but also was early enough for the children not to have yet entered the *Sturm und Drang* of adolescence with whatever special pressures might be attendant upon that period of development.

We centered upon children of middle-class background, finally, for the following reasons. It seemed necessary to concentrate on one general socio-economic stratum rather than bridging across strata, because differential opportunity and environmental stimulation might well impinge in many ways upon the various aspects of behavior under investigation (see, for example, Miller & Swanson, 1960). From the perspective of the present study, such effects would be extraneous and hence had to be controlled. We could not adopt the solution of conducting parallel studies of middle and lower socio-economic status children, in turn, since our research questions demanded a large sample size for children of both sexes within a given social stratum. It simply was not feasible within the confines of one project to multiply by a factor of two the several years of work our investigation required. Why, then, did we decide to work with children of middle rather than lower socio-economic status? First, because this is the general group that has been the target population in most of the relevant previous research. Second, because the "middle" class is coming to constitute an ever-increasing segment of this country's population, thus making it the one most relevant socio-cultural group for which to establish generalizations.

The children whom we studied were 151 in number: 70 boys and 81 girls. They comprised the entire fifth grade population of a suburban New England public school system, and were divided among six classrooms in two school buildings. The average age of these children was 10 years, 7.60 months, with a standard deviation of 5.42 months. For the boys and girls respectively, the mean ages were 10 years, 8.17 months (S.D., 6.00 months), and 10 years, 7.10 months (S.D., 4.84 months).[1]

The children in our sample came almost exclusively from families whose fathers have the following occupational roles: business manager, executive, sales representative, or accountant (51 percent); engineer, designer, or architect (17 percent); physician, dentist, or lawyer (15 percent); teacher, writer, or researcher (11 percent). The 6 percent not accounted for within these categories included such upper-level blue collar occupations as electrician and carpenter. In sum, the families of our children largely reflect professional and managerial backgrounds. Their religious orientation is by and large Protestant, and all are white.

Approximately six or seven weeks were required in order to carry out our research with each class of about twenty-five children. The administration of all procedures was conducted by two women in their early twenties.[2] Prior to beginning work on the project as a whole, and once again prior to starting work with each particular class, extensive efforts were made to convey to the teachers and principals the viewpoint that the present research effort did not concern the administration of tests or examinations. We deemed it essential to convince the teachers and principals of this matter before attempting to construct a gamelike and relaxed interactional context with the children, since it was evident that the tenor of the casual references made by teachers and principals within hearing of the children could do much to facilitate or hinder our efforts to dissociate the present endeavor from the stressful sphere of evaluative testing. In the sequence of research with a given class, the experimenters would be introduced to the children as visitors interested in children's games. Not only were the teachers and principals requested to avoid references to examinations and testing, but they also were asked not to mention any such terms as "creativity," "originality," "cleverness," or "intelligence" in connection with the interests of the visitors.

During the first two weeks of the research sequence with a given class, the two experimenters functioned solely as observers, independently rating the children's behavior on the scales described in the next chapter. These weeks of observation incidentally served the function of permitting the children to become acquainted with the experimenters and familiar with their presence. This period also provided time for the experimenters to communicate in various incidental ways that they had no concern with intellective evaluation. By the end of the two week period, the children

---

[1] Age was measured to the nearest month as of the time work began with a given class.

[2] The decision to use only female experimenters was based upon the fact that elementary school children are considerably more accustomed to encountering adult females than males.

took the experimenters' presence for granted and treated them quite casually.

Following this period of behavioral observation, the next four or five weeks were devoted to administering the various procedures that involved participation by the children. These included not only the instruments described in the present chapter,[3] but also the techniques that focused upon matters concerning personality functioning, categorizing processes, and sensitivity to the physiognomic properties of visual stimuli. Every effort was made to generate a permissive, gamelike, context in working with the children on most of the instruments comprising the study. There were several procedures where such an atmosphere could not prevail, however, and these were reserved for the end of the sequence of work with a given class. These comprised three subtests from the Wechsler Intelligence Scale for Children (1949), and a story-completion instrument in which various failure situations were depicted that the child had to resolve. By placing these procedures last, the stress that their content generated could not spread to any of the other instruments under consideration.

In all, seventeen procedures were administered to the children during the weeks that followed the observation period. All but one of these were administered individually, each experimenter working with about half the boys and half the girls in a given class. Administration of one procedure to the whole class was completed before work began on another. The two experimenters administered approximately equal numbers of procedures to a given child. The experimental sessions took place in two quiet and similarly decorated rooms.

The sequence of administration of the various instruments in our investigation was so arranged that the five techniques concerned with creativity fell first, fifth, sixth, ninth, and tenth in the sequence of seventeen. It will be noted later that two of these pertain to visual and three to verbal materials. The visual tasks fell at the fifth and tenth positions in the above ordering. An appendix presents a full listing of the administration sequence for the various procedures.

Instruments for Assessing Creativity

The procedures utilized for exploring creativity concerned the generation of five types of associates. In each case, our interest was in measuring two related variables: the number of unique responses pro-

---

[3] The SCAT and STEP tests, described later in this chapter, were not administered by our experimenters but rather by the teachers as part of the school system's general testing program. These classroom test administrations took place at the start of the fifth grade year, prior to the beginning of our contact with the children.

duced by the child, and the total number of responses produced by the child. The nature of these measures is considered further below. All procedures were described as games and were administered individually to each child under circumstances that were free from any time pressure. Further, these procedures did not require the child to respond in writing; rather, all communication by the child was oral. Care was taken to insure that both experimenters had established rapport with a given child before the first of the creativity procedures was undertaken. The frame of reference with which the child approached these instruments was that they were among a number of children's games that the two ladies would be playing with the members of the class, and that the ladies were interested in finding out how children liked to play these various games.[4]

INSTANCES. This is the first of three verbal techniques. In it the child is asked to generate possible instances of a class concept that is specified in verbal terms. It is introduced with the following general instructions:

"In this game I am going to tell you something and it will be your job to name as many things as you can think of that are like what I tell you. For example, I might say 'things that hurt.' Now you name all the things you can think of that hurt." (The experimenter then lets the child try.) "Yes, those are fine. Some other kinds of things might be falling down, slapping, fire, bruises, or a knife." (Here the experimenter varies her suggestions so that they consist of ones which the child has not provided.) "So we see that there are all kinds of different answers in this game. Do you see how we play?" (If the child already indicates strong understanding, the last sentence is replaced by, "I can see that you already know how we play this game.") "Now remember, I will name something and you are supposed to name as many things as you can think of that are like what I've said. OK, let's go."

The experimenter's explanation of the example is provided in such a manner as to convey the feeling of suggestion rather than of finality. The possible answers are given slowly and in a suggesting tone, so as to provide the impression that she is thinking of them at the time. The alternate statement, "I can see that you already know how we play this game," replaces the question, "Do you see how we play?" in the case of those children who obviously understand and hence would be offended by the suggestion that they do not understand the game.

The four items in this procedure, in their order of administration, are as follows:

1. "Name all the round things you can think of."
2. "Name all the things you can think of that will make a noise."

---

[4] Some of the ideas represented in these procedures derive from the work of the Guilford group. That these particular instruments and their conditions of application nevertheless differ in many respects from the work of the Guilford group, will, however, soon be apparent.

3. "Name all the square things you can think of."
4. "Name all the things you can think of that move on wheels."

Here and in the case of the other four creativity procedures, the following general considerations prevail.

The child is given as much time as he wishes for each item. That is, the experimenter exerts no pressure for speed on an item; rather, she encourages the child to continue working on a given question as long as he seems at all motivated to do so. Only if the child indicates with some finality that he is finished with a given question, does the experimenter turn to the next.

The variable of *uniqueness* is defined as follows: For each item in a procedure, a frequency distribution is constructed indicating the number of children in the total sample of 151 who give a particular response to that item. This analysis is carried out for every response provided to that item. Any response to a given item that is offered by only 1 out of the 151 children is defined as a unique response. The number of unique responses provided by a child in his answers to a particular item constitutes his uniqueness score for that item. Thus, to call a response unique for a given item is to say that the response in question was provided in answer to the given item by only one child in the entire sample. The term "unique" hence carries its literal meaning of "one of a kind." In the *American College Dictionary* (Barnhart, 1949), for example, "unique" is defined: "of which there is but one; sole; only" (p. 1326). A child's uniqueness score for a procedure as a whole consists of the sum of his uniqueness scores for the various items which constitute the procedure. In the case of the *instances* procedure, for example, the child's total score for uniqueness consists of the sum of his uniqueness scores on the four items listed earlier.[5]

The variable of *number* is defined as the total number of responses given by a child to a particular item. Recall that this number score is obtained under conditions which encourage the child to work on a given item just as long as he desires. A child's number score for a procedure as a whole consists of his number scores for the various items making up that procedure. For example, in the case of the *instances* procedure, the child's total score for number consists of the sum of his scores for number on the four items contained in that instrument.

Consider some examples of responses to the items of the *instances* instrument. When asked to "name all the round things you can think

---

[5] Initial analysis indicated that orderings of children based upon the present definition of uniqueness are highly similar to those that result from the more arduous approach of assigning weights to all responses in terms of relative infrequency of occurrence.

of,'' we find that ''Life Savers'' is a unique response, while ''buttons'' is not; ''mouse hole'' is a unique response, while ''plate'' is not; ''drops of water'' is a unique response, while ''door knob'' is not. When posed the question, ''Name all the things you can think of that will make a noise,'' we find that ''Dispose-all'' is a unique response, while ''a car honking'' is not; ''cash register'' is a unique response, while ''airplane'' is not; ''snoring'' is a unique response, while ''thunder'' is not. When asked to ''name all the things you can think of that move on wheels,'' we find that ''tape recorder'' is a unique response, while ''wheelbarrow'' is not; ''clothesline'' is a unique response, while ''trolley car'' is not.

ALTERNATE USES. In this second of our three verbal techniques, the child is to generate possible uses for a verbally specified object. The task is introduced in the following manner:

"Now, in this game, I am going to name an object—any kind of object, like a light bulb or the floor—and it will be your job to tell me lots of different ways that the object could be used. Any object can be used in a lot of different ways. For example, think about *string*. What are some of the ways you can think of that you might use string?" (The experimenter lets the child try.) "Yes, those are fine. I was thinking that you could also use string to attach a fish hook, to jump rope, to sew with, to hang clothes on, and to pull shades." (The experimenter varies her suggestions so as not to duplicate any the child has provided.) "There are lots more too, and yours were very good examples. I can see that you already understand how we play this game. So let's begin now. And remember, think of all the different ways you could use the object that I name. Here we go."

In this procedure it was apparent that all the children at the subjects' age level understood on the basis of the above introductory remarks how the game was to be played. Hence, ''I can see that you already understand how we play this game,'' always was said. Again, the experimenter provided her responses to the example slowly and in a suggesting tone, in order to convey the impression that she was thinking of them at the time.

The eight items in the *alternate uses* instrument follow:

1. "Tell me all the different ways you could use a newspaper."
2. "Tell me all the different ways you could use a knife."
3. "Tell me all the different ways you could use an automobile tire—either the tube or the outer part."
4. "Tell me all the different ways you could use a cork."
5. "Tell me all the different ways you could use a shoe."
6. "Tell me all the different ways you could use a button—the kind that is used on clothing."
7. "Tell me all the different ways you could use a key—the kind that is used in doors."
8. "Tell me all the different ways you could use a chair."

As in the previous procedure, we measured the number of unique responses provided by a child to each item, and summed these results to obtain a uniqueness score for the instrument as a whole. We also measured the total number of responses that a child gave to each item, and summed these to yield the number of responses for the procedure as a whole.

Let us note some examples of responses obtained with the present instrument. When requested to "tell me all the different ways you could use a newspaper," "rip it up if angry" is a unique response, while "make paper hats" is not. When asked about uses for an automobile tire, "to grow tomato plants in" is a unique response, while "use inner tube for a life preserver" is not. When queried about uses for a shoe, "to trap a mouse in" is a unique response, while "to throw at a noisy cat" is not. For a button to be used as a "hatch on a model submarine" is a unique response, while for buttons to be used as "puppets' eyes" is not.

SIMILARITIES. In the present instrument, the child is to generate possible similarities between two verbally specified objects. The instructions were these:

"In this game I am going to name two objects, and I will want you to think of all the ways that these two objects are alike. I might name any two objects—like door and chair. But whatever I say, it will be your job to think of all the ways that the two objects are alike. For example, tell me all the ways that an apple and an orange are alike." (The child then responds.) "That's very good. You've already said a lot of the things I was thinking of. I guess you could also say that they are both round, and they are both sweet, they both have seeds, they both are fruits, they both have skins, they both grow on trees—things like that. Yours were fine, too." (The experimenter's suggestions are varied so as not to include any which the child has given.) "Do you see how we play the game?" (If the child indicates clear understanding already, the last sentence is replaced by, "I can see that you already know how to play this game.") "Well, let's begin now. And remember, each time I name two objects, you name as many ways as you can that these two objects are alike."

The experimenter's responses to the example once again were given in such a manner as to convey a tone of suggestion rather than finality.

The *similarities* instrument comprised ten items, as follows:

1. "Tell me all the ways in which a potato and a carrot are alike."
2. "Tell me all the ways in which a cat and a mouse are alike."
3. "Tell me all the ways in which a train and a tractor are alike."
4. "Tell me all the ways in which milk and meat are alike."
5. "Tell me all the ways in which a grocery store and a restaurant are alike."
6. "Tell me all the ways in which a violin and a piano are alike."
7. "Tell me all the ways in which a radio and a telephone are alike."

8. "Tell me all the ways in which a watch and a typewriter are alike."
9. "Tell me all the ways in which a curtain and a rug are alike."
10. "Tell me all the ways in which a desk and a table are alike."

The dependent variables of uniqueness and number were scored for each item in the manner already described, and were summed across items for the instrument as a whole.

As examples of responses to the items of the present procedure, consider the following. For "cat and mouse," "can make women scream" is a unique response, while "have tails" is not. For "milk and meat," "they are government-inspected" is a unique response, while "they come from animals" is not. Given "curtain and rug," "dogs get them dirty" is a unique answer, while "you have to clean them both" is not.

PATTERN MEANINGS. This is one of the two creativity assessment techniques involving visual rather than verbal stimulus materials. The procedure was introduced to the child as follows:

"Here's a game where you can really feel free to use your imagination. In this game I am going to show you some drawings. After looking at each one, I want you to tell me all the things you think each complete drawing could be. Here is an example—you can turn it any way you'd like to." (The experimenter gives the example card to the child. See Figure 2.) "What could this be?" (The child is encouraged to try some suggestions.) "Yes, those are fine. Some other kinds of things I was thinking of were the rising sun, a porcupine, eye lashes, a brush, a carnation, and probably there are lots of other things too. And yours were very good examples too." (The experimenter's particular suggestions are varied so as not to include any given by the child.) "I can see that you already know how we play this game. So let's begin now."

In the present procedure, then, the child is to generate possible meanings or interpretations for each of a number of abstract visual designs. Note that the child is requested to consider each drawing as a complete entity in producing his responses. The experimenter's suggestions for the example are presented slowly, in such a manner as to indicate that she is thinking of them at the time. The *pattern meanings* procedure consists of eight items, in addition to the example. Each drawing appears on a separate 4 in. × 6 in. card. The nine cards are illustrated in Figure 2. Each of the eight cards in the procedure proper is presented to the child with the instruction: "Here is another drawing. Tell me all the things you think this could be."

Once again, the dependent variables of uniqueness and number were scored for each item in the manner previously described, and were summed across the eight items for the procedure as a whole.

Among the responses to the *pattern meanings* procedure, consider these examples. For item 1, "lollipop bursting into pieces" is a unique

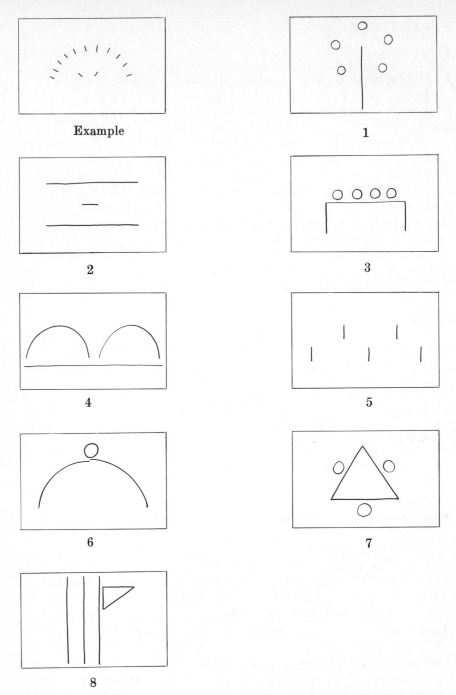

FIGURE 2. *Stimulus materials for the Pattern Meanings procedure. (Original cards, 4 in. × 6 in.)*

response, while "flower" is not. For item 3, "foot and toes" is a unique suggestion, but "table with things on top" is not. In response to item 4, "two haystacks on a flying carpet" is a unique suggestion, while "two igloos" is not. For item 5, "five worms hanging" is a unique response, while "raindrops" is not. For item 7, "three mice eating a piece of cheese" is a unique response, while "three people sitting around a table" is not.

LINE MEANINGS. In our second creativity procedure involving visual stimulus materials, the child is confronted with one or another kind of line and is asked to generate meanings or interpretations relevant to the form of the line in question. The lines were adapted from Tagiuri (1960). Each line is a single continuous unit, in contrast to the discrete elements comprising the patterns in the preceding instrument. The *line meanings* technique is introduced to the child with the following words:

"This game is called the line game. I am going to show you some lines and after you have looked at each one, I want you to tell me all the things it makes you think of. Now take your time, and be sure that when you look at the line you tell me what the whole line makes you think of, and not just a part of it. O.K.?"

The experimenter then presents the first of the nine items in this procedure. Each line is shown on a separate 4 in. $\times$ 6 in. card. See Figure 3 for a presentation of these stimulus materials. The experimenter now proceeds:

"Here is the first line. You can turn it any way you want to. Tell me all the things you can about it. What does it make you think of?"

After the child indicates that he has completed his suggestions for the first line, the experimenter introduces the next stimulus card, again reminding the child that he can turn it any way he wishes. The subsequent items in the series are introduced with similar instructions.

The variables of uniqueness of responses and number of responses were scored for each of the nine items in the manner previously described, and were summed across items to yield total scores for the whole procedure.

Consider the following examples of responses to the *line meanings* instrument. For item 1, "a squished piece of paper" is a unique response, while "mountains" is not. In the case of item 3, "squeezing paint out of a tube" is a unique response, but "a piece of string" is not. For item 4, "a stream of ants" is a unique response, while "a stick" is not. For item 6, "alligator's open mouth" is a unique response, while "arrowhead" is not; "private's stripe" is a unique response, but "hat" is not. In the case of item 9, "fishing rod bending with a fish" is a unique response, while "rising sun" is not; "airport hangar" is a unique response, but "top of head" is not.

Thus, in overview, we have described five creativity instruments, ranging across several different content areas. Each instrument yields

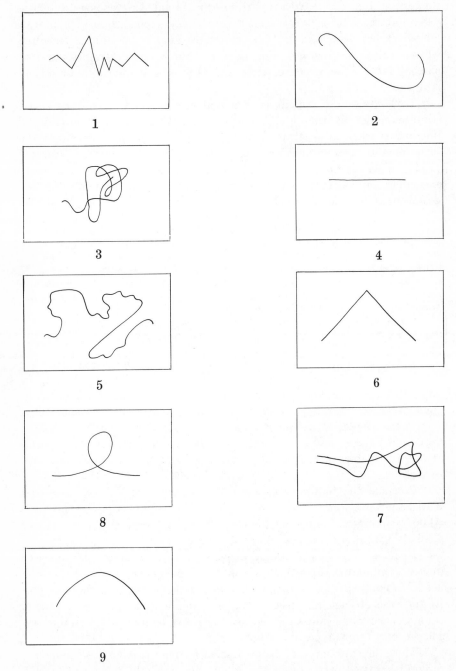

FIGURE 3. *Stimulus materials for the Line Meanings procedure. (Original cards, 4 in.* ✕ *6 in.)*

two types of measures, one concerning the ability to generate or produce associates, and the other concerning the uniqueness of the associates produced. In all, the procedures hence result in ten indices. Three of the five instruments pertain to verbal materials, while two of them concern visual materials. All are administered under conditions of a gamelike and relaxed context, rather than one stressing evaluation. In addition, the experimenter in all cases encourages the child to take as much time as he desires.

It should be stressed that the gamelike instructional context did not eventuate in a flouting of the task constraints inherent in each experimental item. Bizarre or inappropriate responses—those judged inadmissable as possible answers to a given question—were extremely rare.[6] This is a matter of some consequence for the intrinsic validity of the number and uniqueness variables as indices of creativity. If later associates in the response sequence—those most likely to be unique—were to take a bizarre turn, the relevance of our indices for creativity could be seriously questioned. As the various illustrations of unique responses have shown, however, they are quite appropriate to the task requirements.

Of further concern is the general question of whether a response that is unique in the sample as a whole can be considered a creative product for the child who produced it. The answer to this question would obviously require the kind of detailed clinical and biographical study of each child that is impossible to carry out in practice. On the other hand, we propose that, in a sample of 151 school children of fairly homogeneous socio-economic background, a unique response which is at the same time appropriate to task demands will have considerable relevance for the associational conception of creativity outlined in Chapter 1. We are suggesting, in other words, that there is a substantial degree of correspondence between "actuarial" and "personal" uniqueness, when samples derive from a reasonably homogeneous sociocultural matrix.

If one accepts the conception outlined in Figure 1—unique associates emerging later in the associational sequence—then we can proceed to examine the actual magnitude of relations between quantity and uniqueness of associates. Strong positive correlations would empirically strengthen the model portrayed in Figure 1, and thereby would increase our confidence in the relevance of the uniqueness index. Empirical relationships do in fact assume that form, as evidence presented later in the chapter will show.

---

[6] For each item in each procedure, two independent judges found virtually no unique responses that could not conceivably fit the stimulus requirements. With 98 or 99 percent agreement on every item and with any discrepancies resolved by discussion, the percentages of unique responses judged inappropriate round to zero for any item.

Instruments for Assessing General Intelligence

Our assessment techniques for measuring general intelligence were ten in number, and included the following materials: three subtests from the Wechsler Intelligence Scale for Children (WISC); the School and College Ability Tests (SCAT), which provide measures of verbal aptitude and quantitative aptitude; and the Sequential Tests of Educational Progress (STEP), which provide indices of academic achievement in various substantive areas. Our inclusion of "scholastic achievement" indicators within the over-all category of "general intelligence" reflected the fact that typical indicators of aptitude or intelligence, on the one hand, and of academic achievement, on the other, have been found to be rather strongly correlated (see, for example, Cooperative Test Division, 1957c). We will note later that our results yield the same picture. Given these circumstances, the variance shared by aptitude and achievement tests seems to be most appropriately described with the generic psychological label of "general intelligence."

SUBTESTS FROM THE WECHSLER INTELLIGENCE SCALE FOR CHILDREN. One verbal and two performance subtests from the WISC were administered individually to each child. The verbal subtest was Vocabulary; the performance subtests were Picture Arrangement and Block Design. Administered in the order, Picture Arrangement, Vocabulary, and Block Design, these instruments were fourteenth through sixteenth in the sequence of seventeen procedures given to each child. The seventeenth procedure, as we noted earlier, concerned story completions that the child had to provide for various failure situations that were depicted. The stress context potentially present in the case of these four procedures thus was kept specific to the end of the sequence of work with the children in a given class. Care was exercised not to begin work upon any of these potentially stressful procedures until all the children of a given class had completed the thirteen instruments that were to be administered in a gamelike context. We note this here for emphasis, since it already has been stated that administration of one procedure was completed before work on the next in the sequence was begun.

Selection of the Vocabulary subtest was based on the fact that it possesses a very high correlation with the total verbal scale score, and with the full scale score, of the WISC. Wechsler (1949), for example, reports for the Vocabulary subtest a correlation of .89 with the total verbal scale score and a correlation of .87 with the full scale score in the case of a sample of 200 children of age 10½ years, equally divided between the sexes. In a similar fashion, the Block Design and Picture Arrangement subtests from the performance scale of the WISC were selected because of their high correlations with the total performance scale score and with the full scale score. For the sample that we have just described, Wechsler (1949) reports Block Design subtest correlations of .80 and .72 with the total performance scale score and with the full scale score, respectively; and reports that the analogous correlations for the Picture Arrangement subtest are .72 and .70, respectively. The three subtests chosen thus can be said to provide a quite representative sample of the verbal and performance sections of the WISC as a whole.

Administration and scoring for the Vocabulary, Block Design, and Picture Arrangement subtests followed the general procedures set down in the WISC manual (Wechsler, 1949). In the Vocabulary subtest, the child is asked to provide definitions for each of a number of words, arranged in a series of increasing difficulty. In the Block Design subtest, the child is to assemble blocks in such a manner that they look like a design presented to him on a card. A number of different designs are employed. In the case of the Picture Arrangement subtest, the child is requested to arrange a set of pictures in such a way as to "make a sensible story." This task involves a number of different picture sets.

THE SCHOOL AND COLLEGE ABILITY TESTS. These are widely used group-administered tests for assessing the traditionally demarcated areas of verbal ability and quantitative ability. Prepared by the Cooperative Test Division of Educational Testing Service, the test materials are available in forms whose general levels of difficulty are appropriate to different amounts of schooling. The SCAT tests were administered by the school authorities at the beginning of the academic year to the six classes of fifth-graders. As we have noted, this test administration occurred prior to the start of our experimenters' contact with the children. Hence, the children presumably viewed SCAT as part of the school's general testing program. Form 5A of SCAT was utilized. Administration and scoring proceeded in the manner described by the test publisher (see Cooperative Test Division, 1957a; 1957b).

The SCAT materials are used as measures of a student's general capacity for undertaking subsequent academic work. Verbal and quantitative abilities are considered to be the most important yardsticks for estimating such capacity. A form of SCAT appropriate for administration at the beginning of the fifth grade year provided the SCAT scores of verbal and quantitative ability for the present sample of children. The verbal ability score is based upon two kinds of items: sentence completions, which depend upon comprehension of the general meaning of a sentence, and synonyms, which test the child's vocabulary by requesting him to choose the closest synonym to a given word from among multiple-choice alternatives. The quantitative ability score also reflects the ability to deal with two types of items. In the first type, the child is asked to manipulate numbers and apply number concepts in carrying out computations. In the second type of item, the child has to solve problems involving quantities (Cooperative Test Division, 1957a; 1957b).

THE SEQUENTIAL TESTS OF EDUCATIONAL PROGRESS. The STEP materials are companion assessment devices to SCAT in regard to intended educational measurement functions. Whereas SCAT scores are considered to measure capacity for further academic undertakings, STEP scores are assumed to assess past academic achievements. Academic accomplishment in five content areas is evaluated in the tests that were administered to the present group of children: mathematics, science, social studies, reading, and writing. The Cooperative Test Division of Educational Testing Service publishes STEP, and the tests are available in several forms with degrees of difficulty corresponding to different schooling levels. As in the case of SCAT, the STEP tests are group administered and widely used. Our sample of fifth-graders received the STEP tests at the beginning of the fifth grade year, as part of the general testing program during which the SCAT tests were administered. Thus, STEP as well as SCAT administrations occurred before our experimenters began work with the children. STEP and SCAT together constituted the school system's educational assessment program. Form 4A of STEP was used. Again, administration and scoring were carried out in the manner described by the test publisher (see Cooperative Test Division, 1957c; 1957d).

The five STEP areas that were studied include the following kinds of materials (Cooperative Test Division, 1959): The mathematics test measures mastery of such mathematical ideas as number, operation, and measurement. The science test assesses mainly the ability to suggest or eliminate hypotheses and the ability to select methods for the testing of hypotheses in different substantive fields of science. The social studies test focuses upon the ability to see relationships among facts, compare information, and draw conclusions, in the case of such fields as history and geography. The reading test concerns mastery of such reading skills as are involved in summarizing and interpreting passages, as well as in criticizing and evaluating passages with respect to purposes of presentation and motivations of authors. Finally, the writing test evaluates the child's judgment regarding such matters as grammar, punctuation, organization, and effectiveness of written presentations. The form of STEP used was one appropriate for administration at the beginning of the fifth grade year.

In sum, our ten indices of general intelligence covered verbal, visual and quantitative skills, and extended across a range of substantive content. The indices are representative of measures used for assessing "intelligence," "aptitude," and "academic achievement," as these concepts are traditionally defined.

RESULTS AND DISCUSSION

Having described our subjects and the procedures utilized for studying the creativity and general intelligence domains, we turn now to a consideration of the findings. First, we must determine the reliabilities of our several assessment instruments. Then, we can proceed to examine their interrelationships.

Reliability of the Creativity Instruments

The reliabilities of our various measures for assessing creativity are presented in Tables 1 through 6. Reliabilities are especially important to evaluate in the case of these measures, since the purposes of this chapter include establishing the degree of interrelationship among the creativity measures and the degree of their interrelationship, in turn, with conventional indices of general intelligence. Without information about the reliabilities of the creativity indices, we would not know how to interpret whatever findings we obtain concerning interrelationships—their presence or absence, and their degree. For the reliability of a measure, after all, functions as a ceiling or limit upon the extent to which it can reasonably be expected to relate to other variables.

Two approaches to reliability were taken in the case of the creativity indices. The first was to calculate the split-half reliability of each measure according to the Spearman-Brown prophecy formula. This formula considers the degree of relationship between two randomly chosen halves of a set of items—the odd items and the even items. With the sample size of 151 children, the results of these calculations are shown in Table 1. We find that, for each of the two measures in the case of each of the five creativity procedures, the split-half reliability co-

Table 1.

SPEARMAN-BROWN SPLIT-HALF RELIABILITY COEFFICIENTS
FOR THE TEN CREATIVITY VARIABLES ($N = 151$)

Instances–uniqueness	.51
Instances–number	.75
Alternate uses–uniqueness	.87
Alternate uses–number	.93
Similarities–uniqueness	.87
Similarities–number	.93
Pattern meanings–uniqueness	.88
Pattern meanings–number	.93
Line meanings–uniqueness	.82
Line meanings–number	.93

efficient is substantial. All ten of these reliability estimates are .50 or better. Indeed, eight of the ten coefficients exceed .80. Clearly, the measures concerning number of associates and uniqueness of associates for all of the procedures—Instances, Alternate Uses, Similarities, Pattern Meanings, and Line Meanings—possess a high degree of internal consistency.

Our second approach to the reliability of the creativity measures was to carry out, for each, an item analysis that would tell us the extent to which every item is contributing to the score provided by the sum of all items. Such an item analysis consists of item–sum correlations in which the score of each item is correlated in turn with the sum of the scores of all items. The results of these item–sum correlations for each of the ten measures with the sample of 151 children are reported in Tables 2 through 6. In the case of every measure, it is evident that all items are making substantial contributions to the total score. All of the 78 item–sum correlations are .40 or better, and 71 of the 78 are .60 or better. No item in any measure stands out as being unrepresentative of what the measure assesses as a whole. This second source of evidence

Table 2.

ITEM–SUM CORRELATIONS FOR THE INSTANCES
PROCEDURE $(N = 151)$

Item	Uniqueness	Number
1	.68	.74
2	.73	.67
3	.70	.85
4	.50	.76

Table 3.

ITEM–SUM CORRELATIONS FOR THE ALTERNATE
USES PROCEDURE $(N = 151)$

Item	Uniqueness	Number
1	.48	.80
2	.59	.79
3	.69	.83
4	.76	.84
5	.83	.86
6	.79	.83
7	.73	.83
8	.73	.84

Table 4.

ITEM–SUM CORRELATIONS FOR THE SIMILARITIES
PROCEDURE $(N = 151)$

Item	Uniqueness	Number
1	.42	.70
2	.63	.73
3	.67	.78
4	.77	.81
5	.74	.79
6	.66	.81
7	.55	.81
8	.72	.82
9	.75	.85
10	.65	.76

Table 5.

ITEM–SUM CORRELATIONS FOR THE PATTERN
MEANINGS PROCEDURE $(N = 151)$

Item	Uniqueness	Number
1	.64	.74
2	.78	.83
3	.80	.85
4	.69	.83
5	.80	.85
6	.78	.82
7	.75	.75
8	.64	.69

Table 6.

ITEM–SUM CORRELATIONS FOR THE LINE
MEANINGS PROCEDURE $(N = 151)$

Item	Uniqueness	Number
1	.59	.68
2	.65	.79
3	.58	.72
4	.67	.77
5	.60	.80
6	.67	.83
7	.66	.79
8	.64	.76
9	.68	.84

thus again points to the high degree of internal consistency possessed by each measure.

The high reliabilities we have found thus place high ceilings upon the potential relationships of these creativity measures with one another and with other variables. There is nothing in the internal nature of these measures that might act to inhibit the occurrence of such relationships. If, under such circumstances, we find these creativity indices to be strongly related to each other, then it will be especially noteworthy if we find them to be unrelated to or to be weakly related to conventional indices of general intelligence.

Reliability of the Intelligence Instruments

Since all the assessors of general intelligence employed in our study are standard and widely used in intellective testing programs, considerable data are already available attesting to their high reliabilities. We need but give examples of such findings here. We turn first to the three subtests from the WISC: Vocabulary, Block Design, and Picture Arrangement. For a sample of 200 children of age 10½, equally divided between the sexes, the Spearman-Brown split-half reliability coefficients are .91 for the Vocabulary subtest, .87 for the Block Design subtest, and .71 for the Picture Arrangement subtest (Wechsler, 1949). Consider next reliability estimates for the SCAT verbal and quantitative aptitude tests. For a sample of 2,226 fifth-graders using form 5A of these tests (the form we employed), about equally divided between the sexes, reliabilities computed by the Kuder-Richardson Formula 20 are .94 for verbal ability and .88 for quantitative ability (Cooperative Test Division, 1957a). Finally, we consider reliability estimates for the STEP tests concerning Mathematics, Science, Social Studies, Reading, and Writing, again using the Kuder-Richardson Formula 20 (Cooperative Test Division, 1957c). The children studied were fifth-graders, and form 4A of these tests—the form we employed—was utilized. Each of the samples to be mentioned is about equally divided between the sexes. For Mathematics, the reliability is .89 with a sample of 253. For Science, the reliability is .91 with a sample of 252. In the case of Social Studies, and a sample of 263, the reliability is .93. For Reading, the reliability is .95, and the sample size is 277. Turning finally to Writing, the reliability is .89, with a sample of 273.

In sum, the reliabilities for all ten indices of general intelligence are very high. Coupled with the information that we have presented demonstrating the high reliabilities of our ten procedures for assessing creativity, the stage is set for examining the interrelationships among these twenty measures.

The Dimensionality of Creativity and Intelligence for the
Total Sample

Recall the basic questions with which this chapter began. We were faced with the need for a set of procedures that would fulfill the associative definition of creativity which had been proposed, while covering a reasonable range of diversity. Having developed such materials, our task was to determine whether the procedures in question tapped a unified dimension of individual differences, and, if so, whether this dimension was different from the dimension that reflects the conventional concept of general intelligence. Let us consider these issues first in connection with the findings for the sample as a whole.

Table 7 presents the correlations among the creativity measures for the sample of 151 children. We find that the ten creativity indices are very strongly intercorrelated. Indeed, 43 of the 45 correlations in the table are significant beyond the .05 level, and 41 of the 45 beyond the .01 level. In the case of four of the five procedures, the measure concerning uniqueness of responses and the measure concerning number of responses are significantly related ($p < .01$), supporting the general expectation that the chances for production of unique associates should increase as the total number of associates produced becomes larger. We also find that the six verbal indices of creativity—indicators derived from the Instances, Alternate Uses, and Similarities procedures—are substantially correlated with the four visual indices of creativity, as derived from the Pattern Meanings and Line Meanings procedures. We thus find evidence for a unified dimension of individual differences that cuts across any verbal vs. visual type of distinction. If a child produces many associates and many unique associates in connection with procedures that present him with verbal content, then he also does so in connection with procedures that request him to deal with visual content. Such an outcome is indeed encouraging with respect to the question of generality within the creativity area. It represents what we would expect to discover if the creativity domain as we have defined it were to exhibit the same order of generality as the conventional area of intelligence.

Turning to Table 8, we find that our ten indicators of general intelligence are positively correlated with one another for the sample as a whole, and indeed, yield a picture similar to that for the creativity indices reported in Table 7. Thus, 43 of the 45 coefficients are significant beyond the .05 level, and 38 of the 45 beyond the .01 level. The two nonsignificant coefficients involve the WISC Picture Arrangement subtest, which yields the lowest correlations with the other intelligence measures. The findings of Table 8 come as no surprise, of course, since they simply reflect the already well established fact that traditional measures of in-

Table 7.

INTERCORRELATIONS AMONG THE TEN CREATIVITY MEASURES FOR THE TOTAL SAMPLE ($N = 151$)

	2	3	4	5	6	7	8	9	10
1. Instances–uniqueness	08	41	24	33	32	27	07	35	20
2. Instances–number		35	45	22	41	27	30	33	42
3. Alternate uses–uniqueness			67	66	70	46	29	44	52
4. Alternate uses–number				53	74	49	39	39	58
5. Similarities–uniqueness					71	32	20	49	46
6. Similarities–number						45	38	52	58
7. Pattern meanings–uniqueness							29	55	50
8. Pattern meanings–number								25	40
9. Line meanings–uniqueness									64
10. Line meanings–number									

NOTE: For 149 df, r's of .16 and .21 are significant at the .05 and .01 levels, respectively. Decimal points are omitted. In order that correlations between the uniqueness and number variables from a given creativity procedure be uncontaminated, the number measures used for computational purposes in Tables 7, 9, 10, 12, 13, 15, and 16, consist of all responses but those that are unique.

Table 8.

Intercorrelations among the Ten Intelligence Measures for the Total Sample ($N = 151$)

	2	3	4	5	6	7	8	9	10
1. WISC–vocabulary (V)	18	37	56	38	55	53	59	43	44
2. WISC–picture arrangement (PA)		17	15	16	20	24	24	12	16
3. WISC–block design (BD)			34	34	51	37	38	29	26
4. SCAT–verbal (V)				70	71	71	80	70	77
5. SCAT–quantitative (Q)					71	65	69	74	77
6. STEP–mathematics (M)						67	73	60	65
7. STEP–science (S)							76	71	70
8. STEP–social studies (SS)								71	74
9. STEP–reading (R)									80
10. STEP–writing (W)									

Note: For 149 df, r's of .16 and .21 are significant at the .05 and .01 levels, respectively. Decimal points are omitted.

telligence generally tap, in addition to more specific abilities, a single underlying dimension of individual variation. Furthermore, this dimension tends to cut across verbal, visual, and quantitative task distinctions, and tends also to cross the boundary between what have been classified as "ability" indicators (the WISC and SCAT measures) and what have been called "achievement" indicators (the STEP tests). That is, conventional intelligence measures concerning verbal, visual, and quantitative materials tend to be significantly intercorrelated; and these, in turn, are significantly correlated with conventional indices of academic achievement. It should also be noted that correlations across individually (WISC) and group-administered measures (SCAT and STEP) are highly significant, though the magnitude of these r's is quite understandably smaller than those observed within the group-administered domain. The temporal separation of the two sets of measures also contributes, of course, to the differential magnitude of the relevant correlations. Over and beyond these differences within the intelligence domain, however, the variance which all these indices share seems to be most aptly described in terms of the "general intelligence" concept. Is this variance also shared by the creativity measures?

Table 9 indicates quite conclusively that the answer to the preceding query is negative. It is clear from that table that the creativity and intelligence measures are relatively independent of each other. The correlations between creativity and intelligence measures for the sample as a whole are quite low. While 10 of the 100 r's are significant beyond the .01 level, and an additional 11 beyond the .05 level, it can be seen that no correlation exceeds .23. This low relationship between the two sets of measures would not in itself be significant were it not for the following four additional items of information that have been demonstrated: (1) the ten creativity indices are quite highly related among themselves; (2) each of the ten creativity measures is highly reliable; (3) the ten intelligence indices are quite highly related among themselves; and (4) each of the ten measures of intelligence is highly reliable. In the light of these four points, the relative independence of the intelligence and creativity domains becomes a highly noteworthy finding. The dimension of creativity, as presently defined, possesses a degree of internal consistency and pervasiveness which is kindred to that possessed by the conventional intelligence dimension. Yet we find that individual differences in creativity, as operationalized in terms of the ten measures in question, are largely independent of individual differences in the conventionally demarcated domain of general intelligence. We have been able to provide an operational definition of creativity that does justify conceiving of it as substantially independent of the intelligence concept and as possessing a goodly degree of generality.

Table 9.

INTERCORRELATIONS BETWEEN THE TEN CREATIVITY AND TEN INTELLIGENCE MEASURES FOR THE TOTAL SAMPLE ($N = 151$)

	WISC V	WISC PA	WISC BD	SCAT V	SCAT Q	STEP M	STEP S	STEP SS	STEP R	STEP W
Instances–uniqueness	11	12	02	01	−11	06	00	05	00	−09
Instances–number	09	17	15	06	07	07	20	17	08	09
Alternate uses–uniqueness	14	11	−01	05	03	12	12	10	07	06
Alternate uses–number	13	09	06	16	13	22	15	18	14	16
Similarities–uniqueness	09	12	−03	09	02	09	07	08	01	01
Similarities–number	19	14	02	22	13	23	17	21	11	14
Pattern meanings–uniqueness	11	01	06	12	13	15	13	12	09	15
Pattern meanings–number	−13	12	−03	−01	00	−05	01	−04	−02	05
Line meanings–uniqueness	22	21	11	21	21	17	23	21	17	19
Line meanings–number	03	09	04	11	12	02	07	10	11	10

NOTE: For 149 df, r's of .16 and .21 are significant at the .05 and .01 levels, respectively. Decimal points are omitted.

The Dimensionality of Creativity and Intelligence for the Sexes Considered Separately

The findings thus far reported have been based upon the sample of 151 children as a whole, with its approximately equal division between the sexes. Are analogous findings obtained for each sex taken separately? We turn first to the results for the boys. These results are presented in Tables 10, 11, and 12. In a fashion analogous to Tables 7 through 9, Table 10 presents intercorrelations among the creativity indices, Table 11 presents intercorrelations among the intelligence measures, and Table 12 presents intercorrelations between the creativity and intelligence measures, for the sample of 70 boys. The results are quite similar to those found for the total sample. As Table 10 indicates, the various creativity measures are strongly intercorrelated (27 and 33 of 45 r's significant at the .01 and .05 levels, respectively), including the fact of substantial relationships between verbal and visual procedures. The variable with the lowest correlations, instances–uniqueness, was the least reliable of the ten creativity indices. Table 11, in turn, reveals a high degree of interrelationship among nine of the ten intelligence measures. It is evident that the WISC Picture Arrangement subtest is minimally related to the general intelligence domain in the case of the boys. Finally, we find in Table 12 that the creativity and the intelligence measures are essentially independent of each other. The two sets of indicators, each defining a strong dimension, are virtually orthogonal. Only one of the 100 correlations is significant beyond the .01 level, with an additional four being significant beyond the .05 level.

Tables 13, 14, and 15 present the analogous information for the sample of 81 girls. The results strongly resemble those already considered for the sample as a whole and for the boys. In Table 13, we find exceedingly strong interrelationships among the ten indicators of creativity, again clearly bridging verbal and visual task content. Indeed, 44 of the 45 correlations are significant beyond the .01 level. The correlations among the ten indices of general intelligence, as reported in Table 14, are almost equally large. Forty-four of 45 r's are significant beyond the .05 level, and 40 of 45 beyond the .01 level. Once again, however, as revealed in Table 15, these two sets of measures show a substantial degree of independence of each other. Seven of the 100 r's prove significant at the .01 level; an additional 10 are significant at the .05 level. The maximum value of r in Table 15 is .32.

For each sex considered separately as well as for both sexes combined, then, our findings point in the same direction. Our ten creativity measures cohere strongly for the members of both sexes. On the whole, a child who produces many responses, and many responses that are

Table 10.

INTERCORRELATIONS AMONG THE TEN CREATIVITY MEASURES FOR THE BOYS ($N = 70$)

	2	3	4	5	6	7	8	9	10
1. Instances–uniqueness	−10	44	18	32	29	15	−04	23	11
2. Instances–number		25	42	10	41	16	25	26	42
3. Alternate uses–uniqueness			66	73	73	30	25	35	42
4. Alternate uses–number				48	66	47	31	31	54
5. Similarities–uniqueness					68	35	20	43	34
6. Similarities–number						39	31	48	50
7. Pattern meanings–uniqueness							04	50	42
8. Pattern meanings–number								05	22
9. Line meanings–uniqueness									47
10. Line meanings–number									

NOTE: For 68 *df*, *r*'s of .24 and .31 are significant at the .05 and .01 levels, respectively. Decimal points are omitted.

Table 11.

INTERCORRELATIONS AMONG THE TEN INTELLIGENCE MEASURES FOR THE BOYS ($N = 70$)

	2	3	4	5	6	7	8	9	10
1. WISC–vocabulary (V)	02	37	55	36	51	50	55	39	46
2. WISC–picture arrangement (PA)		03	−08	20	05	18	16	03	06
3. WISC–block design (BD)			38	48	60	42	38	38	36
4. SCAT–verbal (V)				71	72	69	82	71	75
5. SCAT–quantitative (Q)					75	68	74	78	76
6. STEP–mathematics (M)						68	78	64	72
7. STEP–science (S)							80	69	69
8. STEP–social studies (SS)								70	76
9. STEP–reading (R)									76
10. STEP–writing (W)									

NOTE: For 68 *df*, *r*'s of .24 and .31 are significant at the .05 and .01 levels, respectively. Decimal points are omitted.

Table 12.

INTERCORRELATIONS BETWEEN THE TEN CREATIVITY AND TEN INTELLIGENCE MEASURES FOR THE BOYS ($N = 70$)

	WISC V	WISC PA	WISC BD	SCAT V	SCAT Q	STEP M	STEP S	STEP SS	STEP R	STEP W
Instances–uniqueness	05	00	—11	—06	—10	01	—03	—04	11	—03
Instances–number	15	21	19	12	06	07	29	15	08	16
Alternate uses–uniqueness	10	12	00	00	—12	04	07	—01	01	08
Alternate uses–number	05	07	13	20	04	19	10	09	10	27
Similarities–uniqueness	06	12	00	07	—03	09	06	06	04	09
Similarities–number	13	08	01	14	—08	15	11	10	00	11
Pattern meanings–uniqueness	17	—08	02	24	14	23	14	17	19	36
Pattern meanings–number	—20	18	—14	—12	—17	—22	—10	—21	—13	—08
Line meanings–uniqueness	20	27	—01	06	09	10	18	12	09	11
Line meanings–number	—05	10	—12	—03	—07	—12	—03	—07	02	—01

NOTE: For 68 df, r's of .24 and .31 are significant at the .05 and .01 levels, respectively. Decimal points are omitted.

Table 13.

INTERCORRELATIONS AMONG THE TEN CREATIVITY MEASURES FOR THE GIRLS ($N = 81$)

	2	3	4	5	6	7	8	9	10
1. Instances–uniqueness	31	43	33	41	43	44	38	57	42
2. Instances–number		43	48	34	41	35	38	37	44
3. Alternate uses–uniqueness			68	59	69	61	35	52	62
4. Alternate uses–number				58	80	51	50	44	63
5. Similarities–uniqueness					76	30	21	54	58
6. Similarities–number						49	48	55	64
7. Pattern meanings–uniqueness							59	58	57
8. Pattern meanings–number								49	59
9. Line meanings–uniqueness									74
10. Line meanings–number									

NOTE: For 79 df, r's of .22 and .29 are significant at the .05 and .01 levels, respectively. Decimal points are omitted.

Table 14.

INTERCORRELATIONS AMONG THE TEN INTELLIGENCE MEASURES FOR THE GIRLS ($N = 81$)

	2	3	4	5	6	7	8	9	10
1. WISC–vocabulary (V)	28	31	60	51	58	60	65	57	57
2. WISC–picture arrangement (PA)		24	32	18	29	31	29	22	27
3. WISC–block design (BD)			33	33	40	34	39	29	30
4. SCAT–verbal (V)				73	72	75	78	72	82
5. SCAT–quantitative (Q)					77	67	69	70	76
6. STEP–mathematics (M)						69	68	65	71
7. STEP–science (S)							73	77	77
8. STEP–social studies (SS)								75	77
9. STEP–reading (R)									83
10. STEP–writing (W)									

NOTE: For 79 df, r's of .22 and .29 are significant at the .05 and .01 levels, respectively. Decimal points are omitted.

Table 15.

INTERCORRELATIONS BETWEEN THE TEN CREATIVITY AND TEN INTELLIGENCE MEASURES FOR THE GIRLS ($N = 81$)

	WISC V	WISC PA	WISC BD	SCAT V	SCAT Q	STEP M	STEP S	STEP SS	STEP R	STEP W
Instances–uniqueness	02	19	00	10	03	–00	07	16	02	05
Instances–number	04	14	12	01	09	08	10	19	09	05
Alternate uses–uniqueness	18	10	–03	09	19	18	18	21	15	06
Alternate uses–number	19	11	–00	13	21	24	20	26	20	10
Similarities–uniqueness	11	12	–06	11	07	09	09	10	–02	–06
Similarities–number	25	18	03	28	29	31	25	31	19	18
Pattern meanings–uniqueness	05	06	07	02	14	07	12	07	02	–00
Pattern meanings–number	01	10	14	14	17	20	18	18	09	16
Line meanings–uniqueness	24	17	20	32	30	23	30	29	24	25
Line meanings–number	12	09	16	20	21	13	16	22	14	12

NOTE: For 79 df, r's of .22 and .29 are significant at the .05 and .01 levels, respectively. Decimal points are omitted.

unique, in the case of a given procedure, also will generate many responses and many unique ones in the case of the remaining four procedures. A child who exhibits a paucity of responses, and a paucity of unique associates, when confronted with one procedure, will show the same lacks on each of the other procedures. The ten indices of general intelligence, in turn, also manifest a generally high degree of unity. Nevertheless, these two domains of measures are relatively independent of each other.

The evidence for these statements is summarized in the entries of Table 16, both for the sample as a whole and for each sex separately. The numbers in a given column are the average of the 45 correlations among all pairs of creativity measures, the average of the 45 correlations among all pairs of general intelligence measures, and the average of the 100 correlations among all pairs of creativity and intelligence measures. These data may be compared to the numerical summaries we provided for the various studies reviewed in Chapter 1. It will be recalled that the studies in question yielded relatively low intercorrelations among "creativity" measures, compared to the correlations of these measures, in turn, with general intelligence. On the whole, we were led to conclude that the indicators assumed to tap creativity actually assessed little in common beyond the variance that they also shared with intelligence. The contrast between that state of affairs and the findings we have obtained in the present investigation is rather striking. The contents of Tables 7 through 15, as summarized in the averages of Table 16, tell a quite different story. We note in Table 16 that average correlations among creativity indices are on the order of .40, and are almost as strong as average correlations among intelligence indices. On the other hand, average correlations be-

Table 16.

AVERAGE INTERCORRELATIONS AMONG CREATIVITY MEASURES,
AMONG INTELLIGENCE MEASURES,
AND BETWEEN CREATIVITY AND INTELLIGENCE MEASURES

	Total sample ($N = 151$)	Boys ($N = 70$)	Girls ($N = 81$)
Among creativity measures ($n = 45$ r's)	.41	.34	.50
Among intelligence measures ($n = 45$ r's)	.51	.50	.55
Between creativity and intelligence measures ($n = 100$ r's)	.09	.05	.13

tween creativity and intelligence indices are on the order of .10. Clearly, a dimension of individual differences has been isolated that possesses generality and yet is quite distinct from intelligence as classically defined. The tests of adequacy that needed to be fulfilled in order for a definition of creativity to be psychologically tenable have been met. The definition that passes these tests focuses upon the ability to generate or produce many associative responses, and to generate many that are unique, within some general set of task constraints.

That the psychological ability just described should turn out to be relatively independent of individual differences in general intelligence, constitutes a finding that is far from obvious. One might well have thought that conventional verbal intelligence would function as a strong component in our creativity procedures, since these procedures call upon the child to make verbal responses and to do so with as much facility as he can muster. Under the conditions of freedom from evaluation and absence of time pressure, however, we find that the ability to generate associative verbal responses comes from a source different from intelligence as traditionally conceived. Such an outcome is all the more impressive when found in the case of elementary school children, since it is reasonable to assume that children are, in general, less differentiated in cognitive functioning than are adults.

We have ascertained that the correlational patterns in regard to the creativity and intelligence measures are highly similar for the two sexes. A further question concerns the possibility of sex differences in means for these measures. Tables 17 and 18 present the relevant information for the ten creativity indicators and the ten intelligence variables, respectively. Consider first the creativity indicators as shown in Table 17. For eight of the ten measures, the means for males and females are highly similar. Note (see the Appendix) that it is the procedure administered first—instances—which yields the significant sex difference in favor of the boys. Conceivably, the girls by virtue of their greater anxiety (see Chapter 6) did not adapt as quickly to the experimental situation, despite our every attempt to create a distinctly relaxed and nonevaluative atmosphere. High anxiety levels might readily contribute to an initially guarded attitude toward the whole experimental setting, with an inhibition of the associative, creative process as the anticipated outcome. Girls may simply require a slightly longer "warm-up" period. In any event, the fact of no sex difference between the means on the subsequent eight measures argues strongly for the conclusion that, in general, the performance levels of boys and girls on the creativity instruments are very much alike.

We turn next to Table 18, which presents the analogous findings in the case of the intelligence variables. The male and female means

Table 17.

SEX COMPARISONS ON THE TEN CREATIVITY VARIABLES

Variable	Boys (N = 70)		Girls (N = 81)		t	p
	Mean	SD	Mean	SD		
Instances–uniqueness	6.36	3.91	3.70	2.70	4.90	<.01
Instances–number	45.13	7.44	42.31	8.22	2.20	<.05
Alternate uses–uniqueness	10.29	9.48	9.67	8.71	0.42	n.s.
Alternate uses–number	46.73	19.54	45.42	20.18	0.40	n.s.
Similarities–uniqueness	4.80	6.40	4.59	5.65	0.21	n.s.
Similarities–number	45.47	18.99	45.52	19.96	0.01	n.s.
Pattern meanings–uniqueness	12.49	9.36	11.88	9.94	0.39	n.s.
Pattern meanings–number	34.60	14.33	35.37	15.41	0.32	n.s.
Line meanings–uniqueness	7.89	6.08	7.91	7.06	0.03	n.s.
Line meanings–number	38.06	13.91	40.86	20.38	0.97	n.s.

Table 18.

SEX COMPARISONS ON THE TEN INTELLIGENCE VARIABLES

Variable	Boys (N = 70)		Girls (N = 81)		t	p
	Mean	SD	Mean	SD		
WISC–vocabulary	43.59	6.53	41.23	5.56	2.39	<.02
WISC–picture arrangement	31.00	5.28	29.86	6.69	1.14	n.s.
WISC–block design	32.71	9.93	28.60	10.32	2.48	<.02
SCAT–verbal	256.74	11.43	256.64	10.72	0.06	n.s.
SCAT–quantitative	256.17	8.70	259.70	9.18	2.42	<.02
STEP–mathematics	255.21	10.65	252.04	10.21	1.87	n.s.
STEP–science	263.09	12.91	263.42	9.57	0.18	n.s.
STEP–social studies	257.91	11.82	257.46	11.00	0.25	n.s.
STEP–reading	262.97	16.48	268.30	14.97	2.08	<.05
STEP–writing	259.19	15.86	267.04	16.05	3.01	<.01

are comparable in the case of five of the ten measures. In the case of the remaining five, where significant sex differences occur, there is no systematic pattern suggestive of greater over-all intellectual power for either sex. Thus, within the verbal sphere, boys do better on the WISC Vocabulary subtest, while girls manifest superiority on the STEP Reading and Writing tests. In the quantitative area, the girls have significantly higher scores on SCAT-Quantitative, yet boys exhibit a distinct trend ($p < .10$) toward superior performance on STEP-Mathematics. Only in the case of WISC-Block Design, where boys are in the ascendancy, is there no balanced superiority for girls on another visual performance subtest. On the whole, therefore, we are led to conclude that the mean performances of the sexes on the intelligence instruments are relatively comparable.

Our consideration of the dimensionality of creativity as we have defined it, and of general intelligence, thus has led us to a very different outcome from that represented by the studies reviewed in the first chapter. Given the empirical warrant provided by the present investigation for conceiving of creativity as a psychological ability that is both pervasive and distinct from general intelligence, we can turn our attention now to studying the psychological correlates of creativity and intelligence considered jointly. Their relative independence permits us to focus on groups of children who are both creative and intelligent, neither creative nor intelligent, creative but not intelligent, and intelligent but not creative. To assign a given child to one of these four groups, we shall develop a single estimate of his level of creativity, and a single estimate of his level of general intelligence. We turn next to the construction of these over-all measures and to the composition of the four groups just described.

Composition of Groups High and Low in Creativity and Intelligence

In the case of both the creativity and the intelligence domains, inspection of the relevant correlation matrices suggests that the ten variables within each domain share sufficient variance in common to warrant giving them equal weights in the computation of over-all index scores.[7]

---

[7] Recall that the WISC Picture Arrangement subtest fell short of this criterion particularly in the case of the boys. We decided to retain this test, however, rather than have the sexes differ in the composition of the over-all index score for intelligence. Since the r's for boys between the WISC Picture Arrangement subtest and the other intelligence measures are (with one exception) in the low positive range, and since the contribution of that subtest to the total is on the order of 0.1, the inclusion of the WISC subtest in question cannot have much of a biasing effect on the over-all index score. Similar remarks apply for the uniqueness variable from the instances procedure in the case of the boys.

To accomplish this end, each of the twenty variables was transformed into standard score form for the sample as a whole. That is, in the case of a particular variable, each of the 151 scores was subtracted from the mean of those scores and the difference was divided by the standard deviation of those scores. The result is a score distribution with a mean of 0 and a standard deviation of 1: a distribution that hence is comparable from variable to variable. An individual child's standard scores for all ten creativity variables then were summed to yield his *creativity index score*. In similar fashion, his standard scores for all ten general intelligence variables were summed to yield his *intelligence index score*.

The comparability of the sexes on these index scores is indicated in Table 19. The boys and girls are very similar in regard to each kind of index score, and this is true both for central tendencies and for variabilities. These findings reinforce the general impression of similarity that we obtained from examining the means for boys and girls on each of the variables in the creativity and intelligence domains. Given the index score results presented in Table 19, it is evident that, in the case both of creativity index scores and of intelligence index scores, the score distributions for the two sexes are highly similar. This implies that median dichotomizations of a given domain's index scores within sex will yield upper and lower halves for the two sexes that are quite congruent.

Our next step was to compose groups, within sex, that would constitute the four possible combinations of high and low creativity and intelligence. Our definition of "high" and "low" for a given sex was a conservative one: the index scores for creativity or intelligence were dichotomized at their median and called "high" if they fell in the upper half of the distribution, "low" if they fell in the lower half. Thus, all

Table 19.

SEX COMPARISONS ON THE CREATIVITY AND
INTELLIGENCE INDEX SCORES

	Boys (N = 70)		Girls (N = 81)			
	Mean	SD	Mean	SD	t	p
Creativity index score	0.60	6.93	−0.52	7.89	0.91	n. s.
Intelligence index score	0.05	7.61	−0.04	7.41	0.07	n. s.

Parenthetically, it might also be noted that the WISC Picture Arrangement subtest was the first evaluative instrument administered following the long series of gamelike procedures. This radical switch in experimental atmosphere might have served to reduce the correlations between that subtest and other intelligence measures below what would ordinarily have been the case where a single testing context prevails.

cases in the sample were utilized, rather than just upper and lower extremes. It is evident that a procedure which retains all cases, rather than eliminating a portion of the sample and working only with the extremes, is the conservative approach in a study of the present kind. For the boys, with an even number of cases ($N = 70$), this meant that 35 individuals were assigned to the high creativity half and 35 to the low creativity half. Likewise, in the case of intelligence, the split for the boys was 35 : 35. Since the sample of girls provided an odd number of cases ($N = 81$), the score that fell at the median was assigned at random and without knowledge of results to the lower half in the case of creativity and to the upper half in the case of intelligence. Thus, the dichotomy for the girls was 40 : 41 for high and low creativity, respectively, and was 41 : 40 for high and low intelligence, respectively.

Given our demonstrations of the relative independence of the creativity and intelligence dimensions, as we have defined them, we now proceeded to distribute the children of each sex in terms of their joint standing on the creativity and intelligence index scores. In the case of each sex, those in the upper half of their sex distribution on the creativity index score were assigned to one group if they also were in the upper half of their sex distribution on intelligence, and to another group if they fell in the lower half of the intelligence distribution. Likewise, those in the low creativity half were assigned to one group if they also were in the lower half on the intelligence index score, and to another group if they fell in the upper half on intelligence. The relative orthogonality of creativity and intelligence implies that approximately equal numbers of children should fall within each of these four groups. The results of distributing the children in the manner described are the group sizes presented in Tables 20 and 21 for the boys and girls, respectively. It is evident from these tables that the four groups within each sex resulting from the median dichotomizations of the creativity and intelligence index scores are, as expected, approximately equal in size.

The stage is now set for a series of 2×2 analyses of variance in which the four subgroups defined by the intelligence and creativity dimensions can be compared on a number of relevant psychological variables. These comparisons will form the basis of most of the material to follow in the remaining chapters of the volume. The sample sizes set down in Tables 20 and 21 will apply in all of the 2×2 analyses of variance to be reported (except for Tables 68 through 81). Since the number of cases varied slightly across the four subgroup cells, Snedecor's (1946) method of unweighted means for 2×2 tables was used.

It should be pointed out that the analysis of variance technique which we utilize is a very "robust" test. This term is used by Box (1953) to characterize statistical tests that are relatively impervious to violations

Table 20.

SAMPLE SIZES FOR GROUPS OF BOYS HIGH AND LOW
IN CREATIVITY AND INTELLIGENCE

INTELLIGENCE

		High	Low
	High	N = 17	N = 18
CREATIVITY			
	Low	N = 18	N = 17

Table 21.

SAMPLE SIZES FOR GROUPS OF GIRLS HIGH AND LOW
IN CREATIVITY AND INTELLIGENCE

INTELLIGENCE

		High	Low
	High	N = 22	N = 18
CREATIVITY			
	Low	N = 19	N = 22

of their underlying assumptions. In particular, it now has been amply demonstrated (see, for example, Boneau, 1960; Box, 1953; 1954a; 1954b; David & Johnson, 1951; Horsnell, 1953) that the F test of analysis of variance and the t test are inconsequentially affected by heterogeneity of variances if the sample sizes in question are approximately equal and sufficiently large (say, no less than 15). This fact has been demonstrated both mathematically and by means of random sampling studies. Given sample sizes that are approximately equal and adequately large, variance differences can be very considerable and still affect the true probability of rejecting the null hypothesis of equal means to only an inconsequential degree. In the light of these demonstrations concerning the t test and the F test of analysis of variance, it is evident that the question of heterogeneity vs. homogeneity of variances is quite irrelevant in connection with the 2×2 analyses of variance performed in the present investigation.

It is especially relevant to note in this connection that typical tests for homogeneity of variance, such as the Bartlett test (Bartlett, 1937), lack robustness—that is, they are much influenced by violation of their underlying assumptions. Thus, Box (1953) and Boneau (1960) indicate that the Bartlett test can yield significant values that imply rejection of the null hypothesis of equal variances under conditions where the variances actually are identical but the distributions vary from normality. The situation is well summed up in the following quotation from Boneau, who in turn also quotes from the Box (1953) article: "Box, realizing that in the case of equal sample sizes the analysis of variance is affected surprisingly little by heterogeneous variance and non-normality, concludes that the use of the nonrobust Bartlett test to 'make the preliminary test on variances is rather like putting out to sea in a rowing boat to find out whether conditions are sufficiently calm for an ocean liner to leave port!' " (Boneau, 1960, p. 62).

In assessing the statistical significance of effects observed in the analyses of variance, we shall attempt to interpret F-values at the .10 level and below. Acceptance of this level appears reasonable here, since the composition of subgroups is based not on extremes, but on median splits. In other words, there will be a substantial number of individuals in the vicinity of the median, but on either side of it, whom we do not anticipate to be basically different from one another with respect to the two dimensions under consideration. This can only serve to attenuate whatever differences may exist among the subgroups. Under these circumstances, we deemed it advisable at the present stage of inquiry to increase somewhat the probability of a Type I error (rejecting the null hypothesis when it is true), and to reduce somewhat the probability of a Type II error (accepting the null hypothesis when it is false).

At this point, then, we have established, within each sex, four groups of children: those who are high in both creativity and intelligence, those who are high in one but low in the other, and those who are low in both. It is relevant to note further that these four groups of children in the case of each sex are homogeneous in age. The data are presented in Tables 22 and 23 for boys and girls, respectively. The mean ages of the four groups of each sex are highly similar, as revealed by the analysis of variance presented below each set of means. All of the effects in the analyses of variance for boys and for girls are nonsignificant, nor does any effect in either analysis even approach significance. We may infer, therefore, that any differences in psychological functioning displayed by the four groups of each sex are not mediated by differences in age.

Table 22.

MEAN AGES OF THE FOUR GROUPS OF BOYS ($N = 70$)

INTELLIGENCE

		High	Low
CREATIVITY	High	10 yr., 7.88 mo. (5.29 mo.)	10 yr., 8.33 mo. (5.94 mo.)
	Low	10 yr., 7.28 mo. (5.14 mo.)	10 yr., 9.24 mo. (7.73 mo.)

ANALYSIS OF VARIANCE

Source	df	MS	F	p
Intelligence	1	1.45	<1.00	n. s.
Creativity	1	0.02	<1.00	n. s.
Interaction	1	0.57	<1.00	n. s.
Within cells	66	2.13		

NOTE: In this and all subsequent 2×2 tables, standard deviations appear in parentheses.

Table 23.

MEAN AGES OF THE FOUR GROUPS OF GIRLS ($N = 81$)

INTELLIGENCE

		High	Low
CREATIVITY	High	10 yr., 7.50 mo. (5.60 mo.)	10 yr., 5.61 mo. (4.79 mo.)
	Low	10 yr., 6.84 mo. (3.85 mo.)	10 yr., 8.14 mo. (4.83 mo.)

ANALYSIS OF VARIANCE

Source	df	MS	F	p
Intelligence	1	0.09	<1.00	n. s.
Creativity	1	0.87	<1.00	n. s.
Interaction	1	2.53	2.17	n. s.
Within cells	77	1.17		

SUMMARY

This chapter both provides us with answers and prods us toward the asking of further questions. We began our investigation against a background of negative results. As indicated in the preceding chapter, an evaluation of previous relevant research left us with the conclusion that no firm evidence was at hand indicating the psychological existence of a "creativity" dimension distinct from general intelligence. Again and again, what was described as creativity dissolved into the intelligence concept or ended up as one or another highly specific trait quite without the pervasiveness and generality that one expects of a basic mode of cognitive activity.

These negative findings stimulated us to search for a clearer and more specific psychological definition of creativity. This search, which followed the route of introspective reports by artists and scientists, led us to an associational conception that focused upon the ability to generate or produce associative content that was plentiful and that was unique, within a criterion of task relevance. The introspective material just mentioned also led us to consider anew the type of context within which creativity might best be expected to display itself. We found ourselves led to concepts such as task-orientation in contrast to ego-orientation, permissiveness and playfulness in contrast to evaluation. Translated into prescriptions for operations, it was clear that attempts at measurement of creativity needed to proceed in an evaluation-free context that was unfettered by such forms of pressure as the imposition of time limits. All this was quite the opposite of the situation that prevailed in the studies that we had been reviewing.

We thus had arrived at a psychological characterization of creativity which offered a possible explanation of why the studies which we had been considering failed to discriminate statistically between the intelligence and creativity domains. It was possible that their starting definition of the term "creativity" was much too diffuse, and that the social psychological context within which they proceeded possessed properties that were quite the opposite of those that would be conducive to the expression of creativity.

In the research reported in the present chapter, we approached creativity in a manner that followed from the considerations mentioned. Procedures were designed in order reliably to study generation and uniqueness of cognitive associates across a sizable range of task content and in a setting free from evaluative stress. Working with a sample of 151 fifth grade children, we have obtained evidence that creativity as herein defined—the ability to generate many cognitive associates and many that are unique—is strikingly independent of the conventional realm of general intelligence, while at the same time being a unitary and pervasive dimension of individual differences in its own right. This evidence holds for members of both sexes. We can assert with high confidence, then, that the ability of a child to display creativity as we here conceive of it, has little to do with whether or not he exhibits the behavior that will earn him high scores on measures of general intelligence.

Such a finding seems especially intriguing in the light of two points that we mentioned earlier but that deserve emphasis in closing this chapter. First, the procedures designed for studying creativity require the exercise of verbal skill on the part of the child, and it is widely recognized that verbal facility plays a large role in assessors of general intelligence. Nevertheless, we find our creativity indicators to be largely independent of individual differences in general intelligence. Second, the relative orthogonality of creativity and intelligence has been demonstrated here at an age level well below that at which we would expect maximum differentiation of types of cognitive performances. Nevertheless, the distinction between the two modes of thinking activity represented by the creativity and intelligence domains seems to be quite clear in an elementary school population.

Having succeeded in defining groups of children within each sex who are creative and intelligent, creative but not intelligent, intelligent but not creative, and neither intelligent nor creative, we now are in a position to set forth toward the second general objective of the present volume: namely, the goal of advancing our understanding of the psychological differences among these four types of children. The pursuit of this goal quite evidently constitutes a voyage of discovery rather than a journey over well-charted terrain. Accordingly, as we noted in the opening paragraphs of Chapter 1, we cast our net widely in terms of the kinds of evidence that we wished to survey. In the chapters that follow, we consider in turn each of the classes of evidence that seemed important to investigate in our attempt to understand the groups in question. We turn first in this connection to a broad perspective: systematic observations of the child's behavior in the school setting. It seemed most appropriate to begin our search for differences among the groups of children by seeking to describe in as adequate terms as possible the behavior that could be viewed by an observer as these children went about their daily activities.

3 ❦

Behavior in
the School
Environment

Do the performances reflected in the experimental and test contexts discussed in the previous chapter have any implications for "real life" behavior? For children of elementary school age, a substantial portion of such behavior occurs in the school setting. How have psychologists attempted to measure behavior under these naturalistic conditions? The prime if not the only method is some variant of rating. In the large majority of cases, these ratings are derived from the child's teachers and peers.

Both of these forms of rating present certain difficulties, if our aim is one of achieving an objective account of the child's actual behavior. Indeed, it is quite possible that these ratings actually tell us more about the persons making the ratings than about the persons rated, or at least tell us as much about the former as about the latter. We strongly doubt, in other words, that an objective descriptive account of *behavior* in a classroom context will be achieved where the rater and the person rated have a prolonged and intensive contact with each other in a context of emotionally tinged social interaction. Of course, if it is the rater's affective preference for the individual rated that is at issue, the difficulties outlined above are not especially relevant. Where the concrete behavior of the "ratee" is of concern, on the other hand, the greater the degree of interpersonal involvement, the more reason to suspect subjectivity of judgment. One pronounced consequence of this subjectivity is the well-known "halo-effect" in which the ratings of a diverse array of behaviors are highly correlated. That teacher ratings may be particularly susceptible to a halo-effect is a conclusion to be drawn from a study by

Holland (1959). Average intercorrelations of each rating variable against all of the other variables ranged from .51 to .70. In short, despite the wide range of behaviors tapped by Holland's scales—for example, originality, popularity, drive to achieve, physical vigor—it is quite evident that the teachers are rating their pupils in terms of some over-all evaluative dimension. Relating this dimension to a variety of other variables, Holland finds that the largest correlations emerge for high school rank in academic achievement. While it is feasible that the behaviors studied by Holland are indeed highly interrelated, a more reasonable assumption is that the positive value attaching to the achievement of good grades in school exerts a distorting effect upon teachers' judgments. In many instances, the teacher is acquainted with a student's scores on standardized aptitude and achievement tests, as well as with his previous school record. Here the teacher's values are especially prone to influence his judgment of the student.

Much of what we have said above also holds in the case of peer ratings. There is a great deal of evidence in the sociometric literature suggesting that no matter which of a number of sociometric criteria are given to the judges as the basis for their ratings, the same individuals tend to be chosen or rejected. Again, knowing whether a particular individual is liked or disliked by his peers, we can make fairly good predictions of how he will be evaluated on a variety of other dimensions. Gronlund (1959), reviewing a number of studies on this problem, reports correlations ranging from the .50's to the .90's between sociometric status scores derived from such diverse criteria as work companion and play companion. Of special relevance for our purposes is the tendency for these correlations to increase as the age of the child decreases. With elementary school children, in other words, a general social acceptability dimension can account for sociometric choices across a variety of criteria.

Given the firm evidence on halo-effects, one can only have grave doubts about studies that employ teacher ratings (such as Piers, Daniels, & Quackenbush, 1960) or peer ratings (such as Reid, King, & Wickwire, 1959) as criteria of creativity. Holland (1959) has demonstrated that "originality" ratings yield correlations ranging in magnitude from .48 to .84 with ratings of other behaviors whose link with "originality" should be quite tenuous indeed (for example, dependability, citizenship, popularity). It is quite clear, then, that teachers have little conception of what behaviors should be subsumed under the categories of "creativity" or "originality." Indeed, even when teachers are given a highly specific definition of creativity (Piers *et al.*, 1960), the correlations between different teachers rating the same pupils are remarkably low. Possibly, teachers are confused by a definition specifying a class of behaviors to which they have given little heed in their classroom activities.

One must also recognize that a pupil's behavior may vary from class to class as a function of differential subject-matter competence, of different teachers' attitudes and behaviors toward a given student, and of the general classroom atmosphere fostered by the teacher. The reliability problem is especially intractable in the case of elementary school samples, for pupils are often exposed to a single teacher for the entire school day. Where the investigation encompasses more than one classroom (and this is usually the case), the issue of teacher differences arises in its most extreme form. Under these conditions, we have no way of ascertaining whether pupils in different classrooms would receive comparable ratings, if the opportunity for equal levels of interaction with two or more teachers were provided.

If teachers encounter considerable difficulty in reliably rating a student's creativity, one can only wonder on what basis a student's peers make "creativity" ratings. The strong relationship between such ratings and various aptitude and achievement test scores in the Reid *et al.* (1959) study suggests the particular criteria that the subjects employed: criteria of general intelligence. When peer ratings of "creativity" are introduced at the elementary school level (Torrance, 1963, for example), one can only have grave doubts about the relevance of such ratings for behavior indicative of creativity as defined in an objective sense.

There are conditions where ratings seem somewhat less suspect as criteria for "creative" performance. In MacKinnon's (1962) research, professional groups (such as architects) were asked to nominate their most creative members. Such a peer-rating criterion for creativity appears justifiable on the surface, since products are generally available for evaluation in these circumstances. As Thorndike (1963) has pointed out, however, the meaning of these "creativity" ratings is by no means unambiguous. While members of various professional groups might well show considerable agreement in rating one another for "creativity," it is quite conceivable that such ratings would be indistinguishable from those based on a criterion of "productivity," for example. Thorndike states the critical question very concisely: "Do ratings and nominations for 'creativity' only have a certain amount of general validity as indicators of professional reputation, or do they have *specific, differential* validity in picking out those who are creative from among all those who are professionally successful and visible (1963, p. 44)?" In the light of the strong evidence presented earlier for consistent "halo-effects" in peer ratings, the likelihood is small that any type of rating measure will be truly adequate as a criterion for creativity.

Given the dubious status of creativity ratings in the case of members of professional groups for whom high-level products are available, teacher and peer ratings of creativity in school contexts must by comparison be evaluated as next to worthless. Bases for judgment in the latter case are bound to be highly idiosyncratic to the rater, and hence reflective of properties of behavior bearing little relation to the creativity dimension that the investigator presumably hopes to measure.

A more reasonable use of ratings with school samples is to treat them as a further source of information about individuals whose thinking styles (''creative'' vs. ''noncreative'') are defined by objective performance. Getzels and Jackson (1962), for example, claim that teachers prefer the ''high IQ'' to the ''high creativity'' types (as defined by those authors' test criteria). The claim has only a weak basis in empirical fact, however. While their data show a significantly greater teacher preference for ''high IQ'' relative to average pupils (and only a nonsignificant trend in the same direction for ''high creatives''), a direct comparison of teacher preferences for ''high IQ'' and ''high creative'' individuals does not yield a statistically significant difference. Getzels and Jackson also obtained teacher ratings of ''social skills'' and ''involvement in learning,'' but these dimensions are not discussed in relation to the IQ–creativity distinction. Presumably, the dimensions in question did not discriminate those authors' criterion groups. While the point is not made explicit, one gets the impression that Getzels and Jackson's intent in the use of teacher ratings was to assess the teacher's value system regarding pupils' behavior rather than the students' actual classroom demeanor.

Torrance (1963) appears to hold a view similar to that of Getzels and Jackson regarding the meaning of both teacher and peer ratings, though elsewhere he conceives of peer nominations as ''intermediate criteria for studying the validity of tests of creative thinking'' (Torrance, 1962, p. 51). In accord with this latter aim, the questions asked of the children required that they nominate others along such dimensions as fluency, flexibility, and inventiveness. Again, we can only express pessimism regarding the ability of elementary school children to use those dimensions in any meaningful way. Unfortunately, Torrance's anecdotal presentation of his findings makes it exceedingly difficult to evaluate whether anything beyond a general ''social acceptability'' factor is reflected in his sociometric data.

Consider, finally, the matter of staff ratings—the type of rating that may be most appropriate for obtaining indices of actual behavior. This method of behavior rating represents nothing new, of course. Where research on creativity is concerned, the Institute of Personality Assessment and Research (for example, Barron, 1955, 1963; Crutchfield, 1962) has long made extensive use of staff ratings of occupational groups (such as Army officers) brought to the Institute for observation and testing. It should be noted, however, that behaviors elicited under these circumstances will partly reflect the atypical setting in which the subjects find themselves. This is not likely to be a problem when studying children in the natural school setting. Where trained raters are given the opportunity to observe school children engaging in a variety of school and recreational activities over a reasonable period of time, we may have achieved the most accurate appraisal of behavior that can be obtained in practice. We assume, of course, that the raters have not been provided with any advance information about the children. Such trained raters should be able to retain the emotional distance from their subjects that is required for a truly objective description of behavior. Of course, the dimensions upon which the subjects are rated must reflect behaviors that are actually revealed in the school setting. Further, such dimensions should directly tap specific observable aspects of behavior. Rating students on such a dimension as "creativity" will necessarily force the judge to make inferences from behavior.[1] Obviously, ratings will become less and less reliable as one proceeds from description to inference. In any event, reliability can be readily assessed when two or more raters make independent judgments of behavior.

Our study has attempted to take account of the strictures outlined above. Subjects were rated independently by two observers on a set of dimensions selected so as to encompass a wide variety of specific behaviors typical of the school setting. These dimensions are in no sense viewed as criteria for the modes of thinking treated in the present report. Our aim, rather, is to explore whether the thinking styles characterizing the four subgroups of subjects under investigation have implications for behavior in the classroom setting.

---

[1] Barron (1955; 1963) has found that a staff rating for "creativity" correlates significantly with a composite score derived from a battery of creativity tests. The author's conclusion that the ratings validate the creativity tests hardly seems justified, however, for no relationships are reported between the "creativity" ratings, on the one hand, and intelligence test data or intelligence ratings, on the other. On the basis of the evidence reviewed in Chapter 1, it is quite conceivable that the creativity ratings and general intelligence are highly related in the present case. We do know, incidentally, that the composite score from the creativity tests is significantly correlated with the Concept Mastery Test, which is considered to be a measure of verbal intelligence: $r = .33$, $p < .01$, for a sample described by Barron (1963). Interestingly enough, the average of the 28 intercorrelations among the eight test scores that are summed in order to make up the composite creativity score used by Barron, is only .19 for a sample that includes the above cases. Once again we have to doubt, therefore, whether the tests in question share anything in common over and above what they also share in common with an intelligence measure. All of this simply adds, of course, to our suspicions that the relationship between the ratings for creativity and the composite score from the creativity tests can be accounted for in terms of the relationship between the creativity ratings and general intelligence.

PROCEDURE

Our intent in the construction of rating scales was to exhaust the repertoire of behaviors observable in the school environment from which the subjects were drawn. A tentative list of dimensions—nineteen in all —was prepared. On the basis of several days of observation in the classroom and other areas of the school, it became necessary to delete thirteen of those dimensions. The deleted dimensions turned out to be inadequate for one of three reasons: (1) the necessary information on *all* children could not be obtained, with the result that a common basis for judgment was lacking; (2) evidence for the dimension could not be found on a strictly behavioral level, thus forcing the rater to make inferential types of judgment; (3) the dimension overlapped too greatly with other dimensions that seemed to get at the behavior in question more directly.

To the six dimensions that remained, three new ones were added. These three reflected aspects of behavior that were overlooked in constructing the original list.

Initially, a five-point scale was provided for each dimension. However, when it became evident that finer discriminations among subjects was possible, the scale was expanded to nine points, every other point having a verbal label attached. The final version of the rating scales is reproduced below.

A. To what degree does this child seek attention in unsocialized ways, as evidenced by such behavior as speaking out of turn, continually raising his hand, or making unnecessary noises?

1	2	3	4	5	6	7	8	9
never		seldom		sometimes		usually		always

B. To what degree does this child hesitate to express opinions, as evidenced by extreme caution, failure to contribute, or a subdued manner in a speaking situation?

1	2	3	4	5	6	7	8	9
never		seldom		sometimes		usually		always

C. To what degree does this child show confidence and assurance in his actions toward his teachers and classmates, as indicated by such behavior as not being upset by criticism, or not being disturbed by rebuffs from classmates?

1	2	3	4	5	6	7	8	9
never		seldom		sometimes		usually		always

D. To what degree is this child's companionship sought for by his peers?

1	2	3	4	5	6	7	8	9
never		seldom		sometimes		usually		always

E. To what degree does this child seek the companionship of his peers?

1	2	3	4	5	6	7	8	9
never		seldom		sometimes		usually		always

F. To what degree does this child depreciate his work and himself, as indicated by such behavior as refusing to show or discuss the work he has done, or making deprecating statements about himself or his work?

1	2	3	4	5	6	7	8	9
never		seldom		sometimes		usually		always

G. To what degree do this child's actions seem to be inhibited by the formal classroom learning situation, as compared with behavior during recess, gym, or other free time?

1	2	3	4	5	6	7	8	9
never		seldom		sometimes		usually		always

H. How would you rate this child's attention span and degree of concentration for academic school work?

1	2	3	4	5	6	7	8	9
poor		below average		average		good		superior

I. How would you rate this child's interest in academic school work, as indicated by such behavior as looking forward to new kinds of academic work, or trying to delve more deeply into such work?

1	2	3	4	5	6	7	8	9
poor		below average		average		good		superior

Two female judges were employed, each making her ratings independently. In the case of a given class, the judges were instructed to rank order the subjects along each dimension, and then to apply the nine-point scale to the ordering. The points on the scale were to be conceived as absolutes. The actual ratings of the children in a particular class followed two weeks of observation in the classroom and in the school environment as a whole. The latter included observation during play before school, and during recesses and lunch. The teachers and pupils had adequate time to adapt to the presence of the two observers, and hence it is most unlikely that the sample of behavior manifested during the two-week period was atypical in any respect. It should be stressed that *the two-week observation period preceded the administration of all of the study's experimental procedures.* Hence, the ratings of the children's behavior were in no way contaminated by knowledge of the children's performance on the various tasks included in the study. Furthermore, the subjects' scores on the aptitude and achievement tests which had been administered by the school authorities at the beginning of the academic year (SCAT and STEP) were not made available to the raters. Finally, communication between the raters and teachers was held to the minimum necessary to facilitate the study. The teachers were informed that they were not to talk to the judges about individual pupils. In sum, every effort was made to avoid biasing the judges' ratings of the children's behavior.

The use of two independent judges to observe and rate the children's behavior permits a check on rating reliability. If substantial interjudge disagreement were found, we would hardly be drawn to a vigorous pursuit of behavioral correlates of thinking. If, on the other hand, the two observers show a reasonable level of agreement in their ratings, we can approach the matter at hand with the assurance that the relevant school behaviors can be reliably measured. This is clearly a critical first step.

Reliability data are reported in Table 24. Shown for each dimension are the intraclass correlation coefficients and the frequency distributions for each rating variable of the number of cases at each degree of discrepancy. Following Haggard (1958), we employed the intraclass (R) rather than the product-moment (r) correlation coefficient in the present context. As a univariate statistic, R is most appropriate here, for we are interested in the extent of similarity or agreement between ratings, each applying to the same child, derived from two independent judges. In contrast, r is a bivariate statistic measuring covariation, and hence is more appropriate where two distinct kinds of dimensions (such as height and weight) are to be correlated. Note that the maximum and minimum values of R are $+1$ and -1, respectively, in the present case.

Table 24.

INTERJUDGE RELIABILITY DATA FOR THE BEHAVIOR RATING SCALES

					Scales				
	A	B	C	D	E	F	G	H	I
Interjudge discrepancy									
0	33	35	38	39	29	54	32	63	49
1	61	55	61	63	59	51	39	51	62
2	34	39	25	36	35	28	41	25	28
3	12	12	19	12	14	10	11	9	7
4	11	7	8	1	10	5	16	2	2
5	0	3	0	0	4	2	4	1	2
6	0	0	0	0	0	1	7	0	1
7	0	0	0	0	0	0	1	0	0
8	0	0	0	0	0	0	0	0	0
Intraclass correlation									
(R)	.68	.67	.55	.68	.43	.62	.10	.78	.72

With the exception of Dimension G, the intraclass correlation coefficients reach fairly satisfactory levels. Note further that the modal discrepancy between judges (with the exception of Dimension G) is either zero or one unit on a nine-point scale. On the whole, then, the two independent observers achieve a quite respectable level of agreement in rating the school behaviors of the children under study.

Having demonstrated acceptable levels of reliability for our rating dimensions, the ratings of the two independent judges were averaged in our subsequent work with each dimension. Given the very low level of agreement between the judges on Dimension G, we shall omit it from further consideration in subsequent analyses of the data.

RESULTS AND DISCUSSION

Internal Analysis of Behavior Ratings

In Table 25, the means and standard deviations for each rating dimension are given separately for boys and girls. For Dimensions A and B, highly significant sex differences in mean ratings were obtained ($t = 3.46$, $p < .001$, for Dimension A; $t = 3.72$, $p < .001$, for Dimension B). All other mean differences are not statistically significant. The direction of the difference in the case of Dimensions A and B makes eminently good sense, thereby increasing our confidence in the validity of the ratings. In brief, the means indicate that boys more than girls engage in disruptive attention-seeking behavior in the classroom, while girls more than boys are hesitant and subdued. For none of the other dimensions would a sex difference have been anticipated on the basis of "common-sense" considerations. We will grant that all of this is *post hoc*, but in any case the results are in support of certain popular conceptions regarding sex differences in classroom behavior.

Consider next the interrelationships among the rating dimensions within the male and female samples. As Table 26 demonstrates quite clearly, the eight rating dimensions are not statistically independent of one another. Independence is somewhat greater for the male than for the female sample. If one selects $p < .05$ as a cutoff point, 32 percent of the r's are nonsignificant for males, whereas 11 percent are nonsignificant for the females. If the more rigorous cutoff of $p < .01$ is used, then the corresponding percentages rise to 43 and 21 for males and females, respectively. The most evident case of overlap concerns Dimensions H and I, where r is .91 for both boys and girls. Clearly, there is no need for two separate rating scales in the present circumstance. Despite the over-all number of significant r's, the correlation matrices do not point to a single general factor that can account for most of the variance in the

Table 25.

SEX COMPARISONS ON THE BEHAVIOR RATING SCALES

Dimension	Boys (N = 70)		Girls (N = 81)		t	p
	Mean	SD	Mean	SD		
A. Attention-seeking	4.51	2.26	3.36	1.84	3.46	<.001
B. Hesitant and subdued	4.03	2.07	5.23	1.91	3.72	<.001
C. Confidence and assurance	4.99	1.66	4.58	1.73	1.46	n. s.
D. Sought as companion	4.76	1.75	4.84	1.74	0.29	n. s.
E. Seeks companionship	6.16	1.45	5.70	1.66	1.77	n. s.
F. Deprecates own work	3.80	1.62	4.23	1.83	1.54	n. s.
H. Concentration on schoolwork	5.67	2.22	5.74	2.06	0.20	n. s.
I. Interest in schoolwork	5.50	2.08	5.28	1.95	0.66	n. s.

Table 26.

INTERCORRELATIONS AMONG BEHAVIOR RATING SCALES

	A	B	C	D	E	F	H	I
A. Attention-seeking	—	−42	−06	−01	67	−06	−23	01
B. Hesitant and subdued	−66	—	−53	−30	−29	67	−53	−69
C. Confidence and assurance	36	−68	—	52	06	−57	61	63
D. Sought as companion	32	−46	68	—	39	−40	35	42
E. Seeks companionship	56	−44	43	72	—	−04	−16	04
F. Deprecates own work	−25	66	−66	−47	−25	—	−27	−25
H. Concentration on schoolwork	03	−48	58	40	15	−35	—	91
I. Interest in schoolwork	15	−59	55	41	24	−37	91	—

NOTE: Correlations for boys (N = 70) appear above diagonal; correlations for girls (N = 81) appear below diagonal. For the boys, r's of .24 and .31 are significant beyond the .05 and .01 levels, respectively. For the girls, the corresponding r's are .22 and .29. Decimal points are omitted.

ratings. Correlations descend to near zero values in both boys and girls, indicating that a simple "halo-effect" interpretation will not do justice to the data.[2]

While there is a sex difference in the magnitude of r's in Table 26, there is no evidence for a sex difference in the patterning of the coefficients. Correlating the matched r's across sex yields a Spearman *rho* of .95.

Behavior Ratings and Modes of Thinking

In the present section, we inquire whether the four subgroups of subjects delineated in the previous chapter can be distinguished on the eight behavior rating variables discussed above. We shall proceed by taking the rating variables one at a time and presenting the mean and standard deviation for each within the four subgroups generated by the intelligence and creativity dimensions. By analysis of variance procedures, we can examine whether the variations in the mean behavior ratings are a systematic function of intelligence, creativity, or a combination of the two (interaction).

We consider in turn the findings for each of the behavior rating dimensions.

A. ATTENTION-SEEKING. The data for females are shown in Table 27. There are no significant effects for the boys. The results for the girls, on the other hand, demonstrate that creativity level makes a significant contribution to the amount of attention-seeking behavior displayed. It is the girls high in creativity who show the greater disruptive attention-seeking behavior (speaking out of turn, continually raising one's hand, making unnecessary noise) embodied in Dimension A.

While we do not wish to push the implications of the present finding too far, consideration might be given to its possible relevance to motivational theories of arousal and activation (for example, Berlyne, 1960; Fiske & Maddi, 1961). Conceivably, our highly creative girls may be more bored by various classroom routines than are their less creative peers. Hence the former might engage in attention-seeking behaviors in the service of a need for variety. Such a conceptualization places a strong emphasis upon an individual's attempts to achieve optimum arousal or activation levels by carrying out various stimulation-increasing behavioral acts. Recently, Maddi, Charlens, Maddi, and Smith (1962) have demonstrated that a period of monotonous stimulation produces an increase in the desire for novelty and a decrease in actual novelty of

---

[2] This conclusion seems appropriate in view of the very high correlations often reported between behavior ratings on various dimensions.

Table 27.

MEAN RATINGS ON DIMENSION A (ATTENTION-SEEKING)
FOR THE FOUR GROUPS OF GIRLS ($N = 81$)

		INTELLIGENCE	
		High	Low
CREATIVITY	High	4.05 (1.81)	3.44 (1.85)
	Low	2.74 (1.94)	3.14 (1.64)

ANALYSIS OF VARIANCE

Source	df	MS	F	p
Intelligence	1	0.01	<1.00	n. s.
Creativity	1	0.65	4.02	<.05
Interaction	1	0.25	1.54	n. s.
Within cells	77	0.16		

productions when these are measured by projective test procedures. In that study, the subjects could only express their desire for novelty at the level of fantasy. Where the environment is less constraining as in the present classroom context, behavior itself might be affected in characteristic ways.

The interpretation proposed above is based on the premise of a mismatch between the teacher's instructional method and preferred modes of thinking on the part of the child. While there does not appear to be any empirical evidence on the issue, it is most unlikely that divergent thinking in pupils would be encouraged by the large majority of teachers. Rather, teachers can be expected to stress the more typical forms of intellectual functioning reflected in convergent thinking. The premium placed upon the latter in standardized aptitude and achievement tests would naturally serve to reinforce the teacher's judgments concerning the value and importance of that mode of thinking.

The differential emphasis given convergent and divergent modes of thinking by teachers will, of necessity, redound to the disadvantage of pupils who favor the latter mode. These are the pupils, it will be recalled (see Figure 1), who are most likely to look for unusual combinations and novel solutions to problems. Relative to their less creative peers, these pupils are likely to exhibit the playful attitude toward knowledge described in the introductory chapter. Such tendencies might well be suppressed, of course, but in a teaching context permissive of student expression, the ideas that "bubble to the surface," so to speak, need not necessarily be inhibited. The possibly disruptive impact upon classroom routines of these attempts at overt communication may be of secondary concern to the student who strongly cathects her own ideational productions. Our highly creative girls, attuned more closely to their own internal states than to situational constraints, might conceivably make more of a nuisance of themselves than do the less creative girls in our sample.[3] For the latter, one can evidently expect a closer match to the modes of thinking and behavior considered most desirable by the teacher. In short, these girls may be tuned to the perceived requirements of the classroom situation. They may have neither the inclination nor the capacity to range beyond the obvious manifest demands of the school toward more fanciful modes of thinking and behavior that are not explicitly sanctioned by the teacher.

B. HESITANT AND SUBDUED. Tables 28 and 29 offer the relevant data for males and females, respectively. Turning first to the boys, those who "hesitate to express opinions, as evidenced by extreme caution, failure to contribute, or a subdued manner in a speaking situation" have the lower general intelligence test scores. The effect, as can be seen in Table 28, is a highly significant one. For boys, then, the intelligence dimension has an impact upon this distinctive class of behaviors.

A comparable state of affairs obtains for the girls (Table 29), but in addition there are some further complexities in the pattern of the results. Again, there is a highly significant effect attributable to the intelligence domain. But now we observe a significant interaction as well. The latter can be explained on the basis of the magnitude of the mean in the upper left-hand cell. For girls, in other words, a high score on both the intelligence and creativity clusters is associated with a sharp reduction in the kinds of behavior reflected in Dimension B.

It is of considerable interest to compare Tables 27 and 29 in the female sample. Note the apparent consistency for the girls who are high on both modes of thinking. These subjects show much attention-seeking behavior and in congruent fashion display little hesitation in expressing their opinions. In contrast, the girls high in creativity but low in intelli-

---

[3] Such an interpretation receives some support in unpublished findings (Propst, 1962) indicating that persons who compose relatively unusual stories demonstrate a kind of introspective richness but avoid active exploration of a nonthreatening external environment.

Table 28.

Mean Ratings on Dimension B (Hesitant and Subdued) for the Four Groups of Boys ($N = 70$)

INTELLIGENCE

		High	Low
	High	**3.12**	**4.67**
		(1.93)	**(1.94)**
CREATIVITY			
	Low	**3.67**	**4.65**
		(1.91)	**(2.23)**

ANALYSIS OF VARIANCE

Source	df	MS	F	p
Intelligence	1	1.60	6.95	<.02
Creativity	1	0.07	<1.00	n. s.
Interaction	1	0.08	<1.00	n. s.
Within cells	66	0.23		

Table 29.

Mean Ratings on Dimension B (Hesitant and Subdued) for the Four Groups of Girls ($N = 81$)

INTELLIGENCE

		High	Low
	High	**3.86**	**6.06**
		(1.93)	**(1.59)**
CREATIVITY			
	Low	**5.37**	**5.82**
		(2.03)	**(1.26)**

ANALYSIS OF VARIANCE

Source	df	MS	F	p
Intelligence	1	1.74	11.77	<.01
Creativity	1	0.40	2.71	n. s.
Interaction	1	0.76	5.12	<.04
Within cells	77	0.15		

gence paradoxically exhibit *both* attention-seeking behavior *and* hesitation in expressing their opinions. These girls, unlike the high-high group, do not compensate for disruptive attention-seeking by forcefully contributing their ideas to the class. Rather, we seem to be dealing with internal ideation that the subject cannot or will not make public. The attention-seeking behavior of these girls seems to be in the nature of an inarticulate protest.

The inability of the low intelligence–high creativity girl to communicate constructively in the classroom stands in sharp contrast to her performance on the various creativity tasks in an experimental context. The latter, it will be recalled, was structured in a specifically nonevaluative manner. One must allow for the possibility, then, that the girl high in creativity and low in intelligence is handicapped both by the underemphasis given divergent thinking processes in the classroom and by the evaluative atmosphere in which most school learning takes place. These two factors are not entirely independent, of course, since evaluative criteria are less sharply defined for divergent than for convergent thinking. Accordingly, we should expect that time spent by the teacher in fostering divergent thinking would be accompanied by a softening, though not the disappearance, of the evaluative atmosphere in the classroom.

C. CONFIDENCE AND ASSURANCE. The outcome of the analysis of variance is given in Table 30 for females. Note that there are no effects

Table 30.

MEAN RATINGS ON DIMENSION C (CONFIDENCE AND ASSURANCE)
FOR THE FOUR GROUPS OF GIRLS ($N = 81$)

		INTELLIGENCE	
		High	Low
	High	5.55 (1.92)	3.33 (1.50)
CREATIVITY			
	Low	5.11 (1.49)	4.18 (1.14)

ANALYSIS OF VARIANCE

Source	df	MS	F	p
Intelligence	1	2.46	20.83	<.01
Creativity	1	0.04	<1.00	n. s.
Interaction	1	0.42	3.52	<.07
Within cells	77	0.12		

whatever for the boys. The girls, on the other hand, yield a massive intelligence effect and a near-significant interaction. Confidence and assurance in the face of criticism and rebuff are much more likely to elude the subjects who are low than those who are high on the intelligence cluster. Of special concern is the implication of the near-significant interaction yielded by the data. Note that the source of the interaction is largely a result of the unusually low mean for the girls who are high in creativity but low in intelligence. These girls, in other words, show the least amount of confidence and assurance in the face of adversity. We can further appreciate now why their attention-seeking behavior assumes the form of inarticulate protest. Oversensitive to possible criticism, these girls apparently would rather keep their ideas to themselves than expose them to the glare of potentially unfavorable publicity. Their disruptive attention-seeking behavior is apparently their only means of advertising their plight. The findings for the present dimension articulate well with those obtained for Dimension B above by lending further support to the inference that the evaluative atmosphere of the classroom might differentially influence the behavior of particular subgroups of children.

D. SOUGHT AS COMPANION. Information concerning this dimension is provided in Table 31 for females. There are no significant effects in

Table 31.

MEAN RATINGS ON DIMENSION D (SOUGHT AS COMPANION) FOR THE FOUR GROUPS OF GIRLS ($N = 81$)

INTELLIGENCE

		High	Low
	High	5.64 (1.36)	3.83 (1.98)
CREATIVITY			
	Low	5.11 (2.05)	4.64 (1.09)

ANALYSIS OF VARIANCE

Source	df	MS	F	p
Intelligence	1	1.29	9.67	<.01
Creativity	1	0.02	<1.00	n. s.
Interaction	1	0.45	3.33	<.08
Within cells	77	0.13		

the case of the boys. In contrast, pronounced differences are observed in the girls. Those low on the intelligence cluster are less sought by their peers. A near-significant interaction effect derives from the fact that the subgroup high in both creativity and intelligence are the most sought after for their companionship, while the subgroup high in creativity and low in intelligence are the least desired as companions. The mean discrepancy across the low creativity subgroups is considerably smaller. The portrait of the girl who is high in creativity but low in intelligence now comes into even clearer focus. Withdrawn, lacking in self-confidence, evoking indifferent or negative responses from their peers, inclined toward disruptive attention-seeking behavior, the girls within the subgroup in question appear to be making the least satisfactory adjustment to the school environment.

E. SEEKS COMPANIONSHIP. Table 32 contains the relevant information for females. Again, the boys yield no significant differences. Note, however, the powerful interaction effect present in the female sample. The high-high and low-low subgroups are rated as more active than the high-low and low-high subgroups in seeking the companionship of their peers.

Table 32.

MEAN RATINGS ON DIMENSION E (SEEKS COMPANIONSHIP)
FOR THE FOUR GROUPS OF GIRLS ($N = 81$)

		INTELLIGENCE	
		High	Low
CREATIVITY	High	6.32 (1.29)	5.17 (2.18)
	Low	5.05 (1.62)	6.09 (1.27)

ANALYSIS OF VARIANCE

Source	df	MS	F	p
Intelligence	1	0.00	<1.00	n. s.
Creativity	1	0.03	<1.00	n. s.
Interaction	1	1.20	9.46	<.01
Within cells	77	0.13		

Particularly relevant is a joint consideration of Dimensions D and E—the comparison between being sought as a companion by others and seeking the companionship of others. There are four possible ways in which these dimensions might be related, and each way in fact is exemplified by one of our four groups of girls. To state the results summarily first, the high creativity–high intelligence girls are both sought after and seek others; the high creativity–low intelligence girls neither are sought after nor seek others; the low creativity–high intelligence group are sought after but do not seek others; the low-low group are not sought after but do seek others. It is understood, of course, that these are relative rather than absolute distinctions. Let us consider these results now in somewhat more detail.

In the case of the high-high group, we find what might be described as an optimally healthy affiliative situation. These individuals are sought out for companionship by others, and in turn also seek the friendship of others. It is likely that in a large number of these instances the choices are reciprocal ones: that is, seeking and being sought occur together. When, on the other hand, we consider the group high in creativity but low in general intelligence, a very different picture emerges: these girls are neither sought nor do they especially seek others. These results make it quite clear that the high creativity–low intelligence girls are the most isolated subgroup in the classroom. Not only are they avoided by others, but they in turn have no use for others either. There is, in other words, a mutuality of shunning. The girls in question are least likely to make positive overtures toward their teachers or classmates, but tend to indulge rather in behavior of a disruptive, attention-seeking kind in relation to others.

Consider next the girls low in creativity but high in intelligence. These individuals are more likely to be sought *by* others than to seek *for* others. Here, then, is a subgroup of girls who appear to be quite confident in their interpersonal relationships. They are, as it were, "sitting on top" of the affiliative situation in the sense that they are chosen by others even though they often fail to reciprocate such overtures. For the low creativity girls who are also low in intelligence, on the other hand, the relationship is reversed. They are more prone to seek than to be sought. Possibly, these girls are externalizers in the sense that they attempt to compensate in the realm of interpersonal relations for their intellectual shortcomings. Their social initiative, in other words, stems from weakness and inadequacy rather than from strength and confidence. Despite their low scores on both thinking styles, however, these girls seem to be somewhat more popular with their peers than are the girls high in creativity and low in intelligence. This latter subgroup appears to be composed of internalizers, for, as we have seen, these girls have little interest in the pursuit of social relationships. In a study employing elementary school children, Singer (1961) has reported that the creativity of stories told to thematic stimuli is positively associated with extent of daydreaming activity. High levels of daydreaming might well distinguish our high creative–low intelligence girls, hence partially accounting for their manifest withdrawal from social interaction in the school environment.

Before proceeding to the remaining dimensions, we should like to give some general consideration to the issue of sex differences. For all of the dimensions treated thus far, the content has largely concerned the child's social behavior in the school setting. As we have seen, thinking styles have had much more of an impact upon such behavior in girls than in boys. One possible reason for this sex difference is the relative importance or salience of the social behaviors in question for boys and girls in the fifth grade of elementary school. By the age of ten or eleven, the child's identification with the same-sexed parent should be quite firm, thus providing the child with distinctive sets of role behaviors that can serve as guiding models. These adult role models are heavily sex-typed, of course, and stress achievement-centered behaviors more strongly in males than females, and affiliative, interpersonally oriented behaviors more strongly in females than in males. We are suggesting, then, that the social world of the classroom provides an arena in which girls can exercise certain "natural" dispositions. Boys, on the other hand, by virtue of their greater achievement concerns, should be less engaged by interpersonal matters. This would imply that social withdrawal in girls, for example, might be more salient and invoke greater censure from one's peers than corresponding behaviors in boys, simply on the basis of distinctive norms and expectations regarding what is desirable for girls and boys. Socially deviant behavior in boys might more readily be condoned, if it appears to be in the service of achievement concerns. The pressures toward affiliation as a positive criterion for femininity could well have unfortunate effects upon those girls whose natural inclinations are toward more solitary intellectual pursuits. Affiliative pressures are likely to be considerably weaker for boys in a middle class, achievement-oriented environment.

F. DEPRECATES OWN WORK. Beginning with the present dimension, the emphasis is on more strictly achievement-centered behaviors. Previous dimensions have been more concerned with the child's interpersonal orientation in the classroom. Tables 33 and 34 report the results for Dimension F in males and females, respectively. For both sexes, it is readily apparent that self-deprecation of work relates to the intelligence cluster. Though the interaction term falls quite short of significance in both sexes, we might just note in passing that it is the subgroup high in

Table 33.

MEAN RATINGS ON DIMENSION F (DEPRECATES OWN WORK)
FOR THE FOUR GROUPS OF BOYS ($N = 70$)

	INTELLIGENCE	
	High	Low
High	2.76 (1.72)	4.61 (1.20)
CREATIVITY		
Low	3.50 (1.79)	4.29 (1.10)

ANALYSIS OF VARIANCE

Source	df	MS	F	p
Intelligence	1	1.74	13.83	<.01
Creativity	1	0.04	<1.00	n. s.
Interaction	1	0.28	2.20	n. s.
Within cells	66	0.13		

Table 34.

MEAN RATINGS ON DIMENSION F (DEPRECATES OWN WORK)
FOR THE FOUR GROUPS OF GIRLS ($N = 81$)

	INTELLIGENCE	
	High	Low
High	3.14 (1.81)	5.28 (1.93)
CREATIVITY		
Low	3.79 (1.55)	4.86 (1.25)

ANALYSIS OF VARIANCE

Source	df	MS	F	p
Intelligence	1	2.59	19.23	<.01
Creativity	1	0.01	<1.00	n. s.
Interaction	1	0.28	2.12	n. s.
Within cells	77	0.13		

creativity and low in intelligence which manifests the greatest self-deprecation.

H AND I. CONCENTRATION ON AND INTEREST IN SCHOOLWORK. We consider these dimensions together in view of their exceptionally high correlation with each other. They both deal with the manner in which the child copes with academic school work. Consider first the results for Dimension H reported in Tables 35 and 36. It is evident that, for boys and girls, high vs. low general intelligence accounts for the large portion of the differences in judges' ratings of the child's "attention span and degree of concentration for academic school work." In the case of the boys, there is, in addition, a near-significant creativity effect. There is no question, however, as to which of the modes of thinking exerts the dominant influence. For the girls, there is no creativity effect whatever.

Turning to Dimension I, the relevant findings are listed in Tables 37 and 38 for boys and girls, respectively. Again there are massive effects attributable to intelligence. Given the high correlation of the present dimension with the previous one, these results hardly constitute a surprise. There is a weak indication of an interaction effect for Dimension I in the case of the girls. Among the high creativity individuals, those girls who also are high in intelligence receive the highest ratings for interest in academic work, while those girls who are low on the intelligence cluster receive the lowest ratings in the sample on the dimension in question. This latter finding must be treated as highly tentative, of course. Nevertheless, it is consistent with other evidence cited, if one bears in mind that ratings of academic concentration and interest do have a social component, for they depend upon the child's overt communications in the classroom context. Hence, a pattern of social withdrawal and verbal inhibition of the sort that distinguishes the girl high in creativity and low in intelligence will also have some effect upon ratings that purportedly deal with academic performance exclusively.

CONCLUSIONS

There can be no doubt, on the basis of the results outlined in the present chapter, that both creativity and intelligence as modes of thinking characterizing elementary school children have implications for behavior in the school environment. Such behavior can be reliably rated by classroom observers who have no prior familiarity with the children and are in no way emotionally involved with them. Accordingly, the ratings obtained can be assumed to constitute a reasonably accurate reflection of actual behavior in the school setting. As we have seen, the "halo-effects" that plague teacher and peer ratings were markedly attenuated in the present rating context.

Table 35.

Mean Ratings on Dimension H (Concentration on Schoolwork) for the Four Groups of Boys ($N = 70$)

		INTELLIGENCE	
		High	Low
CREATIVITY	High	7.12 (1.87)	5.11 (2.35)
	Low	6.28 (1.87)	4.18 (1.67)

Analysis of Variance

Source	df	MS	F	p
Intelligence	1	4.22	19.19	$<.01$
Creativity	1	0.79	3.58	$<.07$
Interaction	1	0.00	<1.00	n. s.
Within cells	66	0.22		

Table 36.

Mean Ratings on Dimension H (Concentration on Schoolwork) for the Four Groups of Girls ($N = 81$)

		INTELLIGENCE	
		High	Low
CREATIVITY	High	7.45 (1.37)	4.11 (1.64)
	Low	6.89 (1.24)	4.36 (1.50)

Analysis of Variance

Source	df	MS	F	p
Intelligence	1	8.63	83.36	$<.01$
Creativity	1	0.02	<1.00	n. s.
Interaction	1	0.17	1.59	n. s.
Within cells	77	0.10		

Table 37.

MEAN RATINGS ON DIMENSION I (INTEREST IN SCHOOLWORK) FOR THE FOUR GROUPS OF BOYS ($N = 70$)

		INTELLIGENCE	
		High	Low
	High	6.82 (2.04)	4.72 (1.87)
CREATIVITY			
	Low	6.06 (2.07)	4.41 (1.46)

ANALYSIS OF VARIANCE

Source	df	MS	F	p
Intelligence	1	3.51	17.36	$<.01$
Creativity	1	0.29	1.44	n. s.
Interaction	1	0.05	<1.00	n. s.
Within cells	66	0.20		

Table 38.

MEAN RATINGS ON DIMENSION I (INTEREST IN SCHOOLWORK) FOR THE FOUR GROUPS OF GIRLS ($N = 81$)

		INTELLIGENCE	
		High	Low
	High	6.77 (1.38)	3.78 (1.86)
CREATIVITY			
	Low	6.16 (1.30)	4.27 (1.52)

ANALYSIS OF VARIANCE

Source	df	MS	F	p
Intelligence	1	5.95	51.77	$<.01$
Creativity	1	0.00	<1.00	n. s.
Interaction	1	0.31	2.68	n. s.
Within cells	77	0.12		

In the preceding pages we have been describing the relationships between the behavior ratings and the modes of thinking under study. For the girls, observed variations in behavior were related to both intelligence and creativity, and to the interaction between them. Interpersonal behaviors engaged the creativity variable as a main effect or in the form of a creativity–intelligence interaction. More strictly achievement-centered behaviors, on the other hand, were relevant mainly to the intelligence domain. For the boys, behavior ratings were associated almost exclusively with the subject's standing on the intelligence cluster. It appears, then, that differences in creativity among boys do not contribute to perceptible behavioral differences in the elementary school setting.

In the remaining portion of the chapter, we shall attempt to integrate the findings for the separate behavior rating dimensions into a composite portrait of the four types of subjects under study. We begin with the female sample. Consider first the girls who are high on both the intelligence and creativity clusters. Relative to the other subgroups, they receive quite positive evaluations along both social and achievement-related dimensions. The highly creative and intelligent girls manifest behavior indicative of "ego-strength." Thus, they are the least hesitant of all the groups in speaking their mind, they show the greatest degree of confidence, and they show the least self-deprecation. This display of "ego-strength" is apparently not perceived as self-aggrandizement, for the companionship of these highly creative and intelligent girls is more avidly sought by their peers than is the companionship of any of the other subgroups. Further, these girls do not adopt a passive stance in the face of their positive stimulus value, but rather they stand foremost in actively seeking out the company of their peers, suggesting that their interpersonal relationships assume a reciprocal form. Turning to achievement-centered behaviors, we observe that the highly intelligent and creative girls again rank at the high extreme. They seem to be very strongly motivated in pursuing their academic school work.

A singular negative note arises in connection with the attention-seeking dimension. The highly creative and intelligent girls apparently can be a disruptive influence in the classroom. There is no reason to suspect that the girls in question are deliberately seeking to disrupt classroom routines. Rather, there seems to be a strong drive toward verbal self-expression, which the highly creative and intelligent girls cannot readily inhibit. Conceivably, they may be somewhat bored by the classroom activities, and hence are eager to propose new possibilities. If, as we suggested earlier, the teacher emphasizes convergent modes of thinking, those girls who are adept at that mode as well as superior in the divergent mode, may seek to "exercise" the latter "faculty," speaking figuratively. Conceivably, these girls are racing ahead of their classmates in their thought processes, and in Bruner's (1957) terms are "going beyond the information given." The child who assimilates knowledge rapidly and reshapes it creatively to her own devices may possibly have a certain nuisance value in classrooms that are imbued with a democratic ideal of equal participation and are concerned with the maintenance of pre-selected work plans and schedules.

We turn next to the highly creative girls who fall below the median on the intelligence cluster. In almost every respect, these girls stand at the opposite extreme from the subgroup just considered. As we have seen, the girls high in creativity but low in intelligence are the least communicative members of the sample, the most subdued, the most easily upset by rebuff and criticism, neither sought by nor seeking the company of their peers, the most deprecatory of self and work, and the least motivated with regard to academic tasks. It is, then, evident that level of intelligence in a context of high creativity has a very significant impact upon a host of school-relevant behaviors. The highly intelligent among the highly creative girls appear to show the strongest degree of striving and success in both the academic achievement and interpersonal spheres. The less intelligent, but highly creative girls, on the other hand, exhibit the lowest levels of such striving and success in regard to both areas. It is significant indeed that the group at this opposite extreme from the high-high group is not the low-low group, but rather the high creativity–low intelligence group.

Only in the case of the attention-seeking dimension does the high creativity–low intelligence subgroup of girls have anything in common with the girls high in both creativity and intelligence. The fact, however, that this attention-seeking occurs against a context of such distinctively different behaviors in the two highly creative subgroups under comparison, raises the question of whether the attention-seeking dimension has a common meaning across both subgroups. One arrives at the impression that the attention-seeking behavior in the highly creative and intelligent girls derives from an overeagerness to participate, whereas the corresponding behavior in the highly creative, less intelligent girls stems from a basic dissatisfaction with the school environment as a whole. In this latter case, the attention-seeking behaviors, in a sense, are advertising the plight of the child who is highly capable at pursuing a style of thinking that is wholly out of phase with the thinking mode emphasized in the classroom.

Consider next the subgroup of girls high in intelligence and low in creativity. There are many similarities between the present subgroup and the girls high in both intelligence and creativity, but a few fundamental differences also stand out. Turning first to the similarities, we observe that girls high in intelligence and low in creativity show confidence and assurance in relations with teachers and classmates, and exhibit little tendency to deprecate their work or themselves. Their self-assurance, however, considered in relation to the two sociometric-type dimensions, has a distinctly "cool" and "aloof" quality. Unlike the highly creative and intelligent girls, for whom seeking and being sought both are strong, the present subgroup tends to be sought more than they tend to seek.

There is, in sum, a basic reserve in the highly intelligent–low creative girls, which when viewed against a context of self-assurance, suggests an unwillingness to overextend or overcommit oneself. Note, in this connection, that these girls comprise the subgroup least likely to seek attention in potentially disruptive ways, and are reasonably high in the tendency toward caution and hesitancy in expressing their opinions. In these respects, the girls in the present subgroup diverge quite sharply from their like-sexed peers who are both highly intelligent and creative. The latter, it will be recalled, express their views quite freely and, in fact, seek attention to an excessive degree.

With respect to more strictly achievement-centered behaviors, the highly intelligent and low creative girls perform quite well. Their attention span, concentration, and interest in academic school work seem to be quite high. Their lack of creativity does not appear to be a handicap to effective academic performance. Within the classrooms employed in the present study, it is quite clear that low intelligence is considerably more debilitating than low levels of creativity. Recall that the subgroup of girls high in creativity and low in intelligence appeared to be having the most serious difficulties of all in both social and academic areas. The present subgroup, on the other hand, has achieved an admirable level of adjustment, though possibly at a severe price. There is an indication of a certain lack of spontaneity in these girls, and one somehow comes away wondering whether they ever venture outside of the teacher's frame of reference in their academic pursuits. To do so might signify a loss of control, and possible alienation of the teacher. Correspondingly, in relation to their peers, there may well be a reluctance to commit oneself in interpersonal encounters unless quite sure of the other's intentions. In sum, the highly intelligent–low creative girl seems to be closely attuned to the explicit requirements of the school situation, and appears to show little inclination to test the limits of those requirements.

Finally, we turn to the subgroup of girls low in both intelligence and creativity. Paradoxically enough, we note certain respects in which the low-low child is better off than her low intelligence counterpart who is high in creativity. This is consistent with our earlier observation that creativity in a context of poorer than average intelligence confers few advantages, and, indeed, can be viewed as disadvantageous within the school context under study. More specifically, the girls low in both intelligence and creativity do not manifest the delicate sensitivities that distinguish the highly creative girl who is low in intelligence. Thus, the former subgroup exhibits higher levels of confidence and assurance and is less upset by criticism than is the latter. In the realm of interpersonal relations with their peers, the girls low in ability at both thinking modes are more likely to seek the companionship of others than to be sought, whereas the highly creative–low intelligent subgroup are not only unsought by others *but also* unseeking of others. While the low-low girls do show considerable caution and inhibition in the formal learning situation, they appear to be compensating for these shortcomings in the interpersonal sphere. Their efforts are not meeting with unqualified success, however. The highly creative–low intelligent girls, on the other hand, do not seem to show these overt compensatory effects, possibly because they prefer more internal modes of coping (such as withdrawal into fantasy).

To conclude our treatment of the results for the girls, it is evident that the modes of thinking under investigation have distinctive implications for overt behavior in the school setting. Particularly interesting is the observation that, in addition to main effects attributable to intelligence and creativity, a significant interaction often obtains. Thus, it makes a considerable difference whether creativity is located in a context of high or of low intelligence. These results call into serious question the Getzels and Jackson (1962) procedure of selecting "creativity" and "intelligence" criterion groups who show maximal discrepancies between those modes of thinking. Such a procedure would have been quite legitimate, if Getzels and Jackson had confined their generalizations to those maximal-discrepancy subgroups. Those authors' work, however, leaves no doubt that they intended to draw generalizations concerning the nature of creativity and intelligence as distinct thinking processes. Our results unequivocally demonstrate that such generalizations are unwarranted, at least in a female population.

Let us now turn our attention to the boys. As we have seen, only the intelligence variable exerts an influence on the behavior rating domain in the present case. It should be stressed, however, that the behavior dimensions related to intelligence in the boys are correspondingly related in the girls. Hence, there is no basic inconsistency between the sexes, but rather a greater number and a greater complexity of relations in the case of the girls than the boys, for the obvious reason that the creativity variable plays an important role in the female sample.

In view of the relative simplicity of the results for the boys, there is no need to follow the practice of delineating psychologically the four subgroups generated by the intelligence and creativity variables. Rather, we shall examine the particular dimensions that discriminated the boys high and low in intelligence. These dimensions bear directly upon how the child copes with academic school work (Dimensions H and I), or concern symptoms indicative of inadequate coping (Dimensions B and F).

It is quite likely that the highly intelligent boy finds that his style of thinking is approved and rewarded in the classroom, with the consequence that he displays a great deal of confidence in coping with classroom requirements. The boy of low intelligence, on the other hand, exhibits behaviors suggestive of difficulty in meeting the school's academic demands. Whether the withdrawal and self-deprecatory behaviors of these boys are antecedents or consequents of poor performance cannot be readily gauged from our data. We strongly suspect, however, that children become sensitized to the reward structure in the classroom, and begin to display various symptoms when their performance does not conform to it. In the middle class elementary schools we have chosen to study, the symptoms are frequently intrapunitive. At lower social class levels, the behaviors might conceivably take a more extrapunitive form (aggression and truancy, for example). Such behaviors would, of course, meet with severe condemnation in a social environment that puts a heavy premium upon academic performance.

Why does creativity have so few observable behavioral consequences in the elementary school boys under study? One way of approaching the issue, admittedly speculative, is in terms of deviations from sex-typed modal behaviors. Similar behaviors on the part of boys and girls, in other words, might be evaluated differently largely on the basis of discrepancies from differential normative expectations for the two sexes. Earlier, we observed significant sex differences in two of the behavior rating dimensions, differences that seemed to make good sense in terms of these normative expectations. However, even in the case where sex differences in rating are not statistically significant, one clearly should not assume behavioral identities. Thus, it is conceivable that the withdrawn behavior of the high creativity–low intelligence girls is highly salient relative to implicit affiliative expectations for girls as a whole. Hence, they receive the kind of extreme rating which, as we have noted, leads to significant interaction effects. Similar behavior on the part of boys may not be perceived as quite so deviant, since boys in general are presumed to be more strongly achievement-oriented than are girls.

SUMMARY

The major question posed by the present chapter concerned the implications of creativity and intelligence as modes of thinking for behavior in the school environment. Nine dimensions were eventually selected for use in rating the school behavior of the subjects. These behavior rating dimensions were chosen on the basis of their exhaustiveness and relevance to the school setting. Two independent judges manifested moderate to high levels of agreement in their ratings on eight of the nine dimensions. These were then retained for further analysis. The eight dimensions were intercorrelated to a moderate degree, but the range of correlational values was substantial, and not at all suggestive of a single evaluational factor—the "halo-effect."

Relationships between the behavior ratings and modes of thinking were examined separately for each sex. In the case of the girls, variation in the behavior ratings was attributable to intelligence, creativity, and the interaction between them. The highly creative and intelligent girls behaved in ways indicative of high levels of "ego-strength," though there were signs of a lack of inhibition in the behavior of those subjects. The girls high in creativity but low in intelligence appeared to be having the most difficulty (of all the female subjects) in coping with the achievement and the social demands of the school situation. Their academic motivation was low, and they were the most withdrawn and hesitant pupils in the classroom. For girls with high intelligence and low creativity, in turn, school apparently presents few problems despite evidence of some constriction in intellectual functioning and in interpersonal relationships. Finally, the girls low in both creativity and intelligence appeared to be compensating for poor academic performance by seeking, with qualified success, for satisfactory interpersonal outlets.

In the case of the boys, only intelligence effects were noted. The less intelligent boys manifested significantly lower levels of concentration and interest in academic work, and were considerably more intrapunitive than their highly intelligent peers. Such intrapunitiveness might be considered a typical outcome of poor academic performance in a middle class elementary school.

Some consideration was given to the issue of sex differences. We proposed that differential normative expectations for boys and girls in the achievement and affiliation areas might have contributed to the observed differences.

4

Categorizing
and
Conceptualizing

The present chapter will explore the implications for intelligence and creativity of the way in which young children come to grips with similarities and differences in their environment. This similarity-difference issue is basic to much of the recent work on styles or strategies[1] of categorization and conceptualization. Although these terms—categorization and conceptualization—are often employed interchangeably in the recent literature on cognition, we can draw an analytic distinction between them that should prove helpful in delineating their possible relationships to the intelligence and creativity domains.

---

[1] The distinction between style and strategy derives essentially from the theoretical background of the investigator making the distinction. Those who have come to the present problem area from psychoanalytic ego psychology (for example, Gardner, 1953) employ a "style" interpretation. For these workers, categorization and conceptualization are adaptational control mechanisms or "cognitive styles" of the ego that mediate between need states and the external environment (see Klein, 1958). The strategy interpretation, on the other hand, characterizes the work of those investigators (for example, Bruner, Goodnow, & Austin, 1956) for whom categorization and conceptualization are conceived of as involving such matters as types of error minimization and risk taking in the making of cognitive decisions. The style and strategy approaches are not mutually incompatible, of course. Rather, two levels of analysis may be involved, with strategies reflecting a finer-grained view of the psychological processes represented in categorization and conceptualization styles. Alternatively, one might conceive of styles as operating without the subject's awareness, and of strategies as implying some form of conscious choice. The entire issue is quite complex, but fortunately of only tangential relevance to the concerns of the present volume.

Categorizing

Categorization, whether conceived as style or strategy, can be treated as a problem in "breadth"—that is, in the range of discriminable events assigned to a common class. Within this general framework, at least two further distinctions are feasible. The first concerns the case in which the category is clearly specified (it may be learned by or directly provided to the subject during an experimental session). The question at issue concerns the category's "band width." Consider, for example, the Wallach and Caron (1959) study—subjects initially learned that geometric figures which possess a particular angle are "poggles," and then had to judge whether a subsequent series of geometric figures, identical but for variation in a single criterial attribute of acuteness of angle, belonged or did not belong to the "poggle" class. Obviously, the larger the number of instances admitted to that class, the broader the subject's "poggle" category. Comparable procedures were developed by Bruner and Tajfel (1961) and by Tajfel, Richardson, and Everstine (1964). Those authors used dot numerosity and line length as their dimensions of judgment. Patterns containing a specified number of dots and lines of a particular length were made criterial (served as "target" stimuli), and subjects were required to judge a series of dot and line patterns in terms of their belonging or not belonging to the "target" class. Individuals vary, of course, in the range of patterns judged criterial. Narrow category breadth is reflected in high rejection rates, while wide category breadth implies high rates of acceptance. The Bruner-Tajfel study further demonstrated that neither form of categorization preference conveys an over-all advantage in arriving at accurate judgments. Accuracy here implies delegating the criterial patterns to the "target" class and assigning the noncriterial patterns to the "nontarget" class.

The Pettigrew (1958) Category Width Test is structurally similar to the experimental procedures just outlined, but is constructed in a simpler paper-and-pencil format. In brief, the test's twenty items present the central tendency value for a category, the subject's task being one of estimating the most deviant members of that category from the multiple-choice alternatives provided. Note that the scores for category "band width" on the "poggles" and the Pettigrew procedures were positively and significantly correlated in a sample of sixth grade children (Wallach & Caron, 1959). Further evidence for the generality of category "band width" may be found in that portion of Fillenbaum's (1959) work classified under the label "coarseness–fineness" of categorizing.

Consider next the other approach to the "category-breadth" problem. Unlike the preceding case where the category was specified for the subject we now engage him in what might be termed a category-search operation. Presented with a diverse array of common objects to be sorted into the most "comfortable" number of groupings, the subject must generate his own categories and decide upon the particular exemplars each category shall contain. Essentially, subjects must decide how narrow or broad a range of objects can be justifiably grouped together as "equivalent" in some respect. Breadth of categorization, in other words, is reflected in the number of groupings used in fulfilling the task requirement. As the number of groupings formed increases, the number of objects placed within each will obviously tend to decline. Broad categorizers, in sum, should produce fewer groupings, while narrow categorizers produce more.

This second form of categorization style was first studied by Gardner (1953), who labeled it the cognitive control principle of "equivalence range"; more recently (Gardner & Schoen, 1962), it has been relabeled "conceptual differentiation." Since the early Gardner work, a number of studies have appeared relating "equivalence range" ("conceptual differentiation") to other cognitive and personality variables (for example, Clayton & Jackson, 1961; Gardner, Holzman, Klein, Linton, & Spence, 1959; Gardner, Jackson, & Messick, 1960). With regard to the generality issue, both Gardner and Schoen (1962) and Sloane, Gorlow, and Jackson (1963) have shown that "equivalence range" behavior is highly consistent across a variety of stimulus domains—common objects, object names, photos of people, sets of described human behaviors. Concerning stability over time, Gardner and Long (1960) report an r of .75 for number of groups formed on two administrations (three years apart) of the Gardner Object-Sorting Test.

It is possible that the distinctions observed between "category band width" and "equivalence range" phenomena are merely minor variations within a general "breadth of categorization" dimension. On the other hand, it is evident that the psychological processes engaged are far from identical in the two cases. What then is the evidence concerning their empirical relationship? Regretfully, the published findings are equivocal. Thus, Sloane, Gorlow, and Jackson (1963) report that the two styles of categorization distinguished above are independent of one another. Subjects who are broad in "equivalence range" on object-sorting tasks (where categories derive from the subject) do not necessarily emerge as broad categorizers on "band-width" measures (in which the categories are inherent in the assigned tasks). Gardner and Schoen (1962), on the other hand, obtain a strong factor on which both object-sorting and "band-width" tests have substantial loadings. Individuals with broad equivalence ranges (that is, persons who form few groupings) tend to have broad band widths on the Pettigrew Category Width Test, for example. In an earlier study reported within the same monograph, however, the evidence for generality was quite weak. Finally, Tajfel, Richardson, and Everstine (1964) report low to moderate levels of consistency between some of their "band-width" indices, on the one hand, and conceptual measures related to equivalence range, on the other. Since it is not at all clear, then, that categorization breadth generalizes across "equivalence range" and "band-width" behaviors, we included instruments representative of each in the design of the present study.

Creativity, Intelligence, and Categorizing Breadth

Let us return now to the question with which the chapter opened. Does categorization breadth bear any relationship to the modes of thinking under study—intelligence and creativity? Consider first the evidence for the "band-width" type of category breadth. In the case of intelligence, a relationship between quantitative aptitude and one of the Pettigrew (1958) category-width factors has been well substantiated both in the original Pettigrew study and in later work (Kogan & Wallach, 1964; Messick & Kogan, 1965). High quantitative aptitude is associated with broad categorizing. No relation to verbal aptitude has ever been demonstrated, possibly because the Pettigrew instrument requires strictly quantitative estimations. Recently, Messick and Kogan (1965) have explicated the relation between quantitative aptitude and category width, giving the latter a possible causal role. It was proposed that broad categorizers on the Pettigrew index may perform better on traditional quantitative aptitude tests because their characteristic cognitive strategy facilitates solution of quantitative problems.

In marked opposition to the results obtained with the Pettigrew test, Bruner and Tajfel (1961) report that tendencies toward narrow categorizing are significantly related to IQ.[2] Very conceivably, the Bruner-Tajfel categorization measures are contaminated with such response styles as acquiescence and criticalness. Acquiescence may be roughly described as a "yea-saying" tendency, criticalness as a "nay-saying" tendency. Although the evidence for the generality of such tendencies to agree and disagree is still quite tentative (McGee, 1962a; 1962b), the fact remains that any experimental situation in which the subject can respond "yes" or "no" to an ambiguous stimulus presentation must allow for the possibility that such responses are not specific to the particular stimulus context in which they are elicited. There is some indication that acquiescence may be negatively related and criticalness positively related to intelligence (Frederiksen & Messick, 1959; Messick & Frederik-

---

[2] Bruner and Tajfel give no indication in their article of the particular IQ metric employed.

sen, 1958), which could conceivably account for the correlation obtained by Bruner and Tajfel between narrow categorizing and IQ.

In the context of the Bruner-Tajfel work, acquiescence would be expressed as a general willingness to accept stimulus patterns as members of the target category. Criticalness, on the other hand, implies an inclination to reject stimulus patterns for the target category unless certain of a "good fit." Since the dot and line patterns do force difficult discriminations upon the subject, it is entirely conceivable that stylistic consistencies other than category breadth as such will influence experimental outcomes.

The Pettigrew instrument does not allow for the operation of acquiescence or criticalness as styles of responding, and hence may well be a more pure index of category breadth than are those procedures calling for acceptance–rejection responses on the part of subjects. A children's version of the Pettigrew test was used in the present investigation.

To the authors' knowledge, there has been no empirical attempt to relate conceptual band width to creativity. The present chapter will direct itself to this issue. Inherent in the notion of broad band-width behavior is a type of testing of category limits which at the very least bears a metaphorical relation to the associative conception of creativity outlined in the introductory chapter. Persons willing to entertain the possibility that highly deviant instances deserve category membership might well turn out to be most capable of conceiving of manifold and unusual possibilities in connection with the creativity tasks described in Chapter 2. The major difference between the conceptual band-width and creativity constructs, as we have employed them, concerns the issue of who shall impose category limits or boundaries. For band-width tasks, various limits or boundaries are specified by the experimenter and the subject must decide which are the most appropriate. The more extreme the limits selected relative to a typical instance or central tendency value, the larger will be the number of possibilities accommodated by the category. Creativity tasks, on the other hand, offer the subject virtually unlimited freedom in the imposition of category boundaries. Hence, the subject can try out numerous possibilities and is restrained largely by internal criteria of what is inappropriate or bizarre. Although the cognitive operations reflected in conceptual band width and creativity are far from identical, there is sufficient stylistic similarity between them to warrant detailed study of their empirical relationship.

We turn next to the evidence for relationships between intelligence and creativity, on the one hand, and the type of category breadth represented by equivalence range or conceptual differentiation, on the other. With regard to intelligence, Gardner, Jackson, and Messick (1960) have explored the interrelationships among a variety of cognitive controls and intellectual abilities. Included among the assessors of cognitive styles was an object-sorting measure of equivalence range. Correlations between the latter and the various ability indices were almost uniformly nonsignificant. Consistent with the above, Sloane, Gorlow, and Jackson (1963) found no relationships between vocabulary skill and several different forms of object-sorting behavior. Thus, object-sorting indices of equivalence range (conceptual differentiation) appear to be quite independent of traditional intelligence indices.

Does this independence also obtain in the case of creativity? One suggestive result in the Gardner and Schoen (1962) monograph points to a possible link between conceptual differentiation and a variable based on TAT performance. Individuals who tell TAT stories that are quite "distant" from the concrete physical properties of the "stimulus" tend to form few groupings on the object-sorting test. Gardner and Schoen explicitly state that "highly imaginative stories . . . were ranked as most distant." Although the foregoing result conforms to expectations (a relationship between broad categorizing and creativity), it must be noted that the TAT measure was based upon a single card presentation. Further, we know little about the relation between imaginativeness of TAT stories and creativity as defined in the present investigation. On the basis of the Gardner-Schoen work, then, only a highly tentative link has been established between broad equivalence range (low conceptual differentiation) and creativity.

Possibly militating against the emergence of relations between conceptual differentiation and the two modes of thinking under study are the complexities inherent in the scoring of the object-sorting task, complexities that have gone unrecognized by Gardner and his colleagues. In this connection, Messick and Kogan (1963) have recently shown that the usual object-sorting index is composed of two independent components— the number of groupings containing at least two objects and the number of singles (miscellaneous objects left ungrouped). It was proposed that the term "conceptual differentiation" be confined to the former component, while the latter be considered a possible indication of "compartmentalization." In a male adult sample, "conceptual differentiation" was significantly related to performance on a vocabulary test (those who formed more groupings tending to have higher vocabulary scores). Conceivably, subjects with superior verbal knowledge may be more critical in restricting the meaning of class rubrics. It is also possible that narrow equivalence ranges offer an advantage in critically coping with the synonym alternatives of a multiple-choice vocabulary test.

Turning to the "compartmentalization" variable, we find a very different pattern of correlates. Those subjects who leave larger numbers of

objects ungrouped tend to do more poorly on an "Unusual Uses" measure of "Spontaneous Flexibility"—"the ability to produce a diversity
of ideas in a relatively unstructured situation" (Frick, Guilford, Christensen, & Merrifield, 1959), and on a "Bricks Uses" measure of "Ideational Fluency" (French, 1951), in which the subject lists as many ways
as he can think of for using a brick. Given the relevance of the above
divergent thinking tasks for creativity, the findings obtained represent
a further link between cognitive style indices and measures having possible implications for creativity.[3]

The Messick-Kogan results do not constitute the definitive study of
the conceptual differentiation–intelligence–creativity issue. Note that they
were obtained only in the case of males. Although the two components
of the over-all object-sorting score were also found to be independent in
females, the relations of these component scores to intelligence and creativity were, if anything, the reverse of those obtained in the case of the
males. It appeared from the female data, in other words, that intelligence
may have some bearing upon the tendency to leave many miscellaneous
objects ungrouped, while creativity may have implications for the number
of groupings formed (exclusive of singles). These statements have an
eminently reasonable quality, for leaving many singles does represent
a failure in conceptualization—an important ingredient of any intelligence construct—and forming few groupings (many objects per group)
will probably imply that the subject has constructed categories encom-
passing unusual combinations of objects—an outcome not too remote
from the emission of unique associates in creativity tasks.

It is quite conceivable that the categorization, intelligence, and
creativity variables are not associated in the same way in males and
females. Under any circumstances, however, a further delineation should
be attempted of the nature of relationships between conceptual differentiation and compartmentalization, on the one hand, and creativity and
intelligence, on the other. The present chapter will later present evidence
relevant to the issue.

To sum up at this point, we have considered two classes of operations
concerned with categorizing breadth: "band width" and object sorting,
the latter in turn being further separated into conceptual differentiation
and compartmentalization. The literature extant on possible linkages
between these aspects of categorizing and indices in the intelligence and
creativity areas has been passed in review. While suggestive leads have
appeared, the situation remains unclear. For one thing, we cannot be sure

---

[3] It should be stressed that the Spontaneous Flexibility and Ideational
Fluency procedures employed in the Messick and Kogan (1963) investigation
were timed, group-administered tests, and hence subject to the criticisms of such
"creativity" measures detailed in Chapter 1.

of the relationships between the possible measures of creativity noted in the preceding studies and those defining the creativity dimension described in Chapter 2 of the present volume. In the case of band width, moreover, the authors know of no attempt to study potential relationships with creativity. Further, effects that may be dependent upon an individual's *joint* status with regard to general intelligence and creativity dimensions have yet to be investigated.

Conceptualizing

In the opening paragraph of the chapter, the authors suggested that a distinction could be made between categorizing and conceptualizing. Thus far, we have dealt exclusively with the former, and particularly with the breadth of a subject's categories. When category breadth is viewed as a problem in band width, conceptualizing as such is ruled out, for the reason that the concept (for example, speed of flight of birds) is directly provided by the experimenter. The subject's task is one of establishing appropriate conceptual boundaries. Where object-sorting behavior is concerned, on the other hand, the subject must both formulate concepts and differentiate them from one another. The activity of formulation—what we choose to call conceptualizing—can be distinguished in terms of the structural properties and content of the concepts selected. The activity of differentiation—previously designated as part of the meaning of categorizing—concerns the breadth of the concepts that get formulated. The foregoing distinction, it should be stressed, is made strictly for expository purposes, and does not conform to any standard usage in the relevant psychological literature. Categorizing and conceptualizing, as delineated above, are related but analytically separable processes. In the case of object-sorting performance, these processes may be invoked sequentially, as the subject scans his repertoire for concepts appropriate to the objects provided, and then, having selected a concept, decides on the particular exemplars to include within it. One can imagine a feedback, trial-and-check operation in which the subject puts forth a concept to encompass a few related objects, proceeds to try it out with one or more additional objects, finds that the concept is applicable or inapplicable to them. Concepts may be retained, modified, or abandoned as a result of this search-and-trial process. We must also allow for the possibility that characteristic category breadth influences the kinds of concepts likely to be invoked. Conceivably, the broad categorizer may favor concepts capable of accommodating a wider range of exemplars. Whatever the causal sequence, however, it is evident that conceptual (as opposed to categorizing) style ought to be studied in its own right. It is to this issue that we now turn.

Various approaches have been taken to the problem of assessing conceptual style. One of the most popular is based upon object-sorting performance. It is a quite simple matter to inquire of an individual, after he has completed his groupings, the particular basis or reason for each of the groupings formed. The number of such reasons for any person will total to the number of groupings containing two or more objects.

How shall the bases or reasons for groupings be scored and interpreted? The method favored by Gardner and Schoen (1962) derives from the work of Rapaport, Gill, and Schafer (1945). According to this latter scheme, reasons given for any grouping can be placed into one of three rubrics: concrete, functional, and conceptual. The last of these was reserved for "true abstraction, i.e., a definition based on a common attribute of objects with disparate other properties." The "functional" classification applied to definitions based on object usage, and the "concrete" classification to definitions of location, belongingness, or simple association. The abstraction score employed by Gardner and his coworkers consists of a ratio of conceptual reasons to the total number of reasons given.

The foregoing abstraction index was included in the Gardner, Jackson, and Messick (1960) study, and proved to be unrelated to all the various intellectual ability indices represented in that investigation. This is a rather puzzling finding, for we would certainly expect a level of abstraction score to bear some relation, at the very least, to performance on inductive reasoning tasks. Undaunted by this negative evidence, however, Gardner and Schoen (1962) employed the identical abstraction score in their large-scale investigation of conceptual differentiation. In addition, those authors also constructed a "Behavior Sorting Test" requiring subjects to categorize phrases describing a variety of human behaviors that were then scored for level of abstraction in the same manner as groupings derived from the object-sorting test.

The results of the Gardner-Schoen work again pointed to the relative independence of level of abstraction from the other variables included in the test battery. A significant relation obtained only with the number-of-groups score on a difficult Photo Sorting Test, in which grouping evidently required abstraction. As in the earlier study (Gardner *et al.*, 1960), no relations were found between level of abstraction and ability (Wechsler IQ). Even the similarities subtest (Wechsler, 1944)—a commonly used score for capacity to abstract—failed to relate to the Gardner abstraction index.

The rather poor relational fertility of the abstraction index preferred by the Gardner group forces a consideration of the merits of the Rapaport *et al.* (1945) scoring scheme for object-sorting performance. The distinctions drawn between conceptual, functional, and concrete responses appear quite arbitrary. There is no evidence in the Gardner-Schoen monograph concerning interscorer reliability.[4] Test–retest reliability, according to those authors, is .30 over an eight-month period. In short, there appears to be little justification for continued application of the Rapaport *et al.* (1945) scoring procedure in research on problems of conceptual style with normal subjects. Where differentiation among normal, schizophrenic, and brain-damaged individuals is the focus of interest, the abstract-concrete dimension may have some value (see Goldstein & Scheerer, 1941). The more recent work of McGaughran and Moran (1956; 1957) suggests, however, that an abstraction dimension as such may even be inadequate for distinguishing among psychopathological groups.

Brown (1958) offers a conceptual analysis of language development that provides a possible reason for the intractability of the abstraction dimension. In very direct terms, abstraction can represent the most primitive of responses (for example, the child who labels all four-legged animals as ''dogs''). This is a type of abstraction indicative of a failure to differentiate. At the same time, abstraction, when following upon differentiation, can represent the highest form of intellectual functioning. Conceivably, these distinctly different types of abstraction might be displayed in object-sorting performance and yet fail to be separated adequately in the scoring system. When a dimension can incorporate such highly divergent sets of processes, it is not likely to be a useful vehicle in the study of conceptual style.

A second possible method of studying conceptual style from the reasons provided for object sortings is to consider the accuracy of an individual's groupings. If a person says that he has sorted in terms of a given criterion, and if it turns out that the actual sorting made is not accurately described by the reason that he provides, then the sorting may be called inaccurate. Thus, Kennedy and Kates (1964) asked twelve-year-old children to group the objects that belong in their estimation with a target object, and then inquired as to the reason for each child's particular grouping. Groupings were scored as ''inadequate'' if not made at all, if irrelevant objects were included, or if relevant objects were excluded. Inaccuracies of sorting, as thus defined, were found to be greater among the least intelligent children, and were found to be greater among the most poorly adjusted children, with adjustment evaluated in terms of a personality inventory and teacher ratings.

Accuracy of sorting, however, does not necessarily tell us much about style of conceptualization per se. It is an aspect of conceptual

---

[4] In an unpublished study of object-sorting behavior, Messick and Kogan attempted to apply the Rapaport *et al.* (1945) scoring scheme, but were forced to abandon it as unwieldy.

performance that one might well expect to have much in common with degree of accuracy as manifested in other forms of cognitive activities. In considering what psychological interpretations one can make concerning reasons given by individuals for object groupings, we hence shall want to look beyond the accuracy–inaccuracy question.

Are there dimensions other than level of abstraction and accuracy–inaccuracy that can be effectively employed in the study of conceptual style in normal subjects? A potentially useful classification scheme has been offered by Kagan, Moss, and Sigel (1960). The scheme describes two basic orientations—egocentric vs. stimulus-centered—and three structural conceptual classes under each of the foregoing orientations. The egocentric orientation "includes concepts which are based on the individual's personalized, affective classification of a group of stimuli and/ or the inclusion of the individual as part of the grouped stimuli" (pp. 262–263). It should be noted that an egocentric orientation is likely to reflect the use of affect-laden stimuli in a conceptual sorting test. Kagan *et al.* worked with a human figure-sorting task, and hence obtained frequent egocentric responses in a sample of children. Where an object-sorting task is employed, as in the present investigation, egocentric responses can be expected to decline sharply and stimulus-centered responses to increase proportionately. In the stimulus-centered orientation, "the concepts are based on aspects of the external stimulus, and the individual's personal traits or feelings are not used as the basis for categorization" (p. 263).

Turning to the three formal conceptual categories, Kagan *et al.* designate them as descriptive, categorical-inferential, and relational. Descriptive concepts are based on similarity in objective, physical attributes among a group of stimuli. Objects are grouped, in other words, in terms of some shared physical property (such as color, size, or shape) which is abstracted from the objects in their entirety. Categorical-inferential concepts do not rest on a single abstracted physical property shared by the objects, but rather represent groupings that take account of the objects as whole entities. Any object in a group can be considered an independent instance of the conceptual label (kitchen utensils, or pieces of furniture). Finally, the relational category refers to concepts based on the functional relationship among the objects in a group. The functional relation may be spatial or temporal. The objects located within any grouping are not independent instances of a concept, but rather each object derives its meaning from its relationship to the other members of the group. The relational category has a thematic quality, for the subject essentially links the objects together in a story theme.

The foregoing tripartite classification served as the basis for subsequent work on the problem of conceptual style in children and adults

(Kagan, Moss, & Sigel, 1963). Proceeding on the assumption that a "descriptive" response implies the analytic differentiation of an element of similarity from irrelevant aspects of the stimuli, Kagan, *et al.* decided to relabel the "descriptive" classification as "analytic-descriptive." Such concepts are presumed to involve an "active conceptual analysis," and are contrasted with relational concepts which are presumed to involve a "passive acceptance of the entire stimulus." Further, analytic-descriptive concepts are claimed to be based upon more subdued attributes, whereas relational concepts are described as a response to the most obvious aspects of the grouped stimuli. Note, finally, that the inferential-categorical classification receives only secondary consideration in the Kagan *et al.* work, as those authors seem to prefer the more straightforward analytic vs. nonanalytic distinction to which descriptive vs. relational responses lend themselves.[5]

Creativity, Intelligence, and Conceptual Style

Turning now to the issue of correlates, is there any indication that the classification schema proposed by Kagan and his colleagues bears a relation to the intelligence and creativity domains? All the reported evidence concerns intelligence. This evidence is particularly difficult to evaluate, for both children and adults were employed as subjects, and different procedures were sometimes used to assess analytic vs. nonanalytic functioning in the two types of samples. The figure-sorting procedure discussed earlier in the chapter was administered to adult subjects, and a modified version was adapted for children. But in addition, a new procedure was devised for children in which pictorial stimuli were presented in triads, the child being required to select which two of the three stimuli were most similar and to specify the basis for his decision. The triads were so constructed that the child could base his similarity judgment upon analytic-descriptive, inferential-categorical, or relational grounds.[6] Although this classification schema was identical to that derived from the figure-sorting procedure, it is evident that the latter and the triad procedure do not involve identical processes. Despite these compli-

---

[5] Kagan, Moss, and Sigel (1963) claim that their classification scheme bears upon the constructs of analytic vs. global functioning as these have been defined by the Witkin group (Witkin, Dyk, Faterson, Goodenough, & Karp, 1962; Witkin, Lewis, Hertzman, Machover, Meissner, & Wapner, 1954). There is evidence, however, that different operational measures of analytic functioning—for example, embedded figures vs. object-sorting performance—yield different patterns of correlates. The complexities surrounding this issue are discussed by Wallach (1962).

[6] In fact, the triad procedure was given under conditions that actively discouraged the emission of the more popular inferential-categorical responses.

cations (which are acknowledged by the Kagan group), we shall attempt to glean from their presentation as much as is relevant to the issues posed by the present chapter.

Considering first the results for adults in the Fels longitudinal study, men above the median on descriptive-analytic concepts were rated significantly higher on "intellectual mastery," and had "slightly higher IQ's than the other men in the sample." As children (aged six to fourteen), these men had been rated significantly higher in persistence in problem situations, confidence in approaching challenging intellectual tasks, and motivation to obtain achievement-related goals. In contrast, men above the median on relational concepts seemed to be more dependent, anxious, and lacking in ambition. Results for women were generally nonsignificant. Summing up, the adult results as a whole point to a rather weak association, if any, between a preference for descriptive-analytic concepts and objective intelligence indices.

We turn next to results reported for sixth grade children. Correlations are given between IQ scores from the California Test of Mental Maturity and the conceptual style variables derived from the triad and figure-sorting tests. Relationships emerge more strongly for boys than girls, paralleling the adult data cited earlier, but the results can best be described as equivocal. The evidence indicates quite clearly that the relation of the conceptual modes to IQ depends upon the way the former are measured. IQ is positively related to categorical-inferential responses deriving from the triads procedure, but negatively related to such responses when they stem from the figure-sorting task. The results are more consistent in the case of analytic-descriptive responses, though even here it can be noted that a significant positive relation obtains only for Performance IQ in the triads task and only for Verbal IQ in the figure-sorting procedure. Relational-nonanalytic responses were scored only in the case of triads and were found to be inversely related to IQ scores. For reasons not entirely clear, the relational conceptual style was not scored in the figure-sorting test. In sum, the foregoing data relating conceptual style to intelligence indices do not permit any firm inferences respecting relationships between those domains. Such a conclusion is further reinforced by the outcomes of a study of third grade children in which no significant relations whatever were found between conceptual style and IQ variables.

Despite the equivocal results reported in Kagan, Moss, and Sigel (1963), a reading of the monograph soon reveals that they believe the analytic child to be superior to the nonanalytic child. Analytic children, according to those authors, are at a developmentally higher level than the nonanalytic, and hence it is reasoned that their superiority should be manifest in the realm of general intellectual functioning. A great deal of evidence is brought to bear on this issue, some of it demonstrating a link between analytic preferences as an adult and intellectual striving as a child. Virtually all the data favoring the Kagan *et al.* position derived from males. Conceivably, analytic functioning does not confer the same kinds of advantages on girls as on boys. Even in the case of boys, however, the findings are often equivocal.

We have found, then, that relational or thematic conceptualizing is viewed by Kagan and his associates as a distinctly inferior mode of conceptual functioning. Relational concepts are thought to reflect a passive acceptance of the stimulus in contrast to attempts at active analysis, and to constitute a response to those stimulus properties that are more obvious or more prominent. It is of interest to consider that this negative evaluation of relational conceptualizing is rather widely held. Thus, for example, Bruner, Goodnow, and Austin (1956) report an experiment demonstrating that individuals can, as it were, be tempted into error in concept attainment, when the instances are provided to them in thematic rather than in abstract form. Performance in determining the defining attributes of a concept from testing members of a given array of instances was evaluated for two conditions. In one, the subjects worked with visual instances of an abstract geometric kind, varying in terms of such attributes as, for example, shape (triangle vs. rectangle) and color (yellow vs. black). In the other, the subjects worked with visual instances that were strictly equivalent logically in terms of number of attributes and number of values of each attribute to the geometric instances just considered, but whose content concerned meaningful pictorial material instead of abstract forms. For instance, one attribute of variation was the male vs. female sex of a depicted human figure, another was whether the figure was in day dress or in night dress. While a concept with abstract content hence might be "yellow triangles," a concept with thematic content might be "male figures in day dress."

Comparing subjects in the two conditions, Bruner, Goodnow, and Austin report that when working with thematic instances, subjects require a larger number of choices in order to attain a given concept, make more choices which are redundant (logically unnecessary in terms of the information already in hand), and offer a larger number of incorrect hypotheses before achieving the correct one. Further, in the thematic case, subjects are loathe to test the relevance of one attribute compared with their willingness to test the relevance of another, even though each attribute has the same likelihood of being involved in the concept. As the authors remark, ". . . the thematic material will, more readily than abstract material, lead certain attributes to have nonrational criteriality: the subject will 'hang on' to these and will formulate hypotheses around them" (Bruner, Goodnow, & Austin, 1956, p. 111). In short, it is found in the present context that the availability of thematic material seduces the individual into logical errors and inefficient strategies. Once again, thematizing tendencies are viewed as intellectually inferior manifestations.

Is there any reason to expect that creativity, as defined in the present investigation, might be relevant to issues of conceptual style? Possibly, the question can be rephrased as: How will creativity be manifested on a test of conceptual style? Working with the scoring scheme proposed by Kagan and his colleagues, we would very likely assume that the analytic-descriptive response is much more relevant to the domain of intelligence than to the area of creativity. The foregoing conceptual mode requires that the subject detect common aspects inherent in the stimuli, an operation suggestive of convergent rather than divergent thinking. Similarly, inferential-categorical responses imply a search process in which the subject attempts to find a superordinate concept to handle a set of exemplars. This is abstraction in the classic sense, a process most psychologists would again link to intelligence rather than to creativity.

We turn, finally, to the relational response, what Kagan and his co-workers have designated as "passive acceptance of the stimulus." Recall that relational responding involves the construction of a thema in which the stimulus elements are placed in a functional relationship to each other. Where the stimulus elements are few in number and the thematic aspects highly salient (as in the Kagan *et al.* studies), it is quite conceivable that the relational response will represent a low-level global approach to the task at hand. On the other hand, suppose one were to increase the number of stimulus elements in a sorting task and eliminate or markedly reduce compelling thematic interrelationships. Would relational responses have the same psychological meaning in that case? Is it not likely, in fact, that the creative individual will take advantage of the opportunities afforded by the relational conceptual mode for forming unique combinations of elements? Such opportunities are obviously much smaller in the analytic-descriptive and inferential-categorical modes, because both of these are considerably more stimulus-bound. Of course, one must take account of natural inclinations toward abstraction in object-sorting tasks with instructions to group stimuli on the basis of their similarity. The subject might well suppress tendencies toward relational groupings in an instructional context encouraging abstraction. On the other hand, the emergence of relational preferences under such conditions could be taken as evidence for their considerable strength in the individuals concerned. Relational or thematic responding, under these circumstances, might constitute a relatively free-wheeling type of response to the task at hand, in contrast to the more conventional response of grouping stimuli in terms of common elements—whether the latter are of the analytic-descriptive or inferential-categorical variety. In sum, the authors anticipate that creative children will more frequently indulge in relational responding than do noncreative, whereas highly intelligent children will prefer analytic-descriptive and inferential-categorical modes of responding to a greater extent than do less intelligent children.

The present chapter has focused exclusively upon the approaches to conceptual style that originated with Rapaport, Gill, and Schafer (1945) and with Kagan, Moss, and Sigel (1960). The authors stressed these two approaches because both sets of investigators used the object-sorting procedure in their research. There are, of course, other approaches to the problem of conceptual style. Bruner and Olver (1963), for example, used associative grouping techniques. Two words (bell and horn, for example) were presented together, and the child specified in what way they were alike. A third word was then presented, and the child had to indicate how it differed from the first two and then how all three were alike. This process was continued through a series of nine words that were progressively more distant semantically from the original pair. The study was conducted on children at three grade levels (first, fourth, and sixth). As might be expected, grouping strategies changed with increasing age. Younger children were more likely to employ a variety of complexive groupings whereas older children tended toward genuine superordinate concept formation. In this respect, the Bruner-Olver data are quite consistent with observations by Inhelder and Piaget (1958) and by Vygotsky (1962) concerning the child's progression from spontaneous (complexive) to systematic concepts.

It is quite evident that the Bruner-Olver work was pursued from the perspective of the development of intelligence. It is the general superordinate concept that characterizes abstract intelligence in the adult, and the above authors take special pains to show how such concepts make for cognitive economy and new combinatorial possibilities in processing information. Once again, however, we must note that the research which has been conducted on conceptual style has had very little to say about the creativity issue. Bruner and Olver do distinguish a category of thematic grouping (which bears some similarity to the relational classification in the schema by Kagan *et al.*), but thematic groupings are viewed as the most uneconomical ones imaginable. From the standpoint of forming simple rules that encompass a multiplicity of stimuli, the thematic grouping does indeed have little value. Of course, Bruner and Olver deliberately constructed their stimulus materials to foster categorical superordinate groupings, and indeed, where intelligence is the focus, these groupings may represent an optimal mode of responding. As we indicated earlier, however, creativity may very probably be expressed through the mechanism of thematic groupings on conceptual style indicators, if indeed creativity has any implications whatever for conceptualizing activities.

Is it possible to construct a procedure within the conceptual domain that will optimize thematic-relational modes of responding? The present authors have made an attempt at such a procedure, which consists of sets of four disparate nouns to be embedded by the subject in a meaningful story of his own construction. A subject's responses can then be scored for thematic excellence (degree to which all component words are integrated, and imaginativeness of thematic content). Unlike the procedures discussed previously, where thematic-relational responding may represent only a preferred mode of coping with the stimulus materials, the present task requires that the subject bring a thematic-relational set to bear, if he is to achieve a high score. We shall later note whether our highly creative children perform better than the less creative on the foregoing task.

The next section of the chapter will offer a description of the procedures employed to assess categorizing and conceptualizing in our sample of children. It should be stressed that these activities were measured in the same nonevaluative context that characterized the measurement of creativity in the present study. To the extent that categorizing and conceptualizing have been investigated under evaluative conditions, a common occurrence in much of the previous research, relations with intelligence indices will be enhanced. The results reported in the present chapter should show, therefore, whether such relationships involve more than shared method or situational variance.

Following the description of categorization and conceptualization procedures, the empirical associations among the relevant variables will be examined. The contributions of intelligence and creativity to styles of categorization and conceptualization will be determined. Of special interest is the exploration of possible intelligence–creativity interaction effects with respect to the cognitive styles under investigation here. There is presently no empirical information whatever pertaining to this important question.

PROCEDURE

The present section of the chapter offers a description of the instruments used to measure categorizing and conceptualizing. Scoring methods will be presented for all of these instruments, and discussed in considerable detail for the conceptual style indices. These indices are based upon content analyses of "free" response materials, and hence the authors will elaborate upon the scoring categories employed to code the data. Some of these were briefly sketched in the introduction to the chapter. Finally, appropriate reliability information will be provided for each index. The reliability coefficients will be of the internal consistency and/or interscorer form, in accordance with the type of variable under consideration.

Measures of Breadth of Categorization

BAND-WIDTH PROCEDURE. Used as an index of the "band-width" type of category breadth was the Wallach and Caron (1959) adaptation for children of the Pettigrew (1958) category-width test. The present instrument was the eleventh in the sequence of procedures, and was administered in the classroom to the children in aggregate. The experimenters attempted to maintain a gamelike atmosphere for the administration of the category width task. Thus, the instrument was described as a "guessing game" to the children. Since all of the subjects had experienced considerable individual contact with the experimenters in a relatively relaxed context before the category width task was given, the precautions taken should have served to minimize the apprehensions of children for whom the category-width task might otherwise have had a testlike character.

The experimenter read the instructions for the "guessing game" to the children. These instructions were also reproduced on the instrument itself, so it was possible for the children to follow the experimenter as she presented the instructions orally. The instructions for the category width task ("guessing game") follow.

"This game asks you to guess about a lot of things in our world. For instance, if you knew that most grown-up men in the world are around 5 feet and 7 inches tall, you might guess that the tallest man in the world is 7 feet tall, or 8 feet tall. And you might guess that the shortest man in the world is 4 feet tall or only 3 feet tall. In this game you get a chance to guess about things like that. Why don't you just begin reading now, and circle your guesses for each of the things printed below. Take your time, and ask me any questions you want about things that aren't clear to you."

Listed below are the twelve items comprising the children's version of the category width test.

1. Most birds fly at the speed of about 17 miles per hour.
    a. How fast does the fastest bird fly?
        1. 30 miles per hour
        2. 21 miles per hour
        3. 60 miles per hour
        4. 18 miles per hour

b. How slow does the slowest bird fly?
   1. 15 miles per hour
   2. 5 miles per hour
   3. 10 miles per hour
   4. 2 miles per hour
2. Most whales are about 65 feet long.
   a. How long is the longest whale?
      1. 69 feet
      2. 150 feet
      3. 76 feet
      4. 90 feet
   b. How short is the shortest whale?
      1. 37 feet
      2. 8 feet
      3. 51 feet
      4. 58 feet
3. Usually about 58 ships arrive in New York City harbor every day.
   a. What do you guess is the largest number of ships ever to arrive in New York City harbor in one day?
      1. 102 ships
      2. 65 ships
      3. 74 ships
      4. 60 ships
   b. What do you guess is the smallest number of ships ever to arrive in New York City harbor in one day?
      1. 5 ships
      2. 49 ships
      3. 38 ships
      4. 18 ships
4. Most dogs are about 3½ feet long.
   a. How long is the longest dog?
      1. 4½ feet
      2. 4 feet
      3. 5½ feet
      4. 6½ feet
   b. How short is the shortest dog?
      1. 1 foot
      2. ½ foot
      3. 2½ feet
      4. 2 feet
5. Most cars are able to go about 90 miles per hour.
   a. How fast will the fastest car go?
      1. 213 miles per hour

2. 95 miles per hour

3. 394 miles per hour

4. 132 miles per hour

b. How slow will the slowest car go?

1. 3 miles per hour

2. 18 miles per hour

3. 9 miles per hour

4. ½ mile per hour

6. Most roads are about 18 feet wide.

a. How wide is the widest road?

1. 51 feet

2. 27 feet

3. 20 feet

4. 36 feet

b. How narrow is the narrowest road?

1. 16 feet

2. 7 feet

3. 2 feet

4. 11 feet

7. Most states have about 4 million people in them.

a. How many million people are there in the largest state?

1. 5 million

2. 15 million

3. 8 million

4. 30 million

b. How many million people are there in the smallest state?

1. 1 million

2. 2 million

3. ⅛ million

4. 3 million

8. Most buildings are about 50 feet high.

a. How high is the tallest building?

1. 421 feet

2. 1253 feet

3. 157 feet

4. 63 feet

b. How short is the shortest building?

1. 40 feet

2. 6 feet

3. 29 feet

4. 17 feet

9. Most windows are about 34 inches wide.

a. How wide is the widest window?

1. 110 inches

2. 36 inches
3. 43 inches
4. 57 inches

b. How narrow is the narrowest window?

1. 3 inches
2. 21 inches
3. 12 inches
4. 28 inches

10. Most sailboats go about 9 miles per hour.

a. How fast will the fastest sailboat go?

1. 22 miles per hour
2. 39 miles per hour
3. 11 miles per hour
4. 14 miles per hour

b. How slow will the slowest sailboat go?

1. 7 miles per hour
2. 8½ miles per hour
3. 6 miles per hour
4. 4½ miles per hour

11. Every year about 300 new schoolbooks are written.

a. What is the largest number of schoolbooks written in one year?

1. 524 books
2. 330 books
3. 392 books
4. 980 books

b. What is the smallest number of schoolbooks written in one year?

1. 94 books
2. 25 books
3. 9 books
4. 180 books

12. Most people spend about 55 minutes out of a whole day eating meals.

a. What is the longest time anyone spends eating meals in a whole day?

1. 60 minutes
2. 105 minutes
3. 240 minutes
4. 73 minutes

b. What is the shortest time anyone spends eating meals in a whole day?

1. 3 minutes
2. 29 minutes
3. 47 minutes
4. 11 minutes

In scoring the procedure, the two parts of each item are keyed 1, 2, 3, and 4, representing responses that are least to most discrepant from the central tendency provided for each item. These twenty-four values are simply summed to yield the total score. A large score reflects a preference for broad band widths; a small score reflects a preference for narrow band widths. The odd–even reliability coefficient for the present variable was .76 for the sample of 151 children.

EQUIVALENCE RANGE PROCEDURE. The present procedure (described as a "picture game") was fourth in the experimental sequence. Fifty words referring to fifty familiar objects in the Clayton and Jackson (1961) Object Sorting Test were transformed into pictorial form. A line drawing of each of the fifty familiar objects appeared on a separate card.

The objects were as follows: a fork, a door, a tire, a scissors, a TV set, a spoon, a cigarette, a spool of thread, an arrow, a lamp, a flashlight, a flower, a clock, a lipstick, a rake, a jacket, a screwdriver, a wallet, a letter, a sled, a hanger, a refrigerator, a hammer, a pot, a key, a picture, a coin, a radio, a rowboat, a telephone, a canoe, a rug, a golf club, a comb, a shoe, a chair, a baseball, a cup, a pistol, a hat, a pencil, a lamppost, a purse, a candle, a ruler, a glass, a book, a watch, a tree, a stool. Instructions to the subjects were the following:

"Now let's play the picture game. While I spread these pictures out for you I'll name them off so that we will be sure to agree on what each object is." (The experimenter sets down five rows of ten pictures each before the subject, naming each as it is put down. The same initial arrangement is used for every child.) "Now your job is to look the pictures over and then put all the pictures that seem to belong together into groups. The groups may be large or small, any size you want as long as the pictures in each group belong together for a reason. There aren't any right or wrong answers in this game. Every time I play it with someone the groups turn out differently. So you see, any way you feel like making groups is fine, as long as you have some reason for it. Once you make the groups you can add to them or change them, and if there are any pictures left over at the end that don't seem to fit into any of your groups, you can just leave them separately. Do you see how we play the game?—Good. Now take your time, there's no need to hurry. And remember that your groups can be all different sizes. O.K., go ahead."

Subjects then proceeded to rearrange the cards to form groupings. If the subject had any difficulty in keeping the groupings separate from one another, the experimenter suggested that the child build a pile of cards for each group. When the subject completed the grouping task, the experimenter inquired into the reasons for the particular groupings formed. These will be discussed in the section on conceptual style to follow.

Two measures are derived from the number of groupings provided. The number of groups containing two or more objects constitutes the *conceptual differentiation* score; the number of singles (objects left un-grouped) constitutes the *compartmentalization* score.

Turning to matters of reliability, an index of internal consistency obviously could not be obtained in the present case. Note should be taken, however, of the correlation of .75 between alternate forms of the object-sorting test in the work of Sloane, Gorlow, and Jackson (1963). While these were group-administered paper-and-pencil versions for adults, correlations with the individually administered Gardner (1953) object-sorting test were substantial (*r*'s of .55 and .53). These various correlations concern number of groups including singles. One can feel quite confident, then, that the object-sorting task administered in the present investigation would meet a fairly stringent criterion of internal consistency.

Measures of Conceptual Style

REASONS FOR OBJECT SORTINGS. The categories proposed by Kagan, Moss, and Sigel (1960) were employed in scoring the reasons provided by a child for his object sortings. These categories—descriptive, inferential, and relational—were not devised for the particular object-sorting procedure used here, and hence it was necessary to amplify the Kagan *et al.* scheme somewhat for scoring purposes. The scoring rules for the *descriptive* category were as follows:

Groupings in this category are based on similarity in objective, physical attributes among a group of stimuli. The concrete attribute shared by objects can be perceived through any of the senses. For example, "hard objects" (lamp-post, door, hammer) would be tactile knowledge, "they all make sounds" (radio, television, phone) would be auditory, and "give light" (lamp, flashlight, candle) would be visually perceived. All descriptive labels must contain a reference to a commonly shared physical attribute of the grouped stimuli. Where a visual perception is the basis for the grouping, the shared attribute does not have to be drawn onto all the objects grouped. In this way a group such as "all have knobs" (radio, television, clock) is labeled "descriptive" even though the knob is not visible from the angle at which the object is viewed in the drawing. It is "descriptive" because the knob is an integral and necessary part of the physical structure of the object.

Turning next to the *inferential* category, the scoring rules were as follows:

These concepts classify objects because of some characteristic shared by all, but what they share is not inherent in the physical nature of the stimuli grouped. These labels do not contain a direct reference to an objective, physical attribute of the group of similar stimuli (unlike "descriptive" labels), and yet each object *is* an individual instance of the label (unlike "relational" concepts). The classifications made fall generally into the areas of usage and location. Examples of groupings based on usage would be "for eating" (fork, spoon, cup, glass), or "boats" (canoe and rowboat). This second group is indirectly based on usage since the general class of boats is composed of objects that can do and are used to do a similar task—travel on water. Examples of location would be "objects you would find indoors" or "things you might see outside."

Finally, we consider the scoring rules for the *relational* category:

The distinguishing characteristic of these conceptual labels is that they grow out of the relationships between or among the stimuli grouped together, and then serve as a kind of umbrella over the collection. Because of this, no stimulus is an independent instance of the concept, and some have had greater weight in determining what the concept became than did others. These relationships among the stimuli grouped together are functional, and build on connections of a temporal, spatial, or complementary nature. The temporal–spatial complexes are concrete or situational in nature, generally thematic. A typical theme might be "getting ready to go out" (comb, lipstick, watch, pocketbook, door). No single object is an example of the label that envelops it. A typical complementary relationship might give rise to the label "to put money away," where the stimuli (coin, purse) are both clearly necessary to achieve the single goal suggested.

What is the interjudge reliability for coding responses into the three rubrics of conceptual style outlined above? The 151 subjects of the study generated a total of 1730 groupings (exclusive of singles) in the object-sorting task. Of this total, 1561 yielded agreement between two judges in regard to the kind of conceptual style—descriptive, inferential, or relational—reflected by the response.[7] In short, agreement on the conceptual style indices is equal to 90 percent. All scoring was carried out without awareness of the given child's identity. The 169 disagreements were resolved by discussion between the judges. Most of the disagreements, as might be expected, occurred in the case of responses falling near the boundary between two of the three conceptual modes. In resolving discrepancies, the judges evolved a set of informal rules to assist in the classification of these boundary responses. Some of these rules are illustrated below.

We consider first the case in which the "descriptive" classification approaches the "inferential" one. Here the judges set the border at the point where a concrete, physical attribute could no longer be directly implied from the reason given for the grouping. An example of this outer limit to the "descriptive" category would be a grouping (glass, cup, pot) with the reason "they hold something." The quality of hollowness so directly implied here suggested inclusion in the "descriptive" class. However, the same stated reason that "they hold something," if refrigerator is included as a member of the group, would not be "descriptive" since the quality of the concrete space suggested is different for the refrigerator than for the pot, glass, or cup. With the refrigerator included, abstract space is suggested—that is, enclosures *in general*; with-

---

[7] When two different types of reasons were given for a single group, the first one was taken if both were adequate or inadequate. If one was adequate and the other not, the adequate one was selected.

out the refrigerator, the shared attribute is concrete, similarly shaped space—therefore ''descriptive.''

Comparable classification difficulties occasionally arose when ''inferential'' responses seemed to shade into ''descriptive'' ones. Thus, ''inferential'' classifications based on usage may indirectly reflect something shared by the stimuli in their physical natures. The border between ''descriptive'' and ''inferential'' depends on whether the child's primary interest is in the physical nature of the object or in the usage to which it gives rise. For example, the objects (radio, phone, television) can be presented with the labels ''all make sounds'' or ''you can hear things over them.'' The first reason focuses on the sound-making character of the stimuli and would be ''descriptive.'' The second label, however, stresses what one can *do* with the stimuli, and would be ''inferential.''

''Inferential'' location responses shade into ''relational'' ones if the child seems to be more interested in relations among or between objects seen outside, for example, than in their commonly shared location. If he remarks that ''the rake is to clean up the leaves that fall from the tree,'' the label is ''relational.'' ''Inferential'' classifications also can be made for combined usage-location reasons. Such a group would be ''outdoor sports equipment'' (golf club, baseball, canoe, sled, arrow).

In the case of ''relational'' responses, overlapping with the ''inferential'' mode presented judgmental difficulties. As ''relational'' labels approached the ''inferential'' ones in resembling concepts in which each stimulus is an individual instance of a superordinate class, the judges set limits in the following ways: When a child grouped comb, jacket, shoes, clock, hanger, because they were ''what a man wears and uses in the morning,'' he was clearly moving toward classifying objects and away from themes. But the group is well within ''relational'' bounds because the thematic situation is still strong, and because even if one accepted the implied classes of ''things one uses'' and ''things one wears,'' all the stimuli in the group are not individual instances of *both* classes. In the multiple-group label ''for building something and cleaning things out'' (hammer, screwdriver, rake), the two activities do not readily lend themselves to a thematic interpretation. But even though focusing on the classification possibilities afforded by the stimulus materials, the child has not arrived at a single label of which all items are representative. This marks the ''relational'' side of the border. On the ''inferential'' side, the child might give the reason ''in or on top of a desk'' for a book, ruler, pencil, and scissors. This would be ''inferential'' because, even though it is a multiple label, all the stimuli are instances of both parts of the label; they can *all* go either ''in or on top of the desk.''

A child's scores regarding conceptual style in object sorting consist of the percentages of his groupings (exclusive of singles) categorized as descriptive, inferential, and relational.

THEMATIC INTEGRATION. The present procedure was third in the experimental sequence and concerned the telling of stories. The instructions to subjects were as follows:

"In this game I am going to show you a card that has four words on it. It will be your job to tell a very short story using up all four words without changing them at all—you know, don't add 's' or things like that. The story shouldn't be longer than 2 or 3 sentences. Here is an example: armchair, ranch, watch, cards." (The experimenter shows the words printed on a card to the subject.) "Now you might tell the story like this: 'The man in the *armchair* looked at his *watch* and decided to go back to the *ranch*. He put the *cards* in the drawer, cleaned up his desk, and soon left the office.' You see, all four of the words are used in this little story." (In presenting the example, the experimenter tells the story slowly, as if thinking it up herself and offering it only as a suggested solution to the task. She points to the words on the card as they are used in her story.) "Now on the next card it will be your turn to tell a story. You can tell any kind of story you would like and use the words in any order you would like as long as you use all of them. There's no need to rush. O.K., here we go."

The experimenter then showed the subject the first set of words printed on a card and instructed him to make up a story using all four words. Four more sets of four words each followed in sequence. The five items comprising the instrument were as follows:

1. job, sky, sand, people
2. book, gun, pool, dream
3. ring, car, grass, rope
4. night, dog, medicine, flower
5. lamp, fence, overcoat, cup

When reading the words on the card to the subjects, the experimenter varied their order to insure that the child did not expect them to be used in a fixed sequence. Since the use of all four words was crucial in scoring the present task, this aspect was emphasized again at the end of the instructions.

The children's stories were analyzed in terms of two clearly defined categories, labeled 2-type and 0-type stories. When a story was not clearly within either of these groups, it was rated as a 1-type story. In using the scoring criteria, care was taken to avoid being misled either by the child who had a slick or sophisticated story-telling style or, at the other extreme, by the child whose lack of story-telling finesse obscured the qualities that did exist in his or her stories.

Turning first to the 2-type category, this score was intended for stories which were well integrated and imaginative in theme and/or details. Those details meriting a 2 value fell in the areas of humor, fantasy, fancifulness, and drama. In general, it was impossible to separate a detail from a total theme—a fanciful detail will be part of a story with a generally fanciful flavor. Stories with details different in tone from the bulk of the story do occur, however, and these were given a 1 rating unless the child thoroughly integrated the detail into the story's action. A few examples of different types of 2-stories are listed below.[8]

Humor: "A few nights ago my father acted a little unusual. He was reading in bed and fell asleep over his book and left the *lamp* on all night. In the morning he took his *cup* of coffee and almost drank the cup with it. Then he put his *overcoat* on backwards and as he said goodbye to us crashed into the board *fence*."

Fantasy: "One *night* when I was sleeping a *dog* came barking at my window. I jumped out of bed and ran to my window to see what had happened. The dog had found a bottle of strange *medicine* with an ugly color. I opened my window and took it from him. Then I went to my *flower* bed and poured it on them. In a very short time they had grown 20 feet tall. From then on I had the tallest flowers in the whole country."

Fanciful: "The very tired man opened the *fence* on the walk to his house. He came in and threw off his *overcoat*. Accidentally his overcoat hit a *lamp* and the lamp hit a *cup* that was very valuable. The dog was standing nearby wagging his tail. By sheer miracle the cup fell on the dog's tail and it held there until the master could get to it. The dog was rewarded greatly by his master."

Dramatic: The dramatic stories rated as 2's were of three general types. First, there are stories with a single violent action supported by the general theme:

"I tied a *rope* onto the *car* and onto the garage, and I had the car and went 102 miles per hour. The rope broke and the car went all over the *grass*. I had bet a *ring* that the rope wouldn't break."

Next, there are stories with lesser focus on any single outstanding event, but which nevertheless move toward a general culmination:

"Once my father went out in a *car* for a drive. When he came home he told us of the *ring* he found in the *grass*. The ring was down on the other side of the mountain. It had very precious stones in it so he went to get it. We put the *rope* in the car, got in, and started over to the grassy mountain. I climbed down and found the ring. A rope was tied around me so that I could come up. When we got home I gave the ring to my mother."

Finally, there are stories which achieve a dramatic effect by convincingly or vividly describing various events:

"One day my brother and I decided to make a tree hut. We used part of our old *fence* to build it. In it we had a *lamp* and a table with a *cup* and some dishes on it. I decided to go home because it started to rain. My mother told me I could go back to the tree house if I put my *overcoat* on."

We now direct our attention to 0-type stories. A zero score was given where the story lacked integration with the consequence that the words in the story were more prominent than the story theme. The scorer's attention is drawn to story fragments which are not unified

---

[8] The twelve different example stories that follow were provided by eleven different children, seven boys and four girls.

into a meaningful whole. These 0-type stories may make little sense or may lack a flavor of wholeness. An example of a 0-type story having meaning but lacking integration follows:

"My *job* is to *sand*. *People* look at the *sky*."

A 0-type story manifesting integration but little meaning is the following:

"This lady had a *dream* that she found a *gun* and shot a *book* and then read the book and went to the *pool* and finished it."

Most stories rated zero because of poor integration were really "skeletonized" versions which could conceivably achieve wholeness by addition of details. However, some stories sufficiently integrated to warrant a score of 1 also were lacking in detail, so that brevity as such was never an adequate cause of a zero rating. At the same time, it is typical of 0-stories that the poorness of the integration draws attention to the skeletal structure. These structures can be schematically depicted as shown below.

"His *job* was to fly in the *sky* and he liked *people* and he loved hot *sand*."

In the above example, only two of the words are meaningfully integrated, and the structure assumes the form

Another 0-type structure, somewhat better integrated, is reflected by the following story:

"The *car* went over the *grass*. We put a *ring* around a *rope*."

Note here that the child has achieved integration within two sets of two words each, but has not unified the couples into a single idea. The form can be depicted as

In the next 0-type structure, a still higher level of integration can be noted.

"This lady had a *dream* that she found a *gun* and shot a *book* and then read the book and went to the *pool* and finished it."

It can be seen that the child has essentially created overlapping couples in the form of a chain complex

Finally, there are those structures which are sufficiently integrated to fall on the border between a 0 and 1 rating.

"A guy has a *dream* that he wished he had a *gun*, a *book* and a swimming *pool*."

"The *people* were looking at the *sky* and thinking of a *job* and began to make a *sand* castle."

The first example received a 0-score, the second a 1-score on the basis of the complexity of detail represented. Note in both examples the presence of a key word meaningfully related to the other three words, with the latter poorly connected to one another. The schematic depiction might be

In sum, one is constantly aware in 0-type stories of the elements from which the story was constructed; the four critical words stick out and often seem awkwardly or arbitrarily placed in the story. In 2-type stories, on the other hand, one's attention is directed to the total situation described rather than to the separate parts; the story is a Gestalt representing considerably more than the words constituting its building blocks.

For the "Telling Stories" procedure, the authors are able to report both interscorer and internal consistency reliability. Agreement between two judges in scores of low, medium, and high quality across the total of 755 responses was 80 percent. Once again, the materials were scored without knowledge of the identities of the particular children. If we ask about agreement in classifying stories as 0-type or non-0-type, the value rises to 97 percent. Agreement in classification as 2-type or non-2-type is 83 percent. Judges evidently agree quite well in judging the quality of stories produced, though they show a somewhat greater consensus in regard to responses of low quality. The latter observation, however, is largely a function of the greater frequency of 2-type than of 0-type stories. The relevant data are shown below for the five items, after interjudge discrepancies in judgment were resolved by discussion.

Item	No. of 0's	No. of 1's	No. of 2's
1. job, sky, sand, people	7	123	21
2. dream, gun, book, pool	19	114	18
3. rope, ring, grass, car	8	96	47
4. night, dog, medicine, flower	4	121	26
5. fence, lamp, overcoat, cup	5	97	49

It can be seen that items 3 and 5 appear more conducive to 2-type stories, items 1, 2, and 4 less so. Although the twenty words employed in the task are common nouns, it seems that the words job, dream, and night provide an organizing focus in items 1, 2, and 4, respectively. One might anticipate that this would help in the creation of a 2-type story, yet the effect is in the opposite direction. Apparently, a key organizing word leads the child astray by making it more difficult for him to combine the remaining words in a thematic way. These remaining words are made to fit the association begun by the organizing word. The creation of 2-type stories is facilitated when the four component words contribute more or less equally to the theme produced, as in items 3 and 5. Under these conditions the subjects seem less handicapped in making combinations and developing integrated relationships among the component words.

Despite the foregoing item differences, it should be stressed that the present procedure displays a high degree of internal consistency. The Spearman-Brown odd–even reliability coefficient is .74, a very respectable level for a five-item measure. Item scores of 0, 1, or 2 were summed in obtaining this coefficient.

Three scores are derived for each child: number of low, number of medium, and number of high quality stories. Given the differences between the 0-type and 2-type scoring categories, it seemed more informative to keep these three scores separate rather than combine them.

RESULTS AND DISCUSSION

Sex Differences in Categorizing and Conceptualizing

The authors turn first to the examination of possible mean differences between boys and girls in the various categorizing and conceptualizing activities described in the foregoing section of the chapter. Table 39 offers the relevant data.

It can be seen that the boys manifest broader band-width behavior than do girls on the children's version of the Pettigrew test. This is an oft-replicated finding—apparently one of the most stable in the cognition-and-personality literature. An interpretation of the sex difference is available in Wallach and Caron (1959), though it should be noted that later work with adults (Kogan & Wallach, 1964) suggests that the basis for the sex difference may be considerably more complicated than has been previously assumed. The authors will have more to say about the meaning of sex differences in band width at a later point in the chapter.

Turning to object-sorting indices of categorization breadth, it is evident that sex differences are negligible in the case of both the number of groupings containing at least two objects and the number of singles (objects left ungrouped).

The conceptual style indices derived from the object-sorting procedure reveal a significant sex difference in the case of descriptive responses. Boys tend to employ a descriptive style to a greater extent than do girls. The difference in question offers indirect support for the attribution of analytic properties to the "descriptive" category on the part of Kagan, Moss, and Sigel (1963). The Witkin groups (Witkin *et al.*, 1954; Witkin *et al.*, 1962) have consistently stressed the superior analytic functioning of boys relative to girls.

Table 39.

SEX DIFFERENCES IN CATEGORIZING AND CONCEPTUALIZING

Variable	Boys ($N = 70$)		Girls ($N = 81$)			
	Mean	SD	Mean	SD	t	p
Band width	44.94	10.68	39.72	11.15	2.93	$<.01$
Object sorting						
No. of groups	12.01	4.01	12.21	3.15	0.34	n. s.
No. of singles	3.59	4.50	2.85	3.15	1.17	n. s.
% Descriptive	20.41	17.57	14.85	12.55	2.26	$<.05$
% Inferential	56.13	19.35	59.79	20.26	1.13	n. s.
% Relational	23.41	14.41	25.42	19.57	0.71	n. s.
Thematic integration						
No. of 0-type stories	0.30	0.82	0.28	0.60	0.14	n. s.
No. of 1-type stories	3.59	1.49	3.63	1.29	0.19	n. s.
No. of 2-type stories	1.11	1.40	1.09	1.32	0.13	n. s.

Finally, there is no indication of any sex difference in performance on the thematic integration task.

Interrelationships among Categorizing and Conceptualizing Indices

Relationships among the various categorizing and conceptualizing tasks are shown in Table 40. With the exception of some of the experimentally dependent measures, correlations are fairly low. Thus, the band-width index of categorization breadth is unrelated to the equivalence range indices and to the conceptual style and thematic integration measures. The present results do not support the Gardner and Schoen (1962) claim that band-width and equivalence range indices of categorization breadth tap the same underlying construct. Note further that the independence of the number-of-groups and number-of-singles scores in males is consistent with the Messick and Kogan (1963) proposition that the foregoing scores may reflect different processes. On the other hand, the independence of those scores is not maintained in the female sample ($r = .31$, $p < .01$), though the relationship is not a particularly strong one in absolute terms. The Gardner-Schoen work is based exclusively upon female samples, and hence their practice of deriving a combined index (treating each single as a distinct group) may have some justification. On the other hand, as Table 40 indicates, two scores may show a low-level significant association with one another, and yet yield differential relationships with other variables. Thus, in the case of the girls, it is only the number-of-groups score (conceptual differentiation) that is significantly linked with the conceptual style indices. The larger the number of groups formed (and hence the fewer objects per group), the greater the likelihood of descriptive and relational groupings; correspondingly, the smaller the number of groups formed (and hence the more objects per group), the greater the likelihood of inferential groupings. For girls, a preference for superordinate concepts permits the inclusion of a relatively larger array of objects within the concept class; descriptive and relational concepts, on the other hand, apparently cannot accommodate as many exemplars. It is tempting to conceive of these relationships as dictated by the structure of the object-sorting task. However, the absence of such relationships in the case of the boys suggests that the findings for the girls derive more from the latter's mode of responding to the object-sorting procedure than from structural constraints in the task itself.

For the boys, the number-of-groups and number-of-singles indices manifest significant associations with the thematic integration task. Forming more groups (greater conceptual differentiation) is related to the construction of 2-type stories in the thematic integration task. Apparently, it is the more differentiated boy who can better handle a task

Table 40.

CORRELATIONS BETWEEN VARIABLES IN THE CATEGORIZING AND CONCEPTUALIZING DOMAINS

Variable	1	2a	2b	3a	3b	3c	4a	4b	4c
1. Band width	—	—20	10	06	—03	—04	—15	02	07
2a. No. of groups	—07	—	14	—08	05	04	—07	—23	28
2b. No. of singles	—17	31	—	—10	13	—07	36	—19	—01
3a. % descriptive	03	35	19	—	—70	—29	08	05	—10
3b. % inferential	—20	—46	—03	—37	—	—49	—11	09	—03
3c. % relational	19	26	—09	—26	—80	—	05	—18	16
4a. No. of 0-type stories	—18	—01	—06	—12	12	—05	—	—38	—18
4b. No. of 1-type stories	15	—16	23	24	—06	—09	—19	—	—84
4c. No. of 2-type stories	—07	16	—20	—18	00	11	—27	—90	—

NOTE: Boys ($N = 70$) are above diagonal; girls ($N = 81$) are below diagonal. Correlations enclosed within blocks involve relations between experimentally dependent measures. For boys, r's of .24 and .31 are significant at the .05 and .01 levels, respectively. For the girls, the corresponding r's are .22 and .29. Decimal points are omitted.

requiring integration of a thematic sort. Boys who leave more singles, on the other hand, are prone to give more 0-type stories. The act of leaving objects ungrouped (compartmentalization) does imply a failure to find linkages between common objects, and hence one would indeed expect "compartmentalizers" to perform quite poorly on a thematic integration task. Quite surprisingly, the compartmentalization index is related to 1-type stories in females. The relationship is of borderline significance, however, and could conceivably be a chance phenomenon.

In the case of both boys and girls, the indices of conceptual style derived from reasons for object-sorting are largely independent of the quality of stories produced in the thematic integration task. We had a mild expectation that subjects who grouped objects on relational bases would be better able to integrate disparate words into an imaginative theme. The operations involved in the two cases are psychologically similar in many respects. Yet we see that the relevant measures are clearly unrelated. Apparently, there is a considerable difference between grouping objects relationally (thematically) where alternative modes of grouping are available, on the one hand, and grouping where the required mode is thematic, on the other.

Finally, we come to the correlations enclosed in boxes in Table 40. All the correlations are negative within the conceptual style and within the thematic integration domains as a consequence of dependencies among the scores employed. Although the correlations are of varying magnitude, this result cannot readily be given any psychological interpretation given the differential variabilities of the measures (see Table 39). The experimental dependencies among the scores derived from each of the foregoing domains do imply that caution must be exercised in the interpretation of findings. If two of the conceptual styles in object-sorting are positively related to some external measure, for example, the third style must necessarily be negatively related to that measure. The relationship between conceptual differentiation and the three conceptual styles in object-sorting by girls is a case in point. Despite the statistical constraints inherent in these relationships, however, it is nevertheless worth knowing *which* particular style or styles relate positively and *which* negatively.

Relationships with Intelligence and Creativity

Given the multidimensionality of the categorizing and conceptualizing domains, the authors will relate each of the categorizing and conceptualizing variables in turn to the intelligence and creativity clusters. We begin with the band-width index.

BAND WIDTH. Tables 41 and 42 provide the relevant data for males and females, respectively. A creativity main effect is present in both sexes,

Table 41.

MEAN BAND-WIDTH SCORES FOR
THE FOUR GROUPS OF BOYS $(N = 70)$

INTELLIGENCE

		High	Low
	High	46.59 (10.95)	47.61 (10.01)
CREATIVITY			
	Low	46.22 (11.35)	39.12 (8.94)

ANALYSIS OF VARIANCE

Source	df	MS	F	p
Intelligence	1	9.25	1.50	n. s.
Creativity	1	19.62	3.19	<.08
Interaction	1	16.51	2.69	n. s.
Within cells	66	6.15		

Table 42.

MEAN BAND-WIDTH SCORES FOR
THE FOUR GROUPS OF GIRLS $(N = 81)$

INTELLIGENCE

		High	Low
	High	41.73 (10.88)	43.11 (12.49)
CREATIVITY			
	Low	37.74 (9.43)	36.64 (11.18)

ANALYSIS OF VARIANCE

Source	df	MS	F	p
Intelligence	1	0.02	<1.00	n. s.
Creativity	1	27.38	4.52	<.05
Interaction	1	1.54	<1.00	n. s.
Within cells	77	6.05		

the highly creative children exhibiting broader band width. In the case of the boys, a nonsignificant trend toward a creativity–intelligence interaction may be noted. Inspection of the means in Table 41 indicates quite clearly that it is the low-low boys in particular who deviate from the remaining three subgroups. For the girls, on the other hand, low creativity contributes to narrow band width regardless of intelligence level (Table 42).

In the introduction to the chapter, we proposed that creativity might have implications for band-width performance, because the latter concerns such matters as tolerance for deviant instances. The results for the girls are certainly in support of this view. The highly creative girls apparently prefer to stretch category boundaries to accommodate instances that lie substantial distances from the central tendency value. These girls, in other words, are more willing than their less creative peers to risk the inclusion error—that is, the possibility that the extreme instance does not really belong in the category. The less creative girls, on the other hand, tend toward more narrow categories. For them, an error of exclusion seems to be the more desirable risk.

Performance on the various creativity tasks used in the study can also be viewed in terms of an inclusion–exclusion error model. The set encouraged by these creativity tasks is one of pushing category limits as far as feasible. The child is implicitly encouraged to risk inclusion errors by formulating as many instances as possible for each item in the creativity procedures. Where the subject's natural proclivities are in the direction of preferring exclusion errors, we are dealing with an orientation that is incongruent with the experimental context in which the creativity tasks are administered. We might well expect, then, that narrow band-width subjects will perform more poorly in the creativity area than do those subjects whose natural cognitive strategy of broad band width is consistent with the requirements of the creativity tasks.

The obtained relationship between band width and creativity also raises the possibility of what might be considered an ''obsessive'' component in the associational behavior that leads to high creativity status. Both greater band width as well as the generation of greater numbers of associates and of unique associates require that the individual keep turning over the given problem in his mind rather than let it go. In the case of band width, the person must stick to an item until he can envision atypical instances—that is, instances that are sufficiently deviant as to fit multiple-choice alternatives that are further away from the average instance of the class. This ''refusal to relinquish'' a topic of thought may well be characteristic of the kind of motivational state that can provide the opportunities for novel insights. Such a state would not be without its attendant pain.

The results obtained for the girls thus suggest that a fuller understanding of creativity processes may be achieved by considering relations with the band-width dimension of categorizing style.

As we have seen, the results for the boys were not as clear-cut. It was only in the case of both low intelligence and low creativity that a differential effect was observable. Possibly, the nature of the band-width task—quantitative estimation—endows the task with somewhat different properties in the case of boys and girls. It may be noted that while performance on the SCAT quantitative ability test is nonsignificantly correlated with band width in the case of both sexes, performance on the STEP mathematics achievement test is significantly correlated with greater band width in the case of the boys ($r = .24$, $p < .05$), while the corresponding correlation for the girls is not significant ($r = .05$). It is possible, therefore, that the association with mathematics achievement contributes to greater band width for the high intelligence–low creativity boys. One should also allow for the possibility that broad (or narrow) band width may mean different things in the context of high intelligence than in the context of high creativity. The mediating link between creativity and broad band width may be stylistic, whereas the link with intelligence may indicate a rational approach to the band-width task in which extreme alternatives are deemed more likely to be correct. Indeed, one might argue that such extreme judgments are likely to be more accurate, in fact. At least one highly deviant instance can be found for many categories of human and natural events.

OBJECT-SORTING PERFORMANCE. In the present section, the authors will discuss the results for conceptual differentiation, compartmentalization, and the three conceptual style indices derived from the object-sorting procedure. Only the results for boys will be discussed in detail. The female sample yielded uniformly nonsignificant relationships between object-sorting measures, on the one hand, and intelligence and creativity, on the other. These latter results stand in sharp contrast with those reported earlier for the band-width variable. It will be recalled that broad band width was associated with high creativity in females. It would seem that the tolerance for deviant instances which characterizes the band-width procedure does not come into play in the case of object-sorting performance. A close comparison of the two procedures suggests that the number of groupings formed on the object-sorting task cannot readily be viewed in terms of a tolerance for deviant instances. Whereas the rejection of instances in the band-width task is an assignment to limbo, the object-sorting procedure permits the subject to provide his own categories, and hence an object rejected for one category will generally find a place in another.

Let us now turn to the findings for the males. The compartmentalization index (number of singles) yielded no relations whatever to intelligence and creativity. Table 43 provides the results for conceptual differentiation. A significant interaction is obtained in which both the high-high and low-low groups show greater conceptual differentiation (form more groupings) than do the high-low and low-high groups, who in turn are quite similar to one another. Since it is virtually impossible to make sense of these results in isolation, we shall consider them in conjunction with the findings for conceptual style. It is evident at this point, however, that the distinction between compartmentalization (number of singles) and conceptual differentiation (number of groups excluding singles) measures in object sorting is pivotal in regard to relationships with creativity and intelligence. The creativity and intelligence groups differ significantly on conceptual differentiation, but do not differ on compartmentalization. How do these groups differ regarding the reasons they provide for the conceptual differentiations that they make?

The descriptive category does not bear any relation to the intelligence and creativity dimensions. All F values are less than 1. There is, on the other hand, a near-significant effect in the case of inferential reasons and a distinctly significant effect for relational reasons. The relevant data are shown in Tables 44 and 45. Consider first the case of relational reasons (Table 44). The significant interaction effect here

Table 43.

MEAN CONCEPTUAL DIFFERENTIATION SCORES (NUMBER OF GROUPS EXCLUDING SINGLES) FOR THE FOUR GROUPS OF BOYS ($N = 70$)

		INTELLIGENCE	
		High	Low
	High	13.18 (3.91)	10.94 (4.61)
CREATIVITY			
	Low	10.89 (3.55)	13.18 (3.54)

ANALYSIS OF VARIANCE

Source	df	MS	F	p
Intelligence	1	0.00	<1.00	n. s.
Creativity	1	0.00	<1.00	n. s.
Interaction	1	5.11	5.78	$<.03$
Within cells	66	0.88		

Table 44.

MEAN PERCENTAGE OF RELATIONAL RESPONSES FOR
THE FOUR GROUPS OF BOYS ($N = 70$)

		INTELLIGENCE	
		High	Low
	High	28.18	23.50
		(18.37)	(15.51)
CREATIVITY			
	Low	15.44	27.00
		(10.52)	(8.71)

ANALYSIS OF VARIANCE

Source	df	MS	F	p
Intelligence	1	11.83	1.08	n. s.
Creativity	1	21.31	1.95	n. s.
Interaction	1	65.87	6.04	$<.02$
Within cells	66	10.91		

Table 45.

MEAN PERCENTAGE OF INFERENTIAL RESPONSES FOR
THE FOUR GROUPS OF BOYS ($N = 70$)

		INTELLIGENCE	
		High	Low
	High	56.12	54.72
		(19.16)	(20.93)
CREATIVITY			
	Low	63.50	49.82
		(19.77)	(16.14)

ANALYSIS OF VARIANCE

Source	df	MS	F	p
Intelligence	1	56.79	2.71	$<.11$
Creativity	1	1.54	<1.00	n. s.
Interaction	1	37.71	1.80	n. s.
Within cells	66	20.92		

appears to mirror the interaction observed for the dimension of conceptual differentiation. The high-high and low-low groups give the most relational reasons, suggesting that the use of the relational category in those groups contributes to greater conceptual differentiation (a larger number of groupings). Note further that the subgroup high in intelligence and low in creativity shows the least inclination to employ relational responses, whereas the low intelligence–high creativity subgroup uses the relational mode to an intermediate degree.

When account is taken of the inferential category (Table 45), the differences among the four subgroups are highlighted. Although falling slightly short of statistical significance, the intelligence difference observed is sufficiently suggestive to be worthy of some consideration. Thus, the high-high and low-low subgroups, which were identical in percentage of relational reasons, now begin to diverge. It is the high-high subgroup that gives more inferential responses. Indeed, the low-low subgroup provides the lowest percentage of inferential responses. Similarly, in the case of the low-high and high-low subgroups, we note that the high intelligence–low creativity subgroup gives the largest percentage of inferential responses, the low intelligence–high creativity subgroup using the inferential mode on a more modest basis.

In the introduction to the chapter, we proposed that creativity might relate to relational responding whereas intelligence might relate to inferential and/or descriptive modes of responding. As we have shown, the results are considerably more complex than the foregoing hypotheses. It appears that we must take account of the relational–inferential balance, if we are to distinguish the four groups of subjects under study. Thus we noted that the boys high in intelligence and low in creativity showed the greatest discrepancy on a relative basis between relational and inferential responding. These boys refrain from building thematic groupings, preferring rather to concentrate on finding exemplars for·superordinate concepts. Indeed, they are the lowest of all four subgroups in the percentage of thematic responses, and the highest of all four in the percentage of inferential responses. Their performance can be contrasted with that of the boys low in intelligence and high in creativity, who, while forming the same number of groupings as the high intelligence–low creativity boys, maintain a more even relative balance between relational and inferential bases for grouping. That the relational mode is not necessarily a primitive, low-level approach to the grouping task is strongly suggested by the performance of the high-high group. Recall that these boys ranked high in both relational and inferential modes of responding. The low-low group resembled the high-highs in level of conceptual differentiation and in percentage of relational reasons, but it should be stressed that the percentage of inferential reasons was markedly depressed in the low-low group.

One of the shortcomings of the Kagan *et al.* scoring scheme when applied to the object-sorting task used here is that no provision is made for the quality or adequacy of the groupings formed. In the case of relational groupings, for example, one can readily conceive of quality differences in thematic content. Although high-high and low-low boys produce the same number of relational groupings on the average, it is entirely conceivable that the former group constructs more imaginative themes than does the latter. Further work with the object-sorting task should very probably take account of the quality dimension when scoring reasons for grouping.

It is of some interest that the descriptive category—which the Kagan group has taken to be indicative of an analytic orientation—should fail to discriminate the four subgroups under consideration in the present investigation. If the argument is advanced that descriptive responding should relate only to the more analytic intelligence measures, we can point out that no relation was found between frequency of descriptive reasons and any of the measures comprising the intelligence cluster. It should be emphasized that the Kagan group used triad and figure-sorting procedures whereas the authors employed an object-sorting task. In the latter case, inferential responding may be more indicative of an analytic bent.

Our results clearly suggest that the attempts by Kagan, Bruner, and others to treat the relational or thematic category as developmentally primitive may be misguided. If an investigator is interested in creativity as well as intelligence, he must allow for the possibility that the creative individual will sometimes break away from a strictly analytic or inferential approach to engage the stimulus materials in a more playful, imaginative manner. Assuming that the stimulus materials do not offer obvious themes, the consequences of such a playful attitude are most likely to be felt in the relational or thematic area. As we have seen, the boys high in intelligence and low in creativity rarely select the thematic option, preferring rather to engage the task on a more strictly inferential plane. Here, then, is further evidence (see Chapter 3) suggesting some constriction in the cognitive functioning of the child high in intelligence but low in creativity. The two high creativity subgroups manifest a lower relative discrepancy between relational and inferential responding. These are the boys who seem to be relatively capable of generating inferential groupings, but at the same time seem to give their imagination freer rein in the form of thematic responding. These two subgroups can in turn be distinguished from the boys low in both intelligence and creativity, whose thematic responding may derive from a difficulty in conceptualizing at the inferential level.

It is apparent from the preceding section that assessment of an individual's status with respect to conceptual differentiation will, at least under some circumstances, provide an incomplete picture of this aspect of his object-sorting behavior. Subgroups that were indistinguishable in regard to conceptual differentiation scores turned out to be building their concepts in terms of different types of content. The relative balance between thematic and inferential bases for grouping objects was important to consider in conjunction with information about degree of conceptual differentiation.

THEMATIC INTEGRATION. Unlike the case of object-sorting performance, where thematic responding represented one possible mode of conceptual functioning, the thematic integration procedure forces the subject into the thematic mode. The authors have used the designation of "thematic integration," because the scores derived from the procedure inform us of the extent to which the subject has integrated the four component words of each item into a unified and meaningful theme.

It will be recalled that subjects' stories were classified as 0-, 1-, or 2-type, from lowest to highest quality. An examination of the results for the boys indicates a lack of significant effects for 0- or 1-type stories. Note, however, the results for 2-type stories in Table 46. An intelligence effect is quite apparent. The highly intelligent boys produce a larger number of high quality stories. The creativity dimension, on the other hand, seems to have no connection whatever to thematic integration.

Table 46.

MEAN NUMBER OF HIGH QUALITY STORIES (2-TYPE) FOR
THE FOUR GROUPS OF BOYS ($N = 70$)

		INTELLIGENCE	
		High	Low
	High	1.41	0.94
		(1.62)	(1.26)
CREATIVITY			
	Low	1.44	0.65
		(1.46)	(1.17)

ANALYSIS OF VARIANCE

Source	df	MS	F	p
Intelligence	1	0.40	3.62	$<.07$
Creativity	1	0.02	<1.00	n. s.
Interaction	1	0.03	<1.00	n. s.
Within cells	66	0.11		

These results come as a mild surprise in the light of the findings for relational reasons reported in Table 44. It is now quite evident that the boys high in intelligence but low in creativity are quite capable of high quality thematic productions when the task demands it. The low output of relational groupings in the object-sorting task on the part of those boys is apparently a reflection of preference rather than of incapacity. The high intelligence–low creativity boy may prefer to function at the analytic or inferential level, though clearly capable of coping constructively with a strictly thematic task. When given the option, he avoids conceptualizing in thematic terms.

Turning to the other subgroups of boys, recall that the high-high and low-low boys yielded the same percentage of relational responses on the object-sorting task. Now we note that the thematic integration procedure splits the two subgroups widely apart. The high-high boys construct substantially more high quality stories than do the low-low boys. Hence, the authors are forced once again to raise the question of a quality criterion for relational or thematic responding in an object-sorting context. The results obtained with the thematic integration procedure lend credence to the view that thematic conceptualizing may range from low-level primitive functioning to cognitive functioning of the highest order.

For the girls, it is the number of low-quality (0-type) stories that is related to intelligence and creativity (Table 47). Although there is a

Table 47.

MEAN NUMBER OF LOW QUALITY STORIES (0-TYPE) FOR
THE FOUR GROUPS OF GIRLS ($N = 81$)

	INTELLIGENCE	
	High	Low
High	0.18	0.00
	(0.39)	(0.00)
CREATIVITY		
Low	0.16	0.73
	(0.37)	(0.88)

ANALYSIS OF VARIANCE

Source	df	MS	F	p
Intelligence	1	0.04	2.63	n. s.
Creativity	1	0.12	8.65	<.01
Interaction	1	0.14	9.87	<.01
Within cells	77	0.01		

significant main effect for creativity, the interaction effect is of greater practical import. The table shows quite clearly that the girls low in both intelligence and creativity produce a disproportionately large number of low quality themes. Evidently, the presence of either intelligence or creativity in girls militates against the production of 0-type stories. These findings indicate that we learn substantially more about thematic integration ability by considering a girl's joint standing on the creativity and intelligence dimensions than we do by taking note of intelligence status alone. Indeed, the effect for intelligence per se is clearly not significant. Creativity status is at least as important as intelligence level in contributing to thematic quality. It is only when both creativity and intelligence are low that the incidence of fragmented, atomistic stories becomes substantial.

CONCLUSIONS

Some general points deserve mention by way of highlighting the progress made in adding to the descriptive pictures of various creativity and intelligence subgroups. Of particular interest is the high intelligence–low creativity subgroup of boys, who emerge in this chapter as displaying a similar dynamic to that exhibited by the comparable subgroup of girls in Chapter 3. The findings from the object-sorting procedure support a view of this group as least willing to engage in cognitive behavior of a free and unconstrained kind. Conceptualizing on a thematic basis is, after all, a relatively freewheeling type of response to the task at hand, inferential concepts reflecting a more conventional mode of approach, given task instructions that encourage abstraction. The high intelligence–low creativity boys exhibit the lowest proportion of thematic conceptualizing, and the highest proportion of inferential conceptualizing, among the four male subgroups.

What type of import should we ascribe to the relative absence of thematizing found for the high intelligence–low creativity boys on the object-sorting task? In principle, this absence could reflect either an inability to invoke thematic bases for grouping, or a disinclination to invoke such bases. The fact that this same subgroup shows a high level of thematic integration on a story task in which thematizing is required for high quality performance, indicates that the ability to thematize certainly is present in the members of this subgroup. We are led to conclude, therefore, that it is the desire to thematize which is lacking. When required to thematize, these boys can do so. However, when given the option of using inferential concepts instead of thematic ones, they prefer inferential and avoid thematic conceptualizations.

In terms of current views of cognitive development (for example,

Bruner & Olver, 1963), the conceptualizing style revealed in the object-sorting behavior of the high intelligence–low creativity boys would tend to be defined as exhibiting the greatest maturity of cognitive functioning of all four subgroups. Large numbers of objects are placed within particular rubrics, these rubrics are very often defined in terms of inferential abstraction, and these rubrics are very seldom defined in terms of relational themas. The texture of this chapter's findings leads the authors to question seriously the appropriateness of such a view. Comparison with the subgroup of boys high in both intelligence and creativity is instructive. There we find the relative incidence of inferential conceptualizing still rather high, but in addition the relative incidence of thematic conceptualizing also is high. In respect to this balanced usage of thematic and inferential reasons for object groupings, the high creativity–low intelligence boys are relatively similar to the high-high subgroup. The low-low subgroup, on the other hand, may consist of individuals who are rather inflexibly locked in thematic modes of responding and relatively incapable of switching to inferential bases for grouping.

In general, then, balanced usage of thematic or inferential conceptualizing styles seems to characterize the two high creativity subgroups, and especially the high-high group. An apparent distaste for thematic responding when other response options are available seems to characterize the high intelligence–low creativity subgroup. Finally, a possible inability to make more use of inferential conceptualizing, with a consequent concentration on thematic responding, appears to characterize the low-low subgroup.

While object-sorting behavior proved unrelated to the creativity–intelligence distinctions for the girls, such was not the case for the band-width measure of categorizing breadth and for thematic integration. Findings in both areas confirmed the importance of considering creativity differences as distinct from the general intelligence dimension. Perhaps of particular interest is the fact that wider acceptance limits for assigning instances to a given class—broad band-width behavior—is linked with greater creativity (a finding also obtained for the boys, but not as strongly). The association tasks defining the creativity domain and the band-width procedure seem to share in common the characteristic of permitting a subject to entertain hypotheses to the effect that deviant instances deserve category membership. The creativity tasks, in fact, encourage such hypotheses, in that the child is urged to generate as many associates as he can, without time limitation. The operation of some kind of ''boundary-setting'' process in creativity hence seems indicated by the obtained linkage with band width. The setting of wide tolerance limits for acceptance in a class, with the attendant possibility of an ''obsessive'' style of cogitation—a tendency to hang on to a problem or topic and look at it from different angles—hence may belong to the psychological nature of creativity.

Creativity comes to appear, then, as a mode of thought that possesses negative as well as positive connotations. The positive side of the coin—the idea of a playful acceptance of the possible—has already been introduced. Now we glimpse the presence of a dark side as well—that a concern with possibilities can obsess a person and prevent him from putting an idea aside until all kinds of unlikely ramifications have been pursued. Somewhere within the playfulness and the obsessiveness—or perhaps in the alternation between them—may lie the chance of making those connections between disparate elements that lead to new and useful integrations of knowledge.

We have no reason to expect, therefore, that creativity should be linked with anxiety-free and tension-free states of motivation: a typical definition of "psychological health." The authors have considered some aspects of this issue in describing the findings on observed behavior in Chapter 3. The matter will be confronted in more detail when we consider findings on personality variables in Chapter 6.

SUMMARY

The major focus of the present chapter was the examination of possible empirical links between the domains of categorizing and conceptualizing, on the one hand, and intelligence and creativity, on the other. On pragmatic grounds, the authors distinguished between categorizing and conceptualizing, treating the former as a problem in preferences for narrow vs. broad categories and the latter as a matter of the structural and content characteristics of concepts employed when grouping or integrating diverse arrays of stimuli. A review of relevant literature produced a number of studies concerned with the relation of intelligence to categorizing and conceptualizing. The evidence derived from these studies proved equivocal. Studies relating categorizing and conceptualizing to creativity were very scarce, and as in the case of intelligence, far from conclusive. None of the previous work was concerned with the effects on categorizing and conceptualizing of an interaction between intelligence and creativity.

Used as measures of categorization breadth in the present investigation were a children's adaptation of the Pettigrew category-width test and a modified form of the Gardner object-sorting test. Conceptualization was measured by applying the classification proposed by the Kagan group—descriptive, inferential, and relational—to the reasons given by subjects for the groupings formed in the object-sorting task. Finally, a measure of thematic integration—another aspect of conceptual style—

was devised in which subjects were required to build a story around sets of words. The stories were scored in terms of a quality criterion. Reliability levels (internal consistency and/or interscorer agreement) were fairly high for all the procedures employed.

A number of hypotheses were formulated linking categorizing and conceptualizing to the intelligence and creativity domains. Some of these hypotheses were derived from prior research, others from an intuitive analysis of psychological processes presumed to be common to tasks taken from the separate domains of interest. Thus, the authors proposed that children exhibiting broad band width on the Pettigrew test would rank higher on the creativity index, on the grounds that performance in both areas involved a concern with category limits or boundaries. The hypothesis was confirmed for both boys and girls, but much more conclusively in the case of the girls. The authors suggested that the band-width index might be measuring a tolerance for deviant instances, hence accounting for its association with creativity.

No explicit hypotheses were formulated for the conceptual differentiation (number of groups) and compartmentalization (number of singles) indices derived from the object-sorting procedure. For the girls, no significant relationships were obtained. The boys, on the other hand, yielded a significant creativity–intelligence interaction in the case of the conceptual differentiation index. This finding resisted interpretation in isolation, and so we turned to the three conceptual style indices in the hope of achieving clarification.

In harmony with the Kagan group, we predicted that descriptive and inferential modes of responding would relate to intelligence. On the other hand, we disagreed quite radically with the Kagan group concerning the meaning of the relational mode. To Kagan and his co-workers, this latter mode of responding was identified as a ''passive acceptance of the stimulus.'' While relational responses might have such meaning in the case where themas are obvious, it seemed reasonable that relational responding on an object-sorting task might have much in common with creativity, since such responding would represent a freewheeling, nonconventional approach in the face of instructions encouraging abstraction.

These hypotheses concerning the relation of conceptual style to intelligence and creativity were only partially confirmed, and then only for the boys. A near-significant association was found to hold between inferential responding and intelligence in accordance with prediction. Relational responding yielded a significant interaction in which boys either high or low in both intelligence and creativity were responsible for the largest percentage of relational responses, while boys high in intelligence and low in creativity were least likely to use the relational mode. The authors' interpretation of the conceptual style results placed considerable stress on the child's inferential–relational balance. For the boy high in intelligence and low in creativity, the balance was strongly weighted on the inferential side, suggesting, when taken in conjunction with the thematic integration results (summarized below), an aversion against thematizing. For the boy low in both intelligence and creativity, the balance was skewed to the relational side, suggesting an inability to construct inferential groupings. The two high creativity groups, in turn, fell between these extremes, suggesting a more balanced use of both thematic and inferential conceptual styles.

Finally, the thematic integration results were considered. A clear-cut intelligence effect was obtained for the boys, with the highly intelligent producing the more integrated and imaginative stories. These results strongly suggested that the rarity of relational (thematic) responding by high intelligence–low creativity boys in the object-sorting task was a matter of preference rather than of incapacity. Where the task requirements called for thematic responding, the foregoing group of boys were equal to the assignment.

The boys low in both creativity and intelligence performed quite poorly in the thematic integration task, despite their predilection to relational responding in the object-sorting procedure. This finding called attention to the need for a quality criterion in connection with the conceptual style indices. The identity in percentage of relational responses for high-high and low-low boys could well be concealing substantial differences in the type and quality of the relational responses emitted.

The thematic integration results for the girls indicated that a high incidence of poorly integrated, fragmented stories occurred only in the joint absence of creativity and intelligence. Once again, the relevance of considering an individual's joint status with respect to both dimensions was demonstrated.

In sum, it is quite evident that categorizing and conceptualizing activities have much to do with creativity and intelligence. Investigators working in the area of creativity in particular have often tended to seal off this area, treating it as a separate discipline, rather than exploring possible points of articulation with other relevant traditions. As we have shown, creativity, both alone and in interaction with intelligence level, bears upon matters of categorizing and conceptualizing styles. Conceivably, there are other aspects of cognition that also should be examined for their possible relevance to creativity and intelligence. Clearly, the time is now ripe for the creativity–intelligence issue to assume its proper perspective within the domain of the cognitive processes.

5 ⋘

Sensitivity to
Physiognomic
Properties

A broad distinction can be drawn between two classes of properties in the visually perceived environment of the individual.[1] On the one hand, there are properties that provide information of what Werner and Kaplan (1963) would call a "geometric-technical" kind; information concerning such matters as the form, arrangement, height, width, configuration, color, of visually apprehended stimuli. On the other hand, there are properties that provide information about the affective or emotional significance possessed by such stimuli; whether, for example, they portend joy or sadness, anger or fear, strength or weakness. It is properties of this latter type that are meant when the term "physiognomic" is used.

The term has its origins in the idea of discovering inner temperament and character from a person's outward appearance, particularly from his facial features. More generally the term has come to convey the notion of learning about inner feeling and affect states from perceivable externals, and it is in this sense that the term has its application here. Physiognomic properties are in some sense definable with reference to the "geometric-technical" or physical properties of visual stimuli, since the former can be specified in terms of values of the latter. This is not necessarily to imply, however, that the perception of physiognomic properties of environmental stimuli must proceed by a process of learned inference from particular aspects of the geometric-technical properties of those stimuli. For it also is possible that physiognomic sensitivity may

---

[1] While our discussion and research are confined to the visual modality, the same considerations also should hold with regard to auditory perception.

at least in some instances be "genetically primordial," as Werner and Kaplan (1963) would put it—that is, a developmentally early ability not dependent upon learning for its exercise.

It is not our purpose here to take sides in the debate on whether physiognomic sensitivity is an innate, primitive kind of ability or a derivative product of learning; most likely it involves elements of both. We shall consider a psychological description of what sorts of events seem to be involved in the making of physiognomic discriminations, whatever the etiology of such discriminations may be. The major interpretative conceptions that others have offered for these phenomena will, however, be reviewed. Next, we shall turn to a sampling of the kinds of systematic studies that have been carried out with the aim of exploring sensitivity to physiognomic properties in the case of adults and children. And finally, we shall examine the thinking that led us to be interested in physiognomic sensitivity in relation to creativity and intelligence. We then will be in a position to take up the research that we conducted in this area.

THE MAKING OF PHYSIOGNOMIC DISCRIMINATIONS

To respond to the physiognomic properties of things and events involves an act of metaphor, an act of simile, or an act of signification. The poet who describes a stormy sky as angry, or as like a jealous giant, is ascribing to certain color and form combinations an affective significance that goes beyond the given colors and forms as such. The same is true of the writer for whom a blue and sunny sky is smiling, the artist for whom a particular heavy, jagged line is upset rather than serene, the dancer who views the walking of another person across the room as reflecting an ebullient and gay rather than a sad and depressed state of mind. In all these instances, internal emotions are being "read" from aspects of visual stimulation. A particular visual configuration is said to "be," to be like, or to signify, a particular affect. Readings of this kind hence involve the positing of an identity relation, a similarity relation, or a symbol–referent relation, between visual pattern and emotional state. A gap is being bridged between two distinct kinds of psychological entities—visual experiences on the one hand, feeling states on the other. Whether we believe that the translation rule is a product of learned inference or represents an innately given linkage, the fact remains that a distinction does exist in our subjective experience between the two classes of events under consideration. We treat the visual as a metaphor for the affective experience, as an analogue of it, or as a representation of it.

It may well be, furthermore, that there is no single unified ability to which the label of "physiognomic sensitivity" ought appropriately to be attached. Turning visual experiences into metaphors, similes, and symbols of affective happenings may come about in more than one way and for more than one reason. Indeed, it is this very fact that may be responsible for the unresolved debate on etiology mentioned above. To our knowledge, no one has investigated the question of dimensionality within this realm of sensitivity to physiognomic properties—that is, the extent to which different measures of such sensitivity will turn out to be correlated or uncorrelated.[2] It is a matter to which we shall turn later in connection with our own research on the topic. Were the domain to reflect many dimensions rather than just one, it would become likely that the etiological picture is complex, involving more than a single type of cause. Whatever the answer to the dimensionality question may turn out to be, however, the psychological character of the phenomenon in question is relatively clear: two different classes of psychological experiences —one visual, the other emotional—are put into relationship with each other.

Views on Etiology

Several proposals have been made concerning a mechanism to bridge the gap between these two classes of experiences. We do not feel that the evidence is at all of such a nature as to permit one to choose among these proposals. They should receive some discussion at this point, however, since two of the three major views of the matter provided the initial impetus that led researchers to become interested in the area.

The two views in question both presume that physiognomic properties of the environment are directly perceived on an innate basis. The first of these nativistic theories, stated most extensively by Werner (1948) and by Werner and Kaplan (1963), proposes that the reading of emotional content from visual stimuli is possible because visual perception in the young human is inextricably wedded to the perception of affective and postural events originating in one's own body. In the early stages of ontogenesis, there is little differentiation between cues arising from postural and affective sources within oneself, on the one hand, and visual cues arising from the external environment, on the other. Perception of external stimuli is intermingled with perception of the affective and postural states that those external stimuli elicit on an innate basis. Such a view of perception has been discussed at length by, for instance, Wapner and Werner (1957) and Murphy and Hochberg (1951).

---

[2] A recent study by Beldoch (1964) has demonstrated consistencies in physiognomic sensitivity across three media—speech, music, and graphic—but has not been concerned with the issue of relations among various physiognomic indices within a given medium.

As the latter writers put it, information from visual, postural, and affective sources, and hence from exteroceptive, proprioceptive, and interoceptive sense receptors, respectively, initially is ". . . present in an undifferentiated or partially differentiated state," and ". . . subsequent differentiation gradually achieves more and more separation of these factors. We would expect that in primitive stages, perception of environmental objects would prove inextricably fused with the motion, position, and feeling-state of the observer" (p. 336). On such a view, awareness of physiognomic processes is a genetically primitive manifestation originating from a mixing of the postural-affective responses with the visual responses elicited by external stimuli. Hence the expectation of such psychologists as Werner that physiognomic sensitivity should be most pronounced in very young children and in those adults who may be presumed to be in a developmentally regressed state, such as the brain-damaged, the drug-intoxicated, and primitive peoples.

The second nativistic proposal, stated in the writings of such Gestalt psychologists as Köhler (1937) and Asch (1952), holds that awareness of physiognomic properties arises from strictly visual experiences, without any involvement of postural or affective responses on the part of the observer. The interplay among visually given stimuli is presumed to be sufficient to define the conditions that will produce physiognomic perception. Thus, Asch (1952) for example, argues that ". . . the forms of objects and their movements often directly excite us to perceive expressive properties. . . . Although the stimulus-conditions for expressive properties are relatively complex, they are nevertheless definite" (p. 185). Such a view implies the same expectations as were presented above concerning the kinds of individuals for whom physiognomic sensitivity should be maximized, given an adult culture that urges its members to pay maximum attention to "geometric-technical" qualities such as size and shape. For, as Asch says, "It would seem that the properties we call expressive are among the first we note and respond to. Objects are friendly and forbidding as directly as they are tall and elliptical" (1952, p. 183). So also, Köhler (1937), in discussing the environment of African primitives, states that ". . . their environment will have many aspects to which they attribute full objective value, while our scientific civilization denies such value and accordingly tends to impoverish our perception" (p. 277).

A number of writers subscribe to a nativistic interpretation of physiognomic sensitivity without seeming to distinguish between the two views just outlined. Thus, for example, Arnheim (1949) has remarked, "Expression seems to be the primary content of perception. To register a fire as merely a set of hues and shapes in motion rather than to experience primarily the exciting violence of the flames, presupposes a very specific, rare, and artificial attitude'' (p. 164). So too, the art critic Gombrich (1960) writes that ''. . . the poet's metaphor of the smiling sky suggests, as do all metaphors, a looser network of categories than do the tighter meshes of literal and rational language . . . metaphors are not necessarily 'transferred' meanings, linkages established, as the classical theory of metaphorical expression has it. They are rather indicators of linkages not yet broken, of pigeonholes sufficiently wide to encompass both the blueness of a spring sky and a mother's smile'' (p. 232).

Consider finally the third kind of hypothesis that has been proposed concerning the origins of physiognomic sensitivity. Rather than assuming some kind of innate linkage between visual and affective experience, it assumes that the two become connected through a learning process. Whereas the other views suggest that the visual and emotional experiences possess a close primordial connection, the present view suggests that they are quite separate and apart to begin with and must be united by some sort of learning. In considering, for example, the description of a particular abstract line pattern as being gay or sad, or the reading of an emotional state from the postural attitude reflected in a person's stoop, the present view would argue that the visual and affective events in question are disparate and discrete classes of information that find a connection only through some type of associative mechanism. For instance, it may be proposed that particular visual configurations presented by other human beings are associated in our experience with other behavior on their part which rewards or punishes us, engendering appropriate affects in each case. Then, with repetition of this linkage, the visual configurations alone can come to function as metaphors, similes, or symbols for the emotional states in question.

Examples of Prior Studies

What kinds of systematic studies have been carried out in the present area? The majority of them have been concerned with demonstrating a goodly degree of consensus in adults concerning the connections to be made between visual materials and attributions of feeling states. Two main methods have been used: what Werner and Kaplan (1963) have referred to as ''production'' and ''comprehension.'' In the production approach, emotional states are described with the request that the subject draw an appropriate nonrepresentational visual analogue. In the comprehension or matching approach, nonrepresentational visual materials are presented with the request that the subject make the emotional attributions he deems appropriate, from among given possibilities. The demonstration of considerable consensus or uniformity in the adult performances studied has been taken by Werner and Kaplan (1963), Asch (1952), and others, as evidence in support of a nativistic interpretation of the origins of physiognomic sensitivity. It need not, however, carry this implication, since conditions of learning might well be sufficiently general as to yield the degree of uniformity obtained in adults. Let us turn now to an overview of the kinds of studies that have been conducted.

Among the findings on production, Lundholm (1921) asked eight adult subjects to draw representations of given clusters of relatively synonymous adjectives. One such cluster, for example, consisted of the adjectives "sad," "melancholy," "mournful," "doleful," and "sorrowful"; another cluster consisted of "merry," "cheerful," "gay," "jolly," and "joyous"; a third cluster consisted of "quiet," "calm," "tranquil," and "serene." There was high agreement regarding certain characteristics of the graphic productions used to represent such affects. For instance, line patterns that were directed downward from left to right constituted the customary expression for the cluster of "sad" adjectives, while the usual mode of expression for the cluster of "gay" adjectives consisted of line patterns that were directed upward from left to right or were horizontal. The typical mode of linear expression for the "calm" adjectives was horizontal in direction. In related findings by Krauss (1930), involving a larger number of adult subjects, certain linear qualities were provided with high frequency as expressions for given affect referents such as "raging" (*wütend*) and "filled with longing" (*sehnsuchtsvoll*). Thus, the drawings for "raging" typically included jagged lines with sharp angles, while the drawings for "filled with longing" tended to involve a single line, gently curving or relatively straight.

Other, more recent, studies using the production approach have yielded comparable results. Thus, Scheerer and Lyons (1957) reported that their college student subjects tend to provide angular, heavy, irregular lines as a graphic expression for the word "massacre"; while providing curved, light, repetitive lines as a graphic rendering for "happy." So also, Peters and Merrifield (1958) found that their adult subjects tend to draw lines sloping downward from left to right to express the words "sad" and "sorrowful," lines sloping upward from left to right as expressions for "joyous" and "strong." Their linear expressions for the words "lively," "agitating," and "angry" tend to be on the angular and irregular side, while the lines drawn to express "grave," "idle," and "quiet," tend to be straight. With regard to heaviness–lightness of lines, heavier lines tend to be employed as expressions for "angry," "furious," and "cruel"; lighter lines, for "delicate" and "quiet."

Consider next some of the results obtained with the comprehension method. Poffenberger and Barrows (1924) were interested in determining the comparability of Lundholm's findings to those that might be obtained with a matching technique. Using almost the same adjective clusters as had Lundholm, the adult subject was to select from among eighteen line stimuli the one that "best expressed the feelings indicated" in a given group of synonymous adjectives. The task was repeated with each of a number of adjective clusters in turn, and the subject could utilize the same line to express the meaning of as many adjective clusters as he wished. With a sample of 500 respondents, the results were quite similar to those which Lundholm had obtained. Among these congruent findings were the following. For the adjective cluster of "sad," "melancholy," "mournful," "doleful," and "sorrowful" the typical choice was of a gently curved line descending from left to right. For the cluster of "quiet," "calm," "tranquil," and "serene" the typical choice was a gently curved but basically horizontal line. Given the cluster, "merry," "cheerful," "gay," "jolly," and "joyous," the typical selection was a curved, undulating line that was horizontal or ascended from left to right, as also was the case for the adjective "playful." In the case of the cluster, "agitating," "exciting," "fiery," "brisk," "vivacious," "lively," and also for the cluster, "furious," "angry," "cross," "vexed," "enraged," the preferred selection was an angular, undulating line.

In another part of the research by Krauss (1930), adults were provided with various words, including several terms describing emotions, and were requested to match abstract line drawings to these words. The drawings actually had been originally made by other subjects as linear expressions for the verbal referents in question. There were high degrees of agreement between the matches made by the present subjects and the referents for which the drawings actually had been made. Scheerer and Lyons (1957), in further results from their study cited earlier, also obtained high degrees of agreement among adult subjects in the matches of three abstract lines with three words depicting materials that carry different networks of meanings: "gold," "silver," and "iron." Comparably high degrees of consensus in matching have been reported in work by Hall and Oldfield (1950).

The kinds of agreement at issue here also tend to hold across cultural boundaries. Osgood (1960) reports comparisons of Anglo-Saxon Americans, Navajo Indians, and Japanese persons currently residing in the United States. A concept would be verbally defined in the subject's native language and he would then be requested to choose the one of two abstract visual patterns that better characterizes the concept in question. A number of different pairs of visual patterns would be presented in succession for a given concept. With adults as subjects, members of the three cultural groups tended to agree, for example, in characterizing "noisy" with a crooked line rather than a straight line; in depicting "bad" with a thick rather than a thin line, and with a crooked rather than a straight line; and in expressing the concept of "fast" with a thin rather than a thick line.

In a study that varies somewhat from the framework of the "comprehension" approach as described above, Tagiuri (1960) asked adults to construe given abstract lines as paths made by individuals moving from a starting point to a goal. Here, then, the line is to be taken as representational of a person's movement through space, rather than as an abstract pattern. The subject is requested to describe the "personality" and "character" of a person who would move in the manner depicted by the line, and, rather than being given multiple-choice alternatives, the subject is free to respond in whatever manner he sees fit. There tends to be a substantial degree of agreement regarding the personality attributions made in the case of particular different paths. Thus, for example, a person traversing a straight-line path is described in such terms as "well-reasoned," "aggressive," "persevering," "determined"; while a person traversing a path that meanders and oscillates is described in such terms as "immature," "very emotional," "stupid," "irresponsible."

It is clear from the work reviewed in the preceding pages that adults exhibit a strong degree of consensus concerning the appropriate linkages between certain visual materials and certain emotional states. Is there any evidence, in turn, on the developmental course with respect to such physiognomic sensitivity? Recent research by Honkavaara (1961) has led her to conclude that there is a developmental increase in general physiognomic sensitivity across the years from an age of five or six to adulthood. One of her studies requested children of several age levels and adults to describe photographs of persons. Younger children tended to restrict themselves to descriptions in terms of what Honkavaara calls "matter-of-fact" qualities: labels such as "man," "woman," "auntie," "uncle." With increasing age, one finds an increase in the occurrence of descriptions in terms of expressive qualities such as "happy," "sad," "laughing," "crying." Another of her studies requested the subject to judge whether a given photograph depicted a face that was more on the sad or the happy side. In the case of each of a number of photographs the child or adult was asked, "Is this person more miserable than happy?" With increasing age, there was an increase in the degree of consensus displayed.

Although Honkavaara takes findings such as these as evidence for a development-linked increase in general physiognomic sensitivity, there seems to be a basic interpretational problem that renders such a conclusion untenable. Age-linked differences in comprehension of the nature of the task, in comprehension of the specific instructions, and in vocabulary, always remain as possibilities when a developmental span bridging the range from young childhood to adulthood is at issue. And it is only across this very broad age range that age-linked differences in the tasks at issue are clear. While Honkavaara argues that her findings indicate that physiognomic sensitivity is not a developmentally primordial, primitive phenomenon, but rather a manifestation that makes its appearance late in development, we are forced to conclude for the reasons stated that her findings do not firmly support this argument.

In sum, the present state of knowledge regarding sensitivity to physiognomic properties informs us that there is a considerable degree of consensus among adults with regard to the making of physiognomic attributions, and that, for whatever reasons, young children display a lower degree of such consensus and are not as inclined to make physiognomic attributions in general. We have pointed out that such findings do not really provide much leverage regarding questions of underlying psychological mechanisms, however. That consensus regarding physiognomic attributions is reasonably high among adults could be the case for numerous reasons, and may well be the case for different reasons in different instances. Thus, for example, among Osgood's (1960) conclusions from his cross-cultural research, he notes that ". . . there are many specific relations between human organisms and their generally similar environments whose stability can be the basis for synesthetic and metaphorical translations. These may be either innate to the species or developed by learning under similar conditions'' (p. 168). That, in turn, physiognomic sensitivity seems to be greater in adults than in young children could tell us something about age-linked increases in such sensitivity or, on the other hand, could simply arise as an artifact of the patent differences in understanding of tasks, in understanding of specific instructions, and in vocabulary skills, that exist between young children and adults.

The findings that we have reviewed—considerable adult consensus in physiognomic attributions and apparently lower physiognomic sensitivity in children—actually constitute a mandate for a type of research on the present topic that to our knowledge had not yet been carried out in any extensive way: namely, the study of individual differences in physiognomic sensitivity as exhibited in children. Given the high level of consensus displayed by adults, the question of individual differences does not become a prominent one in their case. The findings with respect to children, on the other hand, suggest that at an age intermediate between early childhood and young adulthood—say, ten or eleven years— there will be a reasonable degree of uncertainty regarding the extent to which physiognomic sensitivity will be displayed, if at all. In a child of this age, one hence can begin to investigate the psychological significance that may attach to the presence or absence of various manifestations of physiognomic sensitivity. With age and amount of schooling held approximately constant, one can be reasonably certain that differences in performance on the tasks provided are not reflecting blatant differences in comprehension of task and comprehension of instructions—the kinds of differences that age comparisons might well generate if one extended the age level down to five years at one end and up to twenty years at the other.

Creativity, Intelligence, and Physiognomic Sensitivity

The considerations just described lead one to the age group of children under study in the present volume, and to an individual-differences approach, in the exploration of physiognomic sensitivity. Is there any reason to believe, however, that sensitivity to physiognomic properties of the environment will be related to the interplay between creativity and intelligence as we have defined and operationalized those concepts? We felt that the answer to this question was an affirmative one, and that the obtaining of such relationships hence would further our understanding of the associational conception of creativity, on the one hand, and of the psychological nature of physiognomic sensitivity, on the other. What were the bases for this belief?

We have described both nativistic and empiricistic interpretations of the etiology of physiognomic sensitivity. We also have noted that such sensitivity may be multidimensional rather than unidimensional, so that the actual causal picture may involve learning in some cases, innate factors in others. *Both* classes of causal interpretations, however, are such as to suggest that creativity, either alone or in its interrelationship with the general intelligence dimension, may be a prominent correlate of sensitivity to physiognomic properties.

Consider first the nativistic theories. Both varieties of nativistic views emphasize the assumption that awareness of the environment's physiognomic properties is a developmentally primitive characteristic, which hence should be most pronounced in very young children and in primitive peoples. Assimilation of the values of Western culture is assumed to inhibit physiognomic sensitivity, or to reduce its accessibility, since ours is a civilization that emphasizes a concern with "geometric-technical" properties of visual stimuli. It is for these properties that Western culture reserves the status of full objectivity and reality. On the assumption that physiognomic sensitivity represents a "genetically primordial" phenomenon, the persons who display it are better able to maintain their contact with this ontogenetically early mode of experiencing the world. They are more attuned to, or more able to get in touch with, those perceptual paths that tend to become less accessible with socialization into the cognitive ways of the West. One is reminded of the concept of "regression in the service of the ego" (see Hartmann, 1958; Kris, 1952; 1953; Schafer, 1958). It would be intriguing indeed to find that behavior which may reflect the ability to utilize naive or developmentally primitive types of perceiving is associated with greater creativity.

Let us consider now the empiricistic approach to physiognomic sensitivity. If visual and affective experiences are quite disparate to begin with, so that learning is required in order to forge a connection between them, then individual differences in physiognomic sensitivity would be reflecting the differential ease with which such learning takes place. To the extent that the individual is open to his affective states and able to discriminate their changes, specific linkages will be more easily established between visual patterns and affects generated in response to other stimuli which are part of the same situation. It would be most interesting to discover that behavior which may reflect openness to one's affective states and discrimination of their variety is correlated with greater creativity.

The two kinds of bridges we have postulated between creativity and physiognomic sensitivity actually are more similar than different in their nature. Both have to do with the availability to the person of a particular range of experience: primitive ways of construing the world, or sensitivity to one's emotional states, respectively. The hypothesis here proposed, then, is that increased availability of one or both of the ranges of experience just described should be related to the associational conception of creativity. The basis for this hypothesis lies in the assumption that the generation of many associates, and many that are unique, is a process which should be enhanced by the availability of wider ranges of experience as sources which may be drawn upon.

We turn now to a consideration of the techniques used in our research on sensitivity to physiognomic properties.

PROCEDURE

Our methods for exploring physiognomic sensitivity were four in number. They represented an attempt on our part to sample major lines of potential variation in this domain, both with regard to stimulus materials and with regard to type of response.

We shall discuss first two procedures in which we study whether the child is able to go beyond "geometric-technical" descriptions of visual data to descriptions that take account of affective properties. The two procedures differ considerably in their stimulus materials: in one case, line drawings of stick figures are presented; in the other, a path of movement traversed by a person viewed from above is represented by a line. Thus, the nature of the visual stimulus is more abstract in the second task than in the first. In the first procedure, the posture or stance of a stick figure is the visual characteristic that may be seen as implying a feeling state. In the second, the figure becomes a point in space, as it were, and we examine whether the perceived movement path of this person-as-a-whole carries an affective tone for the child. In the case of both tasks, the child's free descriptions of the visual data are subjected to a content analysis.

In the third task to which we shall turn, the child must choose which of two abstract patterns better fits an emotional expression depicted in a picture of a face. In this instrument, we examine the extent to which the child's choices coincide with appropriate linkages as defined by consensus among adult judges. Here the visual stimulus is even more abstract than in the second task. The visual material no longer carries any human reference but is entirely nonobjective. Since this third procedure's visual data are quite devoid of human reference, we cannot use in this procedure the free-description technique of assessing whether the child does or does not attach affective connotations to the materials. It is too unlikely that any children would do so. Hence, we must change from the free description technique of the first two procedures to a forced-choice technique in which the child is requested to decide between two physiognomic translations of a given emotive state; one which adults consider appropriate and one which adults consider inappropriate.

Finally, as our fourth task we shall consider an instrument in which seemingly bizarre attributions of emotional states are made to line drawings of stick figures, and we inquire whether the child is willing to accept these attributions. Whereas the three tasks just mentioned study physiognomic sensitivity under conditions of increasingly abstract stimulus materials, the fourth task raises somewhat different considerations. Here we propose bizarre emotive attributions for visual data and determine whether the child is willing to entertain them, where entertaining them does not require him to reject more fitting affective attributions. Note the contrast in this respect with the third procedure, in which the child is forced to choose between a good and a poor translation, in terms of visual patterns, of a given affect state. In the fourth task, the child can accept emotive attributions that are fitting, and also accept ones that are bizarre. Acceptance of one kind does not constitute rejection of the other kind.

We turn now to a description of each of the instruments.

Free Descriptions of Stick Figures

The stimulus materials in this procedure are thirty-five line drawings of human-like stick figures derived from the work of Sarbin (1954) and Sarbin and Hardyck (1955). With an open circle for a face, the expressive potential of each stick figure is conveyed solely by means of postural cues. To adults, the stance of each stick figure readily carries an emotive connotation (Sarbin, 1954). Figure 4 reproduces four of the thirty-five stick figures to illustrate the nature of these stimuli. The numbers refer to their positions in the sequence of thirty-five. Each stick figure is presented on a card.[3]

The present task, which came second in the series of seventeen procedures, was introduced to the child with the following instructions:

"This game is a stick figure game. Do you know what a stick figure is?" (The child is permitted to answer.) "Well," (or "Yes,") "a stick figure is a drawing of a person made with simple lines. Here is one." (An example figure not used in the procedure proper is shown to the child.) "Now in this game your job is to describe each stick figure—to tell me all you can about each one. You may have a lot to say about some of the stick figures, and nothing at all about some of the others. You just say as much as you want to. O.K.? Let's begin now.

"Here is the first one. Now tell me all you can about this stick figure."

The first card is handed to the child as the last sentence is spoken. When the child finishes his description, the experimenter hands him the second card, saying: "Here is another. Now tell me all you can about this stick figure." Analogous instructions prevail for the remaining thirty-three cards in the set. The gamelike character of the procedure was emphasized by having the child turn each card upside-down and add it to a pile after using it.

The child's descriptions of the stick figures were recorded verbatim by the experimenter. The thirty-five descriptions for each child were subjected to a content analysis that proceeded in terms of the following scoring considerations. Our basic concern was with the extent to which the child would respond exclusively in terms of physical characteristics of the stick figures or rather would also include or even emphasize the attribution of emotional states. In order to measure this kind of difference, scoring definitions were prepared which contrasted three types of descriptions, assumed to vary along a dimension ranging from concentration on "geometric-technical" properties to concentration on the physiognomic. Presented below are the scoring definitions learned by each judge:

The description of each stick figure will be scored "low," "medium," or "high." If the child includes material in a description that should receive more than one type of score, assign him the score of the highest ranking answer given.

Score "low" if the stick figure is described in terms of physical characteristics and the description is specific to parts of the body considered in isolation. The description is in "geometric-technical" terms and is atomistic. For example, "finger bent," "elbow bent."

---

[3] We are grateful to Theodore R. Sarbin for permission to use his stick figure materials.

12

16

22

28

FIGURE 4. *Examples of four of the stick figures.*

Score "medium" if the stick figure is described in terms of physical characteristics, i.e., not in terms concerning affective states or personality qualities, but the stick figure is described as a whole. Usually in this kind of answer a state of action is described (e.g., "leaning," "bending") or an occupation (e.g., "he looks like an umpire"). Also score "medium" for description of the stick figure as a nonhuman entity (e.g., "a flower").

Score "high" if the stick figure is described in terms that *directly* (not implicitly) express the stick figure's emotive response to any situation. For example, "he's angry at someone." Mention of affective qualities as such also earns a score of "high." For example, "happy," "sad," "stern," "graceful." As the example of "stern" indicates, judgments of character are included here. Quotations which define the internal affective state of the stick figure also are included. If an affective state description is deemed stereotypical by the judge, so that it may reflect merely a verbal habit rather than a response to the stick figure, it is scored "medium" rather than "high" (e.g., "bigshot").

The 35 descriptions provided by each of the 151 children (hence 5285 descriptions in all) were scored by two independent adult judges. Each judge worked "blindly," that is, without knowledge of the identities of the children whose protocols were being scored. Scoring reliability was assessed by counting the number of agreements between the judges in scores of "low," "medium," and "high," assigned to the total set of descriptions, and dividing by the total number of descriptions. This agreement quotient was .95, hence indicating high interjudge reliability in use of the three scoring definitions. Scoring discrepancies were resolved by discussion between the judges.

Three measures were derived for each child: the number of descriptions scored "low," the number scored "medium," and the number scored "high." The total of these frequency counts must, of course, be thirty-five. It seemed appropriate to keep these three measures as separate variables since it was possible that individual differences would display themselves more clearly in the case of one of them than another.

Consider the following examples of descriptions for the stick figures presented in Figure 4. They are chosen so as to provide a contrast between descriptions found for children at the two extremes. For 12, 16, 22, and 28 respectively, one child's descriptions were as follows: (12) "hands over head, cupped together—feet moving—looks like he's dancing—body twisted" (scored "medium"); (16) "elbows bent—head going back—hands out—wrists are bent and knees bent" (scored "low"); (22) "body, knees, elbows bent—hands curled" (scored "low"); (28) "his knees are bent—body at an angle—hands curled up" (scored "low"). Another child's descriptions were these: (12) "he looks as though he's dancing—seems very happy" (scored "high"); (16) "he doesn't want something—he's trying to get away from it" (scored "high"); (22) "he seems very mad, as though a friend of his had a fight with him and he wants to get him" (scored "high"); (28) "he seems as though he's mad and a bad sport, as though he lost a game or something" (scored "high"). For a third child, the respective descriptions were: (12) "doing a ballet—one leg straight and the other bent—arms over her head and bent" (scored "medium"); (16) "legs slightly bent—leaning back and looking back" (scored "low"); (22) "The person has one leg straight, the other bent—back bent forward—arms bent" (scored "low"); (28) "one leg bent in the air—the other in the ground—arms are bent and hanging" (scored "low"). A fourth child described the figures in these terms: (12) "a cheerleader—happy, awful happy" (scored "high"); (16) " 'no, I don't want it'—looks like it's something awful and he doesn't like it" (scored "high"); (22) "a person mad and ready to fight, like somebody took away his ten dollars—real angry" (scored "high"); (28) "a person mad and ready to have a fist fight—somebody stole his car—real mad" (scored "high").

Free Descriptions of Paths

The stimulus materials for this task comprise the cards from the Line Meanings procedure presented in Figure 3. These lines are among a number that were developed by Tagiuri (1960) in connection with research reviewed earlier in this chapter.[4] The present task came eleventh in the sequence of seventeen, following the Line Meanings procedure in the same session. It was introduced to the child in the following manner:

"Here is another question about these lines. This time I would like you to imagine that each line is a trail of footprints a person has made by walking through a desert. Pretend that you are up above looking down and seeing the trail this person has made. Here, I will show you what I mean."

At this point the experimenter puts a sheet of white cardboard, fifteen inches by twenty inches, on the table before the child. The cardboard has drawn on it a heavy black line that follows a somewhat undulating path. The child is asked to stand in front of this cardboard so that he is looking down upon it. Then the experimenter takes out a stick figure constructed from a pipe cleaner and standing about two inches tall. She moves the stick figure in such a way that it follows a route on the cardboard from the start of the path at the child's left to the end of the path at the child's right. When the figure has been moved to the end of the path it is left standing there. This same procedure, with the path in the same orientation, is followed with each child. The experimenter then continues:

"You see, you are looking down on the trail this person has made just as though you were high above it. Do you see what I mean?" (If the child indicates that he does not, then the experimenter repeats the demonstration just described,

---

[4] Thanks are due Renato Tagiuri in connection with the present procedure.

with the explanation that was just indicated.) "Fine. Now, when you look at the little cards, there won't be any person there—but it will be your job to imagine that he is there and to guess what sort of person he is to have made this particular trail. You just look at the trail of footprints and it will help you to tell me what the person who made it must be like. Do you see how we play this game? Good. Then let's begin."

The experimenter presents the child with the first card, and goes on:

"Here is the first trail of footprints. Hold the card straight, like this, and imagine that this is a trail some person has made—that you are looking down from up high and seeing how it goes along from where it started (the experimenter points to the path's beginning) to where it ends (the experimenter traces the path to its end). What sort of person do you think made this trail?"

Analogous instructions are provided for each of the remaining paths. The child's description in each case is recorded verbatim by the experimenter. The nine descriptions generated by this procedure were subjected to a content analysis similar to that used for the Free Descriptions of Stick Figures procedure. A two-category distinction proved appropriate for the present materials: presence vs. absence of a physiognomically sensitive description. "Presence" corresponded to the scoring category of "high" defined for the preceding task. The scoring definitions learned by each judge follow:

The description of each path will be scored "high" or "not high." If the child includes material in a description that should receive both types of score, assign him the "high" score.

Score "high" if the person is described in terms that *directly* (not implicitly) express his emotive response to any situation. For example, "he's unsure of himself." Mention of affective qualities as such also earns a score of "high." For example, "happy," "sad," "stern," "graceful." As the example of "stern" indicates, judgments of character are included here. Quotations which define the internal affective state of the person also are included. If an affective state description is deemed stereotypical by the judge, so that it may reflect merely a verbal habit rather than a response to the path of the person's movement, it is scored "not high" rather than "high" (e.g., "he likes to walk"). If the criteria for a score of "high" are not met, score "not high."

Nine descriptions were provided by each child (hence 1359 descriptions in all). These were scored by two independent adult judges, both once again working without knowledge of the identities of the children. Reliability of scoring was measured by dividing the number of interjudge agreements in scores of "high" and "not high" by the total number of descriptions, yielding an agreement quotient of .85. Scoring reliability hence was quite satisfactory. Discrepancies between the judges were resolved by discussion. The measure for each child consisted of the number of descriptions scored "high." The range of this variable was, of course, 0 to 9.

To illustrate the nature of these descriptions, some examples follow. The eighteen descriptions that appear were provided by eighteen different children. We present first a description scored "high," then a description scored "not high," in the case of each of the paths 1 through 9, respectively.

1. "He's scared of something and trying to get away; he can be nice when he wants to, but usually he's grumpy; along here (the right-hand extreme of the path) he was getting more relaxed" (high). "He was looking for an ending to the desert" (not high).

2. "A gay person; just left his family and is going to a big job across the Sahara; it's a job that'll give him lots of money and he won't have to work hard; and he's poor, so he's skipping along gaily" (high). "A man who was back-tracking; a person was going around something; a person who was going in between mountains" (not high).

3. "He was in a hurry; couldn't find his directions and so he didn't go in a straight line; in a hurry because he wanted to get home; he was excited; he wanted to get home; he was in a mess and in trouble and walked like this" (high). "Must have liked to go over his trails—retrace his steps" (not high).

4. "Someone very tense; because if he were relaxed he might wander all over; somebody mad" (high). "Man was traveling on a highway; he met people in a huge car; it had a lot of people and it was crowded; they traveled together and got food in restaurants; when they got where they were going, they had a nice vacation" (not high).

5. "His mind is wandering; he doesn't care about anything; he's happy; he's letting his imagination go; walking in any direction he wants; he's quite cheerful until he comes to the straight part—then he's thinking of something serious—then he becomes happy again" (high). "He might be going on some sort of journey and there are a lot of hills that block the way so he has to go in curves instead of just going straight" (not high).

6. "Maybe anxious; maybe hurrying and running and keeping as much as the person can in a straight line" (high). "He might have seen something so he went there; but he didn't see anything there so he went here" (not high).

7. "Maybe he was carefree; and maybe he just went around something" (high). "Probably riding on a road, and detoured to take a special view of the woods and then came back on the road again" (not high).

8. "Adventurous; an Arab; dark-eyed; brown skin; exploring" (high). "He's going into the desert and suddenly has no water so he starts going in circles and finally finds his way back" (not high).

9. "A wandering person; instead of going straight he'd rather go around; you could say, 'curious'" (high). "A person might have started a picture on the sand and never finished it; he wanted to make a big picture, so he walked; he might have started to go around in a big circle and never finished it; he stopped half way" (not high).

Emotive Connotations of Abstract Patterns

Whereas the posture of a stick figure concerned us in the first task, and the movement path of a person-as-a-unit concerned us in the second, the stimulus materials in the present procedure consist of nonrepresentational patterns. As we noted earlier, one can think of the stimuli in these three tasks as forming a series that increases in abstractness as far as relevance to human affective states is concerned. As also noted previously, the abstractness of the stimuli in this third procedure requires us to change our dependent variable from a free description approach to a forced choice between two visual pattern translations of a given state of emotion, one translation considered appropriate and the other inappropriate by adult judges. The affective states were indicated to the child by means of photographs of the face of an adult female representing diverse emotions.

The five abstract patterns used in this procedure are presented in Figure 5. While original with us, it is evident that their style owes much to the work of the cartoonist Saul Steinberg, as represented in, for instance, his delightful collection *The Labyrinth* (1960). The four facial photographs representing affective states were taken from the Lightfoot series developed by Engen, Levy, and Schlosberg (1957; 1958). Most of the pictures in this series are reproduced in Morgan (1956). The four photographs used in our work are numbers 1 ("happy-a"), 39 ("happy-b"), 51 ("angry"), and 56 ("sleepy") as presented in Morgan (1956, pp. 32–33).[5] The first two clearly depict a happy emotional state, the third, an angry state, and the fourth, a state of sleep. All are photographs of the same actress. The patent differences in emotional expression which they represent (with, of course, the two "happy" photographs being highly similar) are attested to in ratings by ninety-six college students on nine-point dimensions representing pleasantness–unpleasantness, attention–rejection, and sleep–tension (Engen, Levy, & Schlosberg, 1958). The photographs described as "happy-a" and "happy-b" received median rating values at the pleasantness, attention, and tension ends of the respective dimensions. The photograph labeled "angry" received median ratings at the unpleasantness, attention, and tension extremes. Finally, the photograph labeled "sleepy" received a middling median rating on pleasantness–unpleasantness and extreme median ratings at the rejection and sleep ends of the remaining dimensions.

The task involves presenting the child with two of the patterns and requesting him to select the one that better fits the expression in a given facial photograph. Twenty-two such choices are made, each involving a different constellation of two patterns and one face. The twenty-two stimulus triads in question were arrived at by reference to adult consensus. We began with a somewhat larger group of triads composed

[5] We are grateful to Harold Schlosberg for advice in connection with the use of these photographs.

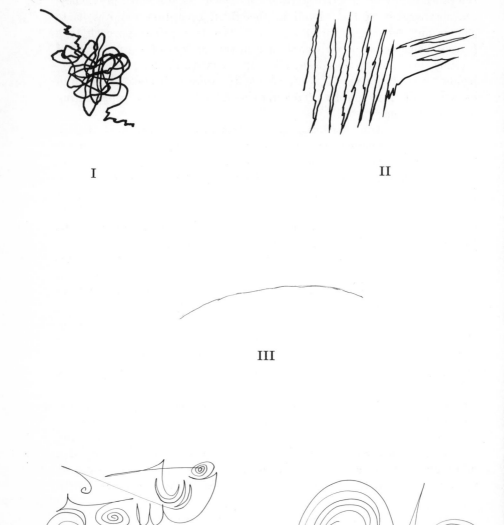

I

II

III

IV

V

FIGURE 5. *The five abstract patterns used in the Emotive Connotations of Abstract Patterns procedure.*

from six faces and six patterns. The twenty-two triads retained for the task were those on which three independent adult judges agreed regarding which choice for each triad was the physiognomically appropriate one. The latter triads are based on the five patterns presented in the illustration and the four facial expressions described in the preceding. In those triads wherein a particular pattern appears, it does so sometimes as the left-hand member of the pattern pair, sometimes as the right-hand member, so that left–right positions for a given pattern are approximately balanced. The number of left and right side appearances for each pattern in the twenty-two triads are as follows:

Pattern	Left	Right
I	5	3
II	3	5
III	5	5
IV	5	4
V	4	5

The correct pattern in each triad appears as the left-hand pattern in twelve of the triads, and as the right-hand pattern in the remaining ten. Left–right positions of the correct choices hence are approximately balanced.

The instructions for the task and the actual choices offered are presented below. Each triad is referred to by the term describing one facial expression followed by the numbers of two patterns from Figure 5 in their left–right arrangement. The correct choice in each case is italicized.

"This is a matching game. I have some lines drawn on cards (these are shown to the child) and I also have some pictures of a lady's face (these too are now shown). I am going to show you two of these lines together with one picture of the lady's face, and it will be your job to pick the line that seems to be most like the way the lady feels.[6] There are no right or wrong answers in this game. Everybody has a different idea about it, but since you'll be seeing the same lines and faces more than once you'll want to be sure to look carefully each time. Just remember always to pick the line which seems to you to be most like the way the lady feels. Let's try one now and you'll see how easy it is.

(1) "Here are the two lines and here is the lady's face. Which of the lines is most like the way the lady feels?" Happy-a: I, *IV*

(2) "And here are two lines and here is another picture of the lady. Which of the lines is most like the way the lady feels in this picture?" Sleepy: *III*, V

---

[6] With a choice between two stimuli, it is evident that "more like," rather than "most like," would be appropriate grammatical form. We found in pretesting, however, that "most like," even though grammatically inaccurate, is a more apt vehicle for communicating the idea to children of this sample's age.

(3) "Which of the lines is most like the way the lady feels in this picture?" Happy-b: *IV*, II

(4) The query for each successive item is similar to the one given above. Angry: *I*, III

    (5) Happy-a: II, *V*
    (6) Sleepy: *III*, IV
    (7) Happy-b: *V*, I
    (8) Angry: *II*, III
    (9) Happy-a: I, *V*
  (10) Sleepy: *III*, II
  (11) Happy-b: *IV*, I
  (12) Angry: V, *II*
  (13) Happy-a: *IV*, III
  (14) Happy-b: III, *IV*
  (15) Angry: V, *I*
  (16) Happy-a: *IV*, II
  (17) Sleepy: I, *III*
  (18) Happy-b: II, *V*
  (19) Angry: *I*, IV
  (20) Happy-a: *V*, III
  (21) Happy-b: III, *V*
  (22) Angry: IV, *II*

The procedure fell seventh in the sequence of seventeen. The score for a subject can vary, of course, from 0 to 22.

Bizarre Emotive Attributions for Stick Figures

Our interest in the present procedure was to invite the child to entertain the possibility of relatively bizarre attributions of emotional states for given stick figures. In contrast to the procedure just described, the question here was not one of discriminating between an appropriate and an inappropriate physiognomic translation of an emotional state. Rather, the child was permitted to accept both kinds. Our question was: If a child is allowed to accept obviously appropriate linkages between the posture of a stick figure and an affective happening, will he also accept bizarre possibilities or will he reject the latter? More particularly, which children—as defined in terms of creativity and intelligence—will be more accepting of the bizarre possibilities, and which children more rejecting of them?

A set of twenty-four stick figures was chosen from among the larger number used in the Free Descriptions of Stick Figures procedure. For each figure, three labels were assigned describing affective states: one state deemed bizarre for that figure, another deemed highly appropriate for that figure, and a third deemed moderately appropriate for the figure in question. Three independent adult judges had been given the three labels pertaining to each figure, and had been requested to select the label whose affective attribution was most bizarre, and the label whose affective attribution was most appropriate, for the stick figure in question. The twenty-four figures and their respective sets of labels were those in the case of which all three judges had agreed in their choices of the most bizarre and the most appropriate emotional attributions.

As examples of the kinds of descriptions provided, we present the labels that were assigned for each of the figures illustrated in Figure 4. The label that was judged most appropriate for a given figure appears first, and the label that was judged most bizarre for a given figure appears last, in the set of three. Stick Figure 12: Does he seem to be joyous? Does he seem to be excited? Does he seem to be angry? Stick Figure 16: Does he seem to be taken by surprise? Does he seem to be scared? Does he seem to be happy? Stick Figure 22: Does he seem to be very angry? Does he seem to be ordering someone around? Does he seem to be peaceful? Stick Figure 28: Does he seem to be very angry? Does he seem to be excited? Does he seem to be searching?

The three labels for a stick figure were not presented in succession. Rather, all twenty-four stick figures were presented one at a time with a question about one of each figure's three labels. Then the twenty-four stick figures were again presented one at a time (in the same order) with a question about a second of each figure's three labels. Finally, the twenty-four figures were presented once more in the same sequence, and the child was asked about the third of each figure's labels. The inquiry about a stick figure's bizarre label took place for eight of the figures during the first presentation of all twenty-four, for another eight during the second complete presentation of the figures, and for the remaining eight during the last presentation. The eight questions about bizarre labels were spaced in a random sequence within each series of twenty-four presentations.

Instructions for the present task, which occupied the eighth position in the sequence of seventeen procedures, are as follows:

"This is another stick figure game. You remember that a stick figure is a drawing of a person made with simple lines. I am going to show you a stick figure and ask you a question about it. Your answer should be either *yes* or *no*, nothing else but either *yes* or *no*, depending on what you think about the stick figure. There are no right or wrong answers. Everybody has a different idea about it, so any way at all that you want to answer is fine. All right. Here we go now.

"Here is the first stick figure. I'd like your opinion about him. Does he seem to be thinking?"

Analogous questions then were asked for each of the twenty-three remaining stick figures in the series. The sequence of twenty-four figures then was repeated a second and a third time. To emphasize the gamelike quality of the procedure, the child turned each stick-figure card over and added it to a pile after responding.

Three scores are derived from these materials: the number of bizarre labels accepted by the child, the number of highly appropriate labels accepted by the child, and the number of moderately appropriate labels so accepted. In each case, of course, the possible score range extends from 0 to 24.

Response Reliabilities

How reliable is the behavior assessed by the foregoing measures of physiognomic sensitivity? We already have ascertained that the scoring systems developed for content analyzing the two procedures that involve free descriptions are reliable in the sense that different scorers will apply them in the same way and thus obtain the same scores from a given protocol. To what degree, however, are these scores, and the scores obtained from the remaining two physiognomic procedures, internally consistent for a given child?

Table 48 gives the Spearman-Brown split-half reliability coefficients for the various physiognomic indices. In the case of the Free Descriptions of Stick Figures procedure, reliability was estimated for a single total score obtained by translating item scores of "low," "medium," and "high" into numerical values of 0, 1, and 2, respectively. This was necessary since the number of instances of each type of score varied, of course, from child to child. For the remaining procedures, the reliability coefficients pertain to the scores as described in the preceding section. It is apparent from Table 48 that the reliabilities are generally adequate. Each of the scores in question, in other words, possesses a reasonable degree of consistency across its various items. While the first procedure's reliability coefficient is very high, the remaining coefficients all are in

Table 48.

SPEARMAN-BROWN SPLIT-HALF RELIABILITY COEFFICIENTS
FOR THE PHYSIOGNOMIC SENSITIVITY MEASURES
$(N = 151)$

1. Free descriptions of stick figures	.92
2. Free descriptions of paths	.55
3. Emotive connotations of abstract patterns	.58
4a. Bizarre emotive attributions for stick figures	.40
4b. Highly appropriate emotive attributions for stick figures	.37
4c. Moderately appropriate emotive attributions for stick figures	.60

the moderate range. The response reliabilities for these various measures function as ceilings, of course, upon their capacity to vary systematically with other factors.

RESULTS AND DISCUSSION

Internal Analysis of Physiognomic Sensitivity Measures

If the physiognomic sensitivity indicators cohered in the sense that a child high on one would be high on all, then it evidently would be inappropriate for us to treat these indices separately. They would be reflecting a common dimension of psychological variation. It will be re-called that we raised earlier the question of whether a uni- or multi-dimensional conception of physiognomic sensitivity would turn out to be more appropriate. Little prior evidence has been available on this ques-tion, since previous work in the area has not studied the relative standing of the same individuals on different measures of such sensitivity. Rather, any single study typically has been confined to a given kind of indicator. Clearly, the dimensionality question must be answered before we can proceed to investigate relationships with creativity and intelligence.

The two sexes are compared on the various physiognomic sensitivity indices in Table 49. It is evident that their mean scores are highly similar with the exception of one measure, sensitivity in the Free De-scriptions of Paths procedure. There we find a significant difference in favor of the girls ($t = 2.99$, $p < .01$). Sex differences in the present do-main, then, are relatively absent. In the one procedure where they do occur, their direction is consistent with the general cultural expectation that girls should excel boys in the type of sensitivity under scrutiny. With this material as background, we can turn to the question of relation-ships among the various measures.

As Table 50 indicates, these relationships are quite low. Turning first to the correlations for boys, the Free Descriptions of Stick Figures procedure is unrelated to any of the remaining tasks. Within that pro-cedure, number of highs is inversely related both to number of lows and number of mediums, an expectable outcome in the light of the experi-mental dependencies among these scores. Scores on the Free Description of Paths task are correlated at the .05 level with the number of highly ap-propriate emotive attributions made for the stick figures, measure 4b, but with none of the other indices. The number of "correct" matches in the Emotive Connotations of Abstract Patterns procedure turns out to be unrelated to any other measure. Finally, degrees of acceptance of bizarre, of highly appropriate, and of moderately appropriate emotive attribu-tions for the stick figures, are unrelated to the various other tasks, with

Table 49.

Sex Comparisons on the Physiognomic Sensitivity Measures

Measure	Boys ($N = 70$)		Girls ($N = 81$)			
	Mean	SD	Mean	SD	t	p
1a. Free descriptions of stick figures: lows	1.60	4.07	0.93	2.99	1.17	n. s.
1b. Free descriptions of stick figures: mediums	21.44	5.25	20.91	5.62	0.59	n. s.
1c. Free descriptions of stick figures: highs	11.23	6.05	12.48	6.38	1.23	n. s.
2. Free descriptions of paths	3.09	2.52	4.40	2.81	2.99	<.01
3. Emotive connotations of abstract patterns	19.69	2.41	19.02	2.85	1.53	n. s.
4a. Bizarre emotive attributions for stick figures	0.96	1.21	1.01	1.04	0.30	n. s.
4b. Highly appropriate emotive attributions for stick figures	21.66	1.82	21.54	1.53	0.42	n. s.
4c. Moderately appropriate emotive attributions for stick figures	18.73	2.90	19.07	2.74	0.75	n. s.

Table 50.

INTERCORRELATIONS AMONG PHYSIOGNOMIC SENSITIVITY MEASURES

	1a	1b	1c	2	3	4a	4b	4c
1a. Free descriptions of stick figures: lows	—	—13	—51	—11	16	—01	—07	—13
1b. Free descriptions of stick figures: mediums	03	—	—73	—17	—05	07	—15	01
1c. Free descriptions of stick figures: highs	—47	—84	—	20	—03	—05	20	05
2. Free descriptions of paths	—04	—01	11	—	10	—09	33	15
3. Emotive connotations of abstract patterns	—17	04	08	20	—	—03	07	13
4a. Bizarre emotive attributions for stick figures	—09	00	07	—12	—02	—	—05	21
4b. Highly appropriate emotive attributions for stick figures	—23	—17	24	—04	04	00	—	35
4c. Moderately appropriate emotive attributions for stick figures	—09	—03	13	—01	—06	17	50	—

NOTE: Correlations for boys ($N = 70$) appear above diagonal; correlations for girls ($N = 81$) appear below diagonal. For the boys, r's of .24 and .31 are significant beyond the .05 and .01 levels, respectively. For the girls, the corresponding r's are .22 and .29. Correlations within block involve relations between experimentally dependent measures. Decimal points are omitted.

the exception of the one significant correlation already noted between the Free Descriptions of Paths task and number of highly appropriate emotive attributions for the stick figures. Considering relationships among the three measures comprising the fourth procedure, the only significant correlation is that between number of highly appropriate and number of moderately appropriate attributions accepted for the stick figures. The fact that, in this fourth task, acceptance of bizarre attributions is not significantly related to acceptance of highly appropriate or moderately appropriate attributions, argues against the operation of an acquiescent bias (Couch & Keniston, 1960; Jackson & Messick, 1958) in connection with the entertaining of bizarre attributions. That is, boys who are more willing to accept bizarre attributions are not simply boys who are more willing to accept attributions in general.

Taking the correlations for boys as a whole, only four out of twenty-eight are statistically significant. With two of these four reflecting dependencies among scores, it is clear that the evidence at hand indicates the presence of multidimensionality rather than unidimensionality in the domain of measures under study.

The correlations for girls tell a similar story. Once again, the Free Descriptions of Stick Figures procedure is unrelated to the other indices. The experimental dependencies among that procedure's scores once more are reflected in the finding of inverse correlations between number of highs and both number of lows and number of mediums. The Free Descriptions of Paths procedure is unrelated to any other index, and this also is the case for the task concerning Emotive Connotations of Abstract Patterns. Each of the three measures comprising the fourth procedure is unrelated to any of the other tasks. Once more, the only significant correlation among those three measures is a relationship between number of highly appropriate and number of moderately appropriate attributions. Acceptance of bizarre attributions once again is not significantly related to acceptance of highly appropriate or moderately appropriate attributions, thus providing further evidence that the entertaining of bizarre attributions is not a product of a generalized willingness to accept attributions.

Only three out of twenty-eight correlations are statistically significant for the girls. With two of these three again reflecting score dependencies, we may conclude that, for the girls as well as the boys, our indices of physiognomic sensitivity define many dimensions rather than one.

There is little warrant on the basis of our findings, then, for conceiving of sensitivity to physiognomic properties in terms of a single ability. When measures found to be reasonably reliable are constructed so as to sample various kinds of stimulus materials and types of responses, these measures turn out to possess little relationship with one another. This despite the fact that each of them can be said to have face validity as reflecting some aspect of the potential interconnections between affective and visual experiences. The important point at this juncture thus is the demonstration that no justification exists for combining the scores on the various physiognomic indicators into a single index. The variations in abstractness of stimulus materials, as well as in other aspects of the physiognomic procedures, all seem to be sufficiently extensive as to preclude any clear consistencies of individual differences in the handling of these tasks. We also have been able to demonstrate that differences among children in the willingness to entertain bizarre affective attributions for stick figures are relatively specific to attitudes toward the bizarre linkages per se, rather than simply reflecting individual differences in "yea-saying"—in readiness to accept any attributions.

Sensitivity to physiognomic properties can be a multidimensional affair, and yet these various dimensions may nevertheless vary in systematic ways with groupings of children in terms of intelligence and the associative conception of creativity. It is to this issue that we turn next.

Physiognomic Sensitivity and Modes of Thinking

FREE DESCRIPTIONS OF STICK FIGURES. Consider first the results for the four groups of boys. No creativity or intelligence effects are observed for the number of lows on the present procedure. The groups do differ, however, in number of mediums and of highs (Tables 51 and 52). The high creative groups give a significantly smaller number of descriptions that earn scores of "medium," and a near-significantly larger number of descriptions that earn scores of "high," compared with the low creative groups. Differences as a function of intelligence, while not at all significant, do follow the same trends: that is, the high intelligence groups offer fewer descriptions that earn scores of "medium," and more descriptions that earn scores of "high," than do the low intelligence groups. Given the orthogonality of the creativity and intelligence dimensions, we therefore find that the largest number of "medium" scores occur in the low creativity–low intelligence group, while the smallest number of "medium" scores occur in the high creativity–high intelligence group. In complementary fashion, the largest number of "high" scores are found in the high creativity–high intelligence group, while the smallest number of "high" scores are found in the low creativity–low intelligence group. The major effect in each of these cases, however, occurs as a function of creativity differences.

For the boys, then, free descriptions of the stick figures reflect crea-

Table 51.

MEAN NUMBER OF MEDIUMS IN FREE DESCRIPTIONS OF
THE STICK FIGURES BY THE FOUR GROUPS
OF BOYS ($N = 70$)

		INTELLIGENCE	
		High	Low
	High	19.65	20.06
		(6.02)	(5.73)
CREATIVITY			
	Low	22.72	23.35
		(4.07)	(4.33)

ANALYSIS OF VARIANCE

Source	df	MS	F	p
Intelligence	1	0.27	<1.00	n. s.
Creativity	1	10.15	6.81	<.02
Interaction	1	0.01	<1.00	n. s.
Within cells	66	1.49		

Table 52.

MEAN NUMBER OF HIGHS IN FREE DESCRIPTIONS OF
THE STICK FIGURES BY THE FOUR GROUPS
OF BOYS ($N = 70$)

		INTELLIGENCE	
		High	Low
	High	13.53	11.78
		(7.02)	(6.14)
CREATIVITY			
	Low	10.33	9.29
		(6.33)	(3.85)

ANALYSIS OF VARIANCE

Source	df	MS	F	p
Intelligence	1	1.95	<1.00	n. s.
Creativity	1	8.06	3.96	<.06
Interaction	1	0.13	<1.00	n. s.
Within cells	66	2.04		

tivity differences. High creatives provide descriptions that depict affective states of the stick figures, while the descriptions given by low creatives are more likely to emphasize the physical characteristics of the figures.

We turn next to the comparable data for the girls. Considering first the mean numbers of lows in the various groups (Table 53), we find an interaction with a p value beyond the .07 level. The main source of contribution to this interaction would seem to be the fact that the high creativity–high intelligence group provides almost no descriptions at all that receive scores of "low." Almost none of this group's descriptions of stick figures, in other words, concern isolated parts of the body. Turning to the number of scores of "medium," the four groups are very similar. Finally, we note the results for the number of scores of "high" (Table 54). A significant intelligence effect is found, the high intelligence groups offering a larger number of descriptions that receive scores of "high" than the low intelligence groups. The creativity dimension yields a trend in the same direction, the high creativity groups providing more descriptions that earn scores of "high" than do the groups low in creativity. Once again, then, the largest number of "high" scores is found in the high creativity–high intelligence group, while the smallest number of "high" scores is found in the low creativity–low intelligence group. While the major contribution to this contrast fell along the creativity dimension in the case of the boys, however, it falls along the intelligence dimension in the case of the girls. Unlike the boys, on the other hand, the variable of number of lows provided a further discrimination in the case of the girls. As we have seen, the high creativity–high intelligence group stood apart from the others in its virtual absence of scores of "low." The girls who are high in both creativity and intelligence thus earn the smallest number of "low" scores and the largest number of "high" scores.

The findings for the two sexes regarding free descriptions of the stick figures, while divergent in regard to the strength of the creativity and intelligence effects, are nevertheless parallel in an important respect. In the case of both, the high creativity–high intelligence groups exhibit the greatest concentration of descriptions that refer to affective states or personality qualities, though it should be noted that this reported trend is not powerful enough to produce statistically significant effects for both thinking modes.

FREE DESCRIPTIONS OF PATHS. Turning first to the boys, the evidence points to a near-significant intelligence difference (Table 55). Boys high in intelligence give a larger number of path descriptions that express emotive responses on the part of the figure traversing the path than do boys low in intelligence. As in the case of the preceding stick figures procedure, the high-high and low-low groups again stand at the extremes on the present measure of physiognomic sensitivity.

Table 53.

MEAN NUMBER OF LOWS IN FREE DESCRIPTIONS OF
THE STICK FIGURES BY THE FOUR GROUPS
OF GIRLS $(N = 81)$

		INTELLIGENCE	
		High	Low
	High	0.05	1.78
		(0.21)	(3.95)
CREATIVITY			
	Low	1.42	0.68
		(3.55)	(2.98)

ANALYSIS OF VARIANCE

Source	df	MS	F	p
Intelligence	1	0.25	<1.00	n. s.
Creativity	1	0.02	<1.00	n. s.
Interaction	1	1.53	3.48	$<.07$
Within cells	77	0.44		

Table 54.

MEAN NUMBER OF HIGHS IN FREE DESCRIPTIONS OF
THE STICK FIGURES BY THE FOUR GROUPS
OF GIRLS $(N = 81)$

		INTELLIGENCE	
		High	Low
	High	15.59	11.11
		(6.84)	(5.82)
CREATIVITY			
	Low	12.42	10.55
		(7.15)	(4.64)

ANALYSIS OF VARIANCE

Source	df	MS	F	p
Intelligence	1	10.10	5.33	$<.03$
Creativity	1	3.49	1.84	n. s.
Interaction	1	1.70	<1.00	n. s.
Within cells	77	1.89		

Table 55.

MEAN NUMBER OF HIGHS IN FREE DESCRIPTIONS OF
PATHS BY THE FOUR GROUPS OF BOYS ($N = 70$)

		INTELLIGENCE	
		High	Low
	High	3.82	3.11
		(2.79)	(2.35)
CREATIVITY			
	Low	3.50	1.88
		(2.85)	(1.65)

ANALYSIS OF VARIANCE

Source	df	MS	F	p
Intelligence	1	1.36	3.91	$<.06$
Creativity	1	0.60	1.74	n. s.
Interaction	1	0.20	<1.00	n. s.
Within cells	66	0.35		

Consider next the findings for girls in the paths procedure. We note in Table 56 that the high intelligence groups again earn a significantly larger number of "high" scores for their descriptions than do the low intelligence groups. Further, it is again the high-high group that yields the largest number of "high" scores. This outcome parallels the female data for free descriptions of stick figures. Turning to the groups obtaining the smallest number of "high" scores on the paths procedure, we find that the two groups low in general intelligence are relatively indistinguishable in this regard, the high creativity–low intelligence group actually earning a slightly lower score than the low-low group. Note that in the female data for the free descriptions of stick figures (Table 54), the two groups low in general intelligence were also similar in their showing on number of "highs," both groups again earning fewer such scores. In the case of the girls, then, the two low intelligence groups —those high and those low in creativity—are found to be in the bottom rankings and to be relatively indistinguishable in regard to awareness of the affective meanings that may be carried by human expressive behavior, whether of gesture (free descriptions of stick figures) or of a person's total path of locomotion in space (free descriptions of paths).

It is intriguing to consider these results in the light of our findings concerning social interaction patterns manifested by these two groups of girls. Recall that behavior ratings of girls in the high creativity–low

Table 56.

MEAN NUMBER OF HIGHS IN FREE DESCRIPTIONS OF
PATHS BY THE FOUR GROUPS OF GIRLS ($N = 81$)

INTELLIGENCE

		High	Low
	High	5.64 (3.05)	3.50 (2.09)
CREATIVITY			
	Low	4.74 (2.84)	3.59 (2.70)

ANALYSIS OF VARIANCE

Source	df	MS	F	p
Intelligence	1	2.69	7.33	$<.01$
Creativity	1	0.16	<1.00	n. s.
Interaction	1	0.25	<1.00	n. s.
Within cells	77	0.37		

intelligence group indicated that they were least sought after as companions and least likely to seek companionship themselves. This group, in other words, tends to avoid others and has this avoidance reciprocated in kind, suggesting that these are the most isolated girls in the classroom. The members of the low-low group, in contrast, although not particularly sought out by others for companionship, nevertheless do themselves seek the companionship of others. Recall also that the high creativity–low intelligence group engages in much behavior of a blatantly disruptive and attention-seeking kind, while the low-low group does not. An interesting contrast between the two groups begins to emerge when these various social interaction findings are put in juxtaposition with the physiognomic findings on human expressive behavior.

It may be that the relatively poorer performance of these two groups in translating the physiognomics of human expressive behavior on the two free description tasks comes about for quite different reasons. The high creativity–low intelligence group may not especially want to read the emotive significance of the behavior of other persons, while the low-low group may find it difficult to read the emotive significance of such behavior. We proposed earlier (Chapter 3) that the disruptive behavior of the high-low group may reflect a basic dissatisfaction with the total school environment. Withdrawn from social participation and pursuing solitary fantasy activities that impinge upon others only in disruptive ways, these children may well have only a minimal desire to read the affective significance of the social behavior of others. For, after all, this group of children is inclined to reject others. In contrast, the low-low group demonstrates a desire to make social overtures to others. The members of this group do not partake of the kind of intense associative life that can motivate disruptive behavior and can be served by the solitary pursuit of fantasy in preference to affiliation with others. Yet they too experience difficulties in reading the expressive cues provided by the gestural behavior and movement patterns of others. In their case there can be no lack of desire to do so; rather, it may well be the ability that is lacking.

Taking the results for both sexes in perspective at this point, the outlines of some generalizations begin to emerge concerning physiognomic sensitivity to human stimuli—bodily gesture and movement of the total person. Quite consistently, such sensitivity is found to be maximal in the joint presence of high creativity and high intelligence. In all cases, it is greater when both are present than when one is present without the other, though it must be noted that only one or the other thinking mode is making a statistically significant contribution to the observed effects. For boys, the high-low and low-high groups seem to yield a degree of sensitivity approximately midway between that found in the high-high group and that found in the low-low group. The trend is toward maximal sensitivity for the high-highs, minimal sensitivity for the low-lows, and an intermediate degree for the remaining two groups. On the other hand, for girls, high creativity without high intelligence does not seem to yield the same intermediate results as high intelligence without high creativity. Rather, performance in the high creativity–low intelligence case essentially drops down to the level found when creativity and intelligence both are absent. The high creative but low intelligent girls may be motivated to avoid reading the emotive meanings of other people's behavior, while the girls low in both creativity and intelligence may be unable to read these meanings. For both sexes, however, sensitivity in translating such meanings is maximal in the case of the high-high group.

It may be, therefore, that the two correlates under study of the tendency to make these physiognomic translations—creativity and intelligence—operate in a manner that is in some respects additive and in other respects interactive. Presence of either creativity or intelligence may indicate that the ability to make such translations is possessed by the child. A fortiori, then, presence of both means that the ability is maximal. Absence of both, in turn, means that the ability is minimal.

Presence of one without the other, however, may mean that an intermediate level of ability is operating, or, alternatively, when it is creativity that is present in the absence of high intelligence, may mean that motivational forces are operating that will hinder the ability from being utilized.

EMOTIVE CONNOTATIONS OF ABSTRACT PATTERNS. We turn now to a considerably different class of stimulus materials. The stimuli dealt with in the present task are fully abstract in the sense that no depictive referent in human behavior is provided for them by the experimenter. We measure in the present context the extent to which the child can make matches between abstract patterns and emotional states that agree with those made by adult judges. As we have noted, it was necessary to adopt agreement with a criterion as the dependent variable for the present type of stimuli, since free descriptions by children of completely abstract stimuli would not be at all likely to contain affective connotations.

The results for boys are presented in Table 57. It is apparent that both intelligence and creativity exert an influence in the present case. Inspection of the means indicates that the significant findings are brought about by the depressed score for the low-low group. The group low in

Table 57.

MEAN NUMBER OF CORRECT ABSTRACT PATTERN CHOICES
BY THE FOUR GROUPS OF BOYS ($N = 70$)

		INTELLIGENCE	
		High	Low
CREATIVITY	High	20.29 (1.83)	20.56 (1.34)
	Low	20.06 (2.48)	17.76 (2.80)

ANALYSIS OF VARIANCE

Source	df	MS	F	p
Intelligence	1	1.03	3.78	<.06
Creativity	1	2.29	8.43	<.01
Interaction	1	1.63	5.99	<.03
Within cells	66	0.27		

both creativity and intelligence is considerably inferior in performance to any of the remaining three groups. The latter three, in turn, are relatively indistinguishable in performance. Presence of creativity and/or intelligence, therefore, is sufficient to raise performance to a point close to the ceiling of 22. Absence of both, in turn, leads to a poorer performance.

The present results are reasonably parallel to those obtained for boys with the preceding two tasks. Once again, the low-low group makes the poorest showing. With scores running so very close to the ceiling of 22 in terms of the average number correct, it is evidently not possible to distinguish the high-high group of boys from the low-high and high-low groups. The task in general, in other words, turned out to be easier than would have been ideal, with the consequence that its items possessed only a limited capacity to discriminate individual differences. Under these circumstances, the finding of a considerably depressed performance on the part of the low-low group is a most intriguing datum. Despite the high over-all average score obtained on the present task, this one group falls significantly short in performance. Presence of a high level of either creativity or intelligence is sufficient to push the score level up toward its effective ceiling, but absence of both leaves the individual sufficiently deprived to depress his score.

No comparable findings are obtained for girls. The four groups are very similar in performance. Once again, the over-all performance mean approximates the ceiling, so that the present task simply may not have been sufficiently discriminating to yield intelligence and/or creativity effects for the girls.

Our findings concerning the Emotive Connotations of Abstract Patterns task thus do not require any further interpretative principles beyond the ones introduced in examining the results for the preceding two tasks. For boys in the present instance, low levels of *both* intelligence and creativity produces a lessened sensitivity to the physiognomic properties of visual stimuli. Unfortunately, the relative ease of the present task for the sample of fifth grade children under study led to ceiling effects that made it impossible to ascertain whether high levels of both creativity and intelligence would bring about the highest levels of physiognomic sensitivity. Still, a reasonably congruent pattern of results has been obtained across three procedures varying considerably in the degree of abstractness of their stimulus materials. These are, furthermore, procedures that, as we have seen, possess little correlation among themselves. One may surmise, therefore, that the functional relationships between these procedures, on the one hand, and creativity and intelligence, on the other, are stronger than the functional relationships among these procedures as such. The latter tap empirically distinguishable aspects of physiognomic sensitivity, but these aspects, distinct as they are from one another, vary in ways that are relatively similar to one another as a function of the creativity–intelligence groupings.

The interpretative approach that we have followed invokes the idea of creativity and intelligence as additive contributors to physiognomic sensitivities, with the implication that such sensitivities will be maximal in the presence of both, and minimal in the absence of both. There is a further indication in the data that the high creativity–low intelligence females may possess a motivationally grounded aversion to the making of physiognomic discriminations, possibly as a consequence of their preference for relative social isolation and their generally asocial behavior.

EMOTIVE ATTRIBUTIONS FOR STICK FIGURES. The final physiognomic sensitivity task addresses itself to a different type of issue than has been considered thus far. If an individual is given an opportunity to entertain bizarre affective attributions for stick figures, to what extent will he accept or reject this opportunity? Acceptance of the opportunity is not contingent upon rejection of more appropriate attributions, but rather is entirely independent of acceptance or rejection of the latter. The relative degree of acceptance of appropriate and bizarre attributions informs us of the extent to which an acquiescent response set characterizes the behavior of the subjects apart from consideration of the status of the given attributions as bizarre or appropriate. We have already been able to provide evidence which suggests that no such response set is operating, since for neither sex are there significant correlations between degree of acceptance of bizarre attributions, on the one hand, and degree of acceptance of highly appropriate or of moderately appropriate attributions, on the other (Table 50). We now inquire whether the creativity and intelligence groups vary in their degree of acceptance of highly appropriate, moderately appropriate, and bizarre attributions.

The results for boys are entirely negative. The creativity and intelligence groups do not vary in the mean number of bizarre emotive attributions which they accept for the stick figures, nor do they vary in the mean number of highly appropriate or of moderately appropriate attributions which they accept. Bizarre attributions are entertained very seldom by each of the four groups; highly appropriate and moderately appropriate attributions, in turn, are accepted with high frequency by each of the four groups. Either the groups of boys have no differential likelihood of acceptance for appropriate and bizarre attributions, or the measuring instrument is not sufficiently sensitive to detect the variations that exist.

The girls present a somewhat different story. It can be seen in Table 58 that the groups differ in regard to their willingness to entertain hypotheses of bizarre affective attributions for the stick figures. On the

Table 58.

MEAN NUMBER OF BIZARRE EMOTIVE ATTRIBUTIONS
FOR STICK FIGURES BY THE FOUR GROUPS
OF GIRLS ($N = 81$)

		INTELLIGENCE	
		High	Low
CREATIVITY	High	1.14 (1.21)	1.11 (0.90)
	Low	0.42 (0.84)	1.32 (0.99)

ANALYSIS OF VARIANCE

Source	df	MS	F	p
Intelligence	1	0.19	3.78	$<.06$
Creativity	1	0.06	1.28	n. s.
Interaction	1	0.21	4.23	$<.05$
Within cells	77	0.05		

other hand, there are no significant effects whatever in regard to the degree of acceptance of highly appropriate and of moderately appropriate attributions by the four groups of girls. Evidently, the differences found for bizarre attributions define a phenomenon specific to that class of attributions rather than some more general response characteristic. The groups strongly resemble one another in the case of highly appropriate and in the case of moderately appropriate attributions; it is only in the entertaining of bizarre attributions that they differ.

What kinds of differences are suggested by Table 58? The basic statistical evidence is an interaction effect significant beyond the .05 level. Clearly, it is this interaction which also is reflected in the p value of less than .06 for the intelligence dimension, since only one of the four group means is clearly different from the remaining three, the latter in turn being relatively homogeneous. The high intelligence–low creativity group stands out as being least willing to consider bizarre attributions. While each of the other groups entertains an average of more than one bizarre attribution, the high intelligence–low creatives entertain very few indeed.

That the high intelligence–low creative group is particularly avoidant of bizarre attributions adds an intriguing datum to our picture of the group in question. Faced with the opportunity to consider bizarre hypotheses concerning the emotive significance of stick figures' gesture patterns, they are particularly likely to turn this opportunity down. The present finding suggests a type of strategy on the part of this group that may play a causal role in their low creativity status. These are the girls who are most unwilling to consider highly unusual possibilities in making affective attributions; they eschew that which is "far-out" or bizarre.

Notice that a similar phenomenon was found in regard to thematic ("relational") categorizing in the case of the high intelligence–low creativity boys (Chapter 4). The object-sorting behavior of this group was less likely to be based on thematic considerations than that of any of the remaining three groups. The other two possible bases for object-sorting—"descriptive" or "inferential" conjunctive concepts—are more conventional ways of establishing sortings than is the weaving of a theme into which different objects can be fitted. Thus, the high intelligence–low creativity boys stand out from the remaining groups as engaging in fewer "far-out" or unconventional ways of sorting objects, while the high intelligence–low creativity girls stand out from the remaining groups as offering fewer "far-out" or bizarre hypotheses about affective connotations of visual stimuli. The underlying mechanisms in these two cases may be similar, our measures happening to be such that they are able to catch the high intelligence–low creativity boys in one case, the high intelligence–low creativity girls in the other. The common factor uniting these instances is the reduced likelihood of a bizarre or "far-out" type of cognitive behavior for the subgroup high in intelligence but low in creativity. Our proposal is that the reduced likelihood in question may be reflective of an avoidance tendency with regard to the given kinds of cognitive materials. The evidence just noted supports the contention that children of high intelligence who are motivated to avoid that which is unconventional and possibly bizarre will exhibit the kind of associational behavior that leads to low creativity status.

Also relevant to recall in the present connection is the behavior observed on the part of the high intelligence–low creativity girls in the school environment (Chapter 3). We were led by the behavior observation evidence to characterize this group as exhibiting a basic reserve, an unwillingness to overextend or overcommit oneself. The members of this group were least likely to engage in potentially disruptive attention-seeking behaviors, were cautious and hesitant in expressing opinions, were sought by others but tended not to seek others themselves. They also, however, were self-assured and confident in relations with peers and teachers, as well as quite competent and motivated in connection with academic work. The total effect, therefore, was one of lack of spontaneity, overcontrol, conformity to classroom norms and teacher expectations. Such a picture certainly reinforces the present evidence. It is quite consistent for the group in question to be the least likely of the four to entertain bizarre hypotheses concerning affective attributions.

Let us turn now to the remaining three groups of females. While all three are more likely to entertain bizarre hypotheses than the high intelligence–low creativity group, and the means of all three are relatively homogeneous, it is possible that different mechanisms may underlie their behavior. Note that the highest mean is found in the case of the low-low group, while the means of the two groups high in creativity are slightly lower and essentially the same. While we hesitate to make too much of such a difference, it does raise the possibility that the scores of the low-low group arise from a simple failure to discriminate the bizarre character of the attributions in question, while the scores of the two groups high in creativity arise from a more discriminative entertaining of bizarre or unusual attributions. This possible distinction offers a provocative lead for further study.

CONCLUSIONS

Sensitivity to physiognomic properties has proven to be a complex psychological domain. We have found that diverse means of operational-izing the physiognomic sensitivity concept lead to dimensions of individual differences which possess little relationship with one another. There is more warrant, then, for talking about a plurality of sensitivities than about a single characteristic. All of this serves to underscore the probable complexities of etiology involved. Nonetheless, consideration of the joint roles played by creativity and intelligence in connection with physiognomic perception has furthered our understanding both of the latter and of the creativity–intelligence distinction. Ordering children in terms of creativity and intelligence levels leads to predictable patterns of physiognomic sensitivity differences that are relatively consistent across different physiognomic indicators, or congruent in terms of given explanatory principles, even though the indicators possess almost no interrelationships themselves. The significance of the creativity–intelligence distinction for the present domain thus is apparent.

Three tasks were designed in such a way as to provide physiognomic indicators that cover a range extending from stimulus materials that possess a concrete depictive referent in human behavior to stimulus materials whose linkage with human behavior is only abstract and nondepictive. For the boys, the findings on all three tasks offer an ap-proximate fit to what we have called an additive model: according to this model, creativity and intelligence both will make contributions to physiognomic sensitivity, with the result that such sensitivity will be greatest when creativity and intelligence both are high, and will be at its lowest level when creativity and intelligence both are low. The present model accords no special status to the high-low and low-high groups, since it simply implies that their levels of physiognomic awareness will be intermediate between those of the high-high and low-low groups. That the model gains some support from the male findings on each of the three sets of stimuli designed to sample the concrete–abstract range mentioned previously constitutes some evidence for its generality of applicability across differences in the nature of stimuli.

It is clear from the findings in question that we learn more about individual differences in physiognomic sensitivity by taking account of the joint variation of creativity and intelligence than by considering a person's intelligence status alone. Providing information about both creativity and general intelligence level contributes in an additive fashion to our ability to sift out the individuals whose physiognomic sensitivity will be highest and those whose physiognomic sensitivity will be lowest in a general sample. That is, while high intelligence boys will tend to show greater physiognomic awareness than low intelligence boys, those high in creativity as well as intelligence will tend to exhibit the greatest physiognomic awareness of all. Commensurately, while the low intelligence group will show less physiognomic sensitivity than the high intelligence group, those low in creativity as well as intelligence will tend to show the least physiognomic sensitivity of all. Similar statements hold, of course, when we consider the creativity dimension. While high creativity boys tend to be more physiognomically sensitive than those low in creativity, that subset of the high creativity group whose intelligence level also is high shows the greatest physiognomic awareness of all. Similarly, that subset of the low creativity group whose intelligence level also is low exhibits the least physiognomic sensitivity of all.

A cautionary note must be sounded at this juncture, for a strict additive model obviously requires that both intelligence and creativity yield statistically significant effects. On two of the three tasks, this did not happen. Rather, in those cases one of the modes of thinking made a significant contribution, while the operation of the other was reflected only in nonsignificant mean differences in the appropriate direction. It should be stressed, however, that we have proceeded in a very conservative manner by dividing our samples at the median into high and low intelligence and creativity subgroups. More stringent criteria of classification—upper and lower thirds or quarters, for example—could be expected to enhance the magnitude of differences observed. Sample sizes did not really permit these fine subdivisions in the present investigation. However, the results reported here should provide a point of departure for more rigorous tests of the proposed model.

The results for the girls, although consistent in some respects with those of the boys, led to a somewhat different formulation. While findings on the task involving completely abstract stimuli were inconclusive for the girls, results for the two tasks whose stimuli provided depictive referents for human behavior suggested that the high creativity–low intelligence group may avoid making physiognomic discriminations for motivational reasons. Their physiognomic sensitivity was about as poor as that found for the low-low group. Such an interpretation was congruent with the general view of the high creativity–low intelligence group that had emerged from earlier evidence: namely, that they were socially avoidant, that this avoidance was reciprocated, that they were wrapped up in solitary fantasy pursuits, and that they were most likely to relate to peers or teachers in disruptive ways. We proposed, therefore, that while the poor physiognomic sensitivity of the low-low group reflected a general lack of capacity not specific to the physiognomic domain as such, the poor sensitivity of the group high in creativity but low in intelligence reflected an avoidance of specifically physiognomic discriminations.

Further evidence suggesting the role of motivational considerations in the present domain appeared in connection with a procedure that permitted study of the child's willingness to entertain bizarre or "far-out" hypotheses about the affective states that might be depicted by given instances of human gestural behavior. While the male results for this task were inconclusive, the female findings indicated that one group seemed to be particularly avoidant of entertaining such hypotheses: the girls of high intelligence but low creativity. Earlier evidence concerning this particular group had suggested that it comprised individuals who were overcontrolled and conforming to classroom norms—reserved and fearful of overcommitment on the one hand, but self-assured concerning routine classroom activities on the other. Here was a group, in other words, which might avoid certain physiognomic possibilities for motivational reasons.

The data at hand for the females, therefore, were too complex to order in terms of the assumptions of an additive model. Although congruent in part with this model, the data seemed to call for additional explanatory principles to account for the behavior of the high-low and low-high groups—principles that possessed a motivational flavor. While in some instances the effects of creativity and intelligence upon physiognomic sensitivity seemed to be additive, in other instances these effects seemed to be interactive.

In the light of the present chapter's results, what can we say about the relationships among creativity, intelligence, and physiognomic sensitivity? Earlier in the chapter, we introduced the possible role of creativity for physiognomic sensitivity in terms of the hypothesis that high creatives are more able to draw upon developmentally primitive and/or affectively relevant experiences than are low creatives. We postulated the first source as an explication in terms of nativistic interpretations, the second source as a specification based upon empiricistic interpretations of how physiognomic sensitivity comes about. Both ideas, as we noted, had in common the assumption that greater creativity involved increased openness to one or another range of experience. Had the additive model been sufficient to embrace all our findings, the hypothesis just presented would have been sufficient as an interpretation of creativity's contribution. Given the more complex picture that emerges when we consider the female data, however, a somewhat different view of the matter may be closer to the truth. Of particular relevance may be the distinction between those subgroups whose levels of creativity and intelligence are *congruent*, and those subgroups whose levels of creativity and intelligence are *noncongruent*.

When a group is low both in creativity and intelligence, the ability to make physiognomic discriminations may be minimal. The kinds of inferential capacities underlying the general intelligence concept and the associational abilities underlying our conception of creativity are weak. Both kinds of abilities might well be expected to contribute to physiognomic sensitivity, since the display of such sensitivity involves inferential translations from one mode of experience to another, and involves associational freedom in order to bring together the diverse elements of experience in question. When a group is high both in creativity and intelligence, therefore, the two kinds of abilities might well summate to yield the highest levels of physiognomic sensitivity, just as when a group is low both in creativity and intelligence, the joint absence of the two types of abilities would yield the lowest levels of physiognomic sensitivity. So much is consistent with the additive model that we have considered. For the subgroups that are noncongruent in creativity and intelligence, however, some of the abilities that should enhance physiognomic sensitivity are present. When, under these conditions, it is disproportionately low, a reasonable presumption is that motivational forces are operating in an inhibitory fashion. For high creativity–low intelligence individuals, inhibition of physiognomic discriminations may be in the service of tendencies toward the avoidance of other persons and a retreat into solitary fantasy. For high intelligence–low creativity individuals, on the other hand, inhibition of physiognomic discriminations may be in the service of tendencies toward the avoidance of possible sources of errors and mistakes in cognitive activities.

Our proposal, in sum, is that the additive model operates, but within certain motivationally defined limits. If a group whose levels of creativity and intelligence are noncongruent displays disproportionately lowered levels of physiognomic sensitivity, we may suspect that a motivational factor is operating so as to inhibit the display of such sensitivity. A different motivational factor is postulated as relevant for each of the two noncongruent groups. If, on the other hand, a noncongruent group displays an intermediate degree of physiognomic sensitivity, then the additive model seems to apply, since such an outcome would be expected on the assumption that some but not all of the abilities involved in physiognomic sensitivity were available.

SUMMARY

In this chapter we have considered an individual's ability to make physiognomic inferences—inferences about affective meanings—from visual stimuli. Three procedures were utilized which varied in the degree to which their stimulus materials contained a concrete depiction of human expressive behavior, or rather were more abstract. For human stick figure stimuli depicting expressive gestures, and for lines depicting the paths of movement traversed by hypothetical persons, we measured the extent to which the child's free descriptions conveyed information about the affective states of the persons depicted, or rather were confined to statements about their physical characteristics. For visual patterns that were fully abstract—that contained no depictive referent in human expressive behavior—we measured the extent to which the child's choices of affective linkages agreed with those of adult judges. In a fourth procedure, we assessed the child's willingness to go beyond the making of obviously appropriate affective attributions for human stick-figure stimuli and entertain in addition hypotheses that involved relatively bizarre attributions.

The results for the boys suggested that both creativity and intelligence serve to augment physiognomic sensitivity, though one or the other of these thinking modes made a more substantial contribution dependent upon the physiognomic procedure at issue. In general, however, awareness of physiognomic properties tended to be maximal in the subgroup high in both creativity and intelligence, while such awareness tended to be minimal in the subgroup low in both creativity and intelligence. For the girls, the findings were similar in part to those just noted, but in part also suggested that under some conditions, noncongruent subgroups—those in which creativity and intelligence levels are different rather than similar—experience as much difficulty in making physiognomic attributions as members of the low-low subgroup.

To summarize the interpretation to which our results appear to lead:

General intelligence is conceived to further physiognomic sensitivity through the person's ability to carry out inference processes, translations from affective to visual types of experience constituting one class of inferences. Creativity is thought to further physiognomic sensitivity by means of the individual's ability to generate associates that are plentiful and unique, since linkages between affective and visual experiences may well be facilitated by conditions of associational freedom. Given the relative orthogonality of intelligence and creativity, these proposals constitute an additive model according to which physiognomic sensitivity should be maximized in the presence of both creativity and intelligence, minimized in the absence of both, and intermediate when one is present in the absence of the other. Our findings in part were consistent with this model, but in part required the further postulate that particular motivational processes may be operating in those cases where levels of intelligence and creativity are noncongruent—that is, when one is high and the other low. Depressed levels of physiognomic sensitivity under each of the two possible circumstances of noncongruence suggested, when evaluated in the context of earlier results, a distinctive pattern of motivational involvement that hindered the individual's efforts to cope with physiognomic materials. For those of high creativity but low intelligence, the motivational problem seemed to concern a link between the humanlike properties of physiognomic stimuli and a tendency in real life to withdraw from interaction with other people. For those of high intelligence but low creativity, the motivational problem seemed to concern an excessive fear of making mistakes.

The present chapter's findings thus aid in the understanding of physiognomic sensitivity, on the one hand, and of the creativity–intelligence distinction, on the other. Issues bearing upon capacity and motivation may be intertwined within the creativity–intelligence contrast in such a way that questions of capacity are foremost in the cases of the congruent subgroups—those who are both creative and intelligent or are neither—while questions of motivation arise in the cases of the noncongruent subgroups—those who are creative but not intelligent, or intelligent but not creative.

6 ⟪⟪⟪

The Role of
Anxiety and
Defensiveness

It is now common knowledge that a close relationship exists between thinking processes and motivational states. With regard to the modes of thinking inherent in intelligence and creativity, there are two particular motivational or personality variables that appear to have a critical influence—anxiety and defensiveness. Both derive from psychoanalytic theory, and in that theory, stand in a close interactive relationship with each other. It will be our aim in the present chapter to show how this motivational interaction impinges upon the creativity and intelligence domains. In doing so, however, we shall first distinguish analytically between anxiety and defensiveness by attempting a reasonable definition of each of them. Then, we shall go on to consider relevant theoretical speculation and empirical evidence linking anxiety and defensiveness to creativity and intelligence. It is not our goal, however, to carry out an exhaustive survey of studies in the present area. The interested reader may consult Stein and Heinze (1960) or the other sources cited in Chapter 1 for a complete list of relevant creativity references. Ruebush (1963) provides an excellent review of studies bearing upon anxiety and defensiveness as determinants of intelligence. Our intent here is to make a critical selection of the most relevant theoretical and empirical contributions, thereby providing a background perspective for our research findings. It will become clear that previous evidence leaves serious gaps in our knowledge concerning the relation of children's creativity and intelligence to their levels of anxiety and defensiveness. We trust that the present chapter will provide at least a partial remedy to this condition.

Anxiety

Let us turn now to matters of definition. Following Freud (1936), we conceive of anxiety as an experiential phenomenon. It is a state that is perceived as basically unpleasant, with physiological concomitants often present. Little purpose would be served here by a lengthy discussion of psychoanalytic theorizing about the source of this conscious anxiety. In brief, anxiety and fear in the classic psychoanalytic framework are distinguished in terms of dangers stemming from within and outside the individual, respectively. But as Erikson (1950) has indicated, children do not make clear-cut distinctions between inner and outer events or between real and imagined dangers. In their review of the literature on children's anxieties and fears, Sarason, Davidson, Lighthall, Waite, and Ruebush (1960) point out "that the majority of the *specific* fears reported by children have little or no basis in reality . . . these specific fears seem to serve as focal points or screens for anxiety about situations, impulses, and conflicts which possess extremely dangerous implications for the child's security" (p. 47). Given these circumstances, the emphasis has shifted from the study of children's fears (for example, Jersild & Holmes, 1935) to the present-day concern with anxiety in children.

How have psychologists attempted to measure the construct of experiential anxiety? For one group of investigators, the operational specification of the anxiety variable in children has derived from Taylor's (1953) anxiety scale for adults. Castaneda, McCandless, and Palermo (1956) selected those items from the Taylor Manifest Anxiety Scale judged to be most appropriate for children and constituted them as a Children's Manifest Anxiety Scale. The scale presumes to measure the child's tendency to experience a general, chronic state of anxiety, and on that basis has served as an indirect index of drive level in Spence's (1958) theoretical network.

An alternative operational approach is represented by the General Anxiety Scale for Children devised by Sarason *et al.* (1960). In the present case, the items selected for the scale were intended to be consistent with the Freudian conception of children's anxiety. Item content reflected situations that Freud (1936) believed likely to elicit anxiety in many children (such as high places, sight of blood, prolonged parental absence).

A Test Anxiety Scale for Children (Sarason *et al.*, 1960) was developed in a manner comparable to the Children's Manifest Anxiety Scale cited earlier. A questionnaire measure of test anxiety had been constructed for adults (Mandler & Sarason, 1952), and hence the modification of that instrument for use with children was a quite straightforward matter.

The distinction between general and test anxiety could conceivably be of some significance in the study of children, given the major influence of the school situation in our culture. Whereas the generally anxious child might readily generalize his predominantly negative affect to encompass the school situation, there may well be other children relatively low in general anxiety, for whom anxiety is aroused almost exclusively by the evaluative aspects of the educational setting.

Let us turn then to one of the major questions posed by the present chapter. Does a child's anxiety state, when assessed by scales such as those previously described, bear any relation to his cognitive performances in the areas of intelligence and creativity? Such performances, particularly in the sphere of intelligence, are an integral part of the contemporary school scene. There is a vast literature relevant to the question, virtually all of it devoted to the anxiety–intelligence association. In fact, the authors have been able to locate but three papers pertinent to the issue of creativity and anxiety in children. In the first of these, Reid, King, and Wickwire (1959) report relationships between creativity and anxiety in seventh grade children. Creativity was measured by peer nominations,[1] and anxiety was assessed with the Children's Manifest Anxiety Scale (Castaneda, McCandless, & Palermo, 1956). The results of the Reid *et al.* study indicate that the creative children manifest fewer anxiety symptoms. It is doubtful, however, whether this finding should be taken too seriously. When creativity is defined in terms of peer nominations ("classmates who 'have good imaginations. They have new ideas and new ways of doing things' "), it is evidently the child making an impact on the group who will receive the most nominations. These are not likely to be anxious children. Hence, the results can be directly attributed to the rather special meaning of the creativity dimension in this particular study. In the second relevant study, Flescher (1963) reported an absence of relationship between either general or test anxiety, on the one hand, and a composite creativity score, on the other. However, as discussed in Chapter 1, the elements in this composite turned out not to be unified among themselves, thus rendering interpretation ambiguous. In the third study, Feldhusen, Denny, and Condon (1965) found little relationship between general anxiety and four creativity measures in seventh and eighth graders. Again, however, the creativity indices were minimally related to one another.

In striking contrast to the paucity of empirical work on the creativity—anxiety problem, a large number of investigations have been devoted to the examination of relations between anxiety and traditional intelli-

---

[1] See Chapter 3 for a critique of this method of measuring creativity in children.

gence indices. Ruebush (1963) cites nineteen studies that have found small to moderate negative relationships between measures of anxiety and intelligence test scores. Associations tend to be somewhat higher for test anxiety than for general anxiety, a result clearly in accord with expectations. A recent study by Sarason, Hill and Zimbardo (1964) reports the same negative relationships.

The anxiety–intelligence linkage is evidently quite consistent and stable. The prevalent interpretation of this linkage can be directly traced to the work of Sarason and his co-workers (1960), who maintain that anxiety is the etiologically significant variable. Three arguments along with relevant data are advanced in support of the position that the causal sequence proceeds in the direction of anxiety influencing intellective performance.

The first of these arguments states that the performance of highly anxious children on intelligence tests will vary as a function of the degree to which the tests are saturated with testlike cues. If intelligence were the etiological factor, its relationship with anxiety should not be particularly affected by considerations of situational context. The results of several studies show, however, that the test's content and context do make a difference. Thus, Zweibelson (1956) found that the Test Anxiety Scale for Children correlated significantly more highly with the Otis tests (—.28 and —.24 for Beta and Alpha, respectively) than with the Davis-Eells task (—.14). Note that the Otis tests are administered in a testlike atmosphere under speeded conditions and with little praise or reassurance offered the child. The Davis-Eells task, on the other hand, is given in a gamelike atmosphere with ample time and substantial provision for praise and reassurance. In a sequel to the foregoing study, Lighthall, Ruebush, Sarason, and Zweibelson (1959) observed changes in intellective test performances over the fifth to seventh grades as a function of test anxiety level. The results indicated that the low anxious children exhibited greater gains on the Otis Beta than did the children with high anxiety levels, while the reverse effect was obtained in the case of the Davis-Eells task. In the latter case, the highly anxious children manifested improvements in performance exceeding those of the low anxious children. In sum, low anxiety contributes to a progressive facilitation of performance on conventional intelligence tests, while high anxiety appears to enhance performance over time on an intelligence test distinguished by a gamelike format.

Let us now proceed to the second argument for an anxiety-to-intelligence causal sequence as advanced by Sarason and his associates (1960). If intelligence were the etiological determinant, then matching subjects on intelligence should reveal that anxiety bears no relation to performance on an intellective task. The evidence demonstrates, however, that anxiety makes a difference even in the case where subjects are matched in intelligence. Thus, the Yale group (Waite, Sarason, Lighthall, & Davidson, 1958) observed that the matching of intelligence scores on Otis Beta did not eliminate a significant relationship between anxiety and speed of paired associate learning. Subjects low in anxiety learned more rapidly. In a subsequent study, Davidson (1959) found a significant relationship in boys (though not in girls) between anxiety and school grades, with intelligence once again held constant.

We turn finally to the third argument advanced by the Sarason team. If intelligence is the causal agent in the intelligence–anxiety relationship, then one should anticipate that the relationship would disappear in an intellectually superior group (such as a student group which has succeeded in gaining admission to a highly selective Ivy League college). In actuality, the correlations between test anxiety and intellective performance in such samples are negative and statistically significant (Alpert & Haber, 1960; Mandler & Sarason, 1952). This third argument, as advanced by Sarason *et al.* (1960), is clearly somewhat weaker than the other two. The intellectual level of the student bodies of highly selective colleges is not nearly as homogeneous as the Yale group contends. Hence the correlations obtained do not provide unequivocal evidence in favor of the directional interpretation advocated by the Sarason team. Nevertheless, the supportive data available for each of the three arguments posed lend considerable weight to the claim that anxiety exercises a causal influence upon performance on intelligence tests.

On the basis of the foregoing evidence in the intelligence domain, can any inferences be drawn concerning the influence of anxiety on creativity? It has been demonstrated that anxiety's inhibiting effects are much reduced when the testlike attributes of the conventional intelligence test format are removed. The conditions of administration for the Davis-Eells games have very much in common with the creativity procedures employed in the present investigation. The major difference concerns the kind of thinking operation demanded—the convergent form in the Davis-Eells task and the divergent form in the five creativity procedures used. Although the Davis-Eells procedure is presented to the child as a game, the child is required to find the "right" answer. Not surprisingly, Davis-Eells scores correlate significantly with scores on the Otis Beta. In contrast, the composite score on the creativity dimension is statistically independent of the intelligence composite in the present study. This would lead to the expectation that anxiety will have even less of an effect on creativity than on performance in the Davis-Eells task.

Is it conceivable that anxiety could have a facilitating effect on creativity in children? There is no unequivocal empirical evidence available to permit either an affirmative or negative answer to this query. We might, however, approach the question in an indirect way, and inquire whether there is any evidence suggesting that anxiety may enhance intellective performance on particular types of tasks and/or under certain conditions of administration. It will then be possible to compare those tasks and/or conditions with those descriptive of the creativity domain in the present study.

Again, the relevant investigations derive from the work of the Yale group. Thus, Ruebush (1960) compared the performance of low and high anxious children on the Embedded Figures Test (Witkin *et al.*, 1954; Witkin *et al.*, 1962), and observed that the high anxious relative to the low anxious children solved more figures in less time. Ruebush then goes on to interpret these findings on the basis of the greater cautiousness of the highly anxious child, which happened to "pay off" given the particular conditions under which the Embedded Figures Test was administered. These conditions were quite permissive, the child being informed that he could look at the original (simple) figure as often as he liked without penalty, and that guessing was permitted and would not count against him. As Sarason *et al.* (1960) note, "the task is structured so that a cautious approach in which the subject makes sure that he knows the correct response *before* he makes a guess will be rewarded by success (since the watch continues running during guesses). Put in another way, the situation is such that the child who is dependent and cautious is not penalized—if anything these characteristics work in his favor" (p. 170).

Another study reporting an anxiety facilitating effect was carried out by Waite (1959) and is described in considerable detail in Sarason *et al.* (1960). In brief, the Stroop (1935) color-word test and the Porteus (1959) mazes were administered to a sample of low and high anxious children. The results took the form of an anxiety-by-task interaction, the low anxious children doing relatively better on the Stroop than the Porteus and the high anxious children manifesting the opposite pattern. It should be noted that the Stroop and Porteus differ markedly in terms of the amount of time pressure under which the child functions. In the case of the Stroop, a mistake adds to one's error score, and if an attempt is made to correct it, this contributes to a poorer time score. The Porteus mazes, on the other hand, resemble the Embedded Figures Test used in the Ruebush (1960) study. As Sarason *et al.* (1960) note, "the child can correct covert mistakes without showing them overtly merely by looking ahead and engaging in vicarious trial-and-error activity at the choice points of a given maze. He is under no pressure to hurry and as a result the more cautious he is the better he will do" (p. 176).

The foregoing evidence suggests a class of tasks and conditions of administration in which anxiety is associated with higher levels of performance. The tasks are of a sort in which the child can anticipate and monitor the kind of response required, with the result that a cautious approach is rewarded. Conditions of administration are of a type in which the child is not under time pressure and in which the experimenter plays a supportive role. On the basis of the foregoing characteristics of tasks and instructional contexts, Sarason and his co-workers (1960) conclude that it would be a mistaken notion to attribute facilitative effects to anxiety. Rather, they prefer to conceive of task and situational conditions under which the highly anxious child does not really experience anxiety to the degree that it interferes with problem-solving activity. That the high anxious child does better than the low anxious child in the present case is explained in terms of the gratification of dependency needs in a supportive experimental situation and the operation of a cautious style of responding congruent with task requirements.

Does the work described above have any implications for a possible relation between anxiety and creativity in children? A major emphasis in the present volume has been placed upon the conditions under which creativity is assessed. Recall that our creativity procedures have been administered in a gamelike context, with the child permitted to proceed at his natural pace and the experimenter offering as much encouragement as the child requires. As we have seen, these are precisely the conditions under which the highly anxious child performs best in the Yale studies. Hence, the prediction that highly anxious children will be more creative would appear to be warranted. Such a prediction is quite premature, however, in the light of the other characteristic contributing to the superior performance of highly anxious children—a tendency toward cautiousness in venturing responses. It is difficult to imagine just how a cautious style could facilitate performance in creativity tasks of the associative type. Cautiousness would be expected to contribute to a self-censoring response inhibition, and thereby to the generation of few associates. There might, however, be an element of cautiousness involved in the type of obsessive refusal to relinquish a problem that could, under some circumstances, lead to high creativity scores. In sum, one component—the gamelike context—suggests that anxiety might facilitate creativity; the other component—a cautious response style in the anxious child—suggests that anxiety might inhibit or possibly facilitate creativity. On the basis of this divergence, it is virtually impossible to extrapolate directly from the evidence of the Yale studies to the work discussed in the present chapter.

Summing up, it has been quite firmly established that anxiety influences scores obtained on conventional intelligence measures in both children and adults. On the other hand, evidence regarding a possible link between anxiety and creativity in children is quite sparse. Although the interfering effects of anxiety are considerably reduced when intellective performances are assessed under permissive, gamelike conditions, the tasks used in previous research have been quite remote from the creativity domain. Hence, the research results reported in the present chapter should contribute to our knowledge of the relation between anxiety and creativity in children.

Defensiveness

If a broad distinction is made between states and styles in personality dynamics, anxiety may be viewed as an experiential state giving rise to various coping reactions, while defensiveness may be described as a particular pervasive style of coping with anxiety. Thus far, we have focused upon the experiential state and ignored the style of coping. The present section of the chapter will attempt to redress the balance.

Although Freud (1925) appears to have conceived of anxiety as an experiential state, he did make use of the term "unconscious anxiety" to refer to a potential disposition toward anxiety in the event of an increase in strength of dangerous drives and/or a breakdown in ego-defenses. It is evident, then, that Freud implicitly conceived of individual variations in the degree to which the ego-defenses protected the person against overt anxiety. For some persons, the drives and conflicts are so strong and/or the defenses are so weak that the person frequently experiences a state of anxiety. For other individuals, anxiety exercises a "signal function" exclusively; the defenses are invoked at the first indication of impending danger. Such persons would rarely experience anxiety, for their defenses serve the protective function of keeping repressed material out of consciousness. At first blush, this may seem highly adaptive. But as Ruebush (1963) has noted, the defense systems "may be efficient or inefficient in the role they play in the over-all personality functioning of the child. A child whose defense system is rigid and inflexible may use defenses which interfere with other behavioral processes, whereas the child who has acquired a variety of defenses may 'match' the defense to the danger and the over-all situation so as to maximize protection from danger and, at the same time, minimize interference with other aspects of intellectual and personality functioning" (pp. 468–469).

The deleterious effects of processes variously described as defensiveness, denial, or repression have been well documented in the clinical literature. For example, White (1956), building on psychoanalytic theory, conceives of "defensive inhibition" (a concept closely akin to denial or repression) as the individual's basic means of maladaptive protection against threat, and one which is presupposed in any of the other classic defense mechanisms described by Anna Freud (1946). As another example, Rogers (1959a) treats defensiveness and its opposite, openness to experience, as the pivotal dimension in his approach to a theory of personality. It is thus apparent that a construct on the order of defensiveness occupies a central position in theoretical systems as diverse as psychoanalysis and the Rogerian client-centered framework.

Despite the clinical centrality of a concept of defensiveness, the experimental literature has only recently begun to turn up empirical studies relating defensiveness to various cognitive performances. Most of the experimental effort has apparently been concentrated on the assessment of anxiety and its influences. Indeed, defensiveness has been treated as an "error" phenomenon that impinges upon the validity of attempts to measure anxiety states. Thus, we find the label of "lie scale" attached to various psychometric efforts at eliminating the influence of defensiveness on "content" scales (for example, Castaneda et al., 1956; Hathaway & McKinley, 1943; Sarason et al., 1960). Note the implication of conscious intent that the label "lie scale" carries, an implication that clearly is inappropriate when we consider the defensiveness concept.

Let us turn then to the measurement of defensiveness in children. As we have just indicated, both the Children's Manifest Anxiety Scale and the General Anxiety Scale for Children were provided with lie scales. Both of these scales presume to measure the child's tendency to censor or falsify responses to anxiety items, though the lie scale associated with the Castaneda et al. (1956) instrument is intended to tap general lying tendencies while the Sarason et al. (1960) lie scale is concerned with the tendency to be defensive about anxiety-relevant experiences specifically. Under these circumstances, it is perhaps not too surprising that the latter lie scale shows a strong inverse relationship to the anxiety scores derived from either anxiety scale, while the former (the Castaneda et al. lie scale) yields only a slight negative relationship to the anxiety indices.

Given the exceptionally high negative correlation between the General Anxiety Scale for Children and its lie scale, the Yale group (subsequent to the publication of the Sarason et al. [1960] volume) proceeded to develop a Defensiveness Scale for Children to be used in conjunction with their Test Anxiety Scale. This new defensiveness instrument was composed by adding twenty-seven new items to the original eleven-item lie scale. Three of these new items were neutral fillers intended to pick up a negative response set, and the remaining twenty-four were "designed to measure the tendency to deny the experience of negative feelings such as anxiety, guilt, hostility, and inadequacy, even when their expression is appropriate" (Ruebush, 1963, p. 486). Note, finally, that a short unidimensional defensiveness scale, developed independently of the work of the Yale group, was constructed for use with young children in studies of expressive behavior (Wallach, Green, Lipsitt, & Minehart, 1962).

It now appears to be standard practice to administer the Defensiveness Scale for Children along with the General and/or Test Anxiety Scales for Children (Davidson & Sarason, 1961; Ruebush, Byrum, & Farnham, 1963; Ruebush & Waite, 1961; Zimbardo, Barnard, & Berkowitz, 1963). Indeed, one of the foregoing studies (Ruebush, Byrum, & Farnham, 1963) focuses upon defensiveness as the key antecedent variable, test anxiety being relegated to the status of a control. This obviously represents a radical shift in emphasis from the "lie scale" approach.

Thus far, we have focused upon self-report measures of defensiveness. There are, in addition, projective approaches to the measurement of defensiveness that are at least worthy of mention. The approach of particular relevance to the present chapter concerns the cognitive avoidance of particular content in story completion procedures. Miller and Swanson (1960), Kagan and Moss (1961), and Rosenwald (1961), among others, have utilized verbal fantasy or story materials as a basis for inferring a tendency to deny or inhibit the expression of a particular impulse or motive. In the Miller-Swanson (1960) technique, for example, stories were presented depicting a sequence of happenings culminating in failure for the hero. The child was to complete each story, and denial was scored if the story completion ignored, disregarded, or dealt unrealistically with the failure.

There is no basis for assuming, of course, that fantasy and self-report indices of defensiveness will positively relate to each other. We shall later offer empirical evidence relevant to this question.

We are now ready to inquire into the implications of defensiveness for intelligence and creativity. Relevant studies relating defensiveness to intelligence are quite meagre relative to the abundance of papers devoted to the anxiety–intelligence issue. The creativity–defensiveness link, on the other hand, has engendered a great deal of theoretical speculation and a few empirical investigations, though none of the latter have used children as subjects.

Consider first the association between intelligence and defensiveness. If one accepts the view that defensive children have a strong predisposition toward anxiety which is kept in check by a powerful set of defenses, one might expect anxious and defensive children to share certain characteristics in common that set them apart from less disturbed children. Some support for this hypothesis is offered by Ruebush and Waite (1961), who report that dependency needs have a prominent function in the personalities of test-anxious and defensive boys, though expressed more directly in the former and more subtly in the latter subgroup. This finding failed to hold in the case of girls, however. Wallach *et al.* (1962) found defensive first grade girls and anxious adult females to share tendencies toward contradiction in the realm of expressive behavior, but a bridge across age differences is involved in this comparison.

Although there may be evidence for commonalities in anxious and defensive children at the level of deeper needs and motives, it is doubtful whether these commonalities can be extended to include intellective performances. Whereas the test-anxious child is disrupted in an evaluative testing situation, we should anticipate that the defensive child, by virtue of his strong defenses for coping with anxiety, will take a conventional intelligence test in stride, showing little of the performance decrement that characterizes the anxious child. Much to the authors' surprise, very little published evidence relevant to the foregoing hypothesis could be located. Rosenwald (1961) finds no difference between low and high defensive students of high school age in scores obtained on the Information subtest of the Wechsler Adult Intelligence Scale. There is also some indication in the Ruebush *et al.* (1963) study that low and high defensive boys have comparable scores on the Lorge-Thorndike Intelligence Test, but this observation is based on a sample of boys derived by excluding those whose IQ scores were below 100 or above 120. Within the same study, however, low and high defensive boys were contrasted in performance on the Porteus mazes. The findings turn out to be highly relevant to the issue of a possible relation between intelligence and defensiveness. They "suggest that a test situation which is heavily loaded with components unfamiliar to the child is more threatening and consequently more likely to mobilize processes which interfere with quantitative performance in defensive children than are evaluative stimuli; defensive children may not experience anxiety or the threat of anxiety when in a relatively familiar situation—even one loaded with evaluative cues—and thus perform quantitatively at a level commensurate with their ability" (Ruebush, Byrum, & Farnham, 1963, p. 361). As the experiment turned out, the performance of the high defensive boys was inferior to that of the low defensive boys only in the experimental condition where the children experienced a completely unfamiliar situation. This was a condition in which the child was temporarily parted from his mother and subjected to a new task administered by a stranger.

An experiment by Zimbardo, Barnard, and Berkowitz (1963) yields results that are highly consistent with those obtained by Ruebush *et al.* (1963). Boys varying in anxiety and defensiveness were exposed to either an evaluative or permissive interview. In the evaluative case, the child was informed that he would be asked some questions about himself preparatory to taking a test to be used to compare him with other children. In the case of the permissive interview, the child was simply told that the interviewer wished to chat with him about his thoughts and feelings on various matters. The results indicated that the low anxious–high defensive boys yielded considerably higher levels of incomprehensibility and affect under permissive relative to evaluative interview conditions.

Furthermore, these boys also expressed a great deal of inappropriate affect in the permissive interview context. In marked contrast, highly anxious boys showed heightened affect and incomprehensibility levels in the evaluative interview condition.

The interpretation of these results is quite straightforward. The negative behavioral consequences of placing highly anxious subjects in an evaluative situation is highly consistent with all of the evidence presented in the previous section of the chapter. Evidently, anxiety not only hinders effective performance on intelligence tests; it also disrupts verbal communication between the child and an adult figure occupying an evaluative position vis-à-vis the child. For the defensive child, on the other hand, it is not the evaluative aspect that is disturbing. For such children, their habitual patterns of defense are quite capable of dealing with an evaluative situation. It is rather the unstructured and unfamiliar features of the permissive interview that are upsetting, for no specific cues are provided as to what constitutes appropriate behavior. As Zimbardo *et al.* (1963) point out, low anxious–high defensive children "under permissive conditions are concerned not only about failure, but about fear of self-revelation, favorable or unfavorable, and are unable to utilize effectively their established defensive-denial pattern of behavior" (p. 83).

In sum, there is firm evidence in the literature that the cognitive functioning of highly defensive children is most likely to be impaired in contexts distinguished by unfamiliarity and/or ambiguity. The conventional intelligence tests do not belong in that rubric, and, hence, one would anticipate a negligible relationship between intelligence and defensiveness scores. But what of creativity? The kinds of tasks employed as measures of creativity are very likely to impress the child by their strangeness and lack of clear structure. The experimenter, after all, insists that there is no single correct answer. In short, the nature of creativity procedures leads us to expect that defensive children will perform more poorly than their less defensive peers.

The foregoing hypothesis is most certainly not original to the present authors. As we have indicated, there has been much theorizing about the issue of creativity and defensiveness, and, in addition, a few relevant empirical studies with adults can be cited. Still, it is quite surprising that the burgeoning research on creativity in children, on the one hand, and on anxiety and defensiveness in children, on the other, should not have generated a single empirical study bridging the two research traditions. Possibly, the difference in conceptual approach has been too great. Where creativity is at issue, the usual procedure with adults has involved the delineation of high and low creative subgroups and subsequent examination of the personal qualities associated with subjects' creativity statuses. The conceptualization has been of a personological sort, emphasizing the existence of creative and noncreative persons who could then be distinguished further in terms of personality structure and dynamics. The work of the Institute of Personality Assessment and Research (for example, Barron, 1963; Crutchfield, 1962; MacKinnon, 1962) typifies the foregoing strategy. The IPAR studies do not generally make causal statements in which antecedent and consequent status are assigned to the creativity and personality domains, respectively. Nevertheless, the stress upon creativity as a characteristic of persons has led to investigations in which the procedural sequence has generally been in the direction of creativity to personality.

In marked contrast to the foregoing work, the Yale group (for example, Sarason *et al.*, 1960) has focused on anxiety and defensiveness as *determinants* of cognitive performances. Thus, intelligence is not viewed as a "state" variable or an immutable quality of persons, but rather is conceived to represent the outcome of an interaction between motivational and situational factors. The Yale group has been quite explicit in attributing a causal sequence to the motivation–cognition relationship. Cognition is given the status of consequent, motivation the status of antecedent.

The authors have no intention of committing themselves to one or the other causal sequence at the present time. The choice must be made on the basis of theoretical and practical utility, and conceivably the choice might not be the same for the intelligence and creativity domains. We shall proceed to look at the data both ways, and attempt to derive the most meaningful interpretations possible.

Let us return now to the creativity–defensiveness question. Although there has been no previous research with children directed specifically to this question, we might briefly state the basis on which we hypothesize an inverse relationship between creativity and defensiveness, and then go on to note whether the hypothesis derives any support from the rich theoretical literature and/or from the few relevant empirical studies carried out with adult subjects. It is our view that the associative conception of creativity presupposes the availability of disparate and hitherto unrelated strands of experience among which new similarities may be perceived and new connections made. Defensiveness, on the other hand, implies a narrowing of awareness regarding certain kinds of experiences and hence a reduction in the range of cue availability or similarity breadth typical of high levels of creativity. We are suggesting, in other words, that there will be a lack of openness to cue utilization in the defensive child. The expected consequence is a weakness in integrating the diverse elements of experience required for performance of a creative sort.

What support does the foregoing hypothesis muster in the psychological literature?[2] We might begin with Thurstone (1952), who spoke of the creative individual as one standing in good rapport with his own preconscious thinking. Kubie (1958), defining the creative process as "the capacity to find new and unexpected connections," likewise assigns an important role to the availability of preconscious symbolic processes. Kris (1953) and Schafer (1958) refer to the heightened availability of these preconscious symbolic processes in creativity as "regression in the service of the ego." Maslow (1959) considers the most significant forms of creativity to derive from the unconscious, and hence to be impaired for individuals whose primary process material is inaccessible. Likewise, Rogers (1959b) has pointed out that, "when the individual is 'open' to all of his experience . . . then his behavior will be creative." Basing his views on the study of psychotherapeutic cases, Rogers sees the lack of creativity as arising from the repression or denial of aspects of one's experience. Finally, Rosenwald (1961), in contrasting the effects of anxiety and defensiveness upon cognitive performances, notes that "defense may exert its influence through the mediation of cognitive rigidity and the narrowing of attention and associative processes" (p. 671).[3]

Let us turn now to the supporting empirical evidence. It must be noted that most of the relevant research was underway or completed before an adequate index of defensiveness in adults (for example, Crowne & Marlowe, 1960) was devised. Accordingly, investigators tended to use a variety of procedures, objective and projective, to tap constructs more or less closely related to defensiveness. Of course, this heterogeneity in use of instruments makes it difficult to compare studies effectively. Nevertheless, let us plunge into this literature and try to discern whether the findings reported fall into a consistent pattern.

In *Creativity and psychological health*, Barron (1963) summarizes all of his major contributions in the area of creativity. Of particular relevance here are Barron's attempts to measure a dimension labeled "rejection of suppression; tendency towards expression of impulse." A number of measures are reported (p. 211), but the one that appears to approximate a defensiveness construct most closely consists of an MMPI index based on the sum of the Pd and Ma scales subtracted from the sum of the L, Hy, and K scales. When Barron's subjects—United States Air Force captains—are divided into low and high creative subgroups, it is the former who obtain significantly higher scores on the

---

[2] Again, the references cited are a representative, not an exhaustive, listing.

[3] The effects cited by Rosenwald (1961) are attributed to anxiety or arousal states by other investigators (for example, Easterbrook, 1959). A recent review by Korchin (1964) suggests, however, that the mechanisms whereby anxiety influences attentional processes are far from clear.

MMPI index described. It should be further noted that the high creative subgroup achieves a significantly larger mean score than do the low creatives on the Impulsivity Scale of the California Psychological Inventory (Gough, 1957). In a subsequent chapter, Barron goes on to demonstrate that relations hold up for the Impulsivity Scale when intelligence (measured by the Terman [1956] Concept Mastery Test) is partialled out. For some unexplained reason, however, the MMPI index no longer discriminates between low and high creatives. Instead, it is undercontrol on an "Ego-control" Scale and the Rorschach color-responsiveness index (sum C) that relate positively to creativity when intelligence is partialled out. In sum, the Barron work suggests that it may be impulsiveness rather than defensiveness as such which is most directly associated with creativity in adults. Of course, impulsiveness is a trait which might well relate negatively to defensiveness, and so it is of interest that the former is linked to creativity in the expected direction.

Results reported by MacKinnon (1962) in his study of architects conform quite closely to Barron's findings for Air Force captains. It is the more creative architects who are "relatively free from conventional restraints and inhibitions . . . and relatively ready to recognize and admit self-views which are unusual and unconventional" (p. 37). These observations are derived from comparative scores on the socialization, self-control, and communality scales of the California Psychological Inventory. Again, we note that dimensions relevant to defensiveness discriminate between subgroups of more and less creative adults. In the present instance, however, the role of intelligence is somewhat less clear, since the MacKinnon work involves a peer-rating criterion of creativity.[4] Though a negligible correlation of —.08 is reported between rated creativity and scores on the Concept Mastery Test, this does not insure that intelligence plays no role in the association between creativity and the personality variables cited earlier.

A study by Garwood (1964) of undergraduates, graduate students, and postdoctoral fellows in the sciences deviates from the MacKinnon work by basing the creativity criterion on test scores rather than behavioral ratings. The criterion was a composite computed across seven tests taken from the batteries used by Guilford and his associates. With one exception, the tests were quite substantially intercorrelated with one another. As in the MacKinnon work, the high creative subjects in the Garwood investigation yielded significantly lower scores on the socialization and self-control scales of the CPI. In addition, Garwood derived an index of "integration of nonconscious with conscious material." This

---

[4] See Chapter 3 for some of the special difficulties inherent in this type of creativity criterion.

index involves computing the "psychological distance" between conscious evaluations of self and parent figures, on the one hand, and nonconscious evaluations, on the other. Scoring is based on Leary's (1957) "interpersonal system" analysis, and essentially entails score discrepancies between the Leary Interpersonal Check List ("conscious" evaluations) and the Thematic Apperception Test ("nonconscious" evaluations). The "objects" evaluated were self, father, and mother. The results indicated a significant mean difference for "self" and "father" between low and high creative subjects. For both of those "concepts," the conscious and nonconscious responses were less "distant" from each other in high creative than in low creative subjects.

The separation of conscious and nonconscious aspects of the personality is an evident outcome of defensive processes. Hence, the Garwood work represents still another link in the supporting evidence for a creativity–defensiveness relationship. On the debit side, it must be noted that the Garwood study makes no reference whatever to intelligence. It is entirely conceivable that the creativity composite is positively related to intelligence,[5] and hence there is no way of knowing to what extent the personality variables described would have discriminated the more and less intelligent subjects in the Garwood sample.

Most of the studies deriving from the IPAR group at the University of California have focused on the objectively defined traits distinguishing more and less creative adults. There is another tradition, somewhat less prominent, that has emphasized a projective approach to the study of creativity. Rather than speak of a trait of impulsiveness, for example, investigators in the projective tradition are more likely to stress the relative dominance of primary process and secondary process expression (Freud, 1925). Holt and Havel (1960), for example, have devised procedures for scoring these processes in Rorschach protocols. Our interest in this work stems from the general expectation that primary process functioning will be quite rare in defensive individuals. Defensiveness by its very nature implies a strict control over primary process expression. At the same time, low defensiveness does not necessarily imply uncontrolled primary process expression, but rather may reflect a degree of control that transforms primary process material in constructive ways. Of course, this is a conjecture that should be put to an empirical test.

Pine and Holt (1960), working toward an operational specification of Kris' (1952) concept of "regression in the service of the ego," derived

---

[5] The testlike context under which the creativity battery was administered has been shown to enhance correlations between creativity and conventional intelligence indices (see Chapter 1). The possibility of an intelligence differential between the high and low creative groups seems especially relevant to consider since only extreme scorers on the creativity composite were studied.

scores to take account of both the amount of primary process expressed in the Rorschach and the effectiveness with which that primary process is controlled. Congruent with their hypotheses, Pine and Holt observed that it is the control component that relates significantly to an over-all creativity index (based on test performances) in both male and female undergraduates.

Myden (1959) reports similar results when comparing known creative artists with a "control" group of successful persons in other professions. In the present case, however, there is evidence that the creative group yielded more primary process material in their Rorschach responses as well as exhibiting better integration of primary and secondary process thinking. In addition, Myden finds a lesser incidence of repression in the protocols of the creative subjects.

Finally, Pine (1959) adapted the Holt scoring scheme for the Rorschach and applied it to the TAT. Stories were rated for amount of drive content and for two types of control—the level of "directness-socialization of drive expression" and the degree to which the drive content was thematically integrated in the story. These scores were related in turn to various creativity tests, some taken from Guilford's battery. The results appeared to be reasonably consistent with the Rorschach evidence described. Higher levels of creativity were associated with more drive content and with effective control over that content.

On the whole, the studies embodying the projective approach tend to balance the picture of the creative individual that one derives from the strictly trait-oriented studies. Impulsiveness at the trait level does not seem to imply uncontrolled aggressive and libidinal content continually erupting into the consciousness of the creative person. Rather, control functions do operate to render primary process manageable. The chaotic forces of the id must obviously be transformed if true creative products are to emerge.

Despite the complementary evidence offered by those investigators employing the projective approach, their studies as a whole suffer from many weaknesses. The samples have been extremely small, creativity tests (where these constitute the criterion) have not "hung together" well, and the possible influence of intelligence has been completely ignored. It would be of considerable interest to assess correspondences between primary and secondary process indices from projective tests, on the one hand, and defensiveness indices derived from the objective personality inventories, on the other. If a strong relationship can be shown to exist, then the objective index would have evident advantages in examining associations between creativity and psychodynamic processes.

Summing up, we have observed how little is known about the effects of defensiveness in children relative to the amount of information available in the case of anxiety. With regard to intelligence, the sketchy evidence available suggests that defensiveness has little relation to intelligence test scores. The decremental effects of defensiveness appeared to be most pronounced in unfamiliar and/or ambiguous testing contexts, where habitual defense patterns had little adaptive value. Since the creativity procedures employed in the present investigation are distinguished by their unfamiliarity and unstructured quality, we reasoned that an inverse relationship would obtain between defensiveness and creativity in children. Surprisingly, not a single study testing this hypothesis in a sample of children could be found. Accordingly, we turned to the literature on creativity in adults, and found numerous theoretical statements and a few empirical studies that favored the hypothesis. In the latter case, the results of trait-oriented studies indicated that impulsiveness and undercontrol were related to creativity. Psychoanalytic interpretation of projective test responses, on the other hand, suggested that creativity was related to primary process expression in a context of ego-control.

Other Correlates of Anxiety and Defensiveness

Thus far, the present chapter has generally confined itself to an examination of the implications of anxiety and defensiveness for intelligence and creativity. There is no necessary reason, however, for stopping at this point. Anxiety and defensiveness play such a central role in personality functioning that they may well influence other processes under study in the present volume. Consider physiognomic sensitivity, for example. Is it not conceivable that defensiveness will relate to performance in that area as well as in the creativity domain? We have already shown that creativity and physiognomic sensitivity share certain common properties. This would lead to the expectation that defensiveness might hamper effective functioning in the case of physiognomic sensitivity. On the other hand, intelligence also relates to physiognomic sensitivity, suggesting that anxiety too may be involved. The issue is evidently an open one, and in need of empirical exploration.

Categorizing and conceptualizing activities may also be subject to influence by anxiety and defensiveness. Again, there has been little work with children on these matters, despite the very promising findings in adults suggesting possible interrelationships between those domains (Kogan & Wallach, 1964).

Finally, we shall be able to inquire whether anxiety and defensiveness, when assessed by self-reports, have any consequences for children's behavior in the classroom. Recall that all of the children were rated on a set of nine scales reflecting a variety of social-emotional and task-oriented behaviors. The Davidson and Sarason (1961) study suggests that observer and teacher ratings differentiate high and low anxious boys and high and low defensive girls. The present investigation will permit a further examination of this important sex difference, and, in addition, will hopefully lead to new insights concerning the general problem of relations between self-report measures and behavior ratings in samples of young children.

PROCEDURE

Self-report Measures

An 88-item self-descriptive inventory was administered individually to the 151 children in the study. Administration of this instrument took place following the completion of all of the creativity, physiognomic sensitivity, and categorizing and conceptualizing procedures. Since many of the items in the self-descriptive inventory contained negative affect, we placed the inventory late in the sequence of procedures to insure that there would be no adverse effect on the relaxed, gamelike atmosphere maintained for the earlier procedures.

The instructions to the inventory, presented orally by the experimenter but also available for the child to read, were as follows:

"This game is called 'What I am like.' There are a lot of sentences printed below, and you are to pick out all the ones that seem to describe you. If a sentence does describe what you are like, draw a circle around it. But if a sentence does not describe what you are like, then leave it as it is and go on to the next one. There's no need to rush."

The experimenter sat passively by as the child worked on the inventory. If a child seemed to be having a great deal of difficulty making decisions, the experimenter might say: "You don't need to take much time with this. Just do what your first feeling about it is."

The following scales were represented in the 88-item inventory: anxiety (20), test anxiety (19), defensiveness (27), test defensiveness (6), social extraversion fillers (10), general fillers (6).[6] The anxiety, test anxiety, and defensiveness scales were adapted from the work of Sarason and his associates (Davidson & Sarason, 1961; Sarason *et al.*, 1960). For our purposes, the items in those scales were changed from the second-person interrogative form (Are you afraid of school tests?) to the first-person declarative form (I am afraid of school tests). Pressures of time necessitated slight reductions in the number of items contained within the scales devised by the Yale group. Items were selected so as to minimize redundancies in content.

The remaining scales are of secondary interest. We constructed six items in the "test defensiveness" domain to note whether this quite

---

[6] Numbers in parentheses refer to the number of items in each scale.

specific form of defensiveness can be subsumed under a general defensiveness construct. The social extraversion items were adapted from the Minnesota T-S-E Inventory (Evans & McConnell, 1957). Finally, six innocuous items intended as general "fillers" were included in the inventory, but were not scored.

Items were keyed in the direction of the scale label. Higher scores thus reflect greater anxiety, test anxiety, defensiveness, and so on.

Reliabilities (coefficient alphas) computed on the total sample for each of the scales were in the moderate to high range. For the three scales of major interest, the reliabilities were as follows: .86, .87, and .74 for anxiety, test anxiety, and defensiveness, respectively. Turning to the scales of lesser import, the six-item test defensiveness scale yielded a surprisingly substantial coefficient alpha of .63. The social extraversion scale, which was included in the inventory largely for "filler" purposes, yielded a coefficient alpha reliability of .48.

Listed below are the items contained within each scale. The numbers preceding each item indicate the position of the item in the inventory.

Anxiety

7. I am afraid of things like snakes.
8. I get a scary feeling when I see a dead animal.
13. I am afraid of spiders.
19. I worry that I might get sick.
31. When I am in bed at night trying to go to sleep, I often find I am worrying about something.
34. I get scared when I have to go into a dark room.
42. I am afraid of being bitten or hurt by a dog.
45. Some of the stories on radio and television scare me.
46. I think I worry more than other boys and girls.
53. I am frightened by lightning and thunderstorms.
56. When I am alone in a room and hear a strange noise, I get a frightened feeling.
57. I worry that I might get hurt in some accident.
67. When I am away from home, I worry about what might be happening at home.
68. I am frightened when I look down from a high place.
75. I sometimes get the feeling that something bad is going to happen to me.
76. I sometimes worry about whether my father is going to get sick.
77. I get scared when I have to walk home alone at night.
80. Without knowing why, I sometimes get a funny feeling in my stomach.
83. I sometimes worry about whether my mother is going to get sick.
87. I get worried when I have to go to the doctor's office.

Test Anxiety

11. When the teacher asks me to read aloud, I am afraid that I am going to make some bad mistakes.

15. I worry a lot while I am taking a test.

21. When the teacher says that she is going to give the class a test, I become afraid that I will do poorly.

23. I wish a lot of times that I didn't worry so much about tests.

27. I sometimes dream at night that I did poorly on a test I had in school that day.

28. When the teacher says that she is going to call upon some boys and girls in the class to do arithmetic problems, I hope that she will call on some-one else and not on me.·

33. When I am taking a hard test, I forget some things that I knew very well before I started taking the test.

35. I think I worry more about school than other boys and girls do.

43. When I am home and thinking about my lessons for the next day, I worry that I will do poorly on them.

50. I sometimes dream at night that I am in school and cannot answer the teacher's questions.

52. When I am in bed at night, I sometimes worry about how I am going to do in class the next day.

54. I am afraid of school tests.

59. While I am on my way to school, I sometimes worry that the teacher may give the class a test.

60. I worry about being promoted at the end of the year.

61. I sometimes dream at night that the teacher is angry because I do not know my lessons.

71. When the teacher says that she is going to give the class a test, I get a nervous or funny feeling.

73. When the teacher says that she is going to find out how much I have learned, my heart begins to beat faster.

78. When the teacher says that she is going to find out how much I have learned, I get a funny feeling in my stomach.

82. When the teacher asks me to write on the blackboard in front of the class, the hand I write with sometimes shakes a little.

Defensiveness

3. I feel cross and grouchy sometimes.

4. I never worry about what people think of me.

5. I always tell the truth.

6. No one has ever been able to scare me.

9. I never get scolded.

14. I am sometimes afraid of getting into arguments.
16. I have never had a scary dream.
18. There are some people I don't like.
24. I like everyone I know.
26. I sometimes lose my temper.
30. I have never been afraid of getting hurt.
32. There are some things about myself I'd change if I could.
36. I never worry.
37. I don't feel sorry for any of the things I have done.
41. I'm sometimes sorry for the things I do.
44. I always do the right thing.
48. I never worry about something bad happening to someone I know.
49. I don't feel badly when someone scolds me.
51. I am never shy.
58. Sometimes when I get mad, I feel like smashing something.
62. I never worry about what is going to happen.
63. I never hurt anybody's feelings.
64. I sometimes dream about things I don't like to talk about.
69. I am never unhappy.
85. I never have arguments with my mother and father.
86. When I was younger there were some things that scared me.
88. I always know what to say to people.

Test Defensiveness

10. I never worry about knowing my lessons.
12. I never worry about how well I did on a test after I've taken it.
39. I never worry when the teacher says that she is going to ask me questions to find out how much I know.
66. I never worry about my school grades.
74. If I am sick and miss school, I never worry that I will do more poorly in my school work when I return to school.
81. I never worry before I take a test.

Social Extraversion Fillers

17. I like to spend most of my spare time with friends.
20. I am a very lively person.
22. Once I make up my mind to do something, I do it.
29. I usually don't say much when I am together with other boys and girls.
40. I find it easy to make new friends.
55. I like to play pranks on other boys or girls.
70. When I am together with other boys or girls, I am usually the leader of the group.

72. I would rather have a few close friends than many friends.
79. Other people think I am pretty lively.
84. I am a person who likes to talk a lot.

General Fillers

1. I like to watch television before dinner most evenings.
2. I like to play in the snow.
25. I like to go on trips with my mother and father.
38. I love to play games best of all.
47. I like to go to the beach in the summertime.
65. I like cartoon movies best of all.

Fantasy Measure

The children were read the beginnings of five stories, each having as a main character a child who is under stress of failure. At a critical point in each story's development, the child is asked to complete the story. Verbatim instructions to the task were as follows:

"This is another test like the one that you took when I last saw you, and it is the last one that I will give you. I am going to read you the beginning of a story and I am going to test you on how well you can finish it. Let's try the first one now, and remember, this is a test so try to do as well as you can." (The experimenter reads the first story.) "Now you finish the story by telling me how ——— thinks and feels, what happens, and how things turn out." The experimenter recorded all the child's verbal output. Then she read the second story, again instructed the child to complete it, and recorded the child's verbal responses verbatim. This procedure was then followed for the remaining three stories.

The stories were adapted from Miller and Swanson (1960) and follow below. Where only one story is presented—items 1, 3, and 4—the version presented to the boys is shown. The girls received identical versions except for the substitution of a female central character and associated feminine pronouns for the corresponding masculine forms. Where two stories are given—an "a" and a "b" version—the "a" story was read to the boys, and the "b" story to the girls. The names inserted into the stories were selected so as not to include those of any child in the class.

1. All his friends know that ——— likes music and wants to grow up to be a concert piano player. Some of them have laughed at him for thinking he could do this, but ——— has continued his practicing, even though he finds that it is getting harder and harder for him to play the music his teacher gives him. One day a famous musician visits his teacher. It is arranged for ——— to play for him. ——— thinks that he has played very well, but as he is leaving, he overhears the musician telling his teacher that ——— does not have enough

talent to be a concert piano player and that it is a waste of money for him to be taking lessons. It seems to ——— that his teacher is agreeing with the musician. ——— doesn't know what to do.

2a. ———'s father has always wanted him to be good at sports and has encouraged him to go out for the school teams. ———, though, is short and not very strong—in fact, he can't even run very fast. So in spite of practicing more than anyone else and trying very hard, he has been put off every team he has tried out for. He knows his father is very disappointed in him. He is disappointed, too, because he likes sports very much. Finally, he tries lightweight wrestling. After practicing a great deal, he is given a chance in a big match. But, he is too anxious to do well in the match. He gets so nervous that he is easily thrown. ——— feels so disappointed and embarrassed that he bursts into tears in front of everybody. After the match, the coach tells him he should give up sports.

2b. ———'s mother has always wanted her to be a wonderful dancer and has encouraged her to take dancing lessons. ———, though, is not very good at dancing—in fact, she can't even keep time to the music. So in spite of practicing more than anyone else and trying very hard, she has not done very well and has never been asked to dance in the dancing school show. She knows her mother is very disappointed in her. She is disappointed, too, because she likes dancing very much. Finally, ——— decides to give it one more try, and after practicing a great deal she is given the chance to do a dance in the show put on by her dancing school. But she is too anxious to do well at her dance. She gets so nervous that she trips and falls. ——— feels so disappointed and embarrassed that she bursts into tears in front of everybody. After the dance, the dancing teacher tells her that she should give up dancing lessons.

3. ——— is a fifth grader. Everything has gone wrong for him from the very first day in school this year. He's been having trouble with the work and he knows that the teacher, whom he likes, thinks he's dumb. He can never think of the right answers when he's called on in class. And he also has trouble getting along with the other kids. They all seem to have it in for him in class, on the playground, after school, all the time. When anything goes wrong, the kids or the teacher always blame it on him. One day he hears a couple of the boys talking about him and saying that nobody really likes him—and that nobody thinks he's any good. ——— feels like he just can't stand it any more.

4. ——— had always wanted to help his father in his work, so he begged his father to let him work in his office during the summer. His father finally agreed, but only on the condition that if there were any trouble at all, ——— would have to quit. He was very excited at being able to help his father, but somehow from the very first day things went wrong. He mixed up his papers, got in people's way, and just couldn't seem to do anything right. His father was patient with him for a while, until one day ——— accidentally threw away the most important papers in the office. Everyone was very upset about it and ———didn't know what to do. Very soon, ———'s father called him into the office, and he knew that his father had found out about his mistake.

5a. ——— has always felt he was no good. He has tried very hard to make a good impression on the other kids in the class and on his teacher, but usually they just seem to ignore him. He always seems to be making stupid mistakes and not understand the work they are doing. ——— has always dreamed that he would have a chance to show everyone that he is good at something, too.

One day his teacher brings the school's brand new movie projector into the room and announces that they will have a special treat—a movie they have all been wanting to see. She asks if anyone in the class knows how to run a projector, and ——— eagerly raises his hand because he thinks it is like the projector his father has. All the kids laugh and the teacher looks unsure, but he assures her that he knows all about running the machine. But as ——— gets to the machine he realizes that it isn't the same kind as his father's. He is about to admit that he's not sure after all, when he sees all the class and the teacher watching him. Suddenly he knows that he can't fail this time, and he turns and puts the film into the projector. He signals that the film is ready, and the teacher puts out the lights. ——— starts the movie, but even before the picture comes on, the screen, there is a horrible sound of clashing metal, a smell of burning film, and the machine stops dead. The film is ripped and the projector is probably broken. ——— knows what everyone must be thinking of him, and he turns to run out of the room.

5b. ——— has always felt she was no good. She has tried very hard to make a good impression on the other kids in the class and on her teacher, but usually they just seem to ignore her. She always seems to be making stupid mistakes and not understand the work they are doing. ——— has always dreamed that someday she would have a chance to show everyone that she is good at something, too.

One day the teacher brings the school's brand new sewing machine into the room and announces that the girls will have a special treat—a sewing lesson. She asks if anyone in the class knows how to run a sewing machine, and ——— eagerly raises her hand because she thinks it is like the sewing machine her mother has. All the kids laugh and the teacher looks unsure, but she assures her that she knows all about running the machine. But as ——— gets to the machine she realizes that it isn't the same kind as her mother's. She is about to admit that she's not sure after all, when she sees all the class and the teacher watching her. Suddenly she knows that she can't fail this time, and she turns and puts the thread in the sewing machine. She puts the cloth under the needle and starts the machine, but even before she's made one good stitch, there is a horrible sound of ripping cloth, a burning smell, and the machine stops dead. The cloth is ripped and the machine is probably broken. ——— knows what everyone must be thinking of her, and she turns to run out of the room.

The present procedure was the last in the total sequence. The immediately preceding procedure involved the administration of the three subtests of the Wechsler Intelligence Scale for Children included in the intelligence composite of the present study. With the administration of the WISC, a marked change was introduced in the conditions under which the other tasks employed in the study were given. In the case of the WISC, it was quite apparent to the child that he faced an intelligence test, and, hence, the relaxed gamelike context distinguishing the earlier procedures no longer applied. We decided to maintain an evaluative testlike set for the administration of the story completion procedure on the assumption that this would enhance the validity of the instrument as an index of denial (defensiveness) regarding failure. It soon became clear, however, that the denial aspect was not the major differentiating feature of the story completions. Rather, these appeared to vary in terms of the presence or absence of certain qualities reflecting a general concept of maturity. Although denial of failure might influence the maturity of a story ending, this did not seem to be the most essential ingredient of the story.

How then did we proceed to measure the maturity of story completions? Basically, we attempted to gauge the extent to which the story endings were compatible with the character of the protagonist in the story and the situation in which he was embedded. The criterial questions (on the basis of which scoring for maturity was undertaken) were of the following sort: If the story hero perseveres in the child's story completion, for example, is the degree of perseverance realistic in terms of the story beginning, and does it warrant the success achieved? Are the story's characters accurately perceived by the child, and are they made to behave in a manner consistent with their natures and with the situations which confront them? A rating of 1 was given to stories embodying such qualities, and a rating of 0 to stories lacking them.

Let us consider the scoring system in somewhat greater detail. A first prerequisite for a 1-type ending is an adequate and sensitive analysis of the relationships in the given situation. This does not imply that there is but a single way to understand these relationships, though there are obvious limits beyond which a 0 rating is assigned, for the child's omissions or distortions alter the fundamental facts portrayed in the story beginning.

As an example of a 1-type response, consider story 2. Recall in the story that a boy has been advised to give up sports when a long history of failure to make any school teams is climaxed by a particularly dismal failure in wrestling. The "givens" in the story beginning are the boy's desire to be good at sports, his father's pressure in this direction, and the boy's small stature and inability to run fast. A 1-type story might read:

> Bob was very unhappy. He lay down and thought. His father was disappointed but said maybe he could do better next time. Bob said "no," he would quit. A few weeks later he found an ad in a paper on how to build a good body in 10 easy lessons. He did it and got better. His father built him a gym in the basement. He got stronger and ate good foods. Then he tried out for a couple of teams—didn't make it at first. When he came to wrestling this time he was very good at it and finally he became the best lightweight wrestler in the school.

Note that the desires and feelings of Bob and his father have been faithfully worked into the structure of events; success has been realistically achieved because the boy has perceived the causes of failure. In a less qualified 1-type story, the boy might achieve success in some other sport without going through the kind of work that Bob did to ready himself. The story beginning suggests quite strongly that the boy is not at all suited to athletics, but there are always exceptions that a child may reasonably find—ping pong might be an area in which success could be justified. But the ultimate neglect of an important given in the story beginning would be for the child to achieve a kind of success which contradicts factual statements. The following is the beginning of such a 0-type story:

> Bob did not want to give up sports. He was determined not to give up sports. He thought he might go out for track or jumping. And he did. He was put on the team. . . .

We note in the foregoing story that the subject in choosing track and jumping completely omits from consideration the boy's stated size and capacity for speed. The 1-type story, in contrast, meets a reality standard; miracles do not happen. The reality of a success must be judged in terms of the total context of the story, and particularly, the kind of effort put forth to justify success. If the initial causal relations have been sensitively perceived, the story ending impresses the reader with its internal plausibility; events unfold somewhat predictably, and people act in harmony with their natures.

In rating the maturity of a story ending, the judge was often faced with the problem of balancing assets and liabilities. Thus, a very sensitive description of a relationship between two people may have to be balanced against an oversimplification of the amount of success the child has the "hero" achieve. Consider an example for story 5. In that story, a child is described as isolated from his peers. A specific opportunity to "prove himself" is provided, but the child fails before teacher and class, and is about to run out of the room in embarrassment. A 1-type story concludes:

> Then she remembers that often happens and that her mother had taught her how to fix it. So she starts to work, puts the thread in the right place again, and starts the machine again and fixes it. Then she can do it. For once she's been able to do something and have it come out right.

Though the focus of this story ending is on the specific failure incident rather than the total story context of isolation and frustration, it is evident that both of these elements were recognized. The relationship between "doing something right" and being acceptable to her classmates is implicitly present. This in turn indicates the subject's awareness that the child in the story desperately needed acceptance. Thus, the subject constructed her story so as to end with a logical consistency, and simultaneously she fulfilled the criterion of a sensitive analysis of the story beginning, though not making explicit all of the elements on which success is based. This omission is evidently balanced by the subject's careful and perceptive handling of detail.

As a contrast, the following 0-type story is illustrative of a child (male) who has denied the total context of story 5 in the construction of his ending:

> It turns out that George had not broken it, but the projector had already been broken, and that the film had already been torn so that it broke easily. So he wasn't put to blame.

Consider finally the reliability levels for the present procedure. Two independent scorers evaluated all of the story completions for maturity, working "blindly" with respect to the identities of the children. With respect to interscorer reliability, there were 604 actual agreements out of a possible total of 755 (5 stories for each of 151 subjects). This yields a scoring reliability figure of 80 percent. Interscorer discrepancies were resolved by discussion. Turning next to the issue of internal consistency, the present procedure yielded an odd–even reliability coefficient (Spearman-Brown) of .59. This is a quite respectable figure for a five-item instrument.

RESULTS AND DISCUSSION

Sex Differences

We begin the presentation of results with an examination of mean differences between boys and girls on the various personality dimensions (Table 59). Consistent with previous evidence (Cox, 1962; Cox & Leaper, 1959; Sarason *et al.*, 1960), girls obtain significantly higher general anxiety scores than do boys. The basis for this sex difference has been well explicated by Sarason *et al.* (1960, pp. 250–261) and hence need not be given detailed consideration here. Very briefly, the Sarason group interprets the sex difference on the basis of boys' hesitancy in admitting anxiety—in other words, greater defensiveness on their part. A further consideration cited by the Sarason team is the greater relevance to boys of the item content in the general anxiety scale. The items largely concern matters of personal inadequacy and the possibility of bodily harm —issues more central to boys than girls. The latter's anxieties are more likely to lie in the domain of social relationships. Given this differential content relevance for boys and girls, we should expect the girls' defensive tendencies to be weaker with the resultant endorsement of more anxiety items, while the boys defensively resist admitting anxiety and hence endorse fewer items.

Both facets of the interpretation given by the Sarason group receive support in the present study. The reader will note in Table 59 that

Table 59.

SEX COMPARISONS FOR PERSONALITY VARIABLES

Variable	Boys ($N = 70$)		Girls ($N = 81$)			
	Mean	SD	Mean	SD	t	p
General anxiety	5.31	4.55	7.15	4.54	2.47	<.05
Test anxiety	5.37	4.43	5.79	4.89	0.55	n. s.
Defensiveness	5.69	3.81	4.52	3.40	1.99	<.05
Test defensiveness	1.96	1.46	1.59	1.70	1.40	n. s.
Social extraversion	5.07	1.71	4.46	1.70	2.21	<.05
Maturity of story endings	0.80	0.96	1.05	1.31	1.32	n. s.

by girls. Further, a glance at the general anxiety items in the Procedure section of the chapter reveals few statements concerned with anxiety about inadequate social relationships (fear of rejection, for example).

For test anxiety, Table 59 shows no significant sex difference. In this respect, the present evidence departs from other findings (for example, Cox & Leaper, 1959; Sarason *et al.*, 1960) which, while indicating a smaller sex difference than that observed in the case of general anxiety, report a difference which is consistently and significantly in the direction of greater test anxiety in girls. The direction is maintained in the present sample, but the difference falls far short of statistical significance. We have no evident explanation for the deviation of the present findings from those previously reported.

We have already pointed out that the significant sex difference in defensiveness is consistent with previous evidence (Sarason *et al.*, 1960). It must be noted, however, that this earlier evidence concerns the abbreviated lie scale employed by the Sarason group in conjunction with their anxiety scales. The present authors have not been able to locate any normative data for the Defensiveness Scale for Children, which was constructed subsequent to the publication of the Sarason *et al.*, (1960) volume. In short, the present data seem to represent the first published evidence of a significant sex difference on a full-length defensiveness boys receive defensiveness scores significantly higher than those obtained scale. Boys are evidently more defensive than girls. It will be further noted that boys are also more test defensive than girls, though the difference falls considerably short of statistical significance.

Note finally that the social extraversion scale yields a significant difference in favor of boys, and the variable designated "maturity of story endings" does not show a significant sex difference.

Interrelationships among Personality Variables

Correlations between the various personality dimensions are presented in Table 60. An over-all sex comparison reveals greater independence among the personality variables in the male sample. Of the fifteen correlation coefficients, two and nine are significant beyond the .05 level for boys and girls, respectively.

Common to both samples is the substantial association between general and test anxiety, a result very much in accord with previously published evidence (Sarason *et al.*, 1960). Nevertheless, the correlations are not so very high, relative to the reliabilities of the respective scales, as to suggest that the two forms of anxiety are reducible to one. Also common to boys and girls is a significant inverse relation between defensiveness and general anxiety. This finding is congruent with theoret-

Table 60.

CORRELATIONS BETWEEN PERSONALITY VARIABLES

	GA	TA	D	TD	SE	MSE
General anxiety (GA)	—	61	—24	—09	13	—19
Test anxiety (TA)	59	—	—18	—17	—11	—11
Defensiveness (D)	—32	—25	—	23	10	—17
Test defensiveness (TD)	—21	—37	41	—	09	03
Social extraversion (SE)	—10	—22	28	30	—	05
Maturity of story endings (MSE)	—27	—16	—01	—06	10	—

NOTE: Correlations for boys ($N = 70$) and for girls ($N = 81$) are above and below diagonal, respectively. Significance at the .05 and .01 levels requires r's of .24 and .31, respectively, for boys, and r's of .22 and .29, respectively, for girls. Decimal points are omitted.

ical expectations, for defensiveness serves the function of protecting the child from anxiety. The correlations, though significant, are not particularly high, suggesting that some of the myriad forms of anxiety tapped by the general anxiety scale may be attributed to the self by an otherwise defensive child. Consistent with this observation is the decline in the magnitude of correlations when test anxiety, as opposed to general anxiety, is related to defensiveness. In fact, the correlation for males is nonsignificant. Evidently, a form of anxiety focused upon a particular type of life stress is even more likely than general anxiety to be found in both defensive and nondefensive personality structures.[7]

Relations between defensiveness and test defensiveness are highly significant in girls and barely short of significance in boys. It would seem that defensiveness, in comparison with anxiety, exhibits a lesser degree of generality. We hesitate to push this conclusion too far, but it is quite suggestive. The relative degree of generality or specificity in comparing anxiety and defensiveness clearly remains open to further empirical exploration.

Turning to other findings in Table 60, we note that social extraversion in girls is directly related to both types of defensiveness and inversely related to test anxiety. No such associations occur among the boys.

Finally, the maturity of story endings is not related to any of the personality inventory variables in boys, and is inversely related to general anxiety in the girls. It is evident that the "maturity" concept derived from the story-completion procedure has no connection with the

---

[7] Previous research with adults (Kogan & Wallach, 1964) indicates that test anxiety and defensiveness are unrelated in both males and females.

kind of defensiveness tapped by a structured personality inventory. This lack of relationship is hardly surprising, however, for it will be recalled that the scoring scheme for story endings departed radically from a simple "denial of failure" framework.

Personality through Self-report and Behavior Ratings

In the present section, we inquire whether personality revealed through self-report indices bears any relation to overt behavior in the classroom setting. Tables 61 and 62 report the relevant correlations for boys and girls, respectively. We consider first the results for boys. It is quite evident in Table 61 that the test-anxiety variable has distinct behavioral implications. Test-anxious boys tend to be rated as hesitant and subdued, lacking in confidence and assurance, deprecating their own work, and showing a lack of concentration and interest in schoolwork. Clearly, there is a syndrome of behavioral characteristics that is associated with a specific kind of experiential anxiety (or its lack) in the elementary school boy. Test anxiety evidently has an inhibitory and debilitating effect on the male child's general classroom demeanor. Further, the test-anxious boy also appears to be at a social disadvantage. Note that he is less likely than his low test-anxious peers to be sought out for his companionship.

Is the foregoing pattern of relationships also found in the female sample? It will be noted in Table 62 that the associations are considerably weaker. Of the numerous significant relations observed in the boys, only the link between test anxiety and "deprecates own work" remains significant for the girls. The magnitude of the relation is much smaller

Table 61.

CORRELATIONS FOR BOYS BETWEEN PERSONALITY VARIABLES AND BEHAVIOR RATINGS

	GA	TA	D	TD	SE	MSE
A. Attention-seeking	16	00	01	14	10	—22
B. Hesitant and subdued	—10	33	12	—21	—39	—19
C. Confidence and assurance	—11	—31	—03	04	23	29
D. Sought as companion	—12	—24	—14	—13	19	21
E. Seeks companionship	07	05	—06	—05	16	—10
F. Deprecates own work	21	52	14	—09	—18	—35
H. Concentration on schoolwork	—22	—49	—08	—01	08	37
I. Interest in schoolwork	—14	—44	—12	—03	18	36

NOTE: For $N = 70$, r's of .24 and .31 are required for significance at the .05 and .01 levels, respectively. Decimal points are omitted.

Table 62.

Correlations for Girls between Personality
Variables and Behavior Ratings

	GA	TA	D	TD	SE	MSE
A. Attention-seeking	03	18	—11	—19	07	03
B. Hesitant and subdued	01	10	06	—01	—28	—12
C. Confidence and assurance	—07	—09	—03	—02	18	27
D. Sought as companion	—06	03	00	—12	22	25
E. Seeks companionship	15	23	—06	—14	23	00
F. Deprecates own work	10	28	—06	—15	—19	—20
H. Concentration on schoolwork	—03	—16	—15	09	—09	21
I. Interest in schoolwork˙	—07	—21	—11	12	10	15

Note: For $N = 81$, r's of .22 and .29 are required for significance at the .05
and .01 levels, respectively. Decimal points are omitted.

in the female sample, however. Further, test anxiety relates positively
to the seeking of companionship. Recall that test anxiety relates inversely
to being sought as a companion in the male sample. Evidently, test anxiety does not contribute to negative social stimulus value in girls,
whereas test-anxious boys tend to be rejected by their peers.

The foregoing pattern of sex differences is quite consistent with
findings reported by Davidson and Sarason (1961). Those authors also
found test anxiety to be related to a variety of behaviors among boys but
only to a few such behaviors in the case of girls. Their interpretation of
the sex difference stresses the fact "that, in school, boys give more overt
and spontaneous expression to a wider range of feelings and impulses
than do girls. This finding does suggest that observation of children as a
basis for measurement is likely to be more effective for a wider range of
variables for boys than for girls" (p. 209). The results of the present
investigation clearly lend themselves to a similar sort of interpretation.

Turning to defensiveness, we observe, in Tables 61 and 62, that no
overt behavioral correlates emerge. In this respect, our findings deviate
from those reported by Davidson and Sarason (1961). Those authors obtained an array of significant correlations in girls between defensiveness
scores and behavior ratings. We have not been able to formulate a satisfactory explanation for the discrepancy between the two sets of findings.
There is no indication, for example, of greater constriction in the female
sample with respect to behavior ratings or personality scale scores
(Tables 25 and 59, respectively).

Neither general anxiety nor test defensiveness relate to any of the
behavior ratings in boys or girls. Social extraversion, on the other hand,

is inversely related to ratings of "hesitant and subdued" in both sexes, and positively related to seeking and being sought for companionship in the female sample.

Consider finally the "maturity of story endings" variable. In both boys and girls, there is a significant direct association between the quality of story completions and the degree to which the child exhibits "confidence and assurance" in the classroom. In addition, the girls whose story endings rank high in maturity also tend to be sought for their companionship. This suggests that confidence and assurance evoke a positive response from peers in the case of girls who give mature story endings. Results are in the same direction for the boys on the "sought as companion" dimension, but the correlation falls short of significance.

In the case of the boys, maturity of story endings relates to behavior ratings in the more strictly task-related endeavors. Note that the boys who give higher quality story completions are rated as *not* deprecating their work and as showing a high level of concentration and interest in their schoolwork. Conceivably, the "maturity of story endings" variable has more tasklike implications for boys and more social implications for girls.

Personality Viewed as a Function of Creativity and Intelligence

With the present section, we turn to the major findings of the chapter. A decision had to be made as to the sequence in which the principal results should be presented. The heading of the section indicates that we decided to put creativity and intelligence into a "treatment variable" role first. This has been the traditional approach in most creativity research, and hence we shall be able to compare our findings with the small body of relevant evidence in the published creativity literature. It should also be noted that all the previous chapters of the present volume have cast creativity and intelligence as "treatment variables." Given the demonstrated fertility of such an approach, it would seem eminently desirable to try it out in the case of personality dimensions before turning to an alternative in which creativity and intelligence are treated as dependent variables.

We begin with general anxiety in the male sample (Table 63). A near-significant intelligence main effect may be noted, but this result is of secondary concern given the significant interaction obtained. Within the high creative group, intelligence makes little difference—both high and low intelligence subgroups yield equal general anxiety means in the intermediate range. Note, on the other hand, the wide discrepancy in general anxiety for high and low intelligence subgroups within the low creative category. The low creative–high intelligence boys have the lowest anxiety scores, the low-low boys have the highest.

Table 63.

MEAN GENERAL ANXIETY SCORES FOR
THE FOUR GROUPS OF BOYS $(N = 70)$

INTELLIGENCE

		High	Low
	High	5.41	5.33
		(3.30)	(5.10)
CREATIVITY			
	Low	3.22	7.41
		(3.41)	(5.36)

ANALYSIS OF VARIANCE

Source	df	MS	F	p
Intelligence	1	4.23	3.83	$< .06$
Creativity	1	0.00	< 1.00	n. s.
Interaction	1	4.55	4.13	$< .05$
Within cells	66	1.10		

Are these results maintained when test anxiety rather than general anxiety is the dependent variable? Table 64 reveals a somewhat smaller interaction and a larger intelligence effect, but the general pattern of the means is quite similar across the two forms of anxiety.

How shall these findings be interpreted? That the low-low subgroup should achieve the highest anxiety scores is not especially surprising, for these are the boys who have the fewest skills to bring to bear upon the task requirements of the classroom. Of considerably greater interest is the exceedingly low anxiety level in the high intelligent–low creative boys. Those boys who are both highly creative and intelligent actually admit to a wider array of anxiety symptoms. Since one might expect that superior skills in both forms of thinking would contribute to more effective classroom performance and thereby to reduced levels of anxiety, the results obtained constitute something of a paradox. If one is willing to make certain assumptions about the mode of thinking stressed in the classroom, then an approach to the understanding of the paradox is possible. In Chapter 3, we suggested that it is the convergent form of thinking as represented in typical aptitude and achievement tests which most teachers emphasize and reward. The divergent form of thinking is not likely to have any real "payoff" value in the classroom context.

Table 64.

MEAN TEST ANXIETY SCORES FOR
THE FOUR GROUPS OF BOYS ($N = 70$)

		INTELLIGENCE	
		High	Low
	High	4.65	5.83
		(3.37)	(4.69)
CREATIVITY			
	Low	3.06	8.06
		(2.65)	(5.29)

ANALYSIS OF VARIANCE

Source	df	MS	F	p
Intelligence	1	9.58	9.85	$<.01$
Creativity	1	0.10	<1.00	n. s.
Interaction	1	3.64	3.75	$<.06$
Within cells	66	0.97		

Indeed, boys who have a penchant for divergent thinking may find it judicious to inhibit its expression in the school situation. Where a specific answer to a specific problem is being sought, alternative formulations of the problem will have a distracting influence. We are leading up to the suggestion that the creative boy in a context where intelligence is encouraged and rewarded will pay the price of a modicum of anxiety for his creative bent.

Where intelligence is high and creativity is low, on the other hand, we can envision the elementary school boy making a more satisfactory adjustment to the school environment. His preferred mode of thinking fits in quite neatly with the task requirements of the classroom. He is not troubled about realms of possibility, but rather is capable of proceeding efficiently from clearly formulated questions to clearly formulated answers. This is clearly not the stuff of which anxiety is made.

One also can note that the present findings are suggestive of a curvilinear relationship between creativity and general anxiety or test anxiety. Those of high creativity are found to possess a middling degree of anxiety. Those whose creativity level is low, on the other hand, are located at one or the other anxiety extreme. One is tempted by these results to point out the possible analogy with the Yerkes-Dodson law, in that creativity is minimal when the anxiety level is either too low or too high. Such a finding certainly does not support the idea that creativity flourishes best under completely anxiety-free conditions. Of prime importance, however, is the finding that the particular subgroup which stands out as least anxious is the one distinguished by high intelligence and low creativity.

Are the foregoing effects observed in the female sample? The answer is a resounding negative. Creativity and intelligence have no effect whatever upon self-reported anxiety in girls. In this respect, our work is consistent with the evidence reported by Sarason and his associates. Those authors have repeatedly failed to obtain performance correlates of anxiety in girls, whereas many such correlates emerge in boys. The present data constitute further evidence for the differential validity of anxiety scales in boys and girls.

We turn now to defensiveness. Table 65 gives the relevant information for boys. The major finding consists of an intelligence main effect, high intelligence being associated with lower levels of defensiveness. Of special interest is the exceedingly low defensiveness mean in the subgroup

Table 65.

MEAN DEFENSIVENESS SCORES FOR
THE FOUR GROUPS OF BOYS ($N = 70$)

		INTELLIGENCE	
		High	Low
	High	3.76 (2.61)	6.78 (4.51)
CREATIVITY			
	Low	5.72 (3.58)	6.41 (3.86)

ANALYSIS OF VARIANCE

Source	df	MS	F	p
Intelligence	1	3.43	4.35	<.05
Creativity	1	0.63	<1.00	n. s.
Interaction	1	1.35	1.71	n. s.
Within cells	66	0.79		

of boys high in both creativity and intelligence. Where creativity is high and intelligence low, on the other hand, the defensiveness level shows a marked increase. On the basis of these findings, the evidence summarized earlier in the chapter linking creativity with low defensiveness in adults clearly requires some qualification in the case of elementary school children, and possibly in adults as well. For the present sample of young boys, creativity is associated with low defensiveness only in the case where intelligence is also high. Since many of the creativity studies carried out with adults have not controlled adequately for the intelligence factor, creative adults can also be expected to score quite high in intelligence. Accordingly, the negative association between creativity and defensiveness reported in the published literature may hold only for a particular kind of creativity—the kind where a high level of intelligence is also present.

Recall that the results for the anxiety variables in boys were not confirmed in the case of girls. A similar state of affairs holds in the case of defensiveness. Creativity and/or intelligence seem to have little systematic impact upon defensiveness level in girls. The suggestion that anxiety may be a more appropriate variable for boys, and defensiveness for girls (for example, Davidson & Sarason, 1961), hence receives only partial support in the present phase of our work. We observe that creativity and/or intelligence influence both anxiety and defensiveness levels in boys, and affect neither in the case of girls.

The remaining two personality inventory variables—test defensiveness and social extraversion—were unrelated to creativity and/or intelligence in both males and females.

Consider finally the variable designated as "maturity of story endings." The manner in which a child's status on this variable is influenced by his level of creativity and intelligence can be gauged from Tables 66 and 67 for boys and girls, respectively. It is strikingly evident that "maturity of story endings" does not have the same meaning for boys and girls. In the former, there is a strong indication of a creativity effect; in the latter, a main effect for intelligence is obtained. How can we account for this discrepancy between the sexes? Is it possible that intelligence in girls might express itself in literary and fantasy expression to a greater extent than is the case for boys? As Witkin and his co-workers (Witkin *et al.*, 1954; Witkin *et al.*, 1962) have observed, intelligence takes a more analytic form in boys than in girls.[8] Accordingly, for boys to perform well in a story-completion task, something beyond intelligence

---

[8] Recall in Chapter 4 that the boys gave a significantly larger number of descriptive sorts in the object-sorting procedure. Such sorts are indicative of analytic functioning in the Kagan *et al.* (1963) schema.

Table 66.

MEAN SCORE ON "MATURITY OF STORY ENDINGS" FOR
THE FOUR GROUPS OF BOYS $(N = 70)$

	INTELLIGENCE	
	High	Low
High	1.18	0.83
	(1.29)	(0.86)

CREATIVITY

Low	0.61	0.59
	(0.85)	(0.71)

ANALYSIS OF VARIANCE

Source	df	MS	F	p
Intelligence	1	0.03	<1.00	n. s.
Creativity	1	0.16	3.19	$<.08$
Interaction	1	0.03	<1.00	n. s.
Within cells	66	0.05		

Table 67.

MEAN SCORE ON "MATURITY OF STORY ENDINGS" FOR
THE FOUR GROUPS OF GIRLS $(N = 81)$

	INTELLIGENCE	
	High	Low
High	1.41	0.50
	(1.74)	(0.62)

CREATIVITY

Low	1.47	0.77
	(1.26)	(1.11)

ANALYSIS OF VARIANCE

Source	df	MS	F	p
Intelligence	1	0.65	8.06	$<.01$
Creativity	1	0.03	<1.00	n. s.
Interaction	1	0.01	<1.00	n. s.
Within cells	77	0.08		

as such may be required. As we have noted, this "extra" appears to be creativity as defined in the present volume.

The foregoing represents a largely cognitive interpretation of the story-completion results. A motivational interpretation might also be advanced. Such an interpretation in our view might best proceed by accounting in motivational terms for the relatively poor performance of the boys low in creativity and high in intelligence and of the girls high in creativity and low in intelligence. We have observed that the subgroup of boys in question are distinguished by exceedingly low levels of anxiety, suggesting that they are making a reasonably effective adaptation to the school environment. We also have learned (Chapter 4) that this group exhibits an aversion against thematic conceptualizing, with its greater potential for error. Recall that the stories offered for completion entail stressful failure incidents of a kind that the high intelligence–low creativity boys might find particularly remote from their personal experience and particularly intolerable. Given a background of success in school and a strong desire to achieve, an apparently unavoidable failure experience might conceivably disrupt the performance of the highly intelligent–low creative boys to the point that the quality of their story endings suffers. These boys may just not be able to come to grips with failure in any realistic way. The clinical reports in Chapter 7 will offer further support for this interpretation.

Turning to the girls high in creativity and low in intelligence, we noted in Chapter 3 that these are the girls who appear to be having the most serious academic and social difficulties in the classroom. Evidently, the school situation in the case of these girls is imbued with failure. We should like to offer the hypothesis, then, that the failure themes of the story completion procedure and the testlike atmosphere in which the procedure is administered will evoke protective defenses in the high creativity–low intelligence girls, and thereby inhibit the type of constructive fantasy required to produce mature story endings.

In sum, we are suggesting that the highly intelligent–low creative boys cope inadequately with story-completion tasks involving failure themes because the remoteness of failure in the school experiences of these boys and their desire for achievement hinder identification with the story's central character, thus contributing to story completions of low quality. For the highly creative–low intelligent girls, on the other hand, failure is close at hand and perpetually threatening, with the consequence that the story completion material is quite painful and hence evoking of defensive maneuvers which, in turn, interfere with a realistic appraisal and working through of the story theme.

There is clearly no basis for choosing between a more cognitive and a more motivational interpretation. Nor is there any intention of setting up these alternatives as mutually exclusive. In the present context, both are in the realm of speculative probings. We deemed it advisable to offer tentative interpretations, for the reason that theoretical rationalizations are often more encouraging of future research effort than is raw evidence.

Creativity and Intelligence Viewed as a Function of Personality

In the present section, we break away from the model in which results have thus far been cast and consider what can be learned when creativity and intelligence are conceived as ''dependent'' variables. As the introduction to the present chapter made clear, much evidence has accumulated suggesting that cognitive performances of children and adults can be viewed as effects rather than causes of certain personality dispositions. In the previous section, personality was conceptualized as an outcome of intelligence and creativity status interacting with the demands of the school environment. Here, we shall adopt the alternative view of personality as a determinant of creativity and intelligence.

The particular personality variables selected for their possible causal efficacy are test anxiety and defensiveness. There are several reasons why these two personality variables were selected. First and foremost the two variables in question have already demonstrated their utility in the domain of intellective performances. The reader will recall the earlier review of the relevant studies carried out by the Sarason team. Hence, focusing on test anxiety and defensiveness will enhance the continuity of the present work with previous efforts and will permit one to examine effects in the creativity domain. The latter has thus far not been linked to test anxiety and defensiveness in children in any systematic way. We thus have an opportunity to bridge two research traditions that have followed fairly independent lines of development, despite evident points of articulation between them.

Another basis for choosing test anxiety and defensiveness derives from the authors' earlier success with those variables in the domain of risk-taking behavior (Kogan & Wallach, 1964). Of course, this is no guarantee that the personality variables in question will yield equally high payoffs in the study of thinking modes in children. Nevertheless, our earlier work with test anxiety and defensiveness in college students has yielded insights regarding the nature of those dimensions that may prove helpful when studying their effects on children's thinking processes.

We chose test anxiety over general anxiety for the reasons that the former has greater relevance for thinking processes and is less highly correlated with defensiveness (see Table 60). The latter reason has important methodological consequences, for it is possible that test anxiety and defensiveness interact in the course of exerting their influence on the modes of thinking under investigation. Since the correlation between test anxiety and defensiveness is quite low in both boys and girls (see Table 60), we can be sure that joint dichotomization of the test anxiety and defensiveness distributions at the median will apportion individuals reasonably equally over the cells of a resultant 2 × 2 table. Actually, the correlations between test anxiety and defensiveness are on the low negative side, so we can expect to find the number of children low in test anxiety and high in defensiveness or high in test anxiety and low in defensiveness exceeding the number of children who are low or high on both of those dimensions. The actual numbers were as follows:[9]

	Boys	Girls
Low test-anxious–low defensive	12	13
Low test-anxious–high defensive	23	28
High test-anxious–low defensive	21	26
High test-anxious–high defensive	14	14

It can be seen that there are enough cases in the low-low and high-high subgroups to permit the application of Snedecor's (1946) method of unweighted means. Hence, we shall be able to test for the influence of test anxiety and defensiveness (in the form of main effects and interaction) on intelligence and creativity scores.

We turn now to the results. Again, these will be shown in the form of 2 × 2 tables. There will be two tables for each sex. The first will report mean summed standard scores on the intelligence cluster; the second will report mean summed standard scores on the creativity cluster.

Consider first the results for males. Table 68 presents mean summed standard scores on the intelligence cluster for boys varying in test anxiety and defensiveness. Not at all surprising is the statistically significant effect for test anxiety. Highly test-anxious boys achieve lower intelligence scores, a finding quite consistent with the relevant published evidence. Note further that the boys low in both test anxiety and defensiveness show the highest level of intelligence, whereas those high on both of those personality variables manifest the lowest intelligence levels. Defensiveness, in other words, seems to depress intelligence scores somewhat, though not to a statistically significant extent.

Let us turn next to the creativity findings. Table 69 offers the relevant data. The pattern differs quite radically from that obtained in the case of intelligence. Now it is defensiveness that yields the stronger effect. The high defensive boys are less creative than their low defensive counterparts. Particularly interesting is the observation that within both

---

[9] These *N*'s will apply for all of the remaining tables in the chapter.

Table 68.

Mean Intelligence (in Summed Standard Scores) for
Test Anxiety and Defensiveness
Subgroups ($N = 70$ boys)

		DEFENSIVENESS	
		Low	High
TEST ANXIETY	Low	4.52 (6.46)	1.64 (6.89)
	High	−1.38 (8.02)	−4.25 (6.80)

ANALYSIS OF VARIANCE

Source	df	MS	F	p
Defensiveness	1	8.25	2.61	n. s.
Test anxiety	1	34.78	11.01	<.01
Interaction	1	0.00	<1.00	n. s.
Within cells	66	3.16		

Table 69.

Mean Creativity (in Summed Standard Scores) for
Test Anxiety and Defensiveness
Subgroups ($N = 70$ boys)

		DEFENSIVENESS	
		Low	High
TEST ANXIETY	Low	1.37 (8.14)	−1.90 (4.13)
	High	2.99 (8.28)	0.45 (6.62)

ANALYSIS OF VARIANCE

Source	df	MS	F	p
Defensiveness	1	8.42	2.97	<.09
Test anxiety	1	3.92	1.38	n. s.
Interaction	1	0.13	<1.00	n. s.
Within cells	66	2.84		

low and high defensive boys, the presence of test anxiety does not diminish, but rather enhances, creativity.

Are comparable effects obtained in the female sample? Table 70 examines the influence of test anxiety and defensiveness on intelligence. Note that the effects differ somewhat from those observed in the case of the boys. The major finding in the present instance is a near-significant interaction effect. The mean on the intelligence cluster is disproportionately low in the case of the girls high in both test anxiety and defensiveness. Note that test anxiety in a context of low defensiveness has little debilitating effect on intelligence in girls.

Consider finally the influence of test anxiety and defensiveness on creativity in girls. Table 71 indicates that there are no statistically significant effects. It is essential to note, however, that the pattern of findings differs quite radically from those obtained in the case of intelligence (Table 70). The subgroup highest on the intelligence cluster—the girls low in test anxiety and high in defensiveness—is lowest on the creativity cluster. Correspondingly, the subgroup lowest on the intelligence cluster—the girls high in test anxiety and defensiveness—is highest on the creativity cluster. The female subgroups low in defensiveness— those both low and high in test anxiety—are in the intermediate range on both the intelligence and creativity clusters.

It is quite evident that the influence of test anxiety and defensiveness on intelligence and creativity is similar across sex groups in some ways, and different in others. With regard to similarities, the combination of high test anxiety and high defensiveness depresses intelligence level in both boys and girls. By way of contrast between the sexes, on the other hand, test anxiety in a context of low defensiveness has a much greater decremental effect on intelligence in boys than in girls.

How can we explain these similarities and differences? In the case of high test anxiety and defensiveness in both boys and girls, the stressful character of conventional intelligence tests is likely to be most keenly felt. These are the children, after all, who admit to anxiety in evaluational test situations despite generally powerful defenses against anxiety. In order for this anxiety to be expressed in an otherwise defensive child, the evaluational aspects of the school environment must be especially threatening. Failure for these children may well have serious implications for their sense of self-worth and self-respect. If one is willing to conceive of defensiveness as also reflecting a "need for social approval" (Crowne & Marlowe, 1964), then highly test-anxious and defensive children are those for whom failure may imply social alienation and rejection. This is a rather heavy burden for any child to bear, and it is perhaps not too surprising that their performance on intelligence tests suffers as a consequence.

We now ask why test anxiety in a context of low defensiveness has

Table 70.

MEAN INTELLIGENCE (IN SUMMED STANDARD SCORES) FOR
TEST ANXIETY AND DEFENSIVENESS
SUBGROUPS ($N = 81$ GIRLS)

		DEFENSIVENESS	
		Low	High
	Low	0.12	1.22
		(5.61)	(7.06)
TEST ANXIETY			
	High	0.81	—4.29
		(7.47)	(8.61)

ANALYSIS OF VARIANCE

Source	df	MS	F	p
Defensiveness	1	4.00	1.36	n. s.
Test anxiety	1	5.83	1.98	n. s.
Interaction	1	9.62	3.26	<.08
Within cells	77	2.95		

Table 71.

MEAN CREATIVITY (IN SUMMED STANDARD SCORES) FOR
TEST ANXIETY AND DEFENSIVENESS
SUBGROUPS ($N = 81$ GIRLS)

		DEFENSIVENESS	
		Low	High
	Low	—0.30	—2.71
		(5.83)	(8.79)
TEST ANXIETY			
	High	0.39	2.00
		(6.46)	(9.60)

ANALYSIS OF VARIANCE

Source	df	MS	F	p
Defensiveness	1	0.16	<1.00	n. s.
Test anxiety	1	7.28	2.13	n. s.
Interaction	1	4.04	1.18	n. s.
Within cells	77	3.42		

more of a negative effect on intelligence in boys than in girls. Here we may well draw on the work of the Sarason group. Since it is more difficult for boys generally to admit to anxiety, the identical anxiety score in boys and girls may be reflective of greater disturbance in boys. Accordingly, when test anxiety is related to intelligence indices, one should expect the performance of the boys to show stronger decremental effects. This is indeed what happened in the present instance.

There is still another sex difference worthy of comment in connection with the intelligence means shown in Tables 68 and 70. For boys, the combination of low test anxiety and low defensiveness maximizes intelligence test scores; when defensiveness intrudes, test anxiety remaining low, intelligence scores drop. For the girls, the pattern is reversed. The low test-anxious–high defensive girls achieve the highest intelligence scores. The within-sex differences are not especially large, but the pattern reversal across sex may be of some consequence. It appears that defensiveness is somewhat more damaging to intelligence test performance in the case of boys. Since, according to Sarason and his associates, defensiveness is a more natural posture for boys than girls, one might have expected boys to be less seriously hampered by defensiveness when performing on intelligence tests. The findings run directly contrary to this expectation. Possibly, high defensiveness (accompanied by low test anxiety) in girls reflects so firm a control over potential danger signals from within and without that these children are very effectively equipped for dealing with evaluation-laden assessment situations.

We turn our attention next to creativity, and the sex differences revealed in a comparison of Tables 69 and 71. Common to boys and girls is the finding that high defensiveness accompanied by low test anxiety is associated with the lowest levels of creativity. Since these are the *most* defensive subjects (they do not admit to test anxiety), the present evidence constitutes strong support for the creativity–defensiveness hypothesis discussed in the introduction to the chapter. It is the first demonstration of such a creativity–defensiveness relationship in a sample of children.

When we move into the remaining cells of Tables 69 and 71, the sex similarity gives way to sex differences. For boys, the highest creativity mean score turns up in the low defensive–high test-anxious subgroup. For girls, on the other hand, it is the high test-anxious–high defensive subgroup which ranks highest in creativity. Recall that this was the subgroup which ranked lowest on the intelligence cluster.

Boys and girls also appear to differ on the degree to which creativity goes along with the presence or absence of personality disturbance. Low levels of test anxiety and defensiveness represent more of an asset in boys than in girls. In general, however, the present data show quite clearly that there is no one-to-one relation between creativity and the absence of psychological disturbance in children. The boys and girls who perform best on our creativity tasks are not necessarily the best adjusted children in the classroom. It is the quality rather than the degree of disturbance that matters. Overtly acknowledged anxiety under the stress of evaluative school situations does not especially inhibit creativity, and may in fact enhance it. On the other hand, extreme defensiveness (defensiveness with low test anxiety) contributes to lowered creativity levels.

On the whole, the results yielded by the present mode of analysis are reasonably congruent with conceptualizations put forth by the Sarason group and by others. There are certain respects, however, in which the present data will call for substantial modifications in previously formulated theoretical positions. Consider first the assessment of intelligence. As the Sarason team has observed, test anxiety does have a decremental effect on intelligence assessed in the customary evaluational context. Indeed, the effect is considerably more pronounced in boys than in girls, again in keeping with the Sarason conceptualization. Nowhere in the prior literature on the subject, however, is there any indication that the decremental effects of test anxiety are enhanced when defensiveness is also present. In fact, it is only under such conditions that intelligence test performance is markedly reduced in the female sample. Hence, it is very likely that the lesser validity of the test-anxiety scale in girls (so frequently observed in previous research) can be attributed to the moderating role of defensiveness. Since the admission of test anxiety is of lesser consequence to girls than boys, it apparently requires a context of defensiveness in girls for test anxiety to have any impact upon intelligence test performance. The admission of test anxiety in an otherwise defensive girl is evidently more than a glib confession of feminine weakness.

Although the Sarason group has not been concerned with creativity as such, we noted in the chapter introduction that they have placed considerable stress upon the importance of relaxed, gamelike contexts in enhancing the intellective performance of test anxious children. This work is of considerable relevance to the present investigation, given the fact that such a context was employed in the administration of our creativity tasks. Yet these tasks were sufficiently discrepant from any of the instruments used by Sarason and his associates to rule out any direct extrapolations. The evidence of the present study is quite clear in showing that test anxiety does not especially hamper creativity. In this respect, our work supports Sarason's conclusions respecting the differential effects of evaluational vs. gamelike contexts. With regard to test anxiety *facilitating* creativity, on the other hand, the issue is far less clear-cut. In the boys, test anxiety helps somewhat provided that defensiveness is low. The girls, on the other hand, do not yield significant effects, though the direction of the results indicate that defensiveness enhances the creativity-inducing influence of test anxiety. In short, sex differences continue to be a major determinant of results in the present domain. Defensiveness in boys is an unalloyed liability as far as creativity is concerned. In girls, defensiveness is somewhat less damaging.

The findings reported in the present section demonstrate quite clearly that intelligence and creativity may each represent the outcome of an interaction between motivational and situational components. These components are distinctly not identical for intelligence and for creativity. The conditions under which intelligence flourishes may have little value for or may actually hinder creativity. Correspondingly, the ideal condition for the expression of creativity may be far from ideal in the case of intelligence.

It should now be quite evident that the results of the present section could not have been readily generated from previous work on performance correlates of test anxiety and defensiveness. Most of this earlier work has dealt with the two personality dimensions one at a time or has relegated one of the two to a "control" function in relation to the other. The present evidence conclusively shows that test anxiety and defensiveness must be treated in a simultaneous, combinatorial fashion, if we are to understand their effects upon intelligence and creativity.

Effects of Test Anxiety and Defensiveness on Categorizing and Conceptualizing

In the present section, we shall turn from the issue of creativity and intelligence to matters that are of secondary concern to the central focus of the book. Nevertheless, these matters are of considerable theoretical interest in their own right, and furthermore, they may well have important implications for the creativity and intelligence domains. Recall that these latter domains are related to categorizing and conceptualizing activities in certain systematic ways. Since test anxiety and defensiveness influence creativity and intelligence, those personality dimensions may also exert an effect upon categorizing and conceptualizing processes.

Although our purpose here is largely exploratory, there is some basis in the psychological literature for expecting associations between test anxiety and/or defensiveness, on the one hand, and categorizing and conceptualizing activities, on the other. There has been much discussion recently concerning the possible narrowing of attentional and associative processes under states of arousal or anxiety (for example, Easterbrook, 1959; Korchin, 1964). Some investigators have extended this conception to the realm of categorizing styles and strategies, suggesting that anxiety might contribute to a preference for narrow categorizing (Bruner & Tajfel, 1961; Klein, 1958). Finally, Rosenwald (1961) has proposed that it is defensiveness, rather than anxiety, which is responsible for the cognitive effects described.

A direct test of the hypothesis that anxiety and/or defensiveness contributes to narrow categorizing is possible in the present case. Recall that band-width and object-sorting tasks were administered to all the children (see Chapter 4). In Tables 72 and 73, we examine the influence of test anxiety and defensiveness on the band-width measure for boys and girls, respectively. Note that the hypothesis receives strong confirmation in the case of boys (Table 72). Highly test-anxious boys exhibit significantly narrower band width than do their low test-anxious peers. Defensiveness does not exert much of an effect.

Recall in Chapter 4 that, on the basis of the association between creativity and broad band-width preferences, we conceptualized the latter in terms of the extent of tolerance for deviant instances. A state of test anxiety is apparently associated with a markedly reduced tolerance level. Viewed in this way, the present evidence may be compatible with Easterbrook's (1959) hypothesis that arousal results in a "reduction of cue utilization."

Turning to the girls (Table 73), an entirely different picture emerges. It is the highly defensive girls who show broad band-width preferences. This hardly fits the view that defensiveness enhances cognitive constriction. Some earlier work of the authors (Kogan & Wallach, 1964, pp. 146–151) may point the way to an interpretation of the results for females. The authors observed a significant relation in defensive girls of college age between broad band-width preferences and conservatism in decision-making tasks. Narrow band width was associated with greater risk taking. A further piece of relevant evidence in the defensive girls was a significant correlation between broad band width and low confidence in making judgments under conditions where knowledge is lacking. We then proposed that broad band width, which reflects a preference for errors of inclusion in categorizing, represented an attempt to reduce uncertainty by not leaving any potential instances out of a category. In that regard, broad band-width preferences could be viewed as "conservative," and their relation to conservatism in decision-making tasks under payoff conditions seemed to make good theoretical sense. Unfortunately, we do not possess the necessary data in the case of the sample of girls under study here to know whether the mechanisms described definitely apply in their case. The interpretations advanced are clearly intended as no more than working hypotheses.

Particularly perplexing is the strong positive association between

Table 72.

MEAN BAND-WIDTH SCORES FOR TEST ANXIETY AND
DEFENSIVENESS SUBGROUPS ($N = 70$ BOYS)

		DEFENSIVENESS	
		Low	High
TEST ANXIETY	Low	48.50 (7.34)	47.96 (9.88)
	High	44.10 (11.19)	38.21 (11.16)

ANALYSIS OF VARIANCE

Source	df	MS	F	p
Defensiveness	1	10.32	1.61	n. s.
Test anxiety	1	50.04	7.83	$<.01$
Interaction	1	7.12	1.11	n. s.
Within cells	66	6.39		

Table 73.

MEAN BAND-WIDTH SCORES FOR TEST ANXIETY AND
DEFENSIVENESS SUBGROUPS ($N = 81$ GIRLS)

		DEFENSIVENESS	
		Low	High
TEST ANXIETY	Low	36.85 (7.96)	41.57 (10.79)
	High	37.46 (12.99)	42.86 (10.18)

ANALYSIS OF VARIANCE

Source	df	MS	F	p
Defensiveness	1	25.61	3.74	$<.06$
Test anxiety	1	0.90	<1.00	n. s.
Interaction	1	0.11	<1.00	n. s.
Within cells	77	6.84		

broad band width and creativity in girls (Table 42), given the various indications that the former may be indicative of "conceptual conservatism" under conditions of defensiveness. We also know that the latter state (in conjunction with test anxiety) does not especially inhibit creativity in girls (Table 71). These findings suggest as a distinct possibility that creativity in girls may have a special meaning when it occurs in a context of high defensiveness. Creativity under such conditions might well be in the service of uncertainty reduction. Very much in need of the social approval of the experimenter and fearful of failure, the highly defensive and test-anxious girl may obsessively spin out large numbers of associates in an effort to meet the rather vague requirements of the experimental tasks. The possibility that creativity may have such obsessive connotations was spelled out in Chapter 4. Now we have been able to pinpoint the motivational preconditions which are likely to lend an obsessive character to creative functioning.

But how about the defensive girl low in test anxiety? She is a broad categorizer but, as Table 71 shows, least creative of the four subgroups of girls. In the present case, uncertainty reduction seems to operate in different ways in the two experimental contexts. The problem is one of accounting for the decline in creativity in the highly defensive–low test-anxious girls. First, it is the authors' view that these are the most defensive girls in the sample; they do not admit to any form of weakness or imperfection. Conceivably, defensiveness must assume this more extreme form before it will begin to inhibit creativity in girls. Furthermore, these are the girls who should show the strongest image-maintenance tendencies. Confronted by an experimenter whose purpose in administering the creativity tasks is not entirely clear, the defensive, low test-anxious girl might well expend more effort in figuring out the "proper" thing to do than in attending to the tasks themselves. Such suspiciousness must necessarily have an inhibiting effect on creativity. Where test anxiety and defensiveness are high, on the other hand, the "proper" thing to do is to give as many associates as possible in an obsessive fashion, thereby counteracting the fear of failure that test anxiety implies.

The interpretations advanced above are, of course, highly tentative. Future research may prove them wrong. For the present, we are merely trying to show how creativity may be influenced by an array of personality and situational processes, whose relevance for the study of creativity has barely been recognized.

We turn now to other categorizing and conceptualizing procedures. Object-sorting indices do not appear to be influenced by test anxiety and defensiveness. Scores on the thematic integration task, on the other hand, are significantly affected by defensiveness. Tables 74 and 75 offer the relevant data for boys and girls, respectively. It can be seen that defen-

Table 74.

MEAN NUMBER OF LOW QUALITY STORIES FOR TEST ANXIETY
AND DEFENSIVENESS SUBGROUPS ($N = 70$ BOYS)

		DEFENSIVENESS	
		Low	High
	Low	0.00	0.48
		(0.00)	(1.12)
TEST ANXIETY			
	High	0.10	0.57
		(0.44)	(0.94)

ANALYSIS OF VARIANCE

Source	df	MS	F	p
Defensiveness	1	0.23	5.69	<.03
Test anxiety	1	0.01	<1.00	n. s.
Interaction	1	0.00	<1.00	n. s.
Within cells	66	0.04		

Table 75.

MEAN NUMBER OF LOW QUALITY STORIES FOR TEST ANXIETY
AND DEFENSIVENESS SUBGROUPS ($N = 81$ GIRLS)

		DEFENSIVENESS	
		Low	High
	Low	0.15	0.36
		(0.38)	(0.62)
TEST ANXIETY			
	High	0.15	0.50
		(0.46)	(0.85)

ANALYSIS OF VARIANCE

Source	df	MS	F	p
Defensiveness	1	0.08	3.87	<.06
Test anxiety	1	0.01	<1.00	n. s.
Interaction	1	0.01	<1.00	n. s.
Within cells	77	0.02		

sive children manifest a significantly larger number of poor thematic integrations than do children low in defensiveness.

The thematic integration task, it will be recalled, appeared to involve both intelligence and creativity components (Tables 46 and 47). An examination of that task indicates that it has both divergent and convergent aspects. There are a variety of themes that can be woven around the four stimulus words provided, but at the same time the themes can be evaluated on a dimension of quality. We can only wonder whether defensiveness is more harmful to performance on the type of "mixed" task represented by the thematic integration procedure than on creativity tasks of the associative type. As we have seen, performance on the latter may actually be enhanced by obsessive tendencies indicative of motivational disturbance.

Effects of Test Anxiety and Defensiveness on Physiognomic Sensitivity

In the preceding section, we observed how the examination of relations between personality and categorization–conceptualization could shed considerable light on the psychological processes underlying creativity and intelligence. We approach the topic of physiognomic sensitivity in the same spirit. Apart from the general theoretical interest in examining personality determinants of physiognomic sensitivity, the by-product of such study may, as in the preceding section of the chapter, impinge quite directly upon the central issues of the present volume. Recall in Chapter 5 that both creativity and intelligence are associated with sensitivity to the physiognomic properties of stimuli. Let us now see whether test anxiety and defensiveness, both of which influence intelligence and/or creativity, in any way determine the course of physiognomic sensitivity. To the best of the authors' knowledge, there have been no empirical investigations of this topic.

We begin with the procedure in which the children give free descriptions of the stick figures. In the case of the boys, test anxiety and defensiveness appear at first glance to have little systematic effect upon the attribution of affective states to the stick-figure stimuli. There is, however, a nonsignificant tendency for the defensive boys to adhere closely to atomistic physical aspects of the stimuli (Table 76). The evidence for this tendency is bolstered statistically when the correlation coefficients relating defensiveness to number of lows, number of mediums, and number of highs, in stick-figure descriptions, are inspected. For the 70 boys, these correlations are, respectively, .51, —.01, and —.33. The first and third of the coefficients are significant ($p < .01$), indicating the presence of a positive relationship between defensiveness and the tend-

Table 76.

MEAN NUMBER OF LOWS (ATOMISTIC PHYSICAL RESPONSES) IN
FREE DESCRIPTIONS OF STICK FIGURES FOR TEST ANXIETY
AND DEFENSIVENESS SUBGROUPS ($N = 70$ BOYS)

DEFENSIVENESS

		Low	High
TEST ANXIETY	Low	0.00 (0.00)	2.96 (6.24)
	High	1.14 (1.80)	1.43 (3.30)

ANALYSIS OF VARIANCE

Source	df	MS	F	p
Defensiveness	1	2.63	2.65	n. s.
Test anxiety	1	0.04	<1.00	n. s.
Interaction	1	1.78	1.80	n. s.
Within cells	66	0.99		

ency to concentrate upon atomistic physical descriptions of the stimuli, and an inverse relationship between defensiveness and the tendency to provide physiognomically sensitive descriptions. This finding is quite consistent with the evidence reported in Chapter 5 showing a significant association in boys between creativity and the attribution of emotional states to the stick figures. Just as defensiveness inhibits creativity in boys, so it seems to exert a comparable influence on one aspect of physiognomic sensitivity.

Turning to the female sample, the results assume a quite different cast. As Tables 77 and 78 demonstrate, test-anxious girls give more wholistic physical descriptions and fewer affective or emotional descriptions. Recall in Chapter 5 that performance on the stick-figures task was significantly related to intelligence in girls. Accordingly, the dominant influence of test anxiety in the present case is again consistent with expectations. It is not at all clear, however, why test anxiety should affect performance on a task whose manifest properties are so remote from the classic intelligence test format. Very possibly, the test-anxious girl emphasizes the convergent aspects of the physiognomic situation. A stimulus is presented to the child, and she must find the "correct" re-

Table 77.

MEAN NUMBER OF MEDIUMS (WHOLISTIC PHYSICAL RESPONSES) IN
FREE DESCRIPTIONS OF STICK FIGURES FOR TEST ANXIETY
AND DEFENSIVENESS SUBGROUPS ($N = 81$ GIRLS)

		DEFENSIVENESS	
		Low	High
	Low	20.08	19.50
		(7.65)	(6.14)
TEST ANXIETY			
	High	22.04	22.43
		(4.12)	(4.42)

ANALYSIS OF VARIANCE

Source	df	MS	F	p
Defensiveness	1	0.01	<1.00	n. s.
Test anxiety	1	5.98	3.45	$<.07$
Interaction	1	0.23	<1.00	n. s.
Within cells	77	1.73		

Table 78.

MEAN NUMBER OF HIGHS (AFFECTIVE RESPONSES) IN FREE
DESCRIPTIONS OF STICK FIGURES FOR TEST ANXIETY
AND DEFENSIVENESS SUBGROUPS ($N = 81$ GIRLS)

		DEFENSIVENESS	
		Low	High
	Low	14.08	14.32
		(7.99)	(6.97)
TEST ANXIETY			
	High	11.08	9.93
		(5.25)	(4.14)

ANALYSIS OF VARIANCE

Source	df	MS	F	p
Defensiveness	1	0.20	<1.00	n. s.
Test anxiety	1	13.66	6.33	$<.02$
Interaction	1	0.49	<1.00	n. s.
Within cells	77	2.16		

sponse for that stimulus. Such a set is not likely to make for associative leaps into the affective domain. Where a subject focuses on finding the "correct" answer, it will probably not deviate too far from the physical properties of the stick figure.

Test anxiety and defensiveness do not bear any systematic relation to performance on the "free descriptions of paths" procedure. This is not the case in the "matching" procedure, however. The reader will recall that the latter requires the subject to match abstract line patterns with faces conveying emotional states. The appropriate match is based on a consensus of adult judges. Tables 79 and 80 provide the data for boys and girls, respectively. In the case of the boys, a significant effect for defensiveness may be noted. High defensiveness is associated with fewer correct matches. Thus, despite the convergent abilities seemingly involved in the matching procedure, it is defensiveness, not test anxiety, that exercises a significant influence.

This finding may be contrasted with the interaction effect observed in the female sample (Table 80). Girls high in both test anxiety and defensiveness exhibit a disproportionately low number of correct matches. Recall that these are the very girls who rank highest on creativity (Table 71). Despite the gamelike contexts in which both the creativity and physiognomic procedures were administered, personality influences the two in distinctly different ways. Again, it should be emphasized that the physiognomic "matching" procedure has a convergent structure. The child responds in "yes" or "no" terms to the matches suggested to him. It appears that, regardless of content and experimental context, tasks with convergent structures show decremental effects when undertaken by test-anxious girls. Recall that similar effects were obtained in the case of the stick figures, another task with convergent properties. Test-anxious girls performed more poorly there as well.

For boys, on the other hand, content seems to be more relevant than structure. Defensiveness detracts from performance in both the creativity and physiognomic domains. Apparently, the test-anxious boy, unlike his female counterpart, does not bring an evaluational set to bear upon physiognomic procedures despite their convergent properties. Conceivably, the expression of intelligence in boys is more remote from the realm of human emotions, with the consequence that test anxiety does not impinge upon the area of physiognomic sensitivity. For girls, on the other hand, intelligence naturally proceeds along more social lines, and hence considerations of test anxiety may come into play even when physiognomic procedures are administered in a relaxed gamelike context.

We come finally to the procedure in which subjects are given highly appropriate, moderately appropriate, and inappropriate (bizarre) emotive adjectives to be accepted or rejected for particular stick-figure

Table 79.

MEAN NUMBER OF CORRECT ABSTRACT PATTERN CHOICES FOR TEST ANXIETY
AND DEFENSIVENESS SUBGROUPS ($N = 70$ BOYS)

		DEFENSIVENESS	
		Low	High
	Low	20.25	19.61
		(2.45)	(2.41)
TEST ANXIETY			
	High	20.38	18.29
		(1.53)	(3.00)

ANALYSIS OF VARIANCE

Source	df	MS	F	p
Defensiveness	1	1.87	5.62	$<.03$
Test anxiety	1	0.36	1.07	n. s.
Interaction	1	0.53	1.59	n. s.
Within cells	66	0.33		

Table 80.

MEAN NUMBER OF CORRECT ABSTRACT PATTERN CHOICES FOR TEST ANXIETY
AND DEFENSIVENESS SUBGROUPS ($N = 81$ GIRLS)

		DEFENSIVENESS	
		Low	High
	Low	18.77	19.79
		(3.52)	(2.08)
TEST ANXIETY			
	High	19.23	17.36
		(2.72)	(3.30)

ANALYSIS OF VARIANCE

Source	df	MS	F	p
Defensiveness	1	0.18	<1.00	n. s.
Test anxiety	1	0.97	2.27	n. s.
Interaction	1	2.09	4.89	$<.04$
Within cells	77	0.43		

patterns. For girls, test anxiety and defensiveness have no bearing upon the foregoing procedure. Recall, however, our finding (Chapter 5) that the high intelligence–low creativity girls accepted significantly fewer bizarre attributions than the remaining three cognitive subgroups. In the boys, on the other hand, defensiveness exerts a near-significant effect upon the number of moderately appropriate adjectives. As Table 81 shows, the highly defensive boys accept a smaller number of moderately appropriate stick-figure attributions.

Again, defensiveness in boys operates to reduce physiognomic sensitivity, even in the case where the task is presented in the form of a structured list of adjectives. The defensive boy apparently insists upon a closer fit between stick-figure and adjective stimuli before he is willing to accept the latter. One can also view the present findings in a band-width context. The defensive boy, relative to his low defensive peer, manifests narrower band-width preferences. He prefers the error of exclusion to the error of inclusion when it comes to emotive attributions. Recall in the preceding section of the chapter that test anxiety in boys was related to narrow band-width preferences in a quantitative estimation task (a children's variant of the Pettigrew category-width test).

Table 81.

MEAN NUMBER OF MODERATELY APPROPRIATE EMOTIVE ATTRIBUTIONS
TO STICK FIGURES FOR TEST ANXIETY AND DEFENSIVENESS
SUBGROUPS ($N = 70$ BOYS)

		DEFENSIVENESS	
		Low	High
TEST ANXIETY	Low	19.33 (2.61)	18.17 (3.11)
	High	19.52 (2.60)	17.93 (3.08)

ANALYSIS OF VARIANCE

Source	df	MS	F	p
Defensiveness	1	1.90	3.73	$<.06$
Test anxiety	1	0.00	<1.00	n. s.
Interaction	1	0.05	<1.00	n. s.
Within cells	66	0.51		

Now we note that defensiveness is related to narrow band width in a physiognomic sensitivity procedure. We have no ready explanation for the discrepancy, though it might be noted that the band-width task based on quantitative estimations is more closely linked to the intelligence domain than is a procedure employing stick figures and adjectives. This may account for the former's link to test anxiety and the latter's relation to defensiveness. Over and beyond this difference, however, is the common effect exerted in boys by both types of motivational disturbance—a narrowing of category boundaries.

CONCLUSIONS

The present chapter represents the first break with the analytic model developed in the first five chapters of the present volume. With intelligence and creativity shown to be basically independent modes of thinking, we erected a fourfold typological classification of subjects on the basis of high or low status on the intelligence and creativity dimensions. We then proceeded to demonstrate that these four groups of children could be distinguished in their overt classroom behaviors, in their performance on tasks in the categorizing and conceptualizing domain, and in the area of physiognomic sensitivity. A similar approach characterizes part of the present chapter, where we showed that boys' creativity and intelligence status bears upon the scores they receive on anxiety, test anxiety, and defensiveness scales. The direction of causation had been given little consideration up to that point, though there was an implicit tendency (becoming more explicit in the case of the behavior ratings) to assign antecedent status to the intelligence and creativity variables. In this regard, we are clearly the victim of the analytic framework in which our results have been cast. Obviously, it would be sheer folly to treat the relations to categorizing and conceptualizing and to physiognomic sensitivity as anything other than correlational in nature. In the case of behavior ratings, the issue is more equivocal, for it is difficult to conceive of the observed behaviors in other than a consequent role.

We are evidently leading up to the point that the variables of anxiety and defensiveness demanded a hearing as potential causative agents in regard to creativity and intelligence. The case for such a causal relationship had already been made very effectively for anxiety and intelligence by Seymour Sarason and his co-workers. Under the circumstances, we could do no less than explore the full gamut of possibilities—namely, that defensiveness as well as anxiety might have causal efficacy, and that creativity as well as intelligence might be influenced by those personality variables.

The results for the boys were especially clear: test anxiety inversely related to intelligence, and defensiveness inversely related to creativity. We are entirely amenable to the Sarason group's claim that test anxiety is responsible for a decrement in intelligence-test performance. Their research program has shown quite conclusively that the debilitating effects of test anxiety are markedly diminished when intelligence measures become more gamelike in character. The introduction to the chapter furthermore described intelligence tasks that were facilitated by test anxiety.

What implications can be drawn from the foregoing evidence for the measurement of creativity? We strongly suspect that defensiveness does have a causative influence with respect to creativity in boys. Does this then suggest that one embark upon the kind of research program pursued by Sarason and his associates in connection with the anxiety–intelligence issue? We have serious reservations in this regard. If we were to administer our creativity procedures in an evaluational, testlike context, we should expect that the influence of defensiveness would decline and that of test anxiety would increase. At the same time, however, we would bring about the very condition—positive correlations between intelligence and creativity measures—that the present volume set out to elucidate and to eliminate. In short, we are proposing that the kind of creativity undergoing assessment in the present work is precisely the kind of creativity one wishes to assess in a sample of children. We will grant that performance on creativity tasks can be altered by the manipulation of situational conditions, but this in no way detracts from the utility of the particular condition chosen in the present study.

The authors should like to stress that the implications drawn for the study of creativity in no way represent a reflection on the Sarason team's approach to the study of intelligence. One must bear in mind that a particular subgroup of children—those high in anxiety—were performing below their capacity in the classroom not as a consequence of presumed low intelligence, but because they were handicapped by the evaluational pressures of the testing situation. Since teachers are prone to classify children on the basis of intelligence, it was important to demonstrate that intelligence varied with the conditions of its measurement. No such pressing practical problem exists in the case of creativity.

That defensiveness may play a causal role in relation to creativity further contributes to the validity of the latter's method of measurement. The evidence outlined in the course of the chapter points to the debilitating effects of defensiveness in contexts that deviate from the familiar and the expected. Certainly, gamelike conditions and experimenter encouragement deviate substantially from the standard evaluational context of the classroom. If one accepts the view that creativity is a process that will be best expressed where the individual can set his own pace under conditions *initially* free of evaluation by others, the procedures adopted in the present work fit the stated desiderata quite well. They are not the conditions to which children in our schoolroom culture are accustomed, however, and they are evidently disruptive to the defensive child.

Although we make no claim to creativity or intelligence as an immutable quality of persons, we do feel that the particular form of those dimensions tapped by our assessment procedures leads to the most viable typology possible in the domains under investigation. Earlier, we posed the question of the best possible match between personality and thinking modes, on the one hand, and independent and dependent variable status, on the other. It now appears that the issue is fairly well resolved. When test anxiety and defensiveness were cast in an antecedent role, their relationships to intelligence and creativity were in accord with theoretical expectations (more strongly in the case of the boys). This informs us that the type of creativity and intelligence being assessed is in accord with our general specifications for those variables. At this stage, it is perfectly reasonable to deal with creativity and intelligence as characteristics of persons in typological analysis. As we have seen, joint consideration of creativity and intelligence as "treatment" variables reveals information about anxiety and defensiveness that was not uncovered when the analysis was performed in the opposite direction. Thus, we observed that creativity in boys was associated with low defensiveness only in the case where intelligence was also high. Thus too, we observed that intelligence in boys was associated with minimal levels of anxiety and test anxiety only in the case where creativity was low.

One of the more important contributions of the present chapter is the demonstration that creativity and intelligence in children do not imply the absence of personality disturbances. Recall in Chapter 3 that the highly creative girls of low intelligence appeared to be having serious personal difficulties. These difficulties are not expressed in those girls' responses to the personality inventory, for there were no significant differences in such responses as a function of creativity and intelligence in girls. On the other hand, highly creative boys report moderate levels of anxiety, and, if intelligence is low, defensiveness reaches a quite high level. One has the impression that the personality implications of creativity and intelligence are picked up at the level of overt behavior in girls and at the level of personality inventory responses in boys.

In the Sarason group's work, a strong case is made for the superior performance of test-anxious children in performance contexts that reward a pattern of cautious and dependent behavior. Since these contexts have a gamelike character and involve a sympathetic experimenter, we wondered whether test anxiety might also prove a boon to performance in the creativity domain. Our results lend only partial support to such a view.

Test anxiety seems neither to hinder nor to facilitate creative performance in a linear manner, although we do have evidence which suggests
that creativity may be highest in the presence of moderate levels of test
anxiety. Clearly, caution and dependency should not be expected to serve
as unalloyed assets where creativity is at issue, but they may foster a
tendency to stick with a problem. There are conditions where motivational factors (test anxiety and defensiveness in girls) may serve to
contribute to an obsessive style of responding, with higher creativity
scores as a consequence.

In sum, the findings reported in the present chapter have made a
substantial contribution to our knowledge about personality and thinking.
For the first time certain hypotheses concerning creativity and personality have been put to empirical test in a sample of children. Again, for
the first time, the traditional study of anxiety, defensiveness, and intelligence has been brought into close contact with the realm of creativity
research. Finally, we have shown how anxiety and defensiveness also
impinge upon matters of categorizing and conceptualizing and upon
sensitivity to the physiognomic properties of stimuli. These relationships
turned out to have important implications for the creativity–intelligence
distinction.

SUMMARY

Despite the existence of a vast literature devoted to the effects of
anxiety and defensiveness on thinking processes, we found a serious
imbalance in our knowledge of the various aspects of the problem. Thus,
there appeared to be fairly conclusive evidence that anxiety in children
was responsible for a decline in intelligence-test performance. There
were also indications that such anxiety might have facilitative effects
on intelligence under relaxed, nonevaluative conditions. On the other
hand, much less information was available concerning the effects of
defensiveness on intelligence in children. In the case of creativity and its
relation to anxiety and defensiveness, not a single unequivocal empirical
study with children could be found. This was indeed a surprising state
of affairs, given the substantial volume of theoretical speculation and
empirical investigation devoted to the personality correlates of creativity
in adults. A final shortcoming of previous work in the present area was
the general neglect of possible interaction effects between anxiety and
defensiveness as these impinge upon intelligence and creativity.

An 88-item personality inventory was administered individually to
all the children in the study. Included within the inventory were scales
of general anxiety, test anxiety, and defensiveness. A few additional
items were included in the inventory for exploratory or "filler" purposes.

In addition, a story-completion procedure was employed, with the original expectation that it might yield an index of denial of failure (a variant of defensiveness). The children were presented with stories in which the "hero" is in the throes of a severe failure experience, and were then requested to complete the stories. It soon became evident that a simple denial of failure dimension did not adequately account for quality differences in the stories, and accordingly, we arrived at a scoring scheme based on the "maturity" of the story completions.

Reliabilities for the personality inventory measures of interest were quite high. With regard to "maturity" of story completions, both inter-judge and internal consistency indices of reliability reached satisfactory levels.

Boys and girls differed significantly on mean scores in the case of several of the personality scales. These differences were quite consistent with the previously published evidence. Interrelationships among the scales were examined separately for boys and girls. Correlations were somewhat higher in the case of the girls. Though anxiety and defensiveness were inversely related in both boys and girls, the correlations were sufficiently low to allow for the possibility that anxiety and defensiveness might make independent contributions in accounting for variance in the creativity and intelligence domains.

Relationships between the personality measures and behavior ratings (discussed in Chapter 3) were stronger and more widespread in the male sample. Test anxiety in boys, for example, was associated with an array of negative behavioral characteristics. The implications of test anxiety for behavior in girls were considerably less severe. The sex difference in the case of test anxiety was again consistent with previously published evidence. On the other hand, there were no significant relations between defensiveness and behavior ratings in either sex, contrary to previous research suggesting that defensiveness was relevant to the behavioral domain in girls.

Two approaches were taken to the major findings of the chapter. First, we viewed personality as a function of creativity and intelligence, an approach consistent with the one followed in the previous chapters. Since, on the other hand, anxiety and defensiveness might be expected to exert a causal influence on intelligence and creativity, we also presented the data with the latter in the role of dependent variables.

With personality treated as a function of the thinking modes, significant interaction effects were obtained for both general and test anxiety in boys. Highly intelligent–low creative boys were quite low, low intelligent–low creative boys were quite high, and the two highly creative subgroups were intermediate in admitted anxiety. The exceptionally low anxiety level for the boys of high intelligence and low creativity was explained on the basis of a neat match between their area of competence and the type of thinking emphasized in the classroom. In the case of defensiveness, a significant intelligence effect was obtained, the highly intelligent boys being less defensive. The findings ran counter to the defensiveness–creativity hypothesis, suggesting that low defensiveness is related to high creativity only in the case where intelligence level is also high. It should be noted that all of the foregoing effects were obtained only in the case of boys.

Maturity of story endings in the story-completion procedure was found to be relevant to creativity in boys and to intelligence in girls. We attempted to account for the discrepancy between the sexes by invoking both cognitive and motivational interpretations.

Turning to the alternative approach to the data, test anxiety and defensiveness were given the status of antecedents, and creativity and intelligence the status of consequents. For boys, test anxiety was inversely related to intelligence, and defensiveness was inversely related to creativity. Both findings were consistent with stated hypotheses. Results for girls were less clear-cut. In the case of intelligence, a significant interaction effect was obtained, largely as a consequence of an exceptionally low intelligence mean in girls high in both test anxiety and defensiveness. No significant effects for creativity were observed in girls, though the pattern of results was manifestly discrepant from the intelligence findings. A theoretical interpretation of the obtained sex differences was advanced based in part on prior published evidence indicating that anxiety and defensiveness may not mean the same thing in boys and girls. Particularly clear was the evidence that motivational disturbance as such did not necessarily hamper the display of creativity or intelligence. Rather, certain patterns of disturbance may enhance, while other patterns detract from, creativity and/or intelligence.

As a final contribution, we explored the effects of test anxiety and defensiveness upon categorizing and conceptualizing activities and upon physiognomic sensitivity. An array of significant findings was obtained, some having clear implications for the creativity and intelligence domains.

7 ✕✕✕

Studies of
Individual
Children

In the course of the preceding chapters, images have come into focus concerning the various characteristics of boys and girls who are located in one or another of the four creativity and intelligence groupings. In themselves, the groupings defined particular styles of cognitive functioning. Our further sources of evidence concerning behavior in the school setting, categorizing and conceptualizing, physiognomic sensitivity, and personality as assessed from self-description and from fantasy, have contributed to our understanding of the correlates of these thinking styles. It is the purpose of the present chapter to offer a very different kind of evidence. From the systematic inquiry conducted in the chapters preceding, we may presume by this point to possess a picture of the *general* nature of the boys and girls in each of the four cognitive groupings. Now we wish to select children from each of these groups and proceed to say something about them as *individuals*.

In the course of our systematic research, the two experimenters formed clinical impressions of each child in the sample. They proceeded to write these impressions down when the systematic research was completed. The material recorded for each child represents the consensus of the two experimenters as based upon the totality of their experience with a given child, including discussions with current teachers and examination of reports by previous teachers. Such resumés are open to possible bias, of course, in that they were prepared with some awareness of each child's performances on the various procedures comprising the sources of quantitative data that were considered in earlier chapters. They hardly constitute, therefore, fully independent evidence. Rather, they permit us to paint a clinical portrait of particular children who will serve as instances of their respective cognitive types. This information provides us with examples of some of the specific details that characterize the children of one or another grouping.

The bases for choice of particular descriptive materials were various. Several considerations were relevant in preparing the accounts that follow. The vast majority of them pertain to children who were at or near the extremes on the creativity and intelligence scores that determine group placement. Then too, the clinical reports varied in amount of detail, so that much more material, and many more specifics, were available for some children than for others. So also, the subjective confidence with which statements were made varied for different children, although this factor did not always correspond to the amount of known detail. Elements such as these entered as additional considerations into the selection process. The information so selected then was assembled into the accounts which form the content of this chapter.

DESCRIPTIONS OF INDIVIDUAL BOYS

We begin with the boys. In all the clinical accounts comprising the present chapter, the names used are, of course, pseudonyms. In addition, any specific details regarding locale and regarding characteristics and background of particular individuals have been systematically altered or omitted so that no information about personal identity could be revealed.

Boys High in Both Creativity and Intelligence

ALAN. Alan's family is an unusual one. His father, a professional man, also is active in community affairs. Both parents convey a sense of strong commitment to civic matters and are wholehearted participants in such activities, but not at the expense of their several children. Rather, the children seem free to enjoy their parents' interests if they wish. They are neither forced into these adult activities nor excluded from them. Alan has taken advantage of the availability of this adult stimulation, and one finds him well informed, imaginative in his art work and thinking, and with a fine mind for abstracting and organizing. Although the family has high intellectual standards and urges Alan to work hard in developing academic skills, they wisely see him as still a young boy and are sensitive to the emotional needs of a child his age.

Alan's teachers, however, have a harder time remembering his youthfulness. He is large for his eleven years, and displays considerable poise. This, coupled with Alan's wealth of information and understanding of the environment, makes him stand out in any class, and teachers often are unduly intimidated by his competence. When Alan senses their insecurity, it seems to goad him to expressions of arrogance and condescension. These are generally subtly conveyed through the quality of his speaking voice, facial expressions, or little tricks such as reading a book held under his desk during a class discussion but nevertheless following the conversation and entering it at will. When executing such a feat as this, Alan's face reveals a mischievous delight in his own "powers." The delight itself, moreover, seems to be something about which he wants others to know, as if he needs to have his superior qualities seen and recognized as such.

Alan often looks bored by school work. Yet his interest can always be spurred by giving him a leadership role. This provides him with an affirmation of his worth which he might otherwise find, singly, in the successful completion of more challenging tasks. Teachers report that he requires constant intellectual challenging, or, alternatively, a leadership position, if he is to remain stimulated in the classroom. Indeed, Alan frequently is chosen to lead activities. Knowing he can get away with it, he also will sometimes assume leadership over a group assembled for some task, becoming bossy and domineering in the process, and even going so far as to say to his group, "I get all the good ideas."

Toward the end of the fifth grade year, Alan began to show some carelessness in his work. Along with such carelessness, Alan also was found to indulge more often in mischievous pranks. As the school year progressed, Alan seemed to let his hair down and permit himself to engage in spontaneous and boyish mischief-making. It may well be that this behavior reflected a working through of a conflict in his loyalties and identifications. Identification with his family may have been used as a support until he was more certain of what position he should assume with his classmates. Both the mischievousness and the carelessness may be viewed as experiments in being "boyish." In addition to receiving respect from his classmates for his intellectual superiority, Alan would probably like to feel that he is accepted as "one of the guys." It seems quite unlikely that any such desire for group acceptance will dampen his intellectual curiosity or make him a passive conformist. Rather, it seems to imply that his own sense of identity is growing stronger and allowing him greater expressive freedom.

BENJAMIN. Benjamin is a tall, intelligent-looking boy who at first impression may appear cold and condescending toward classmates and teachers. Such a first impression is, however, quickly shown to be false. He is rightfully confident of his intellectual powers, and shows no hesitation in presenting and defending his own position. Benjamin was very eager to discuss intellectual matters with the experimenters, and showed none of the overconfidence in his manner that on first impression had been seen in his face. It was noted that Benjamin was somewhat shy about becoming friendly with the other boys in his class and it may be that his demeanor is, in part, an attempt at hiding this shyness. Some of the time, however, it was very clear that Benjamin's expression reflected quite candidly his insightful sizing up of a person or situation. He is amazingly perceptive of human feelings and qualities, and will express silent but undisguised disdain if he feels that someone is being less than genuine.

The boy has done much thinking about what people are like generally, and about his own nature in particular. He would mention various of his classmates as examples of different kinds of thinkers, using classifications such as "mechanical" and "intuitive," although perhaps not those exact words. Benjamin seems to be concerned with establishing an image of what he wants to be like, and then living up to it. A kind of moralizing seems at times to be uppermost in his ideal self-picture, and he will follow people and partake of activities if he feels that they are "right." While it is likely that Benjamin works for acceptance in school by acting in a way which he feels will be appreciated by the adults around him, he is by no means a passive mimic. His decisions about whom to respect and to seek respect from are completely his own.

In the fourth grade, Benjamin's parents told his teacher that the boy had been very concerned with trying to discover where he as an individual stands. It would appear that he was trying to understand what kinds of relationships he wished to have with peers and with adults, and what he wanted for himself in life. He seems to have arrived at some conclusions. In the current school year he has not been working terribly hard, although he is still easily doing excellent work. When urged to work harder, he responded that he had decided he didn't want to be anyone's genius. Benjamin apparently has determined to set his own pace and make his way according to standards of his own choice. It may be that he has opted for a "better-rounded" image in the eyes of his classmates. Such a decision, however, is not leading him to underestimate intellectual matters. He enjoys learning very much and displays a genuine enthusiasm for work. Humor and visual imagination are displayed in abundance. Regarding his responses on visual tasks, he often sees objects through someone else's eyes, just as he is able to do in social situations.

Lest we have conveyed a picture of Benjamin as overly formal in the school setting, it should be added that frequent mischievous looks are to be found in his eyes. While no plans for mischief are executed in school, he apparently does indulge in some pranks at home. Openness to feelings and experiences thus is present despite a formalness in appearance. In sum, eagerness and enthusiasm seem to be well integrated with intellect in Benjamin.

CHARLES. Charlie is part of a large, closely-knit family whose members participate in such joint activities as chamber music. These activities are a great source of pride to Charlie, as also is his own particular role as cellist. Perhaps it is from such family experiences that Charlie has developed considerable sensitivity to the behavior of others and especially to the ethical issues that arise in personal and group relations. He is not the kind of child who tattles on classmates; nevertheless, he is constantly aware of his own standard of right and wrong and struggles to live by it. In class he has been heard to speak up with earnest conviction on matters concerning the class and concerning the outer world as well. He clearly gives these matters much deliberation before he voices his views. The boy works through his ideas carefully and expresses feelings and opinions with clarity. Furthermore, his intellectual and ethical opinions always are blended with emotional sensitivity; they are not mere verbal formulas.

Charlie works hard and evinces a strong sense of responsibility whether he is enjoying his tasks or not. In those activities where his interest is caught, he shows deep involvement—as in the case of music, dramatics, art, and sports. While his academic subjects arouse less enthusiasm, he nevertheless works at them industriously. Charlie's motivation in connection with school work seems to grow from a desire to meet a certain high standard that he has set for himself, rather than from a desire to succeed in competition with peers. In most instances he avoids the limelight. The boy is quite inward, always watching and listening, rarely verbalizing or volunteering. He enters discussions only when deeply stirred by the topic discussed.

DANIEL. In the classroom, Daniel is involved in his work in a serious and earnest way. He works consistently and well at academic tasks. Perhaps the most striking quality about him, however, is his sense of humor. Sometimes it is quite adult in nature, but more often it is a nervous giggling reaction to situations or ideas. His exuberance is so great that Daniel often is able to involve those around him, or even the total class and teacher, in some hilarious anecdote or another. In the experimental procedures concerning stick figures he would imitate their postural positions, becoming totally and physically involved in acting out the parts of the stick figures in a humorous way as if they were characters in a play, inducing the experimenter thereby to laugh with him. None of this, however, would be at the expense of his performance on the experimental task itself. The humor seemed not so much to be a way of attracting attention as a way of creating a bond between Daniel and those around him. A major factor in Daniel's humor is its impulsiveness. Daniel does not particularly plan what he will do; rather, it pours out of him.

Boys High in Creativity But Low in Intelligence

EDWARD. Ed is a very high-spirited, energetic boy whose clowning, foolishness, and fighting have earned him a reputation as a trouble-maker in school. He can always be very easily distracted from his work and, once distracted, will throw himself with gusto into some activity that is bound to create a classroom disturbance. In his early grades, he seemed to have no awareness of what the boundaries should be for his behavior in social situations.

Various lines of evidence suggest a tense home situation. Reports indicate that discipline at home for the boy has been quite inconsistent. An older brother has had the same kinds of reading problems that Ed is experiencing now. Regarding the father, Ed's projective story responses suggest the picture of a man whom Ed sees as being sad, helpless, and angry about the way things are going in general.

Ed has experienced learning problems in all skill areas, and especially in reading. He visits a remedial reading tutor often, and his reading problems include word reversals. In working with Ed, the experimenters were most impressed by the freedom with which his responses ranged far and wide, and by his interest in exploring the ideas that occurred to him. He was very open in expressing his feelings—happy, sad, and violent. Further, he was unique among all the children in expressing sexual wishes.

The boy has been receiving psychotherapy for several years. According to the school record, psychotherapy has produced dramatic changes in Ed's attitudes toward school and toward people in general. His sensitivity to people, sense of humor, and desire to do well in his work all have increased. As a result, he is now engaged in a battle for control of his impulse to disrupt the class. Being cooperative and "good" have become a real concern to him, not in the abstract but in concrete terms of what he should do at each moment. That the problem of working through his own confusion and arriving at decisions for action is on his mind a great deal, can be seen from various of his projective materials. In one of his failure story endings, for example, he proceeds as follows when, in story 3, he learns that the hero has overheard some boys saying that nobody likes him and nobody thinks he's any good:

> He goes and pounds the kids out. And then he says, "Do you like me?" And they say "No." So day by day he brings in stuff like candy and they gradually begin to like him because of that. And he asks his parents if he could have help from someone who helps guys. And he did and he got smarter. After a year he had the same teacher again and she asked him some problems and he could answer them right off.

Here in microcosm is a recapitulation of Ed's own progression from a stage in which a first impulse must be directly gratified, to the point which, with the aid of therapy, he has been striving to attain where he can carry out a plan and accept help from others toward reaching his goal. Expressed here is the fact that the boy is trying; but the presence of confusing factors in his home life and the compounding of troubles that results from his reading problem make it difficult for him to have experiences of success.

During the fifth grade year, Ed was in the process of terminating psychotherapy. The immediate repercussion was that his behavior in school became worse than ever and he was involved in many fights. He soon began to regain control, however, and it may well be that a factor aiding this was a new external source of self-confidence in the person of an art teacher. During the year a talent for art began to show itself in Ed. Its first manifestation occurred when the class was assigned the task of painting their conception of the ocean. Ed's painting was of a beautifully freewheeling boat moving through the waves. No one knows of his having taken drawing lessons; yet the sense of color, design, and rhythm were incredibly well developed and seemed to be the work of a much more experienced person. The art teacher was very pleased with this picture and with Ed's subsequent art work. The art teacher's pleasure clearly boosted Ed's morale.

FRANK. From the very first years in school, Frank acted rebelliously and aggressively. Reports indicate that he had a fiery temper, did much teasing and poking, and was very easily hurt. It must have been apparent to classmates that Frank's aggressiveness was a cover for easily bruised sensitivities, for they tended to make a scapegoat out of him. Even now Frank rarely seems to act out of strength or confidence. He seems to have a poor estimate of his self-worth, and to use disruptive, attention-seeking behavior as a means of shoring up his confidence.

Early in Frank's school history, the extent to which he disrupted class activities was sufficiently severe for the school to suggest consultation with a counsellor. Various sources indicate erratic and inconsistent discipline in the home situation. In addition to this source of confusion for the boy, Frank had a very serious hearing defect that was not discovered for several years. This condition certainly must have contributed to his tendency toward acting-out in the classroom, and to his difficulty in concentrating on lessons.

There is little that Frank does in school of which he can feel proud. The most disciplined of his attempts at gaining attention in the fifth grade are by means of talking and clowning. The children seem to accept him in the role of class clown, but Frank himself experiences much conflict about his own methods since he is sufficiently sensitive to their shortcomings to be unable to take much pride in them. It is evident that Frank is disappointed in himself and doesn't quite know where to begin to set himself right. He protects himself by the defensive maneuver of proclaiming loudly that he is right in his opinions, and he has very definite tastes and preferences which he defends with stubbornness. He often takes disagreement from another as a personal criticism. One can see that his opinions are loudly voiced in order to cover an underlying fear that he is wrong.

Frank seems to be beset by a deep struggle between a part of him that accepts failure as inevitable and a part that struggles to find a basis for pride and self-confidence. Given much reassurance, warmth, and patience, one can glimpse displays of high competence. But he is very easily upset when the circumstances are less favorable, and then his own emotional breakdown gives him further cause for despair. One incident in an art class will serve as an example. When a painting of his was criticized by the art teacher, Frank defended his work and then began to cry. His own teacher took him from the room and helped him to regain control. After he returned to the room, he sat listlessly at his desk. Apart from his brief verbal self-defense, Frank's reactions were essentially passive. He cried and became listless.

The boy seems to be very perceptive of emotions in other people and in himself, but does not use such sensitivity in a constructive way. His reading of emotional cues from others seems basically oriented toward finding criticisms of himself. And his personal introspections, in their rich affective detail, suggest a passive, almost indulgent, indwelling. For example, he seems fascinated by the details of the experience of fear, describing it as ''a feeling that scares you and you get tense and your muscles tighten.''

GEORGE. George has been a continual problem to his teachers. The boy is highly ''explosive,'' and this anger seems to arise from the conflict between a strong need for recognition and a supersensitivity to rejection. For instance, when not chosen for a desirable position on a baseball team composed of classmates, he stormed angrily from the field into the woods, shouting deprecations such as, ''I'm no good; I'm nothing.'' When criticized or when failure is exposed, he reacts with loud, obnoxious language and rebellious behavior. If not accorded what he deems to be sufficient appreciation by his teachers, he may become sullen, resentful, and quiet.

Much of this angry behavior is exhibitionistic. George seems to use it to create an impression of ''toughness'' and ''manliness.'' There is no doubt, however, that the angry feelings expressed in his behavior are real and intense. The school record indicated a history of extremely violent outbursts in previous years, and that considerable improvement had been shown in this fifth grade year. Such improvement may be due in part to sympathetic handling by his teacher, who has tried to provide George with opportunities for the recognition he needs. Violence nevertheless continues to seethe near the surface, reflected in language that continually alludes to situations of terror and instruments of war and crime. George has few friends, having alienated peers by his boasting and emotional unpredictability. He continually demands reaffirmation of one's relationship with him. It is as if he is helplessly thrashing around in what he perceives as a chaotic and unfriendly environment.

HARRY. This boy is described by his teachers as a "learning problem" child. They report that he seems bright, but that his aptitude and achievement scores do not show this. Difficulty with word reversals is noted in his earlier record. In general, teachers have described Harry as unable to control and channel his thoughts long enough to concentrate on a piece of academic work, and as frequently escaping into daydreams and fantasies. "Short attention span" is a term that has often been used in discussing him. On the other hand, Harry also is described as acutely perceptive, capable of sophisticated humor, and highly imaginative in artistic areas. Various tensions exist in his family situation.

Harry's difficulty in working on academic topics seems to stem from an inability to exert control over the variety of impulses which stir within him. When he feels delight, happiness, anger, violence, sadness, these are quite directly recorded on his face and in his actions. Feelings of violence, for example, are vented through humor, fantasy, and a kind of ritualistic play in which he pretends violence but does not carry it out in reality—such as pretending to hit another boy over the head. Harry's art ability recently has been accorded recognition by the art teacher, and this recognition has noticeably caused Harry to swell with pride. Such a channel of support may help him to overcome the aura of failure and rejection which pervades so much of his school life. The humor which he is able to muster in facing his current academic problems is well exemplified by a desire which he recently expressed for "a full education but no school."

Boys High in Intelligence But Low in Creativity

JAY. In the case of Jay, we find a quite thin, frail looking boy who avoids sports and rough-housing. He is subject to very high parental expectations and demands in the academic area. Descriptions indicate that the parents are very ambitious for their son's academic achievement, but otherwise relatively cold and aloof.

The history of his work in school suggests the gradual emergence or revelation of certain flaws in the nature of his intellective activities. His early teachers raved enthusiastically about his intelligence, variety of interests, articulateness, and easy-going nature. Over the years of elementary school, however, his intelligence has shown itself to be characterized in the main by a mechanical use of factual knowledge; the variety of his interests has eventuated in a superficial familiarity with many things, lacking depth; his articulateness has taken the form of compulsive and often irrelevant talking; and behind a façade of easy-goingness there seems to lurk a frightened little boy.

Jay seems very conscious of his siblings as individuals with whom he must compete for his parents' attention, and of academic success as the prime means of guaranteeing attention both at home and in school. When he was younger, his academic successes were sufficiently pervasive to bring him in full quantity the attention he seeks. In this fifth grade year, however, the fear of going unnoticed seems to be great enough for it actually to interfere somewhat with the academic achievement that constitutes his route to security. Despite the fact that he continues to test very well on typical assessors of intelligence, his school productivity has been dropping. There is some danger of a downward spiral resulting, since the less Jay's production in school, the greater the chance of rejection by his parents, which hence leads to still stronger fear of going unnoticed. It is possible, of course, that Jay is attempting the alternative psychic maneuver of seeking to elicit his parents' protective concern through doing *poorly* rather than well in school. His mother has certainly expressed concern over his current drop in school achievement. If this be the strategy, however, the quality of the parental attention that results must be all the more frustrating to the boy: the upshot of the family's concern has been to hire a tutor to coach Jay for school exams. Whatever the dynamic involved in Jay's behavior, however, it is clear that the domain of academic performance is of overwhelming relevance to his emotional security.

The boy is so anxious for attention in the classroom that he will express the desire to speak on any topic at all that is brought up. It is difficult to stem the rapid flow of his words once he has begun, and his thinking on these occasions reflects the most superficial lines of associative connection. Often, when called on, he has something to say which is completely unrelated to the topic under discussion. The need for attention is so overwhelming that no opportunity to gain recognition can be lost.

Jay was terribly eager to please the experimenters when participating in the various procedures of the study. He frequently inquired whether he was doing well, no matter how often he was told that this is not a test. Despite every attempt to induce a feeling of playing games, he continued to be ever watchful for cues as to his standing with the experimenters. His world clearly was revolving around acceptance versus rejection by adults as based upon the "correctness" of his performance.

KARL. Karl is a boy who has imposed extremely high standards of excellence on himself in all domains. He exerts himself continually to meet these standards. Karl is frail—one of the most frail children in our sample. His aptitude and achievement test scores are very high, and he gives an impression of strong social as well as intellectual maturity in his behavior at school. Karl is frequently chosen by his teachers to lead small groups of children in one or another activity, such as spelling lessons. He appears to be quite self-confident in leading his classmates and in talking with teachers.

Beneath this self-confidence and maturity, however, tension can be found. It seems to emerge from his quest for excellence. Perhaps the very quest itself is in part a compensatory striving after mastery induced by his physical frailty. Adler's (1917) concept of overcompensation for feelings of inferiority may well be appropriate for this child.

Teachers have reported that Karl is very sensitive to insult from others because of his frailty. In the early years of elementary school, this frailty hampered him from doing well in athletic activities, and it was very difficult for Karl to accept the fact of his doing poorly at sports. In an effort to change this state of affairs, Karl sought after-school help from a sympathetic gym teacher, engaging in extra athletic practice over a long period. As a result Karl has developed into a quite competent athlete, and is now reportedly less concerned about his frailty.

The boy has sought excellence in academic matters as well, and, if anything, with even more fervor than he has exhibited in his quest for excellence in sports. Clearly, Karl is concerned with accomplishing as much academically as he possibly can. In a school paper for which the children were asked to describe what they wished for most, Karl expressed concern about getting into college. From any realistic standpoint, with his very high grades and ability scores, it is obvious that Karl will have no trouble at all and has no cause for concern. Yet the possibility of academic failure worries him. To cope with this fear of not succeeding academically, Karl has found that being very well prepared constitutes his only useful source of assurance. If he knows that he has prepared a lesson thoroughly, then he can keep his fears of failure quiescent. Thorough preparation means, in turn, attention to every detail and relation in the material under study. Accuracy and order in his academic work are focal ideals for Karl. His work always reflects precision and the making of fine distinctions.

It should be noted that Karl also imposes high standards of excellence upon himself in the ethical domain. He lives up to, and expects others to live up to, an unbending ideal of justice and fair play among people. One day a girl in a group which Karl was leading displayed open disgust with a large, fat boy beside whom she was to sit. Karl, filled with righteous indignation, delivered a scathing rebuke to the girl.

In sum, excellence in athletics, excellence in moral behavior, and above all, excellence in academics, are the goals Karl seeks.

Louis. This child is tall, good-looking, and well-built. He is viewed by teachers and classmates alike as an excellent student. He is well liked and admired by his peers, enjoying their company when his mood is one in which he desires companionship. He is especially admired for his skill in sports. Consistently chosen as a leader by his classmates, Louis accepts this role easily and carries it out with responsibility. His friends demonstrate a continual eagerness for his companionship. Louis, however, is quite independent, and socializes only when he wishes. At times, he goes off by himself to pursue solitary activities such as reading.

Despite these ample grounds for pride, and despite behavior that exhibits a great deal of confidence and maturity, Louis also has characteristics that suggest a pervasive self-consciousness and embarrassment in his manner of meeting the world. The boy is a strong taskmaster for himself, with much contained anger, which he utilizes as a means of whipping himself toward success. Whenever he encounters frustration in his search for success, self-directed anger is especially in evidence. This contained and self-directed anger is turned outward and expressed toward others only in the realm of sports activities. Louis becomes wildly aggressive in gym class and on the ball field at recess.

In school tasks and in carrying out the experimental procedures, Louis' striving for success is very much in evidence and leads to a particular style of work. When given an intellectual task, he is so eager to achieve success at it that he rushes through to finish quickly and hence often leaves a trail of errors in his wake. This kind of behavior was especially noticeable when Louis worked on the Block Design subtest from the Wechsler Intelligence Scale for Children, as administered by one of the experimenters. He showed great apprehension in beginning the task. It was evident that he felt an intense desire to do well and that possible failure was a real concern to him. His body was tense, he blushed a deep red color, and he was unable to respond to the experimenter's attempts to ease his tension. His mind seemed to be completely concentrated on conquering the task at hand: his whole frame was set to run, as if in a race. When he began working, he carried out manipulations as rapidly as possible. He showed signs of terrible frustration when his first attempts failed to produce the correct result. Frustration and self-directed anger mounted until the tension was too much for him and he expressed the wish to give up.

The tension caused by wanting success thus leaves Louis in a state of agitation as he seeks to do what is necessary in order to achieve it. The agitation itself, of course, makes achievement of success all the more difficult by interfering with his performance on the task at hand, as well as being uncomfortable in its own right. Made uncomfortable in this way, Louis may consciously speed through his tasks in the hope that he may thereby more quickly reach a point of success and thus avoid the pain of frustration. The work created under these conditions tends to be sloppy and superficial, leading his teachers to criticize him for making "careless mistakes." Rather than being a product of his not caring, however, it would seem that such errors arise for just the opposite reason—that he cares too much.

It may be that the stresses described are especially troublesome to Louis in a face-to-face evaluational situation. He does, after all, score high on the intelligence cluster. Hence, Louis must perform well in group-administered intelligence tests, suggesting that he is better able to marshal his resources when not under direct scrutiny by an authority figure.

MARTIN. Here is another frail boy, with a serious, earnest way about him. Martin shows great involvement in whatever he is doing, and his activities usually are solitary ones. He is generally quiet and shy, but an eager spectator. At times Martin is so involved in his schoolwork that he won't stop for recess, but continues at his desk while the other children play.

There seems to be a general quality of "holding back" about Martin. While capable of enthusiastic participation in sports, he seems to have some reluctance about getting his clothes dirty, and this reluctance keeps him at times from taking part. On the playing field he was observed to become very concerned over having fallen in the mud. He spent a great deal of time carefully cleaning his pants off. When friends of his are "fooling around," he will often watch them from a distance with an expression that is half disapproving, half wistful. Occasionally he will join in with what looks like an air of predetermined casualness. Usually, however, he stays apart.

The concentration on studies and the quality of "holding back" in his actions suggest that Martin may feel strongly motivated to make sure that he "goes by the rules" of behavior that have been set up by the adults around him.

Boys Low in Both Creativity and Intelligence

NEAL. Neal has perturbed many a teacher by his impassive face. He seems unable or unwilling to respond to any attempt by a teacher to interest him in schoolwork. He is not a disrupter; rather, he merely sits quietly, unmoved and untempted by the academic activities that surround him.

Neal is slow to understand, shy, and sensitive to rebuff. He stubbornly avoids situations wherein he may expect to encounter difficulty. In a real sense he has given up trying and seeks only to protect himself from discomfort. The offer of individual attention from an adult seems to threaten him. Even his experience with the experimenters, who did their utmost to put him at his ease, was a painful one in which he never relaxed his suspicions. He never responded to their warmth and encouragement, and seemed to come only because he felt that it was expected of him. He adamantly refuses any leadership roles in the classroom, preferring to remain as anonymous as possible. The blank expression which he wears on his face certainly has the effect of inducing the observer to overlook him. A sense of worry and embarrassment are blended in Neal with stubborn resistance. He blushes and turns away from anything that might focus attention on him, shutting himself off from adult overtures.

From Neal's current behavior in the classroom, it is not difficult to reconstruct the probable nature of his early school experiences. He must have been initially bewildered by the demands of the school situation. Shy and understanding the tasks at hand only with great difficulty, he quickly became awed by what was asked of him. He was sensitive to criticism and became ashamed of his slowness. Having encountered school failure early and repeatedly, and apparently finding no adult resource available for support or help, he assumed a resigned attitude in self-protection.

The one island of competence which Neal can claim for himself is in athletics. Gym class transforms him into a wildly active and aggressive boy. He has perfected his athletic skills and puts all his energy into playing the game ''to win.'' It is as if sports constitute the one area where he can show the world and himself his power.

Indications from Neal's family background suggest that his parents expect little of him as far as academic work is concerned.

NORMAN. Norm is painfully aware of how poorly he does in school. He retains very little of what goes on in class, and shows little transfer from one session to another on a given topic. By and large, the teachers feel, with regret, that Norm is a lost cause. This judgment cannot help but be communicated to the child in various ways, no doubt further contributing to his lack of confidence. This confidence level is so low that he will often not even try to carry through on work that he has begun. In working on the Block Design subtest from the WISC, for example, he would stop again and again, declaring ''I can't do it.'' The experimenter had to deluge him with constant encouragement in order for him even to be willing to attempt the task. It is as if he assumes that failure will result from whatever he is given to do, and he doesn't want to try and hence have to face its reality. The boy is most self-conscious about his position in the class. Although he tries to look undisturbed about the matter, he betrays his unhappiness in many ways. The gym teacher, for instance, felt that Norm was the only boy in the grade who, when fighting, could not control his own anger and was really out to hurt others.

As early as the first grade, Norm was not trying in school. Norm may always have been an insecure child who depended very much on his home for support. He seems drawn to sympathetic and warm adults, preferring to reveal his failures to them than to peers. Often he would walk over to his teacher as an admission of failure, just to avoid sitting near students who might ridicule him. Such a fact suggests further that Norm may prefer to accept failure precisely because it allows him to remain close to protecting adults, rather than facing any kind of struggle alone.

Norm is considered to be quite nonverbal by his teachers. He tends to communicate his affects through his eyes and the expression on his face. These facial expressions of his feelings are quite direct in all cases but anger. When Norm is very angry and frustrated, his face will freeze up into a smile. Nonverbal modes of expressing anger that concern the rest of his body then will follow, ranging from inattentiveness, through mischievousness, to violent physical fighting, depending on the situation.

Although Norm seemingly refuses to use words to express what he feels for himself, he was observed to stand up and verbally defend his one and only friend—a boy who was in even worse shape academically and socially than himself. He was very faithful to this friend, and would ask favors for the boy that he would be less likely to ask for himself. Verbal expression was possible for him on those occasions, perhaps because it was not his own reputation or character that he was defending in speaking up for a friend. In contrast, when forced to speak up for himself, as in the case of recitation in class, his voice would be terribly strained, tight, and inadequate. His inability to use words on his own behalf suggests, then, that he has a low estimate of his personal worth. The boy's verbal deficiencies thus certainly are bound up with motivational problems.

OSCAR. This boy is a bundle of energy and activity, wholeheartedly devoted to sports. Classes constitute for him a necessary evil which must be tolerated while eagerly awaiting recess and gym periods. Once these times arrive he becomes totally involved in whatever athletic activity is available, exhibiting strong competitiveness and giving his all toward "winning."

His approach to schoolwork is almost as if it were another sports activity. He somehow feels that the goal in learning is to be the first one through with whatever task is at hand. He rushes headlong through his work and then races to the teacher to deliver it, all the while neglecting the work product itself. Oscar's fifth grade teacher felt that his drive to finish first might stem from a belief that this would be a way of attaining academic status. He apparently has great concern and anxiety over his lack of success in schoolwork. The only way he seems capable of dealing with academic matters, however, is to bring to bear on them the same tactics he uses on the sports field.

Oscar's abounding energy also finds an outlet in mischievous pranks. He seems always to be looking for opportunities to play jokes, and especially enjoys engaging companions in his pranks. This use of humor seems to be motivated once again by a strong desire to be noticed, to win recognition. He seems almost to feel a sense of success when he can disturb the teacher sufficiently for her to stop the class and request him to move to another part of the room. Oscar clearly presents a rather serious discipline problem to his teachers. Attention-seeking through aggressive mischief-making has steadily increased year by year. Despite all this deviltry, however, Oscar is able to retain the affection of peers and adults. Partly this is due to his general good nature, partly to his "choir-boy" look of innocence. He seems well aware that he has kept in everyone's good graces, and it is suspected that he may have come to believe that his mischievous behavior is regarded as "cute."

In sum, all of Oscar's behavior seems to be motivated by a strong desire to gain recognition. He appears to seek this objective by whatever particular means he feels capable of utilizing.

PETER. Peter also is a boy who has been quite anxious to finish first in his schoolwork, rushing through a task in order to be done as quickly as possible. There seems to be parental pressure exerted upon him to excel, and Peter translates this into rushing to be first.

Peter is a rather passive member of the crowd who goes along with demands from peers, a characteristic that no doubt forms the basis for his considerable popularity among his classmates. He can be led rather easily into mischievous activities, but participates in a good-natured, conforming way that lacks malice. He has little confidence on his own, and rarely has the courage to maintain a personal opinion. In both class and playground activities, Peter clearly acts as an easy-going, nondemanding companion.

Not only is Peter happiest when part of a group, but he will go to considerable lengths to avoid being separated from friends. It seemed to be on this ground, for example, that he resisted coming to participate in the experimental procedures. While there may have been some element of fear or suspicion in his hesitancy, his major objection seemed to concern separation from his friends. Since he is a passive follower in classroom activities, Peter may have been loathe to participate in anything intellectual without the presence of other children from whom he could obtain cues as to appropriate behavior.

The frankness with which Peter informed the experimenters that he was not eager to participate in the experimental sessions came as a surprise in the light of his over-all nonassertive character. It may be that his way of handling the anxiety which he felt about the situation was through an act of defiance. There were indeed signs of his adopting a defiant role in his responses to the experimental procedures. He seemed to be trying to present a "little tough guy" image of himself, by means of casual references to such standard teenage preoccupations as the police, cracking knuckles, and gang wars, and by a pervasive cynicism in his verbal behavior.

Overview of the Boys

Some general points may be made concerning the sixteen boys who have been described. Striking among the high-high boys seems to be an acute degree of interpersonal sensitivity coupled with sharp awareness of one's own identity and integrity in the midst of adults and peers. There is a sense of warmth but also objectivity in relations with others, an earnestness and seriousness in matters concerning human beings. One finds maturity coupled with a tolerance for being "boylike"—a simultaneous awareness of adult and peer-group frames of reference, and a capacity to maintain contact with both.

The boys who are equally high in creativity but low on intelligence measures, on the other hand, give the impression of being engaged in battle: battle against others and/or battle against themselves. There is sensitivity to and therefore anger over one's own inadequacies, and there also is angry lashing out at the world and supersensitivity to signs of rejection from others. The confidence of these boys appears shattered, and they are engaged in various defensive and constructive maneuvers aimed at establishing a sense of self-worth. The magnitudes of the forces involved in these battles seem to be particularly great precisely because of the articulated sensitivities these boys possess: detailed assessments of what other people think of them, introspective exploration of themselves, artistic ability.

When the balance is reversed and general intelligence is high but creativity low, there seems to be an overriding concern with academic success. A strong desire for academic excellence and a sense of competitiveness with peers and/or siblings for status in the eyes of adults are to be found. These boys seem to perceive intellective success as a critically important determinant of their standing with the adults who are of significance to them, and these boys also seem to be heavily preoccupied with how such adults view them. A narrowing-down and rigidifying of intellective behavior seems to be in evidence as a consequence of their so sedulous pursuit of success.

In view of the preoccupation with academic success manifested by these boys, how can we account for their exceptionally low levels of general and test anxiety (see Tables 63 and 64)? There is no contradiction here, for as Atkinson (1958, for example) among others has shown, motives to achieve success and motives to avoid failure are statistically independent of one another. The highly intelligent–low creative boys are evidently a success-oriented group, whose behaviors do, in fact, bring them the goals that they seek. It is also worth noting that the present subgroup yields fairly high defensiveness scores (Table 65), suggesting that coping mechanisms are available for the adequate handling of failure stresses encountered in the pursuit of success.

Finally, recall the low-low boys. One attitude found here is that of simple avoidance or giving up, of resignation to a sour fate as far as academic activities are concerned. Another seems to be a kind of blustering hyperactivity. A basic sense of bewilderment seems to pervade these children, and they tend to seek comfort by some means or other—through melting into the peer group in one case, through protection from sympathetic adults in another, through making mischief in a third.

DESCRIPTIONS OF INDIVIDUAL GIRLS

We turn now to parallel sketches of particular girls, and begin again with the high creativity–high intelligence group.

Girls High in Both Creativity and Intelligence

ANNE. Anne is highly admired by all who come in contact with her, peers and adults alike. A recitation of her characteristics conveys the image of a quite ideal human being, and looks almost too perfect to be true. Anne's academic work is superb, and teachers often praise her for it. She is a talented musician, playing the violin quite seriously. In addition, she is an outstanding athlete, while nevertheless remaining entirely feminine in her bodily movement and expression. The most popular boys diligently seek her favors. All of this Anne accepts in a quiet and modest way, carrying herself in a manner that bespeaks good taste and maturity. There is determination and resolve behind her actions, but yet these are very skillfully controlled so as not to offend anyone. Even when relaxing with friends, she does not indulge in excesses of laughter but seems rather to have a more quiet way of expressing her nevertheless genuine pleasure.

This girl has a highly articulated sense of how people view one another and the social effects of particular modes of conduct. Part of this wisdom is summed up in the following statement which she made in the course of telling a story in response to one of the depicted failure situations:

She shouldn't try to make everyone notice her, but do things quietly and people will be sure to notice. People won't admire you if you always try to do things first and be noticed.

Anne's high degree of social perceptiveness and objectivity in viewing herself and others can lend her at times an air of superiority. Her behavior toward the experimenters during the initial period of observation in her classroom was characteristic. Rather than coming over to the experimenters, as the other children occasionally did, she waited until one of the experimenters passed her desk and then began a conversation. Anne commented that the experimenters must be pretty bored by Anne's classmates compared with the last class the experimenters had visited. Despite the tinge of contempt which this remark implies, Anne was quite correct, in that her class contained a considerably higher percentage of children who were passive, less mature, and less interesting, than any other class which the experimenters had visited. In making this comment, Anne seemed to be trying to establish a bond with the experimenters that would separate her from the general level of the class. The social objectivity revealed in her remark was twofold: not only had she assessed her own class, *qua* class, and compared it with another, but also she was confident that the experimenters would have come to the same conclusion.

One of her responses to the paths procedure serves further to illustrate her sensitive awareness of others. Her description (of stimulus 2) was as follows:

This kind of person likes to be free. This person is grim and ready to face everything even though he knows he'll be unhappy from the things he's going to face. He has lots of nerve—cool rather than tense.

Despite an ever-present seriousness, Anne displayed a great deal of warmth toward the experimenters as her acquaintance with them developed. She would speak with much pleasure of her family, and clearly identified quite strongly with the adults in her family, particularly her mother. The family as she described it seemed quite closely knit, and one may also infer that she was given a good deal of responsibility at home, or was at least treated as an intellectual equal.

It is no exaggeration to say that Anne possessed a rather explicit *Weltanschauung*, with a mature awareness that human existence can be painful. Her explanations of what life circumstances might lead a person to make one or another kind of trail in the paths procedure, and her serious concern with how a person can best face a difficult problem in the stories she provided in response to depicted failure situations, conveyed a truly adult philosophy of life. Despite the seriousness, however, Anne also is aware of the support that others can provide in facing life's problems. In the two failure-story situations that take place in a school setting, Anne mentions "a cousin or relative" as helping the child. She seems to understand that someone with whom one can relax can also make it easier for one to learn and to face the world.

BARBARA. Clearly a member of the social elite in her class, Bobby is popular, respected, and frequently chosen by her peers as a leader for group activities. She exhibits an air of confidence that seems quite genuine, rather than a compensation for inner feelings of inadequacy. This confidence is particularly evident and particularly impressive in her relations with adults. One may surmise that her family has been a real source of security for the girl. Her sophisticated humor and witty repartee lend Bobby an adult quality; yet these do not seem to be mere imitations of an adult with whom she identifies. They seem rather to be the mature equipment of a child who is very sensitive to her own feelings and those of others, so that repartee and humor can therefore function as means of coping with affect and awareness of affect.

Bobby's use of humor as a mature way of handling affect can be illustrated by her reaction to the experimenters. She was a bit uneasy because she sensed that the experimenters had a "purpose" which they had not revealed in playing the games with her. Several times she found amusing ways to remind the experimenters that she was aware that they had an unrevealed purpose. Humor served as a way of coping with her malaise and, perhaps, anger at being left out of their confidence.

A restless quality can be seen in Bobby. She moves, talks, and thinks quickly, pouring energy and enthusiasm into every activity—whether play, academic work, or the experimental procedures. Bobby takes an obvious pleasure in roaming freely at all levels of her behavior, physical as well as conceptual. She participates in athletics with great gusto and skill. She equally enjoyed letting loose her thought associations and "giving everything she had" in the creativity procedures. Once involved in something—and genuine involvement comes very readily to Bobby—she will want to follow through until she has exhausted all that she can possibly bring to a subject both in the way of knowledge and in the way of feelings. Indeed, Bobby's penchant for freedom of expression applies just as strongly to her emotional life as elsewhere. She will speak quite freely of her feelings, and is very perceptive of feelings in others. When describing some experience, she seems to be completely involved in it and reporting upon it from within rather than outside. Bobby seems to gain or enhance understanding through projecting herself into others. For example, she identified easily with the various stick figures, appearing to be quite confident that through such identification she would be able to express some aspect of her nature as well as learning about another person.

An interesting complement to Bobby's pleasure in free expression at the physical, conceptual, and affective levels is her awareness of limits, of appropriate boundaries. Bobby displays considerable maturity concerning the channeling of her energy: she expends it in ways that are socially acceptable for the given time and place. Thus, in class she directs her energy into her academic work, while in free time she is gregarious and very active physically. She seems to have internalized a sense of discipline. For example, many of her stick figures are described as engaged in activities they don't particularly want to do. A typical description is the following:

She's sitting and hearing a speech by a counsellor at camp. Talking to her about neatness of the cabin and how they have to be neat. And she has to listen.

She seems to be equally aware, however, of the possible harmful effects of too much discipline. Her description of the person who would make a perfectly straight path in the desert, for instance, proceeded thus:

Very sensible, but he had a blank personality. Very smart and knew where to go but had no imagination; could only think about where he was going and what he was going to do . . .

Bobby seems to have struck a balance, therefore, between freedom and control.

CAROL. Carry is a rather homely girl. Her bearing seems rigid, and she gives a somewhat nervous and fidgety appearance. Despite these tensions, Carry behaves with unusual confidence in class. She is an excellent student, she volunteers often to speak, and she takes strong pride in her work. She sets herself very high personal goals of perfection and efficiency in her academic studies. These goals even extend to orderliness in the visual appearance of her work.

The experimenters had anticipated that Carry's academic success would be found to rest upon a grinding, rote manner of handling the materials. However, the kind of control that revealed itself in goals of orderliness and efficiency did not have an inhibitory character, but rather reflected a general tendency to organize and integrate that would be just as readily applied to fantasy and affective materials as to studies. She proved to be quite capable of generating imaginings of a very wide-ranging kind—to organize and express ideas that were filled with affect. Rather than leading her to deny feeling, the nature of her mode of control was such as to result in the organization and synthesis of feelings into marvelously expressive forms. One of her stories from the thematic integration procedure will provide an example of how she can mould directly emotive words and unusual metaphors into an organized totality:

The boy had just finished reading a terrible *book* which had a man in it who shot someone with a *gun*. In the *pool* of his thoughts that night he had the same terrible *dream* as had occurred in the book.

Carry is a girl with a strong penchant for task involvement. Her own standards with respect to a task were extremely high; yet rather than frightening her from attempting the task, this fact of high standards seemed to spur her to dive in. Carry loved to be involved in the task at hand and would become quite impatient if distracted from her ongoing work. She was not only eager to participate in the experimental procedures, but almost literally would champ at the bit. As time went on she gradually relaxed in her relations with the experimenters, and then would talk with much gusto of her home, her likes and dislikes, and her favorite activities. Even at these relaxed times she seemed filled to the brim with thoughts that were pressing for expression. Her degree of involvement in any activity was always great.

DOROTHY. Dottie represents an intriguing combination of opposites: teen-ager and little girl, disciplined studiousness and loose, almost "wacky," cognitive rambling. Uniting such opposite modes of functioning, however, is the presence in all cases of a driving kind of energy. Whether in the classroom, on the playground, or in the experimental game situations, she exhibits an outpouring of verbal and nonverbal activity. In the experimental games, for example, there seemed to be no end to her desire to explore and pour out answers.

The contrasting modes of her thinking could be found in frequent juxtaposition. In the creativity procedures she would show a great freedom in providing responses, never getting bored but rather always remaining animated. Her ideas and associations would flow from widely separated areas of experience. She would then return to the classroom, however, and take up again with great skill the well disciplined, more conventional kind of thinking that places her at the top of her class academically. She goes about her schoolwork in a conscientious, cooperative manner, and exhibits a high capacity for concentration and attention. As a matter of fact, Dottie seems well aware that she has at her command two different approaches to thinking about things. There is, further, no doubt that she prefers the free over the disciplined manner of thinking. Yet she works energetically within the latter frame of reference when the situation requires.

Her zest for letting her thoughts ramble in a loose way was quite apparent. She loved to use such associational freedom as a means of shocking or impressing the listener. Thus, for example, in a discussion of what would happen if everyone in the world were invisible, she mentioned that no-one would have to wear any clothes. Her story-telling was characterized by an extravagance of violence and explosiveness. She would be wildly fanciful in her stories, dwelling in imaginative detail upon destructive themes. In one story written for the classroom, for instance, she described a sequence in which her father saves her life by killing a snake.

Besides the alternation between Dottie as free and as disciplined in her cognitive functioning, we also mentioned the interplay between Dottie as little girl and as teen-ager. She looks and dresses the part of a teen-ager, and is appropriately boy-conscious. Yet, on the other hand, she can be quite giggly and excitable in a little girlish way, becoming fully absorbed in the kinds of play activities that are common to preadolescent children.

Girls High in Creativity But Low in Intelligence

ELLEN. In her early years at school, Ellen was described by her teachers as a good student with fine work habits. Starting with the fourth grade, however, she became sloppy in her work and careless about completing and handing in assignments. Her test scores dropped. Today, she seems to have no drive at all to work well in school. She seems to resent coming to school, and often is absent due to minor illnesses. The attitude she tries to maintain is one of acting as though the pressures of school work simply do not exist. She avoids bringing attention to herself in connection with any academic matter, and avoids any attempt to cope actively with school work. In a word, Ellen has withdrawn as much as possible from participation in the school environment.

This change of attitude observed in the fourth grade may be a result of the increasing responsibility and amount of work expected of children at about this point in the elementary school sequence. Ellen may be reflecting a belief that growing up is undesirable, and wishing rather to remain a little girl. Indeed, in this fifth grade year, she has focused all her attention on a friendship with another girl in her class who also shows emotional immaturity and an avoidance of academic demands. The two of them would hold hands affectionately at every opportunity, and seemed to use their friendship as a way to avoid viewing themselves within the larger school context.

Ellen's desire to remain a little girl was revealed in many other ways also. Although not small physically, she managed to create, through her bodily movements and facial expressions, an impression of being quite tiny. In stories that she told, Ellen often seemed to identify herself with little things—little children, little kitties, etc. When asked in art class to draw something concerning the sea, Ellen painted a small boat inside the curve of a great wave. Despite the wave's size, it seemed to be more protective than menacing and the little boat appeared safe and calm within it. It does not seem excessive to read a regressive wish into this painting.

To remain a little girl despite school pressure to the contrary, furthermore, requires stubbornness and determination. It is not a passive orientation but rather a posture that one must work to maintain, given the fact that it runs counter to the direction of adult influence. In her quiet way, Ellen seemed to show this stubbornness and determination. Her attitude of grim aggression against the school authorities seemed to be revealed in a favorite recess habit of chipping away at the walls of the school. She could work patiently at this activity for long periods of time, and confided to the experimenters the hope that this chipping would make the building collapse.

Exclusive attention from another person can exert an astonishing effect on Ellen. The experimenters were amazed at her complete freedom and effervescence in the game-playing situation. Anecdotes and answers literally poured from her. The fact that the experimental procedures took place in a test-free setting also may well have contributed to her ease. Ellen would always try to avoid being called upon in class, and would blush when requested to answer a question. Yet, she volunteered often for the experimental games, stayed with the experimenters during recess, and maintained her contact with them even after they had moved on to another class. Clearly, she saw the experimenters as friends, and was responding to their friendship and the freedom of the game-playing context from academic pressure. Given much individual attention, it is conceivable that Ellen would have shown greater interest in her school work.

FLORENCE. Flo is another girl who seems to prefer an infantile state to one of growing up and becoming an active participant in school. She is old for her grade; yet she appears to the casual observer to be one of the youngest looking and acting children in the class.

The girl's school history provides a listing of one severe emotional difficulty after another. In kindergarten she evidenced excessive nervousness by chewing and biting things. She was extremely shy and always played alone. In subsequent grades she developed an attitude of strong hostility toward her classmates, so that she continued to be left alone. Teachers report that she can control her hostility if she must do so in order to gain something that she really wants; otherwise, her negative attitude toward others dominates her behavior and leads to social ostracism. She continues to be very shy, but will, on the other hand, characteristically become quite dependent on whoever sits closest to her. This dependence on her seat-mate results in her being easily led into mischief, and perhaps affords her social support in aggression toward others. At the least, it functions to keep her attention focused upon nonacademic activities.

Flo does little or no school work. When forced to consider an academic topic, her reaction is one of complete listlessness. She seems quite unable to concentrate her thinking for sufficiently long to carry any school task through to completion.

In striking contrast to this approach to academic tasks was her behavior with the experimenters. In the game-playing situation, Flo was active and expansive, high in productivity and uniqueness, sensitive to affective states, and skilled in visualizing. It may well be that this strong difference in behavior stemmed in part from the warmth extended to her by the experimenters, and in part from the lack of explicit demands placed upon her by the experimental procedures. She loved coming to the games and was quite eager to converse with the experimenters at great length. In terms of the foregoing characteristics, and in terms of integration, coherency, and concentration of attention as well, her behavior in the experimental situations was dramatically different from her customary mode of conduct in school.

GLADYS. Gladdie is a girl who has suffered for many years from a liver ailment. Restricted from all physical activity, she is frequently unable to attend school. At least partly as a result of her illness and consequent absences, Gladdie is a very shy girl and not integrated into the social organization of the classroom. She stands apart.

Gladdie's most remarkable characteristic is her free-flowing imagination. Despite her basic shyness, when it comes to the expression of her thoughts she reveals a highly independent and even rebellious air. Once, in front of the class, she reported that a baby kangaroo made leaps that were one mile high. She was so intrigued with the idea that she refused to be dissuaded when her teacher and classmates attempted to correct her. Here and in other instances, it was clear that Gladdie rebels against restrictions on her imaginings. She also dislikes the more painstaking task of correcting and checking her work, preferring rather to let her ideas roam freely in an unpolished form. She commented to the experimenters that she loves to write stories, but hates the process of correcting and finishing them.

In the creativity procedures, Gladdie showed great pleasure in exploring ideas fully and drawing responses from a wide variety of areas. When it comes to story-telling, she develops an intricately woven plot-line that delights the listener. Gladdie, then, is a girl who wants to have her own way imaginatively, will blossom cognitively if given free rein, and who resents questions of detail and accuracy.

HARRIET. Here is a girl who is plagued in her academic work by a complete lack of organization. She is unable to maintain a focus in the school work context and carry a task through to completion. In the experimental game situations, however, although concentration remained somewhat ·of a problem, she revealed herself capable of making unique and rich thought connections. Her fantasy material suggests that she spends a lot of time daydreaming, letting her thoughts skim along from one topic to another with relative abandon.

Socially, Harriet seems very much alive and active. Her anecdotes reveal that she is greatly concerned with the adult social world and perhaps spends a great deal of time dreaming about it. Knowing that she cannot compete with her classmates academically, and hence being ostracized from the social elite of the class, she has gathered around herself a group of other girls who, like her, all are "outcasts" in the class. Harriet is the binding link among these outcasts. It should be noted that in the school system under consideration, social status was directly linked to academic prowess.

Girls High in Intelligence But Low in Creativity

IRIS. As far back as school records indicate, Iris has always been an excellent student. Academic achievement seems to be the route that she utilizes for achieving status. Her behavior in class reflects a single-minded absorption in her school work : she will often skip recess in order to stay at her desk and carry out extra assignments. Determination and drive for academic success can be seen in her face and her manner. On the other hand, she seems to obtain little pleasure from her accomplishments. When she achieves success in academic competition there will be a sign of relief (albeit temporary) in her face, but not of happiness. Her teachers have concluded, and the experimenters concur from their observations, that Iris is completely unable to relax and have fun. In the experimental sessions, she made it very difficult for the experimenters to come to know her in any personal way. She withdrew from any conversational attempts, maintaining a kind of polite distance.

Iris' drive for success will lead her into aggressive acts where these can further her ends. Once she fought determinedly with another girl who vied with her for a piece of paper, possession of which symbolized leadership of their work group. Iris won the fight. In gym class she was observed to cheat when this was necessary in order for her to win. Willful actions such as these were carefully avoided in formal academic situations, however. When interacting with adults who are in positions of authority over her in academic matters, she keeps her aggressiveness well controlled and is always polite. But such politeness is a matter of image-maintenance, for Iris willfully asserts herself whenever the teacher's back is turned.

The following story completion was given by Iris for the third failure situation, in which a girl is described for whom everything has been going wrong in school—she can't do the work and can't get along with the other children. It is revealing of the competitive pressures under which Iris is operating:

The teacher was out; Sue picked up the paper for the next day. She took it home and learned all the answers to the questions. Next day she raised her hand in class all the time and the teacher called on her. The teacher was very pleased with her. At recess, all the girls played with her and asked her how she'd known all the answers. She told them that she'd just known them and never said how hard she'd worked on the paper.

In the story we find absolutely no indication of guilt over having cheated by stealing the teacher's paper. The only concern which Iris describes is that the girl's classmates should believe her success had come easily to her, and not realize "how hard she'd worked." It is not difficult to conclude that Iris is under strong pressure to succeed, and that this pressure drives her to competitive extremes in school. The pressure is by now sufficiently internalized as to be quite self-imposed. There are indications, however, that elements in the home situation foster this drive for success.

The following incident suggests that Iris' academic success may provide her with a means of competitive leverage within her family. A sister of Iris came to the classroom once after school. No greeting passed between the girls. Iris looked up coldly, and then *ordered* the girl to pick up Iris' books and carry them. Hostility as well as coldness were present in this incident. The teacher who witnessed it did not know at the time that the other girl was a sister, and was amazed when she discovered this, so bizarre had been Iris' behavior toward the girl. From what else is known about the family, one gains the impression that competitiveness and strife may indeed characterize the home.

JANE. A quality of not being able to "let go" pervades Jane's behavior. One thinks of such terms as "closed," "constricted," and "constrained" in describing her. In the experimental situations she tended to avoid the expression of feelings, both in her responses and in her general behavior toward the experimenters. She would not open up and chat with the experimenters even in the privacy of the game-playing situation, and even after they had been working with her class for a sizable length of time. This despite the fact that she did indicate in implicit ways that she wanted to be friends with the experimenters. With classmates and teachers, during classes and during recess time, Jane manifests a similar reserve.

This quality of holding back may reflect both fear of potential hurt and an act of defiance. Thus, there are indications that Jane completely shuts herself off from communication with her mother, and that the mother is quite insensitive to her child's qualities. The mother expressed surprise, for example, upon hearing that her daughter was considered "bright" by the school. One gains a picture of the mother as cold and hard, and as generating thereby two reactions in her daughter: stubborn resistance—a silent fighting back; and fear of being hurt if she were to reveal her feelings. Jane's way of maintaining a measured distance from the experimenters suggests that she does not trust adults: when they are warm, she fears that they will suddenly turn cold toward her, and she will be hurt as in a surprise attack. By keeping her distance and closing herself off, therefore, Jane protects herself from being hurt. At the same time, her stubborn silence can function as an implicit way of expressing aggression for being put in this dilemma. The experimenters felt that Jane possesses a great deal of unexpressed anger, as if she fears that expression of this anger would lead to punishment. Thus, personal constriction would function for her both as a defense against possible hurt, and as an implicit means of expressing anger.

KAREN. Karen's father is a school teacher, and reports suggest that he is a warm, confident, and well-liked individual. There is every indication that he enjoys and is proud of the various accomplishments of his daughter, which include high academic achievement, leadership of her peers, and popularity. The girl appears to be very self-confident and mature. Teachers also voice expectations that she will be superior. Her behavior with the experimenters, however, suggested a somewhat more complicated picture.

Alone with either of the experimenters, Karen seemed to lose the confidence which she displayed in class. In sharp contrast to her behavior in class, Karen was not at ease when she was with the experimenters in the game-playing situations. She was tense and quiet, and her eyes sometimes had a frightened look. When at other times, she saw the experimenters in the classroom, she was always very eager to show off her possessions and to emphasize their (and her) uniqueness. This eagerness had a strong quality of protesting too much. The apparent self-confidence with which she took her classmates in hand and assumed leadership roles over them also had an overly commanding, somewhat high-handed quality about it.

These various indications suggest that Karen may be under a considerable strain to keep up an image of herself as an independent and creative person. Parental expectations, teachers' anticipations that her performance will be superior, and her internalization of these high expectations from both sources, may well place her under quite strong pressure to excel. The way in which Karen reacts to criticism seems rather diagnostic in this regard. Criticism shatters her, and she tries to avoid it. In her projective materials, she saw criticism as a significant cause of uncertainty and anger. In response to one of the paths in the desert, for example, she says of the figure that ''he gets offset if people criticize him.'' Such a response permitted her to express the ideas both of the personal upset and the offset path that she saw as resulting from criticism. Criticism leads to confusion and being thwarted in one's efforts to achieve goals. The answer therefore is to appear confident and firm, to strive to be correct, and to seek to communicate that one is doing things that are right and are outstanding.

The preceding may summarize something of the implicit strategy that is guiding Karen's conduct. Noteworthy is the fact that reports by her teachers contain no reference to such a possibility. Instead, they consistently praise her for maturity, intelligence, leadership qualities, self-confidence, and popularity.

LOUISE. Louise places very high demands on her own work. She is a perfectionist, and in earlier years would become very upset whenever she made a mistake. She pays close attention to precise meanings and connotations of words. Her handwriting is exceptionally neat and well formed, even by adult standards. Louise clearly takes great pride in its appearance.

Her completions of the stories depicting failure situations suggest that Louise views academic success as the key to acceptance. Such a world-view certainly would coincide with her own experience. In kindergarten she was painfully shy and nervous, and for all the ensuing years until the fifth grade she was described by teachers as tense and unwilling to stand in front of the class. She was reported, and still is reported, to be very sensitive to criticism. Now, however, she contributes information in class and is able to stand before peers with some confidence. It seems as if this is an ability she has developed through intensive application to academic work. She will generally be found working at her desk in a very concentrated way during class time, and also during some free time. Louise appears to be readily accepted and well liked by classmates, and it is likely that at least some of this popularity derives from the academic prominence she has worked so hard to achieve.

Girls Low in Both Creativity and Intelligence

MARTHA. Looking and acting very much like a little girl, Marty is animated and extraverted in relations with other children. Yet she frequently wears a petulant or worried expression on her face. Beneath her surface animation, Marty seems to lack security in herself and in her position among classmates. For this reason she constantly seeks companionship, flitting from one child to another in a continual search for reassurance of their acceptance. The girl is driven by self-doubt and worry over social isolation.

Academic failure is a further source of frustration to Marty. She has in various ways expressed a wish to be smarter, and seems to feel in general that fate is constantly bombarding her with difficult situations. Most of her life is spent trying to control and cope with what must seem to her a frustrating chaos. She is a perfectionist about neatness and spends a great deal of time "ordering" things. When given an assignment, she is unable to approach the task directly, but rather must go through a ritualistic process of preparing and, as it were, "collecting" herself. Her work is done very slowly and she gives up easily. This collecting and controlling process is exemplified in her drawing, an activity in which she engages during class time as well as during spare time. Her art products resemble the pages of a coloring book. She proceeds by drawing the outlines of an object first, and defining it clearly. Then she fills the insides of the outline with solid blocks of color. These drawings seem to provide her with a source of personal satisfaction, and she will frequently work on them during class activities with which she feels totally unable to cope.

Marty is eager for classroom recognition as well as for success in achievement. She was observed at one point to volunteer to be a leader of a social studies group, and was surprised when she was chosen. Confronted with having to execute the role, she was besieged with confusion. Marty tried to imitate the assertiveness that she had seen in other leaders, but could not bring it off; she seemed to be continually undermined by doubts over the appropriateness of her actions. Eventually a stronger girl took over.

In the experimental procedures, Marty seemed eager to trust the experimenters but yet never succeeded in overcoming her feeling of being threatened. She seemed helpless and inadequate. A basic inhibition pervaded her behavior. It was as if she refused to let her thoughts begin to flow because of the terrible feelings that might result.

Nora. This girl experiences strong fear and tension in school. Each year the work seemed to create pressures that have been increasingly difficult for her to bear. Currently, Nora simply assumes that she won't be able to do a given academic task. Sometimes she copies the work of a friend. At test times her eyes are often filled with fear. Her body becomes very rigid and her neck muscles are visibly tensed. Even in the game-playing situation, with every effort made to reduce tension, she continually was very fearful of doing something wrong.

Despite this traumatic state of affairs for Nora in the academic realm, she has always enjoyed outgoing group activities. In early grades she tended to try to dominate her friends, and became less assertive only when they turned away from her. In her peer interactions, she now exerts control over her aggressive tendencies, but these slip to the surface nevertheless. She seems to want to hurt others as she has been hurt, but holds back as best she can from fear of losing friends. She was observed to make direct comments that were cruel in intent about children in the class, but only when the child whom she derided was helpless in some way and hence an outcast whose friendship she didn't value. She would ridicule the weaknesses of other children with a purposeful cruelty, but it was not so much this cruelty that seemed to characterize her as the total lack of sensitivity which the cruelty implied. She could say such things only if she didn't know—or pretended not to know—how it would feel to be reminded of a weakness so harshly. This same lack of sensitivity in her thinking was reflected in her academic work.

Nora enjoys dramatics, and can stand before the class fearlessly when speaking the lines of a play. The self-assertiveness which she tries to inhibit in other areas is expressed freely in dramatic presentations. It is as if such aggressive expression can be permitted her when she is in a sense pretending to be someone other than herself. Dramatics seems to afford her the freedom to be an uninhibited little girl once more. She also derives pleasure from playing with dolls, again an activity in which one can feel free of inhibitions by representing someone else.

OLIVIA. The prime characteristic of Ol's approach to the school situation is deep insecurity. Every academic year she has required several months to work out some kind of adjustment to her new grade, during which time she frets and cries, complains of various psychosomatic ailments, and quite often is absent from school. After that she becomes somewhat more relaxed in the school setting. Never, however, does she fully lose the constraint and inhibition that are the hallmarks of her reaction to any new situation.

Within the social structure of the class, Ol is quiet and passive. She is receptive to friendly overtures, but is easily hurt by rebuffs, with the consequence that she is hesitant to extend herself freely. She does find clear enjoyment in social participation, however.

Ol's behavior in the experimental game situations showed fear and tension. Encouragements toward expressive freedom and attempts to remove pressure from Ol seemed if anything to have the reverse effect of inhibiting her even further.

PAULINE. A quiet, reserved child, Polly is a hard worker in the classroom. She conveys a sense of strain and tension, however, and seems in general to be excessively inhibited and controlled in her actions. Teacher reports described her as seeming to be in a daze in the classroom, and as becoming easily tired. She played the experimental games very seriously, and had no fun with the experimenters no matter how relaxed and friendly they endeavored to make the atmosphere. In general, she was quite "flat" in emotional tone; quite lacking in affect.

Overview of the Girls

The patterns of differences among the four groups of girls seem to parallel in major respects those found in the case of the boys. Turning first to the girls high in both creativity and general intelligence, one finds a display of strong powers of integration and structuring in combination with an ability to range freely and imaginatively with rich affect and enthusiastic involvement. The question of the *interrelation* between these more and less controlled ways of functioning seems to be an issue with which these children, in one manner or another, come to grips. By and large, they seem able to nourish both modes of cognitive functioning in some kind of simultaneous or successive fashion. The interplay between control and freedom in cognition nevertheless seems to remain of prominent concern for them. They display in addition much social awareness and sensitivity to emotional expression in others.

When creativity is high but intelligence low, the girls in question appear to be reacting negatively to school pressure. There is anger and resentment expressed toward the school setting, regressive listlessness and/or mischief-making in response to academic demands. Social shyness and withdrawal also are prominent. On the other hand, free and even wild imaginings are found, which may be all the more extreme because tinged with rebelliousness. These imaginings are not only a form of rebellion, however, since they seem to reveal themselves most strongly in a nurturant adult environment that does not invoke sanctions of academic failure and success. Something clearly has gone awry with regard to the meaning of school for these girls.

Turning to the instances where general intelligence is high while creativity is low, we find a rather mechanical use of academic achievement as the means of attaining status and success, with the impression that such achievement has for these girls more the meaning of reducing pain than of increasing pleasure. It is as if they must keep achieving academically in order to avoid feeling badly. Indeed, such success has come to signify so much of importance to their emotional balance that they are willing to go to great lengths to obtain it, working long hours at their studies and fearing criticism. Affectively, they give evidence of holding themselves carefully within bounds, both with regard to their own expression and with regard to their perceptions of others. For whatever reasons—and in some cases it looks as if one or another form of family pressure plays a role—it is terribly important to these girls to do well in school, and they concomitantly seem to inhibit themselves emotionally.

In one way or another, the girls low in both intelligence and creativity give evidence of trying to deal with the fact of poor intellectual performance. These girls seem not to know how to cope successfully with academic tasks, and at best resort to imitating the surface behaviors that reflect successful coping by others, such as trying to appear assertive and being neat in one's work. At worst, on the other hand, fear and depression over academic failure are in evidence. There is frustration over one's patent inability to comply with the school's performance expectations, and one result is the use of relatively infantile defenses such as being cruel and vengeful toward other children who are weak, being passive and unresponsive in the classroom, or developing psychosomatic complaints.

SUMMARY

In this chapter we have passed in review clinical descriptions of thirty-two of the children. Eight children representing each of the combinations of general intelligence and creativity levels were considered, equally divided between the sexes. The result, then, is a subsample consisting of approximately 21 percent of the total sample, with score locations at or near the creativity and intelligence extremes constituting the major factor in selection. While not offered as completely independent evidence, the fact that these sketches represent a substantial proportion of the sample and yield fairly clear-cut clinical differences among the four creativity and intelligence types, means that we have been able to add to our knowledge of the kinds of pictures that these different types of children present.

In broad outline, the pictures seem to be these. Presence of both high creativity and high intelligence seems to be reflected in the ability to entertain both control and freedom, both adultlike and childlike modes of conduct, both mature social awareness and direct responsiveness to other children. High creativity coupled with low intelligence, on the other hand, is identified with children in conflict with the school and with themselves. The academic environment, with its structure of rewards and punishments, functions as a kind of red flag for them toward which they express anger and resentment. They are also upset with their own behavior and in various ways express a sense of personal inadequacy and lack of worth. They can, however, be made to blossom in contexts free from typical academic pressures. When, in turn, creativity is low but intelligence high, we find what might be characterized as an addictive relationship to school. Schoolwork must be done in order to avoid pain. A logic has been established wherein academic success is the path to all things of significance and value, while academic failure is tantamount to complete destruction. Finally, low levels of both creativity and intelligence are found in conjunction with bewilderment and frustration over academic inadequacies, leading to various consequences that range from hyperactivity in the social sphere to psychosomatic symptoms.

Thus, the thirty-two children whom we have considered on an individual basis in the present chapter provide instances of the sorts of complex configurations that are to be encountered within the several creativity and intelligence groupings.

8 ⫷⫷⫷

Conclusions

The research described in the preceding chapters may be characterized in a general sense as systematic observation. We have watched children respond to the particular experimental tasks confronting them, and, in addition, have watched them interact in their customary school environment. These observations then have been ordered and analyzed in various ways so as to permit one child to be compared with another. The method lies somewhere between intensive clinical study of the single case through a store of information amassed over a considerable time period, on the one hand, and extensive sampling of persons with a small amount of information obtained in the case of each individual, on the other. We may justly be accused of seeking the best of both worlds—a large amount of information pertaining to a sizable sample of persons. It should not surprise us, then, if some critics claim that we do not have enough information about any single individual, while others insist that we lack a sufficiently large and representative sample. To such criticisms, we can only point out that (1) the reliabilities of our measuring techniques were sufficient to permit an exhaustive analysis of individual differences and similarities in the sample of 151 children, and (2) the relevant data pertinent to each child were sufficient to allow images to come into focus concerning the functioning of particular children.

The extent to which these twin hopes of instrument reliability and information in depth have been fulfilled rests upon the findings presented in Chapters 2 through 7. Interpretations of the studies conducted have been presented in each of these chapters, and it would be inappropriate to attempt a duplication of those materials here. There remain, however, three tasks to which the present chapter will address itself. First, we shall present a synoptic overview, bringing together the major issues, results, and interpretations offered in the earlier chapters. Second, we shall consider the theoretical implications of the findings—what they suggest regarding the nature of thinking processes. Finally, we shall point to possible applications and implications of the study in connection with educational practice.

AN OVERVIEW OF THE FINDINGS

At the outset, we took note of what has assumed the proportions of a controversy in recent psychological history. The nature of the controversy might be put somewhat as follows: Is there an aspect of cognitive functioning, which can be appropriately labeled "creativity," that stands apart from the traditional concept of general intelligence? A close appraisal of the quantitative findings available on this subject led us to a pessimistic answer. Our examination of this literature opened up to us, however, the possibility of a valid distinction between creativity and intelligence that had not, in our view, been sufficiently pursued and developed. The next step, therefore, was empirical research in terms of this distinction. Finally, if creativity and intelligence could be validly distinguished, we were interested in studying the possible psychological correlates that might distinguish individual differences on these two dimensions considered jointly. Specifically, we were concerned with correlates in such areas as the child's observed behavior in school and play settings, his esthetic sensitivities, his categorizing and conceptualizing activities, his test anxiety and defensiveness levels.

We began with a simple question: Did the relevant psychological literature support the assumption of a unified dimension of individual differences describing more and less creative cognitive behavior? To put this question another way, could one demonstrate the existence of greater and lesser degrees of a cognitive capability that was like intelligence in regard to being a pervasive, broad dimension, but yet was independent of intelligence, and which could appropriately be labeled "creativity"? It was clear that to talk of "creativity" was to imply a referent different from that of the general intelligence concept. The typical evidence that we found on this issue led, however, to an opposite conclusion. Let us consider an example.

The volume by Getzels and Jackson (1962), *Creativity and intelligence*, is perhaps the best known of recent efforts in the field. Five alleged tests of creativity were administered to large samples of students ranging in class from sixth grade through the end of high school. Four of the five creativity tests correlated significantly with IQ for the girls, and all five of these tests correlated significantly with IQ for the boys. Consider next the relationships among the instruments in the creativity battery— that is, the question of whether they define a unitary dimension of individual differences. The Getzels-Jackson results showed that the five creativity tasks were virtually no more strongly correlated among themselves than they were correlated with intelligence. To give some averages, for boys the mean correlation was .26 between the creativity battery and IQ, and was .28 among the tasks in the creativity battery; in the case of the girls, the corresponding mean correlations were .27 and .32. In sum, the creativity measures correlated with intelligence on the order of .3, and also correlated with each other on the order of .3. There was no evidence, in short, for arguing that the creativity instruments were any more strongly related to one another than they were related to general intelligence. The inevitable conclusion was that little warrant existed here for talking about creativity *and* intelligence as if these terms referred to concepts at the same level of abstraction. The creativity indicators measured nothing in common that was distinct from general intelligence. Inspection of the creativity battery revealed a quite varied range of materials, including measures of the ability to devise mathematical problems, to compose endings for fables, to detect embedded geometric figures, to think up word definitions, and to imagine uses for an object.

Comparable examination of other research reports in the literature forced us to the same kind of conclusion. Our survey included the study of findings reported by Torrance and his co-workers (for example, Torrance, 1960; Torrance, 1962; Torrance & Gowan, 1963), Guilford and his collaborators (for example, Guilford & Christensen, 1956; Wilson, Guilford, Christensen, & Lewis, 1954), Cline, Richards, and Needham (1963), Cline, Richards, and Abe (1962), Barron (1963), and Flescher (1963). To give but one more example of the kind of outcome obtained, consider a recent study by Cline, Richards, and Needham (1963). With high school student subjects and seven creativity measures, the average correlation for boys between the creativity indices and an IQ measure was .35, while it was .21 among the various creativity tests. For girls, the average correlation between the creativity tests and IQ was .33, while it was .24 among the seven creativity measures. Again and again in reviewing the research in this area, the evidence led to the conclusion that the various creativity measures utilized were almost as strongly, equally strongly, or even more strongly related to general intelligence than they were related to each other. The evidence in hand thus seemed not to permit the very type of conceptualization that Getzels and Jackson (1962) and other researchers were proposing: namely, that there exists a pervasive dimension of individual differences, appropriately labeled "creativity," that is quite distinct from general intelligence. We should note that this same critical point was made by Thorndike (1963) in a recent article.

Appropriate wielding of Occam's razor at this juncture thus dictated the tough-minded conclusion that little of any generality was being measured here beyond differences in the traditional notion of intelligence. Let us pose two issues, however, that made it seem premature to let the matter go at that. First, a potpourri of abilities was being assessed in the good name of "creativity"; second, little attention was given to the social psychological aspects of the assessment situation typically employed in the measurement of "creativity." Consider each of these points in turn.

If we return to the introspections of highly creative artists and scientists, one major focus emerges. The majority of the available introspective accounts have in common a concern with associative freedom and uniqueness. These accounts consistently stress the ability to give birth to associative content that is abundant and original, yet relevant to the task at hand rather than bizarre. The writer's classical fear of "drying up" and never being able to produce another word, the composer's worry over not having another piece of music within him, the scientist's concern that he will not be able to think of another experiment to perform—these are but indications of how preoccupied creative individuals can become with the question of associative flow. Introspections about times of creative insight also seem to reflect a kind of task-centered, permissive, or playful set on the part of the person doing the associating. Einstein refers to "associative play" or "combinatory play." The person stands aside a trifle as associative material is given freedom to reach the surface.

We proposed that the essentials of the creative process might well be contained in the two elements just considered: first, the production of associative content that is abundant and that is unique; second, the presence in the associator of a playful, permissive task attitude. Given a task clear enough so that bizarre associative products do not readily occur, and given a permissive context within which the person works, two variables then would permit us to index individual differences in creativity: the number of associations that the person can generate in response to given tasks and the relative uniqueness of the associations that he produces.

One implication of this view was that productivity and uniqueness of associates should be related variables. Defining uniqueness as a relative infrequency of a given associative response to the task at hand for a sample of subjects, we would expect stereotyped associates to come earlier and unique associates to come later in a sequence of responses. Such an expectation was also consistent with recent work by Mednick (for example, 1962). If unique associates tend to come later in time, then it became clear also that an appropriate assessment context would require freedom from the pressure of short time limits, and perhaps freedom from any temporal pressure at all. The postulated need for a permissive, playful attitude also implied the desirability of freedom from time pressure. Such temporal freedom is one aspect of what a permissive situation would involve. Permissiveness further connotes a relative lessening of evaluational pressures—that is, a focus upon the task rather than upon the self, a relaxed entertaining of the possible rather than tense insistence upon an answer that must be correct if one is not to lose face. The Taoists, as discussed by Rugg (1963), have called such a relaxed attitude a state of "letting things happen." Clearly, we are describing a type of situation in which the individual does not feel that he is being tested, and hence does not feel that what he does will have a bearing upon his self-worth in the eyes of others.

The foregoing analysis of creativity hence suggested a concentration of assessment attempts in the area of associational processes, in contrast to the quite heterogeneous types of tasks that had received the "creativity" label in studies of the kind touched upon earlier. This theoretical analysis also suggested that the assessment context must be quite different from the kind utilized in the studies reviewed; there should be freedom from time pressure and there should be a playful, gamelike context rather than one implying that the person is under test. Interestingly enough, the kind of context present in the case of *all* of the studies on creativity reviewed earlier strongly implied that a test or examination was at issue; the creativity procedures invariably were referred to as "tests," they were administered to large groups of students in a classroom, and temporal constraint was present—either explicitly, through the use of relatively brief time limits, or implicitly, through the use of group administration procedures. In all of this work, there had been the evident assumption that a testing context, with its implication that the respondent is being evaluated in terms of some success–failure criterion, was quite appropriate for studying creativity. The associative approach to creativity, with its emphasis upon an attitude of playful entertaining of possibilities in a task-centered environment, suggested otherwise.

At this point we were ready to begin some experimentation of our own. Following the prescriptions just stated, could one empirically define a dimension of individual differences that concerned the ability to produce many cognitive associates, and many that are unique? Would this dimension possess a substantial degree of generality across differences in types of tasks—for example, verbal vs. visual kinds of procedural formats? Such a contrast was of special interest since the general intelligence concept is defined with respect to a kind of ability that manifests itself in visual (performance) as well as verbal types of tasks, and we were presuming to assess a characteristic possessing approximately the same level of generality as conventional intelligence. Finally, and most important, would the foregoing dimension of associational ability be independent of individual differences in the traditional area of general intelligence? If research findings could provide affirmative answers to these questions, then—and only then—would one be in a position to talk about a kind of thinking ability appropriately labeled *creativity*, with the evident implication of a characteristic different from general intelligence, but yet a characteristic which also possesses a substantial degree of generality across task variations.

Our work, conducted with 151 children comprising the entire fifth grade population of a suburban public school system in a middle-class region, took great pains to establish a gamelike, nonevaluational context for the administration of procedures. The experimenters, two young women, were introduced as visitors interested in children's games. They spent two initial weeks with each class gaining rapport with the children. This initial period of familiarization also provided the basis for observations leading to ratings of the children's behavior on various dimensions. Great effort was expended in communicating to the children that the presence of the experimenters did not concern examinations or tests. The teachers and principals, furthermore, did their utmost to dissociate the experimenters from any concern with intellectual evaluation. Finally, it was our view that the establishment of a gamelike context required the experimenters to work individually with each of the 151 children. We sedulously avoided group administration with its academic testing implications.

Five procedures formed the basis for our exploration of creativity in these children. They concerned the generation of five kinds of associates. Two variables were measured in the case of each: uniqueness of associates and total number of associates. Some of the procedures were verbal, others were visual in nature. One verbal procedure, for example, requested the child to generate possible instances of a verbally specified class concept, such as "round things," or "things that move on wheels." Here, and for every other creativity procedure, the child was given as much time on each item as he desired. Number of unique responses to an item is defined as the number of responses given by only one child in the sample of 151 to the item in question. Total number of responses offered to an item is, of course, self-defining. For "round things," for example, "Life Savers" is a unique response, while "buttons" is not. Another verbal procedure requested the child to think of possible uses for various objects presented orally, such as "shoe" or "cork." "To trap a mouse in," is a unique use suggested for "shoe," while "to throw at a noisy cat" is not. A third verbal procedure asked the child to propose possible similarities between two objects specified in verbal terms. For instance, one pair is "train and tractor," another is "milk and meat." A unique response to "milk and meat" was "they are government-inspected," while "they come from animals" was not unique. The visual procedures, in turn, requested the child to think of possible interpretations or meanings for each of various abstract visual patterns and line forms.

These procedures obviously owe a debt to the Guilford group. They were administered, however, in a carefully constructed gamelike context, with each child taken individually and encouraged to spend as much time as he wished on every item. These administration arrangements were very different from those employed by the Guilford group. It should be emphasized, furthermore, that the use of a gamelike context did not lead to a violation of the task constraints present in the various items of the procedures. Bizarre or inappropriate responses were exceedingly rare.

To assess the traditionally demarcated area of general intelligence, ten indicators were utilized. These included verbal and performance subtests from the Wechsler Intelligence Scale for Children (Wechsler, 1949); the School and College Ability Tests, which provide measures of verbal and quantitative aptitude (Cooperative Test Division, 1957a; 1957b); and the Sequential Tests of Educational Progress, which provide yardsticks of achievement in various academic content areas (Cooperative Test Division, 1957c; 1957d; 1959).

The ten creativity indicators—a uniqueness and a productivity measure for each of five procedures—proved to be highly reliable, in terms of both split-half and item-sum correlations. The reliabilities of the ten intelligence instruments, in turn, were known to be quite high. We now were in a position, therefore, to study the dimensionality of the creativity and intelligence indices. Whether examining results for the sample as a whole, or separately for the 70 boys and the 81 girls, the ten creativity measures proved to be highly intercorrelated, the ten intelligence measures proved to be highly intercorrelated, and the correlations *between* the creativity and the intelligence measures proved to be extremely low. To provide a reminder of the correlational magnitudes involved, the average correlation among the ten creativity measures is on the order of .4; the average correlation among the ten intelligence indicators is on the order of .5; and the average correlation between these two sets of measures is about .1.

We concluded, therefore, that a dimension of individual differences had been defined here which, on the one hand, possessed generality and pervasiveness, but which, on the other hand, nevertheless was quite independent of the traditional notion of general intelligence. This new dimension concerned a child's ability to generate unique and plentiful associates, in a generally task-appropriate manner and in a relatively playful context. It was a considerable surprise that such a dimension should prove to be quite independent of general intelligence, and it seemed indeed appropriate to label this dimension "creativity." The independence of this dimension from general intelligence seemed all the more intriguing for two reasons: first, the creativity procedures almost inevitably called upon verbal facility in some degree, and verbal facility is a very basic element of the general intelligence concept; second, the independence in question was found for elementary school children, and one would expect young children to show less differentiation in modes of cognitive functioning than adults.

In a sense, all that has been described thus far constituted a prelude. Having isolated a mode of thinking in children that is pervasive, independent of intelligence, and appropriately described as a dimension of individual differences in ''creativity,'' we now wished to understand its psychological significance. The appropriate research strategy at this point seemed to require consideration of individual differences on the creativity and the intelligence dimensions taken *jointly*. It was necessary, in other words, to compose four groups of children within each sex: those high in both creativity and intelligence, those high in one and low in the other, and those low in both. In order to define these groups, a single creativity index score and a single intelligence index score were obtained for each child. These index scores were the summed standard scores of the ten measures in each respective domain. The distributions of creativity index scores and of intelligence index scores then were dichotomized at their respective medians, within sex, to yield the groups that exemplified the four possible combinations of creativity and intelligence levels. The two sexes, it will be recalled, were quite similar with regard to the distributions of these index scores. Since all cases were retained, rather than just the extremes, it is evident that the procedure used for composing creativity and intelligence combinations was a conservative one.

Consider now some of the psychological differences that we found to distinguish children who are both creative and intelligent, creative but not intelligent, intelligent but not creative, and neither creative nor intelligent. To begin with, we turn to the behavior of these several groups of children in the school environment. The two experimenters made independent ratings of the children along specifically defined behavioral dimensions during an initial two weeks of observation in each class. This work was carried out prior to any further contact with the children, so that the ratings could not be influenced by the performances of the children on the various experimental procedures. Furthermore, no other possible sources of information about the children were made available to the raters during the observation period. In short, every effort was made to insure that the ratings would be unbiased.

It should also be mentioned that these rating dimensions possess high inter-rater reliability, a very important point that the use of two independent observers permitted us to establish. Without this kind of reliability, investigation of individual differences on these behavioral dimensions would have been fruitless.

The judges rated each child's status on a given dimension in terms of a nine-point scale. For example, one characteristic was defined in terms of the following question: "To what degree does this child seek attention in unsocialized ways, as evidenced by such behavior as speaking out of turn, continually raising his hand, or making unnecessary noises?" The first, third, fifth, seventh, and ninth points on the rating scale for this question were given the verbal labels "never," "seldom," "sometimes," "usually," and "always," respectively. Other questions rated in the same manner included: "To what degree does this child hesitate to express opinions, as evidenced by extreme caution, failure to contribute, or a subdued manner in a speaking situation?" "To what degree does this child show confidence and assurance in his actions toward his teachers and classmates, as indicated by such behavior as not being upset by criticism, or not being disturbed by rebuffs from classmates?" "To what degree is this child's companionship sought for by his peers?" "To what degree does this child seek the companionship of his peers?"

The preceding questions were focused upon issues of social behavior. Several questions of an achievement-centered nature also were included. These inquired about such matters as the following: "How would you rate this child's attention span and degree of concentration for academic school work?" "How would you rate this child's interest in academic school work, as indicated by such behavior as looking forward to new kinds of academic work, or trying to delve more deeply into such work?" For these questions, the first, third, fifth, seventh, and ninth points of the rating scales were labeled "poor," "below average," "average," "good," and "superior," respectively.

Let us look in some detail at the results for the girls. Those high in both creativity and intelligence show the least doubt and hesitation of all the groups, show the highest level of self-confidence, and display the least tendency toward deprecation of oneself and one's work. Concerning companionship, these girls are sought out by their peers more eagerly than is any other group, and this high intelligence–high creativity group also seeks the companionship of others more actively than does any other group. There is reciprocity in social relationships for the members of this group. With regard to achievement, this group shows the highest levels of attention span, concentration, and interest in academic work. In all of these respects, the high-high group obviously is reflecting highly desirable modes of conduct in both the social and the achievement spheres. Interestingly enough, however, this group also is high in regard to disruptive, attention-seeking behavior. The high-high children may well be brimming over with eagerness to propose novel, divergent possibilities in the classroom, in the face of boredom with the customary classroom routines. Against the context of classroom programs that emphasize equal participation by class members and academic values that are likely to center around the traditional intelligence dimension, the cognitive behavior reflected in high creativity levels in the case of these girls may well possess a nuisance value and exert a rather disruptive effect in the classroom situation.

Consider next the group high in creativity but low in intelligence. In many respects it turns out that this group is at the greatest disadvantage of all in the classroom—and, indeed, under more of a disadvantage than the group which is low in both creativity and intelligence. Those of high creativity but low intelligence are the most cautious and hesitant of all the groups, the least confident and least self-assured, the least sought after by their peers as companions, and in addition are quite avoidant themselves of the companionship of others. There is a mutuality of social avoidance in the case of these girls. In the academic sphere, they are the most deprecatory of their own work and the least able to concentrate and maintain attention. In terms of the ratings for disruptive attention-seeking, however, these girls are high, and in this one respect similar to the high creativity–high intelligence group. Most likely, however, the attention-seeking of these two groups is quite different in quality, given the highly different contexts of other behaviors in the two cases. While the disruptive behaviors of the high-high group suggest enthusiasm and overeagerness, those of the high creative–low intelligent group suggest an incoherent protest against their plight.

It affords an interesting comparison to turn next to the group low in both intelligence and creativity. These girls actually seem to be better off than their high creativity–low intelligence peers. The low-low group possesses greater confidence and assurance, is less hesitant and subdued, and is considerably more outgoing toward peers in social relationships, than is the high creative–low intelligent group. The low-low group members appear to compensate for their poor academic performances by activity in the social sphere, while the high creative–low intelligent individuals, possessing seemingly more delicate sensitivities, are more likely to cope with academic failure by social withdrawal and a retreat within themselves.

Finally, we turn to the group high in intelligence but low in creativity. As in the case of the high-high group, these girls show confidence and assurance. In terms of companionship patterns, however, an intriguing difference emerges. While sought quite strongly as a companion by others, the girl in this group tends not to seek companionship herself. She also is least likely to seek attention in disruptive ways and is reasonably hesitant about expressing opinions. Attention span and concentration for academic matters, in turn, are quite high. The impression that emerges, then, is of a girl who is strongly oriented toward academic achievement, is somewhat cool and aloof in her social behavior but liked by others anyway, and is unwilling to take the chance of overextending or overcommiting herself; there is a holding back, a basic reserve.

These results make it clear that one needs to know whether creativity in a child is present in the context of high or low intelligence, and one needs to know whether intelligence in a child is present in conjunction with high or low creativity. It is necessary to consider a child's joint standing on both dimensions. One must seriously question, therefore, the Getzels and Jackson (1962) procedure of defining a "high creative" group as children who are high in creativity *but* low in intelligence, and defining a "high intelligent" group as children who are high in intelligence *but* low in creativity. If one wishes to establish generalizations about the nature of creativity and of intelligence as distinct characteristics, one cannot afford to ignore those children who are high in both and who are low in both.

Let us consider now some evidence in a different area—that of conceptualizing activities. This evidence has cast light on differences among the groups of boys. In one of our procedures, the child was asked to group pictures of everyday physical objects, and was requested to give the reason for his grouping in each case. Among the fifty objects pictured were, for example, a rake, a screwdriver, a telephone, a lamppost, a candle. The groupings were to be carried out in terms of putting together things that seemed to belong together. When this phase was completed, reasons for grouping were obtained. These reasons later were content analyzed—blindly, of course, with respect to the identities of the children—and the reliability of the content-analysis system was evaluated by having all materials scored by two independent judges. Reliability was found to be quite high. Consider briefly now one of the content-analysis distinctions employed.

We wished to contrast relational or thematic reasons for grouping with reasons based upon abstracted similarities among the objects. In the latter type of reason, every object in the group is an independent instance of the label applied, whether the labels refer to shared physical properties or to shared conceptual properties. An example of the physical-descriptive type of category would be the label, "hard objects," for a group consisting of a lamppost, a door, and a hammer. An example of the conceptual-inferential type of category would be the label, "for eating," in the case of a group containing a fork, a spoon, a cup, and a glass. By a relational or thematic type of reason, on the other hand, we refer to a label deriving from the relationship among the objects in the group; no single object is an independent instance of the concept, but rather all of the objects in the grouping are required in order to define it. An example of a thematic category is the label, "getting ready to go out," for a group consisting of a comb, a lipstick, a watch, a pocketbook, and a door.

The distinctions just made derived from work carried out by Kagan, Moss, and Sigel (1960; 1963), with certain modifications necessitated by the nature of the stimuli. It had typically been assumed by these investigators as well as by others that responding on a relational or thematic basis represents an intellectually inferior manifestation. This could indeed be true in the studies just cited, where the stimuli to be grouped were few in number and their thematic characteristics highly salient. Thematizing under such circumstances might well represent a passive, global approach to the materials provided. In the procedure employed by the authors, however, a large number of stimuli—fifty in all—were present, and their nature as well as the instructional context were such as to reduce markedly the *Eindringlichkeit* or prominence of thematic relationships. The child was encouraged to group in terms of abstractions, since the instructions implied to him that similarity be used as the basis for sorting. In addition, the objects were commonplace physical things, and there were many of them. Under these circumstances, it might well be the case that relational or thematic grouping would constitute a freewheeling, unconventional type of response to the given task, in contrast to the more customary practice of sorting the objects in terms of common elements, whether such elements be physical or conceptual. Constraints arising from the nature of the stimuli would be considerably stronger in the case of groupings based upon shared physical or conceptual properties. Groupings based on relationships or themas, on the other hand, would permit greater free play for the evolving of unique combinations of stimuli. With these considerations in mind, let us turn to some results.

The findings for males point to a particularly clear phenomenon. The group of high intelligence but low creativity stands out as avoiding the use of thematic or relational bases for grouping. Rather, they concentrate on conceptual common elements. For whatever reasons—and the reasons may differ in the case of different groups—the other three groups are more willing to indulge in thematic forms of conceptualizing. It is the high intelligence–low creativity group that shows a disproportionate avoidance of thematizing. Such a finding reinforces the hypothesis that thematic responding may, under the conditions of the present procedure, represent a more playful, imaginative approach to the grouping task than does strict common-element sorting.

To suggest that the low incidence of thematizing by the high intelligence–low creativity group is evidence for an avoidance reaction, however, is to imply a further distinction. In principle, a low incidence could reflect either an inability to thematize or an avoidance of it. In another experimental procedure, however, we assessed the ability of the children to integrate a set of words into a unified thema in story telling—that is, in this new task, thematizing was required of the child. Under such conditions, the high intelligence–low creativity group thematizes as well as the group high in both creativity and intelligence. It is when the option not to thematize is available that thematizing drops out of the behavior of the high intelligence–low creativity group. Such evidence, then, suggests that we are dealing with a disinclination to thematize on the part of this group, not an inability to thematize.

It has typically been proposed in work on cognitive development (for example, Bruner & Olver, 1963) that the most mature cognitive functioning involves inferential abstraction—the kind of organizing that would be reflected in terms of sorting objects on the basis of shared conceptual properties. Thematizing has been considered a developmentally primitive response. Our findings suggest, however, that a more critical consideration may be the relative balance between conceptual-inferential and thematizing tendencies. Consider the results for the various groups of boys on the sorting task in somewhat more detail. For both of the high creativity groups, the relative incidence of thematizing *and* inferential-conceptual grouping is fairly high. For the high intelligence–low creativity group, the relative incidence of thematizing is quite low, while the relative incidence of inferential-conceptual sorting is quite high. Finally, for the low intelligence–low creativity group, the relationship is reversed; the incidence of thematizing is high, while the incidence of inferential-conceptual sorting is relatively low.

In sum, the creative boys seem able to switch rather flexibly between thematizing and inferential-conceptual bases for grouping; the high intelligence–low creativity boys seem rather inflexibly locked in inferential-conceptual categorizing and strongly avoidant of thematic-relational categorizing; and finally, the low intelligence–low creativity boys tend to be locked within thematic modes of responding and relatively incapable of inferential-conceptual behavior. Parenthetically, it might be well to offer the reminder that both the incidences of thematic and inferential-conceptual groupings can be high since there also exists the third scoring category of grouping in terms of common physical elements.

Apart from the formulation of concepts, we also were interested in the question of how children set limits or boundaries in the case of concepts already in existence. Do creativity and intelligence impinge upon this boundary-setting process? Given the central tendency value for a class, such as the typical width of windows, the child was asked to specify the upper and lower extremes of the class from among multiple-choice alternatives. At issue, then, was whether the child preferred to set his category limits closer to or further from the central tendency value. The major finding is a relationship between creativity and the setting of broad category boundaries. In general, the creative child is more willing to tolerate deviant instances as possibly warranting membership in the category. In other words, the more creative children seem to display greater cognitive "energy"—they insist upon turning over possibilities until less likely and therefore more deviant and novel cognitive elements have been unearthed. The seeing of connections between disparate events through placing them in a common category—a process implied in the setting of wider tolerance limits for acceptance of potential instances in a class—thus may well be found in the child whose associational processes reflect greater creativity.

When we consider some of our data concerning sensitivity to the expressive potential of visual materials, a result similar to the thematizing findings is obtained for the high intelligence–low creativity group of girls. With line drawings of stick figures in various postures as stimuli, various emotional states were proposed to the child as possibilities for one or another figure, and the child indicated a willingness or disinclination to entertain each possibility. Let us focus our attention upon two kinds of affective labels for each stick figure: a label constituting a highly likely, conventional suggestion, and a label representing a quite unlikely, unconventional possibility. Unconventional and likely emotional attributions for the various stick figures were defined with reference to the consensus of adult judges. Each of some twenty-four stick figures was offered to the child with one affective label upon each presentation. A different type of label was proposed each time a given figure was presented, and a given figure was repeated only after all the others had been shown. More inappropriate and more appropriate kinds of labels for the various figures were offered on a random schedule. Note that a choice was never forced between these two classes of emotional attributions. Each presentation involved one stick figure and one label, with the child requested to accept or reject the label as a descriptive possibility. The child thus was free to accept appropriate and unconventional emotional attributions, to reject both kinds, or to accept one kind and reject the other.

The main results with this procedure for the girls were as follows. Although the four groups did not differ in regard to their acceptance of appropriate or likely affective attributions for the stick figures, they differed in a particular way regarding acceptance of the unconventional attributions—the group high in intelligence but low in creativity exhibited a conspicuously low level of such acceptance. Although the rate of acceptance of such attributions by the other three groups was generally quite low (about 5 percent), the high intelligence–low creativity group accepted virtually none at all. The comparability among the groups regarding acceptance of appropriate attributions acts as a control, indicating that the differential acceptance behavior just described relates to the entertainment of unconventional attributions in particular, rather than simply to the acceptance of any kind of affective labels. Furthermore, there is no relationship between degree of acceptance of unconventional and of appropriate attributions. It is safe to conclude, therefore, that an acquiescence or "yea-saying" response set cannot account for the differential acceptance of unconventional attributions.

The implications of the present finding appear to be quite similar to the thematizing results considered before in the case of the boys. In both cases, the high intelligence–low creativity group is intolerant of unlikely, unconventional types of hypothesizing about the world. This particular group appears conspicuously loathe to "stick its neck out," as it were, and try something that is far out, unconventional, and, hence, possibly "wrong." It is of particular interest that the high intelligence–low creativity group of girls avoids entertaining the possibility of unconventional emotional attributions under the present experiment's conditions. Recall that the entertainment of such possibilities has no effect upon the availability for acceptance of the likely and highly appropriate possibilities; it is not an "either–or" situation. The high intelligence–low creativity girls seem to be so attuned to error that, even where appropriate responses are not sacrificed, they refuse to deviate from a critical standard of "correctness."

Consider next some of the other findings in the domain of expressive sensitivity. Included in this domain were tasks requiring free descriptions of stimuli with implicit emotive significance. We content-analyzed these free descriptions in order to determine the extent to which a child would confine his descriptions to comments upon the physical and geometric characteristics of the various stimuli, as contrasted with the extent to which he would "go beyond" such physical categories and discuss the affective or expressive connotations of such materials. In the case of both sexes, the ability to range beyond the physical and into the realm of affective content tends to be maximal in the group high in both creativity and intelligence. That creativity and intelligence both contribute to such physiognomic sensitivity suggests that two processes may be jointly involved in the display of this sensitivity. On the one hand, the capacity to make inferential translations from one mode of experience to another seems to be reflective of the general intelligence concept; on the other hand, the associational freedom implied by the creativity concept evidently enhances the range of experience available for making inferential linkages.

Let us turn now to some evidence on how the children describe themselves with respect to general anxiety symptoms and to those symptoms experienced under the stress of tests or examinations. Consider the findings for the boys. Standard materials for assessing manifest anxiety and test anxiety were employed, deriving from the work of Sarason, Davidson, Lighthall, Waite, and Ruebush (1960). The results are suggestive of a Yerkes-Dodson function. They are of the same nature for both general manifest anxiety and test anxiety. The level of anxiety is lowest for the group that is high in intelligence but low in creativity. Anxiety level is middling for the two groups that are high in creativity, regardless of intelligence level. Finally, anxiety level is highest for the group that is low in intelligence and low in creativity. The allusion to the Yerkes-Dodson law is made since creativity is found to be maximal in the presence of an intermediate level of anxiety. If anxiety is either too low or too high, then creativity is reduced. Just as interesting, however, are the particular conditions under which anxiety level is lowest. It is the group high in intelligence but low in creativity who, by self-report, are least anxious. At the other end of the dimension, with the highest anxiety scores, stands the group low in both intelligence and creativity.

What are the implications of these findings? First of all, they force us to question whether creativity should be conceptually associated with a state of maximal freedom from anxiety symptoms. It is not those children who are lowest in anxiety level, but those who report a moderate degree of anxiety, whom we find to be most creative in their thinking processes. Traditional conceptions of mental health place considerable emphasis upon anxiety as a debilitator of cognitive performance and as a signal of inappropriate or ineffective adjustment. This no doubt is true when anxiety reaches quite high levels. We need only remember that the strongest degree of anxiety is found in the most cognitively deprived group of children—those who are low both in general intelligence and creativity. However, it may also be the case that a modicum of anxiety is reflecting more the presence of sensitivity to internal states than the presence of disturbance. This should not be construed, of course, as acceptance of the old saw that neuroticism breeds creativity. However, the data in hand do suggest that it is equally unrealistic to assume that the most creative children are the happiest children. There may well be elements of obsessiveness present in the kind of associative freedom that leads to high creativity status. A playful contemplation of the possible, but also an obsessive, task-centered reluctance to put a problem aside, may be involved in the production of many associates and of a large number of unique associates. Creativity need not be all sweetness and light, therefore, but may well involve a tolerance for and understanding of sadness and pain. To think otherwise is to fall prey to the rather widespread American stereotype that suffering is always a bad thing and is to be avoided at all costs.

One possible cost of the avoidance of suffering is evident in the group whose levels of general anxiety and of test anxiety are lowest—the group high in intelligence but low in creativity. This result may well stem from the fact that the group in question is the most closely attuned to the demands of the classroom environment. In that environment, traditionally defined intelligence and its manifestations in the form of high academic achievement most likely are heavily rewarded, while creativity may well be viewed as more of a disruption than a boon. The mode of operation of the high intelligence–low creativity child, therefore, may be such as to minimize the sources of possible conflict between himself and the school environment and to maximize the sources of reward from that environment. It is not surprising that such a close fit between individual and social context would be reflected in a minimal level of anxiety.

Also measured in our work on self-description was defensiveness—the extent to which each child tended, on the one hand, to deny the occurrence of experiences that, although negative, are common to most children of this general age, and on the other hand, to insist upon the occurrence of experiences that, because highly positive, are very rare. An example of a statement of the former type would be, "I am never unhappy"; of the latter type, "I always tell the truth." Boys who are highly creative and highly intelligent tend to exhibit a lower level of defensiveness than the other male subgroups. With defensiveness cast in the role of antecedent rather than consequent, in turn, we find that defensive boys tend to show a lower level of creativity than nondefensive boys. Thus, the kind of disturbance represented by defensiveness is not conducive to creativity, while the type of disturbance reflected in overt anxiety, if present in modest degree, defines an attitude that may actually facilitate creativity.

The damping down of awareness concerning negative experiences and behaviors so characteristic of the defensive child can certainly be expected to inhibit the associative freedom that lies at the basis of creativity. In addition, the defensive boy exhibits reduced physiognomic sensitivity. Hence, nonawareness of one's own affective states is directly linked to nonawareness of affective connotations carried by surrounding evironmental events. This outcome obtains in each of several different physiognomic sensitivity procedures, including one in which the subject was requested to match abstract line patterns with faces conveying the emotional state of anger, joy, or sleepiness. Matches defined as exhibiting greater physiognomic sensitivity were those that agreed with the consensus of adult judges. The positive relationships, in turn, between physiognomic sensitivity and creativity have already been noted. For boys, then, a syndrome emerges in which creativity and physiognomic sensitivity are positively related, creativity and defensiveness are inversely related, and physiognomic sensitivity and defensiveness are inversely related. In sum, the ability to produce unique and plentiful ideational associates shows some commonality with the awareness of negative affective states in oneself and with the capacity to apprehend expressive characteristics potentially carried by visual stimuli in the environment. All three of the foregoing processes reflect an "openness" to stimulation, from either internal or external sources.

From the kinds of results that have been passed in review, pictures began to emerge concerning the psychological nature of the children in the four cognitive groupings: high creativity–high intelligence, high creativity–low intelligence, low creativity–high intelligence, and low creativity–low intelligence. In addition to our quantitative studies, clinical accounts describing various children in the sample also were presented, and these clinical materials tended to reinforce the conclusions derived from the experimental work. The case studies can be summarized in terms of the generalizations presented below. These will also serve to underline the major points of congruence between the clinical and the experimental sources of information concerning the four creativity and intelligence groupings.

High creativity–high intelligence: These children can exercise within themselves both control and freedom, both adultlike and childlike kinds of behavior.

High creativity–low intelligence: These children are in angry conflict with themselves and with their school environment and are beset by feelings of unworthiness and inadequacy. In a stress-free context, however, they can blossom forth cognitively.

Low creativity–high intelligence: These children can be described as "addicted" to school achievement. Academic failure would be perceived by them as catastrophic, so that they must continually strive for academic excellence in order to avoid the possibility of pain.

Low creativity–low intelligence: Basically bewildered, these children engage in various defensive maneuvers ranging from useful adaptations such as intensive social activity to regressions such as passivity or psychosomatic symptoms.

Thus, our work progressed from the definition and operationalization of two types of cognitive activity to an investigation of their correlates in such areas as observable social and achievement-relevant behaviors, ways of forming concepts, physiognomic sensitivities, and self-described levels of general anxiety, test anxiety, and defensiveness. From the findings obtained, it seems fair to conclude that the present definition of creativity denotes a mode of cognitive functioning that matters a great deal in the life of the child. Furthermore, consideration of the child's *joint* status with regard to the conventional concept of general intelligence and creativity as here defined is evidently of critical importance in the search for new knowledge concerning children's thinking.

IMPLICATIONS FOR THE STUDY OF CHILDREN'S THINKING

It is now generally recognized that a wide variety of processes can be included under the general rubric of "thinking." A glance at the chapter headings of textbooks devoted to the psychology of thinking (such as Johnson, 1955; Thomson, 1959; Vinacke, 1952) testifies to the polymorphous quality of the problem area designated by the thinking label. One finds, for example, discussions of problem-solving, concept attainment, imaginative and creative thinking. To these, one might well add decision-making processes (Brim, Glass, Lavin, & Goodman, 1962; Kogan & Wallach, 1964; Taylor, 1963).

While psychologists have acknowledged the multidimensional nature of thought, they have clearly not agreed upon any uniform strategy for extending our knowledge about thinking. The strategies employed can, however, be divided into two fundamental types. On the one hand, there are those investigators who have insisted upon breaking down the thinking concept into its major components in order to study one or more of these in an experimental fashion. The approach consists of a systematic examination of the individual and/or task parameters that affect the course of a particular form of thinking. An example of such an approach in the domain of concept attainment is represented by the work of Bruner, Goodnow, and Austin (1956); an example in the domain of problem-solving is provided by Duncker (1945). In contrast to the foregoing experimental strategy, one might cite the psychometric approach of Guilford (for example, 1964). Using factor analysis as a basic methodological tool, Guilford and his associates have taken the entire domain of thinking as their province and, in so doing, have proceeded to sketch out the "structure of intellect."

Both approaches have their merits and liabilities, of course. Pursuit of the experimental strategy tells us a great deal about the vicissitudes of particular part-processes of thinking, but yields no information concerning the manner in which the part-processes are organized in specific individuals. Psychometrically oriented research, in turn, can be quite revealing of the organization of a multiplicity of thought processes in the person. The price paid for this information is the basic shortcoming that all of the thinking processes under study have been usually measured under one particular standard condition of administration. If these conditions were altered for one or more thinking tasks, the "structure of intellect" might show substantial changes.[1]

In regard to creativity research, the approach has tended, with a few exceptions (for example, Maltzman, 1960; Mednick, 1962), toward a psychometric rather than experimental outlook. Accordingly, we have learned a great deal about the place of creativity and intelligence in the domain of abilities, but it has been the kind of creative thinking that profited from an emphasis upon speeded conditions in a context of

---

[1] It is possible that the importance of the assessment context in the measurement of creativity would have been uncovered sooner if, instead of the standard factor-analytic model, a multitrait, multimethod model (Campbell & Fiske, 1959) had been employed.

evaluation. The motivational characteristics associated with the creativity tasks were highly similar to those typical of intelligence tests. Under the circumstances, it is hardly surprising that intelligence and creativity have not proven to be statistically independent of one another, despite frequent exaggerated claims to the contrary.

One of the most firmly established axioms of psychology states that thinking can be influenced by motivational factors. The latter, in turn, will be determined in part by the particular context in which the thinking process occurs. More specifically, evaluation-laden and permissive, game-like situations can be expected to induce distinctive motivational sets. Thinking that occurs under these different conditions will be affected accordingly. One may conceive of a "thought product," then, as a function of the assigned task, of motivational sets aroused by the environmental conditions under which the subject copes with the task, and of relatively enduring motivational dispositions (such as anxiety and defensiveness) and cognitive capacities (such as problem-solving skill). Further, one can expect relationships to be interactive rather than additive. Thus, assessment conditions can give rise to temporary motivational states that are congruent or incongruent with the more enduring motivational characteristics of the child. We are suggesting, in other words, that thinking of various types may be enhanced or diminished in quality simply by altering the context in which the child's thinking is assessed. Further, we are proposing that this variation in assessment context can affect the degree to which qualities of performance in different types of thinking tasks converge or diverge within a subject population. Where the assessment context emphasizes success and failure, we suspect that differentiation within the thinking domain will be minimized. Under these conditions, the forms of thinking demanded by conventional intelligence tests can be expected to exercise dominance over a wide span of cognitive tasks. As the assessment situation becomes more permissive, however, the overriding effects of intelligence should decline, with the consequence of greater differentiation in the thinking domain.[2] Hence, the creativity-

---

[2] Some readers may object to the above formulation on the grounds that intelligence itself may be composed of independent primary abilities (Thurstone, 1936). It is beyond the scope of this volume to enter the age-old controversy as to whether there is or is not a general factor of intelligence. In the past, the former view has been favored by British, the latter view by American factor analysts. Quite recently, however, McNemar (1964) has defended the general intelligence construct, and Humphreys (1962) has offered a variation on the British position. In this variation, a hierarchical model of abilities is presented in which higher-order factors (where general intelligence can be expected to emerge) are claimed to be of much greater psychological significance than are the primary ability factors. It should also be noted that a higher order *G* factor is more likely to emerge in children than in adults.

intelligence distinction has been turned into a genuine empirical distinction in the present volume by appropriate consideration of motivational and task elements. Creativity procedures based on an associative conception of creativity administered under gamelike conditions generate performances that are statistically independent of performance on intelligence tests administered in the usual manner.

While it has been our major purpose to differentiate creativity and intelligence, consideration should be given to the general question of whether the assessment contexts employed in the present investigation optimize performance respecting those two major modes of thinking. With regard to creativity, we do not believe that there is much doubt concerning the matter. If one wishes to assess a form of creative thinking in children that is independent of intelligence, the assessment procedures and context that we have employed may offer the only course. On those grounds alone, it is probably safe to venture the hypothesis that the kind of creativity assessment described in the present volume optimizes the expression of creative thinking in elementary school children.

But what of intelligence? Does the fact that we have employed conventional intelligence tests administered in the prescribed way necessarily imply that optimal measures of intelligence have been achieved? From the standpoint of differentiating intelligence from creativity, the SCAT, STEP, and WISC evidently served their purpose well. Hence, we now know that the tests employed to assess the aptitude and achievement levels of elementary school children have little relation to the kind of creative thinking explored in the present volume. We must seriously question, however, whether the traditional assessment context for the measurement of intelligence is likely to reveal a child's full potentialities in the problem-solving domain.

If it is possible to push creativity in the direction of intelligence by assessing both in a similar way, should it not also be feasible to make the expression of intelligence more reflective of creativity? There are two possible routes one can follow in this regard. First, presently available intelligence tests could be administered in a permissive, nonevaluative context. It is unlikely that such an approach would have much of an effect on performance, however, for children are very probably sensitized to the readily perceptible cues that an intelligence test offers in abundance. One such fundamental cue is the convergent type of thinking (the one correct answer) demanded by intelligence test items. Recall in this regard the highly significant correlations between scores from the WISC, which was individually administered by nonthreatening examiners already familiar to the children, and scores from the group-administered SCAT and STEP tests.

The alternative route would involve a break with the traditional intelligence tests and a resultant concentration upon problem-solving processes in a variety of contexts. Many psychologists have viewed creative thinking as a special class of highly productive problem-solving (for example, Bartlett, 1958; Crutchfield, 1962; Henle, 1962; Johnson, 1955; Newell, Shaw, & Simon, 1962; Wertheimer, 1959). For the foregoing investigators, the novel, harmonious, and elegant solution to a problem is treated as evidence for creative thinking. From the perspective of the present volume, such productive problem-solving represents a combination of creativity and intelligence. For the novel and elegant solution to a problem will generally involve both associative and evaluative modes of thought. The individual with the larger associative repertoire will generate more possibilities, among which the elegant solution might well be included. But such elegance requires that the individual recognize the most appropriate fit between problem and solution. Such cognizance, in turn, involves the operation of processes that must be subsumed under a construct of intelligence.

It is apparent, then, that creativity and intelligence need not necessarily involve cognitive operations that are orthogonal to each other. There are evidently classes of problems—"adventurous thinking," in Bartlett's (1958) terms—in which associative processes must be brought to bear on the problem if it is to be given an elegant or novel solution. It may actually be necessary to restructure such a problem before efforts toward solution can begin. Most intelligence tests are distinguished by what Bartlett (1958) would probably call thinking in "closed systems." All of the information necessary to solution is inherent in the structure of the problem. The subject must manipulate the given information in the ways that are necessary to achieve the answer defined as "correct" by the test-maker.[3]

The authors have no intention of deriding "closed-system" thinking as unimportant. It is evidently essential that children learn to think within highly structured domains. Many important cognitive operations take place according to formal rules that allow little leeway for associative modes of thought. We are merely suggesting that a mastery of problems requiring thinking within "closed systems" is no guarantor of the ability to think in "open-system" terms. At the same time, the capacity to generate plentiful and unique associates can probably be considered a necessary condition for restructuring and deriving novel, unconventional, and elegant solutions to problems, but there is no evidence that

---

[3] As Wertheimer (1959) has demonstrated, thinking within closed systems may be more or less elegant depending upon whether the subject truly apprehends the structure of the problem or merely applies rote formulas to achieve an answer. Intelligence tests are not concerned with such process distinctions, but concentrate instead on the end-products of problem-solving.

sheer associative freedom is a sufficient condition. For, as Koestler (1964) has made clear, the creative act is characterized by a process of "bisociation"—two domains of thought that had previously led an independent existence are suddenly brought into intimate contact with each other and emerge as an integral whole. There is an implication here of a sense of elegant appropriateness between the domains in question. Any other combination would have fallen short in some respect.

In discussing the act of bisociation, Koestler is striving to elucidate a process capable of accounting for creative accomplishments at many levels of existence. When children constitute the subjects of one's study, the most that can be hoped for is a reasonable approximation to the cognitive capacity likely to be required if "bisociation" is to take place. It is basically a capacity to recognize the presence of similarities between diverse events when the basis for the similarity judgment is not at all obvious but yet is quite appropriate. Our creativity procedures have been designed to capture the essence of the foregoing skill, and we believe that we have succeeded in doing so to an extent well in excess of our initial expectations. Nevertheless, we are quite willing to grant that the creativity of adult life generally occurs within a context of problem construction and problem solution. The creative product rarely, if ever, takes the form of an enumeration of alternative possibilities. Nevertheless, the generation of alternatives is undoubtedly an intermediate step—a precondition for the creative act. By focusing upon the associative flow of children, we have attempted to tap this precondition. We do not mean to imply, of course, that the existence of the preconditions for creativity in a child will necessarily lead to actual creative performances later in life. Such adult creativity is influenced by many factors other than the associative capacities of the individual. Environmental determinants may play a major role. We wonder, however, whether severe inhibitions of associative processes can result in creative products no matter how favorable the environment for the expression of creativity. Evidently, the link between the creative thinking of children and adults must remain an open question, pending the systematic collection of relevant longitudinal data. It is unlikely, however, that we shall soon find a psychologist or team of psychologists to do for creativity what Terman and his associates (Terman *et al.*, 1925; Burks, Jensen, & Terman, 1930; Terman & Oden, 1947) have done for intelligence.

The relations between associational productivity and the achievement of a particular fitting or elegant problem solution have received some preliminary attention in a recent study by Mednick, Mednick, and Jung (1964). According to these authors, performance on the Remote Associates Test (described in Chapter 1), which involves solving the problem of finding a particular association that will be relevant to three different verbally specified concepts, is significantly related to the absolute number of associates produced by adult males to a stimulus word within a fixed time interval of two minutes. Since an attempt was made to control for general intelligence in that study, the finding suggests a congruence between an index related to one of the two types of creativity measures used in the present investigation—namely, productivity of associates—and the problem-solving measure of creativity (Remote Associates Test) utilized in the work of Mednick and his collaborators. Since, in turn, our two kinds of creativity measures— productivity and uniqueness of associates—were highly correlated, we can note the appearance of a bridge between a measure that defines creativity within a framework of solving a problem and a measure that defines creativity in terms of the character of the individual's flow of associations. There is still, however, the fact that associational productivity in the study by Mednick, Mednick, and Jung was measured within a brief time interval. Whether associational productivity under conditions of greater temporal freedom would still correlate with performance on the Remote Associates Test remains to be determined.[4]

To return to the question posed earlier, then, we are of the opinion that conventional intelligence tests provide a good measure of thinking capacity under conditions of success–failure stress on a particular class of problems. If one wishes to assess a form of thinking that is quite independent of associative thinking under relaxed conditions, the standardized intelligence, aptitude, and achievement tests satisfy such a criterion. On the other hand, one may well wish to build new and unorthodox types of problems and administer them in relaxed and gamelike settings. A possible lead is offered by the work of Crutchfield (1964), who devised a set of detective-story problems for children to solve. These problems were intended for training rather than assessment purposes, but there is no inherent reason why such problems could not be adapted for use in assessment.

One of Crutchfield's findings is of special relevance to the present volume. Training on the detective-story problems (a convergent-thinking task) had transfer value for performance on a Guilford-type divergent-thinking task. In other words, associative thinking was enhanced as a consequence of a specific type of problem-solving experience.[5] That such a finding was obtained strongly suggests that classes of problems can be

---

[4] A related study by Freedman (1965) reports that training in the giving of free associations to stimulus words (also within a brief time interval) leads to increased scores on the Remote Associates Test.

[5] Efforts made to facilitate problem-solving performance by training on associative thinking tasks have apparently met with less success (Maltzman, Belloni, & Fishbein, 1964).

devised which require associative modes of thought in order for solutions to be achieved. These problems should lend themselves to administration in a permissive, nonevaluative context with little risk that the children will perceive the problem-solving task in intelligence-test terms. Further, by virtue of demanding both convergent and divergent modes of thinking, the types of problems under consideration might well be viewed as a bridge across the creativity and traditional intelligence domains.

In certain respects, the procedures that we constructed in the domain of physiognomic sensitivity (see Chapter 5) may also be conceived as a bridge between creative and intelligent modes of thinking. A recent statement by Crutchfield (1962) is highly appropriate in this regard: "It may be suggested that one source of original ideas lies in the ready accessibility to the thinker of many rich and subtle 'physiognomic' attributes of the percepts and concepts in his mental world and to the metaphorical and analogical penumbras extending out from their more explicit, literal or purely logical features. For it is partly through a sensitivity to such physiognomic and metaphorical qualities that new and 'fitting' combinatorial possibilities among the elements of a problem may unexpectedly emerge" (p. 124). It will be recalled that creativity was related to enhanced physiognomic sensitivity in our sample of children. We anticipated such a relationship because both creativity and physiognomic sensitivity may be conceptualized in terms of psychological similarity and the obviousness or nonobviousness of the basis for calling one thing like another. Both creativity and physiognomic sensitivity are exhibited when the child describes things or events as similar to one another—through the device of simile or metaphor—on the basis of a nonobvious sharing of attributes.

Given the positive relationship between physiognomic sensitivity and creativity, it is of considerable theoretical interest to obtain inverse relationships for the boys between defensiveness and physiognomic sensitivity, and between defensiveness and creativity. High defensiveness would appear to constitute a condition which inhibits that portion of physiognomic sensitivity which depends upon the ability to cast wide associational nets. To the extent that defensiveness can be lowered, therefore, we can expect physiognomic sensitivity as well as creativity to be enhanced, at least in the case of boys. The forging of associative linkages between various classes of external stimulus events thus seems to possess some dependence upon the extent to which the individual is open to the possibility of acknowledging a wide range of internally experienced affective states—in other words, is low in defensiveness.

Such a connection between physiognomic sensitivity and the capacity to accept internally experienced affect seems to cast light on recent findings reported by Levy (1964) and Davitz (1964). Levy (1964) has obtained a relationship for adults between the ability to identify affects as expressed vocally by others, and the ability to identify feelings expressed by oneself upon an earlier occasion. The former task involved identifying another person's feeling states from a tape recording of that other person's voice reciting the same verbal passage with different expressive qualities. The latter task involved the subject's listening to a play-back of a tape recording of his own voice and attempting to discriminate the various affective states he had previously tried to express in successive readings of the same text. The relationship between the two tasks is maintained even when intelligence is controlled. Although Levy did not conceptualize her findings in terms of an inverse linkage between emotional sensitivity and defensiveness, the congruence between her results and our findings with boys points to the possible appropriateness of such an interpretation. This type of interpretation seems especially warranted when one takes note of the failure reported by Davitz (1964) to obtain relationships between the emotional sensitivity measure (the first of the two tasks described in the Levy study) and a range of traditional personality indicators including the Edwards Personal Preference Schedule, the Guilford-Zimmerman Temperament Survey, and the Psychaesthenia and Hysteria scales from the Minnesota Multiphasic Personality Inventory. Taking the Levy and Davitz findings in the context of our own results, the case for an inverse relationship between sensitivity to physiognomic properties and defensiveness would seem to be strengthened. The common element behind this relationship, in turn, would appear to consist of associational openness and freedom—creativity as defined in the present volume.

But what of the relation observed in our work between physiognomic sensitivity and traditional intelligence indices? The basis for this relationship has much to do with the stimulus constraints inherent in the physiognomic sensitivity tasks. The recognition of affect in human stick figures, or of temporal and enduring human characteristics in line patterns, involves associative processes, to be sure, but also involved is an evaluative judgment—an awareness of which affective attributes do justice to the stimulus requirements. This latter aspect was especially relevant in the procedure calling for matches between human emotive expressions and abstract line patterns.

Thus, the kinds of visual sensitivity operationalized in terms of the physiognomic procedures we have utilized seem to concern both the evaluative processes that are characteristic of general intelligence and the associative processes that are characteristic of creativity. The best indications that we have obtained, then, suggest that physiognomic sensitivity represents a fusion of intelligence *and* creativity.

This kind of conclusion is consistent with some recent work by

Beldoch (1964), who found measures of emotional sensitivity to be related in part to verbal intelligence in adults, but also to possess a substantial degree of independence from intelligence. Our work would lead us to propose that the portion of individual differences in emotional sensitivity which Beldoch found to be independent of general intelligence might well be related to the kind of creativity dimension studied in the present research.

It should be noted that performance on the creativity tasks to some extent must also involve matters of evaluation, for very few bizarre responses were obtained. However, unlike the physiognomic sensitivity domain, the creativity tasks permit a wide diversity of appropriate responses. Hence, associative thinking is considerably more important than evaluative appraisal in affecting performance on the types of creativity tasks employed in the present investigation. Since children constituted the subjects of our study, we deemed it advisable to concentrate first upon the fundamental associative processes underlying creativity, for matters of evaluation already receive considerable emphasis in the child's intellectual life. Creativity in the adult involves both associative (divergent) and evaluative (convergent) modes of thinking, as we have previously indicated. Viewed in developmental perspective, however, it appears to the writers that the associative mode constitutes a basic underpinning which emerges quite early in the child's life (possibly during the pre-school years), whereas the evaluative mode is a derivative of later learning. The foregoing conceptualization is speculative, to be sure, but it is sufficiently compelling to warrant empirical investigation.[6]

Consideration of how cognitive processes develop raises the question of what relationships may obtain between the descriptive model of thinking proposed in this volume and Piaget's delineation of the ontogeny of thought. While much of the Geneva group's work would seem to emphasize the mode of thinking that we have called "evaluative," some of it—in particular, the tasks devised for the study of the development of "formal operations," to use the Geneva group's term—may represent an amalgam of associative and evaluative thinking. The concept of "formal operations" refers to the child's taking account of possibilities

---

[6] Some evidence relevant to the present formulation is offered by the Pine and Holt (1960) study cited in Chapter 6. In the work of those authors, creative thinking abilities in young adults are related to Rorschach indices of psychoanalytic primary and secondary process functioning. A tentative analogy could be drawn between associative and evaluative modes of thought, on the one hand, and the primary–secondary process distinction, on the other. If the Pine-Holt procedures were tried out on children of various ages, our hypothesis would predict that the relation between primary process expression and the associative type of creative thinking will increase in magnitude as the age of the child decreases.

that require him to engage in combinatorial activities that move well beyond the perceptually present environment (see Flavell, 1963; Wallach, 1963). It is possible that taking account of hypothetical possibilities in solving problems of the types where "formal operations" may be used, involves a blend of associative with evaluative modes of thought in a manner similar to what may take place in the work by Crutchfield cited earlier.

In the Geneva tasks, the child is required to generate associative linkages based upon subtle combinations of given elements, and to take account of these hypothetical possibilities in working toward a problem solution. For example (Inhelder & Piaget, 1958), the child is shown five bottles containing liquids that all look like water. Four are labeled "1" through "4," respectively, while a fifth bottle is labeled "g." Two glasses also are present and contain what seems to be the same waterlike liquid. However, when the experimenter pours some of liquid "g" into each of these additional glasses, the liquid in one turns yellow while the liquid in the other remains clear. The child's task is to discover how to produce the yellow liquid. He is free to experiment with the five original bottles in any manner that he pleases in order to achieve this discovery. The situation is not unlike Crutchfield's (1964) work, where the child discovers the solution to a detective story by utilizing the information provided by clues. If administered in a context which is maximally permissive and nonevaluative, then, it is possible that some of the Geneva group's tasks may function as a bridge between the traditional intelligence area and creativity.

According to the Geneva group, systematic solution of the type of problem just described, with its requirement that the child envision possible combinations of bottles *1* through *4* with bottle *g*, does not emerge with clarity until about the twelfth or thirteenth year. Our interpretation would be that its emergence depends upon a suitable integration of associative with evaluative modes of thinking. While the Geneva researchers have devoted much attention to the development of evaluative processes in the child's thinking—his construction of concepts for describing physical reality—it would seem that the developmental history of associative processes in thinking is less well understood. The present work would suggest that one important area in which to look if we seek to understand the development of associative thinking is that of children's play. Are there, for example, "critical periods" in the ontogeny of the associative mode of thinking? If so, then provision of a rich array of play materials should make more of a difference to the later use of associative processes in thinking if such provision takes place before a certain age rather than after. Clearly, intriguing developmental questions concerning associative thinking present themselves for study.

A recurrent theme in the literature on creativity and on problem-solving concerns the decremental influence of excessive motivational involvement upon cognitive functioning. Thus, Crutchfield (1962) remarks that "in problem-solving, it appears that extrinsic, ego-involved motivations, as contrasted with intrinsic, task-involved motivations, are detrimental both to the ability of the creator to free himself from the constraints of old ways of thought and to his capacity to produce original insights" (p. 125). It is precisely such considerations as these that led us to the use of permissive, gamelike contexts for the measurement of creative thinking in children. Although we thereby succeeded in differentiating creativity from intelligence and possibly in maximizing the *overall* level of creative thinking in the sample of children studied, the fact remains that children apparently vary in their perception of an assessment environment which, from the investigator's point of view, has few evaluative features. The child with overly strong ego-defenses has apparently equipped himself to cope quite adequately with the world of aptitude and achievement tests. Indeed, thinking within "closed systems" may actually be facilitated by a defensive posture in the sense of keeping "extraneous" thoughts and images out of conscious awareness during the problem-solving process. When the defensive child is confronted with associative thinking tasks and the unstructured, novel features of a gamelike context in the school setting, however, the situation is apparently endowed with a type of threat for which the child's coping mechanisms are no longer adequate. Under such circumstances, the self is likely to be thrust into a prominent role, the defensive child now expending more energy delineating the relationship between the experimenter and himself and devoting correspondingly less attention to the creativity tasks themselves. Both Wertheimer (1959) and Henle (1962) have noted the necessity for the thinker to forget about himself in thinking and to concentrate upon the structural requirements of the given situation, if an elegant or creative solution is to be achieved.

Complicating the foregoing picture is the evidence that creativity measured in a context of associative flow may (for girls) be enhanced as a consequence of motivational disturbance. The presence of test anxiety in an otherwise defensive girl leads to high scores on associative creativity indices. We suspect that there may well be a counterphobic obsessive reaction in these girls—a need to exhaust their associative repertoire before putting the problem aside. Such a reaction would evidently serve the dual function of alleviating anxiety and, viewed from the subject's perspective, of favorably impressing the experimenter. Interestingly enough, these highly test anxious and defensive girls perform most poorly on the intelligence tests, suggesting the possibility that large discrepancies between creativity and intelligence scores may be indicative of a basis in motivational disturbance for large associative outputs. This interpretation received further support from the classroom behavior data, which revealed, it will be recalled, a pattern of disruptive and withdrawal tendencies in the girls of high creativity and low intelligence. It seems, then, that the inhibitions manifested by those girls in the classroom undergo a dramatic release in the relaxed confines of the experimental room. In the subsequent final section of the chapter, we shall discuss some of the implications that the foregoing results may have for educational practice.

Recall that the motivation–thinking relationships assumed a somewhat different form in the case of the boys. Of prime significance is the observation that anxiety—a proven disrupter of performance on intelligence tests—may actually enhance creative thinking, if the anxiety is not of extreme intensity. As we have previously stressed, creativity is not likely to grow out of a matrix of perfect adjustment or mental health. No one can deny that we are living in an era where the middle-class child is the focus of severe parental and school pressures intended to make him excel academically. For some children, such pressures might well lead to strong anxiety regarding school activities, and hence interfere with both intelligent and creative modes of thinking. The absence of anxiety in the face of academic pressures, on the other hand, is very likely to be reflective of defensiveness, and hence decremental to creativity. Finally, a moderate level of anxiety suggests a realistic "tuning" to the state of the world—a match between internal states and external pressures. It has been shown that the highest levels of creativity emerge under these motivational circumstances. Recall our earlier reference to the Yerkes-Dodson law. Evidently, creative thinking in children (especially boys) flourishes best where the motivational state falls somewhere between defensiveness (unconscious anxiety) and disruption (crippling overt anxiety).

In sum, we have shown that thinking is influenced by motivational determinants in manifold ways. Our evidence makes it clear that creativity and intelligence have unique motivational correlates. Further, there are interactions between those modes of thinking in relation to motivational dynamics. By treating creativity and intelligence within the scope of a single investigation, we believe that it has been possible to attain a level of clarity with regard to the motivation–thinking question that has not been achieved by studying creativity and intelligence separately.

Consider next the points of articulation that our work has provided between the modes of thinking, on the one hand, and the cognitive-style indices, on the other. It has been our intention to show that the study of intelligence and creativity can be brought into fruitful contact with the burgeoning work on cognitive controls and conceptual styles in children. There has been a tendency in the past toward a distinct separation between educational psychologists working on the creativity–intelligence issue and cognitive developmental psychologists interested in cognition and personality organization in the child. Fortunately, the boundaries between the foregoing specialties are being weakened, and, hopefully, the present volume will help to hasten this process.

A recurrent theme appearing in the literature concerned with cognitive growth and organization in children is the salient role assigned to a construct that in one form or another may be designated as an inferential, analytic, or abstract mode of cognitive operation. This construct emerges in the work of the Bruner, Kagan, and Witkin groups, to cite the major influences in the field, though the contributions of those authors differ somewhat in the theoretical rationale and operational specification given the construct under consideration. Beyond theory and method, the major contributors appear to share a value system that relegates the abstract-analytical-inferential cluster to a realm of superior cognitive functioning. In support of this value preference, an impressive array of correlations is marshalled demonstrating significant relations between that form of cognitive functioning and various intelligence indices. Inherent in the indicated value preference is the view that cognitive modes other than the abstract-analytic-inferential represent a more primitive type of functioning or an earlier stage of cognitive development. Included within these alternative modes of cognitive functioning is a disposition toward a thematic conceptual style.

As we have shown, simultaneous consideration of intelligence and creativity forces a modification in the dominant view that the inferential-abstract-analytical complex constitutes the most appropriate, if not sole, criterion of higher-level cognitive functioning in children. Rather, an overconcentration upon such functioning may actually betoken a kind of cognitive constriction. In a similar vein, excessive thematizing seems to be suggestive of a relatively weak intellective capacity. It may well be the extent of balance between inferential and thematic conceptualizing that is the hallmark of "mature" cognitive functioning. Recall that the highly creative boys in our sample were distinguished by their use of both the thematic and inferential modes.

In conclusion, we have tried to show that the broad modes of thinking reflected in the intelligence and creativity dimensions may have wide ramifications in the life of the child. It is now evident that knowledge of a child's creativity and intelligence status permits us to make a variety of probabilistic statements with regard to that child's functioning in the cognitive, affective, motivational, and general behavioral domains. We have been able to capture this broad spectrum of psychological processes in our net by virtue of the *joint* consideration of creativity and intelligence. It would not have been possible to do as well by treating those modes of thinking in isolation from each other.

The considerable relational fertility of our creativity and intelligence indices has made it possible to achieve a fairly comprehensive portrait of the four basic types of children generated by our method of analysis. In the cognitive domain, we have learned how the four types of children differ in their categorizations and conceptualizations of simple environmental stimuli. Information has also been obtained with regard to the child's awareness of the physiognomic, expressive aspects of his perceptual world. Turning to affect and motivation, the four types of children under consideration have been shown to vary in their pattern of psychodynamics as revealed by relative standing on dimensions of anxiety and defensiveness. Finally, the child's overt behavior in the classroom appears to vary as a function of his creativity and intelligence status.

A point of view concerning relative contributions of environmental and ability components has emerged in the course of our interpretations of findings, and hence can be found also in some of the preceding parts of this section. It may be well, however, to put the elements of this viewpoint together rather explicitly in closing this section, because doing so will both highlight the explanatory possibilities of the present investigation and also serve to introduce some of the questions of educational application to which we shall turn next.

In seeking to comprehend the etiology of the four types of children under study, we have made what amounts to an ability distinction between the low-low subgroup and the remaining three. Our interpretation has suggested that the low-low subgroup possesses ability deficiencies with regard to both evaluational and associative modes of thinking. In contrast, we have suggested that both modes of thinking are present at least as potentials in the case of each of the remaining subgroups. Explanations for poor performance in one thinking mode, when performance in the other is superior, have centered upon motivational interferences with accessibility of the thinking mode in question.

For both modes of thinking to be accessible in the case of the high-high group implies that over time the child will switch back and forth from using one to using the other. Flexibility exists in the utilization of each. The line of interpretation for the thinking behavior of the high-high children has suggested further that this flexibility of utilization is not random but rather is tuned in terms of what the given situation seems to call for. Thus, the general intelligence procedures put a premium upon "correctness": there are right and wrong answers or problem-solutions, and one's performance is subject to clear evaluative criteria. In contrast, the creativity procedures are oriented toward associative productivity and freedom, with a consequent ambiguity or increased looseness concerning bases for evaluation. Depending upon whether one or the other kind of task confronts him, the high-high child can respond with the appropriate cognitive strategy.

In the case of the noncongruent subgroups, the postulate that one mode of thinking is relatively inaccessible implies further that the other mode will be utilized in an apparently rigid fashion—that is, will be maintained without consideration of environmental appropriateness or inappropriateness. Why, then, is one of the thinking modes relatively inaccessible in the case of each noncongruent subgroup?

Consider first the children of high intelligence but low creativity. Our interpretation is that these children feel threatened when there seems to be ambiguity or uncertainty concerning what is expected of them. When in a situation where no self-evident evaluational standards or criteria are present, they adhere to those forms of behavior that seem from their past experience to be maximally safe—in other words, maximally likely to result in "correct" performance. When in a situation where it is quite clear what is demanded of them if they are to do well in the eyes of adults, their security is maximized and they can perform with high efficiency.

In the case of children who are of high creativity but low intelligence, on the other hand, the interpretation is that an evaluative framework threatens them. The possibility of error and failure eventuates for them in a kind of cognitive paralysis, so that the form of thinking required under conditions where the evaluational component is prominent becomes difficult for them. When the evaluative spotlight can be lifted from these individuals, however, as tends to be the case in the creativity tasks, they can function effectively.

An intriguing complementarity seems to exist, therefore, in the source of threat for each of the noncongruent subgroups. Presence of unambiguous standards of evaluation threatens the low intelligence–high creatives but reduces anxiety for the high intelligence–low creatives. Commensurately, absence of self-evident criteria of evaluation threatens the high intelligence–low creatives but puts the low intelligence–high creatives at their ease. Could the feeling of threat in each case be eased, the implication of the present interpretation is that the mode of thinking in which each noncongruent subgroup shows poor performance should become more accessible for utilization. The requirement thus would be to render the low intelligence–high creatives able to tolerate evaluation of their performance, and to render the high intelligence–low creatives able to tolerate the absence of clear criteria for such evaluation.

In sum, it is our view that the task of theory formulation in the area of thinking has been rendered both more simple and more difficult as a consequence of the present investigation. The greater simplicity stems from the fact that we have isolated two fundamental orthogonal modes of thinking, whose joint effects are felt in many areas of psychological functioning. Assessment of these thinking modes hence will tell us a great deal about any child. It will not tell us everything about the child, of course, and hence it will be necessary to explore further the relational power of the creativity and intelligence dimensions. The greater difficulty of which we have spoken derives from our enhanced awareness of the complexity of the thinking domain. It appears that an approach which combines a concern for individual differences with a parametric examination of task contexts may be required in order to do full justice to the study of thinking phenomena. Whatever the direction that future theory and research on children's thinking may assume, however, it is the authors' hope that the present volume may offer a few rays of enlightenment.

IMPLICATIONS AND APPLICATIONS FOR EDUCATION

A basic dilemma may be said to exist concerning the role of education on the American scene. Shall education function as an arm of the majority in our society, reflecting those wishes and values that are to be found in the mainstream of the populace? Or shall education function as a minority voice, holding the general culture up to the mirror of constant appraisal and subjecting its values to conscientious questioning? The dilemma exists at all levels of the educational system. Perhaps, at heart, it can be said to be concerned with whether the educational process is to serve ends that are extrinsic to the process itself, or whether this process is to be viewed as constituting an end-in-itself, a sufficient good? To put the matter this way is to imply the authors' point of view. We are, in a word, concerned with the extent to which education in American society has become, and may well continue to become, a tool evaluated in terms of the extent to which it aids the attainment of one or another extra-educational goal.

Consider the current concern in educational circles with "creativity" as a case in point. In large measure, the origins of the concern can be traced to the successful orbiting of a space vehicle by the Russians in 1957. The sudden spate of financial support for "creative" innovations in science and mathematics teaching, and community sponsorship of such enterprises in the schools, thus arose more from the feeling of a competitive national disadvantage than from a concern with the intrinsic subject matter of these disciplines. The interest in assessing and stimulating "creativity" within business and industry seems, at least in part, to share similar kinds of origins.

The irony of the matter is that this kind of concern over creativity may well be the strategy par excellence for killing it. It is relevant to note in this connection a point that has become increasingly clear within industrial research. Concentration upon specific objectives of achieving one or another type of innovation—"applied" research—often leads to dead ends and a drying up of possibilities, while construction of a research environment wherein inquiry is given free rein—"pure" research —often eventuates in new and useful innovations as by-products of an interest in some basic scientific problem. Just as focusing upon the application can decrease rather than augment the innovative yield, so also focusing upon creativity as a goal to be furthered in the same manner as any other educational goal may have parallel adverse effects. The fact is that genuine support of creativity in the thinking of children may require a considerable shift in traditional educational values. To approach creativity with the same mental framework that schools and teachers utilize in trying to further academic achievement is to define creativity as an educational goal that can be nourished in the same manner as other cognitive accomplishments. Our evidence, however, suggests otherwise.

The authors have emphasized that those psychological processes associated with creative functioning require, for their optimal operation, a context free from or minimally influenced by the stresses that arise from academic evaluation and a fear of the consequences of error. To further *this* kind of goal within education, then, is to fashion a learning and teaching environment that will permit children to minimize the bind produced by negative sanctions for error. To be sure, it would be desirable to further such a goal with regard to the traditional domain of intelligence, too. We recognize that it is harder to do so in that area, however, since so much of the nature of the thinking involved is of necessity focused upon the elimination of erroneous inferences. Nevertheless, conventional intellectual functioning would most likely profit from a reduction in this kind of stress as well. For the stress in question inevitably makes it difficult for a child to be interested in problems for their own sake rather than in order to win a competitive advantage by his success. The basic need, then, is to view education as an end in itself rather than as a means for achieving such external ends as raising one's status, increasing one's earning power, or enhancing the prestige of one's nation.

It is important to bear in mind that measurement of creativity as a cognitive characteristic independent of traditionally defined general intelligence required the institution of a permissive environment with a minimization of any sense of competitive examination or evaluative testing. The cognitive ability demonstrated in this manner then was found, operating jointly with intelligence, to possess considerable implications for diverse realms of psychological functioning. The ability in question, therefore, is worthy of assessment and worthy of nourishment —perhaps just as much so, we would venture to propose, as in the case of intelligence itself. As soon as we raise the question of how to accomplish this end in the schools, however, we are face to face with the fundamental issue posed earlier in this section: how to be concerned about creativity, without at the same time subjecting it to the kind of commodity-like promotional campaign that can rob it of genuine value as an educational goal. What, then, should be done about this matter in the elementary schools?

The critical desideratum would seem to involve the development of pedagogical arrangements within which freedom of associative processes can be nourished in a permissive atmosphere. One would hope thereby to accomplish two ends. *First*, the assessment of individual differences in creativity might then be achieved under optimal conditions. As a consequence, we could gain information regarding a child's location on the creativity dimension as well as on the intelligence dimension, under conditions where both of these modes of thinking receive pedagogical emphasis. Clearly, our findings demonstrate that creativity vies with intelligence in furthering understanding of a child's cognitive and general psychological functioning in school. We do not as yet know, however, in what way this pattern of functioning would be affected by a classroom atmosphere highly encouraging of the type of creative thinking described in the present report. *Second*, such pedagogical arrangements may be conceived as training procedures in the sense that repeated exposure to a heterogeneous range of associative tasks carried out in a permissive school environment over an extended period of time may cause sizable increments in children's creativity levels. A further empirical question is the possible differential[7] effect of such training upon children varying in prior intelligence and creativity status. We shall have more to say later concerning this important issue.

Before we spell out some of the implications of training for creativity, the authors should like to stress the manifestly obvious point that superior performance on the creativity tasks employed in the present study cannot be considered an ultimate goal. Creative performance within such a limited operational context is hardly of great social value. The essential issue concerns the degree to which our creativity measures are

---

[7] The finding of associative transfer from an "associative priming" task reported recently by Mednick, Mednick, and Mednick (1964) certainly is consistent with this possibility, although the issues and operations explored in that study were different from those under consideration here. Also consistent is the evidence of transfer to creative thinking tasks from training in the use of novel and uncommon ideas to solve problems (Crutchfield, 1964; Crutchfield & Covington, 1963).

tapping a construct with implications for cognitive functioning in the context of school learning. In short, we must come to grips with the problem of transfer. The manner in which a child copes with our creative thinking tasks is of consequence only if we thereby gain information about that child's preferred mode of thinking in the classroom situation. As we have seen, the creativity–intelligence groupings do have a direct bearing upon observable classroom behaviors. It has not been possible, however, to undertake a systematic examination of the links that may exist between a child's thinking style (derived on the basis of the present study's experimental procedures) and his manner of thinking about academic subject matter. Such an examination would evidently require that we take account of the relative encouragement given by teachers to the two basic modes of thinking under study. The evidence of the present study suggests that the kind of thinking reflected by the intelligence dimension receives greater weight in the classroom than does the type of thinking required to do well on creativity tasks.

Thus, we are faced with a paradox. On the one hand it seems eminently reasonable that training on creativity procedures in an evaluation-free setting should heighten creativity, as measured by such procedures. Still, this is of little educational relevance, if the child's approach to his academic work has not undergone some change as an outgrowth of the training regimen. The likelihood of such transfer, in turn, is not very great, if the classroom teacher exerts a dampening effect upon the associational freedom essential to the creative mode of thinking.

Before we make any proposals to counter the foregoing pattern, there is one further issue deserving of consideration. This concerns the matter of developmental trends. It is most unlikely that the thinking processes examined in the present volume emerged full-blown at the fifth grade level. The individual differences observed in the sample of children under study must in part reflect the children's experiences with all prior formal education. It would be of great interest to know, of course, how far below the fifth grade level the observed differentiation between intelligence and creativity can be maintained. Clearly, one can expect decreasing differentiation with decreasing age and grade level. Still, there may be a point on the age curve where the differentiation between intelligence and creativity becomes especially pronounced. Such differentiation might be expected to correspond with an increased emphasis on the workings of intelligence and an increased salience of the evaluational dimension in the classroom. If creativity is to be given its due, the foregoing stage in the educational sequence might well be the most desirable point for instituting efforts to restore the intelligence–creativity balance.

How can this be accomplished? In the long run, hope must lie in the area of teacher education. If teachers can be taught to deemphasize the success–failure aspects of the learning process and to encourage children to approach school assignments in a spirit of associative play, much will have been gained. Very conceivably, the recommendation put forth by Bruner (1960) that education proceed in part by "inductive teaching" or the "discovery method" may already have had some impact upon teacher training centers. These teaching methods, it will be recalled, require the child to go through the steps by which a particular piece of knowledge was achieved. To quote from the recent report of the Panel on Educational Research and Development (1964), "such teaching is something more than answering intelligent questions intelligently—it is creating the situations in which intelligent questions are likely to be asked" (p. 6). In this respect, the child in coping with a scientific problem, for example, is encouraged to behave as a scientist. Considerable emphasis is placed upon intuitive modes of thinking, while the child's usual preoccupation with possible error is correspondingly deemphasized. As the Panel on Educational Research and Development (1964) has stated it, "the chief activating element in such instruction is the 'teasing value' of uncertainty—presentation of issues that are conjectural, rather than the laying out of hard, dry, finished facts. Such conjectural materials seem to act as a natural stimulant to the impulse to discover on one's own, and curriculum materials can readily be couched in such terms" (p. 12). The method in question may be contrasted with one in which the emphasis is entirely upon the presentation of facts to be stored and retrieved at examination time. It should be evident that the "discovery method" involves associative as well as inferential modes of thinking in the child, and therefore such a method is of relevance for both creativity and intelligence.

It may be quite a long time, however, before instruction at the elementary school level is distinguished by the prevalent use of the "discovery method" in a context that frees the child as much as possible from feelings of evaluative stress and competition with his peers. Hence, one may well ask whether the present study has any practical implications for education of a more immediate nature.

We should like to point the way toward an approach that appears promising. Recall that we were able to create a gamelike, permissive atmosphere within a segment of the school day by bringing into the school setting individuals who were dissociated from the standard intellective-achievement value matrix. Suppose that a school system were to provide personnel who would travel from one class to another on a regular basis for the purpose of "playing games" with the children, the content of these "games" consisting of the kinds of creativity procedures used in the present study. There already exists a precedent for individuals of this kind. Art and music instruction in the elementary school often has been provided by special teaching personnel. This implies, of course, that the presence of adults who direct activities falling outside the traditional categories of academic accomplishment already is a familiar state of affairs for most elementary school children. Indeed, such music and art periods often are viewed by many children as islands of relief from the customary school routines. Hopefully, one could establish a similar frame of reference for the types of creativity tasks utilized in the present volume. Such tasks should from the start be perceived by the children as games which, not unlike music and art activities, are outside of the academic-evaluation payoff matrix. If the rationale for these cognitive procedures is attributed to a concern with the development of children's games, such an explanation should satisfy the children, given a cultural framework in which the school is expected to provide the setting for sports, recreational, and esthetic activities in addition to instruction in academic subjects.

The proposal, then, is to force a wedge open within the school curriculum for conducting enterprises that, although cognitive, are nevertheless free from connection with the stress of academic evaluation. To be sure, we recognize that the matter is a relative one, and we are referring to freedom from evaluational pressure in a relative sense. Some pressure will almost inevitably remain, but the objective will be served if this pressure can be reduced in sizable degree within an oasis of a particular type of cognitive activity—that reflected by the creativity construct defined in the present volume.

There are two critical questions that now merit consideration. First, who are best qualified to conduct the kind of enterprise described above? Second, even if appropriate persons can be found to carry on such an enterprise, is there any assurance that the training will have transfer value for the regular school curriculum?

Consider first the question relating to personnel. It is the authors' view that these should be drawn from the ranks of student teachers. Graduate students in educational psychology might also be drawn into the training enterprise, but their primary function would focus on the evaluation of the program and its relation to other aspects of the educational environment. The choice of student teachers is prompted by two considerations. First, it is evident that Schools of Education must play a cooperative role in the proposed training program, if it is to meet with any success. Second, if the future teacher's initial contact with pupils can be focused upon matters pertaining to creativity, it is conceivable that upon advancing to the status of a regular teacher, the relevance of creativity to cognitive functioning in the classroom will be part of the teacher's "apperceptive mass." In this regard, the teacher as well as the pupil is undergoing a form of training. The issue of transfer value is also pertinent here. If the student teacher is made aware of the importance of associative forms of thinking in a learning context free of evaluation, this should have some effect upon his mode of instruction when he advances to the position of certified teacher. Once associative forms of thinking begin to receive greater emphasis in regular classroom instruction, the problem of transfer assumes a different character. The transfer from special creativity training to school subject matter would be of diminishing relevance, and transfer across school subjects and age levels would correspondingly increase in importance.

There is no intention here of ruling out the possibility that some teachers might presently be able to adopt an appropriate nonevaluational posture themselves. In this case, "games" of the kinds under consideration could be played with the children by the regular teachers. Our expectation would be, however, that only the most capable of teachers would be able to establish the necessary atmosphere by themselves, given their strong association in the children's eyes with questions of success and failure evaluation, and given their own commitments to the more traditional parts of the curriculum.

In proposing that graduate students in educational psychology be implicated in the special training program outlined earlier, we are essentially pointing to the possible merit of a particular kind of fieldwork requirement for graduate students in educational psychology. Hopefully, such placement in the school would sensitize the graduate student to the world of the classroom wherein a whole host of researchable questions stand in need of investigation. Quite clearly, the student teacher cannot be expected to concern himself with the research aspects of any new training program. That is the proper province of the scientific psychologist. As Bruner (1960) has so eloquently noted, psychologists have often done their best to avoid the issues of instruction and cognitive functioning in the classroom, preferring instead to study such processes in the confines of the laboratory. We have no intention of derogating laboratory research, but we do feel that a proper balance should be achieved in which children's cognitive processes are examined under both natural and experimentally controlled conditions. With regard to the discipline of educational psychology, the time has come to break away from a narrowly conceived psychometric emphasis toward more intensive study of the effects of different kinds of educational environments upon children's thought processes. Such a shift in interest is already taking place, and we should like to lend encouragement to the trend.

If a creativity training regimen of the sort described is introduced into the schools, the degree to which such training influences the child's cognitive functioning in the classroom is evidently a research issue that falls squarely in the domain of the educational psychologist. The success of such a training program obviously depends upon a systematic examination of the transfer issue. Unfortunately, the research problems generated by this issue are inherently complex, for one shall have to take cognizance, for example, of individual differences among pupils and teachers, as well as differences in academic subject matter areas and curricular formats. Conceivably, the type of creativity training envisaged will show transfer effects only in the case of particular academic disciplines and/or styles of instruction. Further, the child's location on the creativity and intelligence dimensions may affect the extent to which he profits from special training. We are suggesting, in brief, that the research possibilities opened up by the type of training program proposed are extensive and well worth the attention of those workers interested in the application of psychology to education.

Thus far, we have concentrated on transfer as proceeding in one direction only—from special creativity training under nonevaluative gamelike conditions to performance in more strictly academic tasks. It is entirely feasible, of course, to examine the likelihood that transfer might proceed in the opposite direction. Can performance on creativity procedures be shown to vary as a function of instructional methods? Where "inductive teaching" has been introduced into a classroom, for example, we could compare these pupils' creativity scores with scores of pupils matched in intelligence from other classrooms in which more traditional methods of instruction are employed. Again, we should emphasize that performance on the creativity tasks devised by the authors is not considered an ultimate criterion in any sense. Nevertheless, we should anticipate that children encouraged to think in associative terms in the course of their regular classroom work will perform better on the kinds of creativity procedures employed in the present research relative to the performance of their peers in more traditional classroom contexts. Such a finding would obviously increase one's confidence in the validity of the creativity tasks.

Thus far, the issue of training has been approached with little regard for the individual differences in creativity and intelligence that have been the major concern of the volume. It is entirely fair to ask whether the assessment of children's creativity and intelligence status really matters when a training program of the sort described is contemplated by a school. Is it not likely that all children would benefit from a training regimen in which creativity tasks are practiced in a gamelike environment? In a similar vein, is it not conceivable that a greater emphasis on associative forms of thinking in the classroom will redound to the advantage of all children? A positive answer to these questions is not at all unreasonable. Yet educational resources are evidently limited, and so there is a great deal to be said in favor of training arrangements that focus upon children likely to derive maximum benefit. The identification of such children is clearly a matter of assessment. There is every reason to believe that there will be variations across the four creativity–intelligence subgroups in the degree of cognitive change associated with an induced environmental change. It should be kept in mind that the objectives of assessment and of training can be handled in different ways. Creativity assessment of the kind suggested will require individual work with all of the children in a class under conditions where evaluational pressures are minimized. Once assessment is completed, however, and the children categorized in terms of creativity as well as intelligence, it will be possible to focus more directly on the particular children most likely to profit from training procedures of the type proposed.

With which subgroup of children should one then begin? The high creativity subgroups seem to be least in need of the type of training program envisaged, in view of their already high creativity status. Granted that neither group may be functioning close to a "ceiling," it is nevertheless likely that other children might derive greater benefits from training. Turning to the low creativity subgroups—those high and low in intelligence—the former appears to be a more satisfactory choice. The evidence offered in previous chapters suggests that the child of high intelligence but low creativity is overly preoccupied with extrinsic goals of success. Relief from such pressures in the case of these children may offer the possibility of a more effective and satisfying use of intellect. On the other hand, the children low on both the creativity and intelligence dimensions manifest a degree of deficit that will probably require much more intensive efforts to effect a meaningful level of change. While creativity training may have some value for the low-low subgroup, especially where the classroom teacher is supportive of associative modes of thinking, these children seem to have found socially adaptive outlets that mitigate distress caused by intellectual failure. In short, the high intelligence–low creativity child would seem to be a better bet for a new training venture.

Repeated exposure in a gamelike context to creativity procedures of the kind discussed may be particularly helpful for the high intelligence–low creativity children precisely because such exposure will acquaint them with the experience of cognitive play—of forms of cognitive activity to which the all-too-familiar notions of penalties imposed for error simply do not apply. Once a cognitive island has been established within whose boundaries playful task attitudes can be entertained, it may be possible gradually to widen this domain, keeping the child sufficiently attracted to particular intellective content for his overriding concern with success to begin to wane. It is hard to predict, of course, exactly what can be hoped for from such an enterprise. The preoccupation with success that seems to inhibit associative forms of thinking in the children of high intelligence and low creativity is a phenomenon whose origins may run quite deep and whose current psychological impact may well be fostered by parental values. The fact remains, however, that the school constitutes the major force for intellective achievement in the life of the child. The introduction into part of the school routine of a different approach to the business of thinking may, therefore, carry sizable weight as an influence upon the child's attitudes. At the least, the possibility of such an effect for the high intelligence–low creativity children certainly is worthy of investigation.

Thus far we have discussed training attempts that focus upon the creativity procedures themselves. It may also well be possible to foster creativity in the high intelligence–low creativity subgroup by providing experiences related to some of the materials that were found to be correlates of high creativity levels. For example, the indicators of physiognomic sensitivity studied could provide the basis for training procedures in which the possibility of one or another affective connotation for a given stick figure or a given path is suggested to the child and explored with him. So also, unconventional attributions for stick figures can be discussed with the child who has rejected them completely, and the possible applicability of these unlikely kinds of attributions considered. When it comes to categorizing and conceptualizing activities, the possibility of grouping objects in terms of thematic considerations can be brought up and tried out with the child in an atmosphere of adult-provided support for carrying out these relatively unconventional types of arrangements. In addition, the possibility of more widely deviant instances and how they might fit within a given category can be explored with the child in discussing the band-width settings that might be made for the boundaries of one or another class of objects or events. All these instructional procedures, just as in the case of instruction directed at associational behavior as such, are types of training that could be carried out within the school through individual work in a gamelike context.

What of the high creativity–low intelligence children? It will be recalled that there were many indications of withdrawal and self-depreciation in the members of this subgroup. This was especially so for the girls. It would be helpful to know whether these problems of self-worth take their roots in the general developmental history of the child in the family, or rather represent a cumulation of negative experiences in the classroom. Such information is not available to us, of course, and, quite conceivably, both sources have contributed to the difficulties manifested by the child of high creativity but low intelligence. If the source of the difficulty is primarily school-related, then remedial efforts can be attempted within the setting of the classroom. On the other hand, if the problems experienced by the high creativity–low intelligence group are reflective of deep personality disturbance, then corrective action would evidently involve clinical attention from resources outside of the school system or from appropriate school personnel.

Clinical and/or counseling work with individual children is inevitably expensive, of course, and sometimes not particularly effective. A more appropriate initial approach might be in the direction of modification of the curriculum rather than modification of the cognitive state of the child. Would it not be feasible in certain subject matter areas to develop a course that relies very heavily upon associative forms of thinking? If such courses could be taught under conditions where evaluation is deemphasized to relatively homogeneous groups of children distinguished by high creativity and low intelligence levels, one might conceivably give to these children a sense of a capacity to cope adequately with some school tasks. Along with such specially devised courses, every effort should be made to build upon whatever strengths the child already exhibits in the school setting. If some of the children in the high creativity–low intelligence group show marked talent in and attraction toward art work, for example, this fact should not go unnoticed. While the subgroup of children in question may be attracted to art precisely because of its removal from the matrix of academic evaluation, these children should nevertheless be confronted with the fact that art is a highly significant field of human endeavor. All of these suggestions are intended to emphasize the point that the school environment can be modified in less than drastic ways to increase the likelihood of rewards and ego-gratifications for the child whose creativity level is substantially higher than his level of intelligence.

Counseling and guidance provided by personnel associated with the schools is a supplementary possibility that might accompany curriculum development. If such guidance can be sufficiently intensive, and if the persons providing it can be sufficiently divorced from the evaluative atmosphere of the classroom, the results may be of considerable help. Assessment directed toward defining the children who are of low intelligence but high creativity status may provide an appropriate means of selecting children for whom guidance of a therapeutic kind would be most helpful, and hence may be a means of utilizing guidance and counseling personnel more effectively. It should be emphasized that this group of children deserves every bit as much attention as the high intelligence–low creativity group. One may even suggest that the high creativity–low intelligence group deserves more, since it consists of individuals who at present are receiving a minimum of supportive attention within the school environment.

Finally, there are the children who are high on both the intelligence and creativity dimensions, and those who are low in regard to both of these modes of thinking. Evidence has been presented indicating that the high-high children are doing well in school from both the academic and social standpoint. Hence, one is tempted to conclude that these children require no special attention. Unfortunately, we have no information concerning the degree to which the high-high children are maximizing their full potential in the classroom. Some of the evidence presented in Chapter 3 suggested that the high-high children may be valued more for their intelligence than for their creativity. One is left with the impression that the highly intelligent and creative children would truly blossom under the type of instruction represented by "inductive teaching" or the "discovery method."

Turning to the children who are low in both creativity and intelligence, we must confess that we have not been able to formulate any concrete proposals for constructive improvement. One should not overlook the fact that, while creativity and intelligence may represent two highly important ability domains, they do not necessarily exhaust the "structure of intellect." There may well be facets of intellect untapped by the procedures of the present study, and the low-low children may excel in precisely those respects. Although such abilities will be of lesser importance for academic performance than are the two major modes of thinking examined in the present investigation, whatever sources of strength are present in the low-low children should receive encouragement. No child should be relegated to an academic "waste pile." With the educational scene constantly being subjected to experiment and innovation, the time may come when ways will be found to insure that each child's potential talent will be developed to the fullest degree.

Let us now return briefly to the matter of evaluational pressures in the classroom—a matter that has received very little explicit consideration from those most concerned with educational assessment. We commented upon this point in Chapter 1, when considering previous research in the area of testing for "creativity." This is not to say that the issue of evaluational pressures in the schools has gone entirely without notice, but to point out that the matter has received the least attention among the very group of professionals who should be giving it the most study—those who deal with the problems of assessing the effects of formal schooling. Since those who consider questions of instruction and curriculum are, in turn, subject to very strong influence by whatever procedures for educational assessment are customary, the consequence is that they, too, give little attention to the implications of evaluational pressures for the educational process. To find comments on such implications, one typically must move outside of the professional circles just described and look to the writings of educated laymen or professionals from other disciplines who have observed the current educational scene. It may well be no accident that this kind of distance has been needed in order to facilitate raising the question at hand. Pressures toward intellective achievement and the conquering of stressful examinations are omnipresent in education, a phenomenon congruent with a society where so much depends upon achieved status rather than upon such ascriptively given characteristics as the wealth of one's family and the place of one's birth.

Thus, for example, Bruner (1960) has noted the possibility of an increasing overemphasis upon examination performance as a result of what he calls a "meritocracy" as the prevailing basis of American society. He foresees ". . . a system of competition in which students are moved ahead and given further opportunities on the basis of their achievement, with position in later life increasingly and irreversibly determined by earlier school records. Not only later educational opportunities but subsequent job opportunities become increasingly fixed by earlier school performance" (p. 77). The upshot, then, is the emergence of a new form of ascriptively defined status in which early examination records become increasingly determining of later opportunities, a fact which will then act to render the stresses arising from academic evaluation all the stronger for the student. Teaching, in turn, will become all the more polarized around preparing for competitive examinations. The society's penchant for describing the rewards of education as ones which are extrinsic to learning for its own sake—enhanced income, social position, and professional status—is quite consistent, of course, with an emphasis upon evaluational pressures in the schools. We have noted how the current concern with creativity falls prey to the same problem, as creativity becomes a product to be marketed rather than an intrinsically valuable outcome to be sought by establishing conditions which are maximally propitious for its nourishment.

Some of these same issues have been commented upon by Mayer (1961), who has noted in various ways how the goal of reliability in passing examinations, when treated as a sufficient end, can cripple genuine educational efforts. So, too, Dexter (1964) has observed that the accusation of intellectual inferiority has become a particularly sharp form of criticism in middle-class American society, with the result that extensive pressure to avoid this label devolves upon the child. Once again, however, the nature of the concern is an extrinsic one. It is that the child wishes to avoid condemnation and ridicule in school, rather than that he becomes motivated to think more deeply and meaningfully in school.

All of which returns us, of course, to the dilemma posed at the beginning of this section. As Bestor (1959) has put it, "defects in education are never causeless, they are reflections of weaknesses and shortcomings in the national life" (p. 75). American society as a whole has been moving, and will continue to move, toward increasing opulence. Education comes increasingly to be called upon, under these circumstances, to serve as a rite of passage for the pursuit of whatever the society deems most valuable. To the extent that the basic goals of the society revolve around matters of wealth, status, and national advantage, rather than around matters of intellect, the educational apparatus will be pushed toward serving as a means for the pursuit of essentially noneducational ends. The result is a stimulation of just those kinds of extrinsic pressures for achievement that seem to make genuine creativity so difficult to come by. Spengler (1964) has reminded us how the ". . . conversion of certain types of roses into status symbols has perverted rose culture" (pp. 286–287).

To be concerned with assessing the abundance and uniqueness of a child's associational processes, and yet to place one's assessment and training procedures outside an evaluational framework and the stress that such a framework produces in middle-class American society, constitutes a sizable challenge for educational practice. The research findings of the present volume indicate, however, that, if we are to understand and nourish creativity, this challenge has to be faced. We have learned that it represents not an abstract desideratum, but something quite concrete, affecting the school's categorizing of particular children. To ignore the challenge, therefore, is to ignore much of the cognitive potential of elementary school children. It seems reasonable to expect that if one were to make an accurate assessment of children's creativity and intelligence status and if one were to apply environmental aids appropriate to the child's mode of thinking, many children could conceivably be moved toward higher levels of cognitive functioning. The implications of such change for education could be far-reaching.

Appendix ⟪⟪⟪⟪

SEQUENCE OF WORK WITH EACH CLASS

A. SCAT and STEP tests administered to the class by the school authorities at the beginning of the academic year, prior to any contact of the experimenters with the children. (Chapter 2)

B. Two weeks of observation of the children in the class by the experimenters, followed by their filling out the Behavior Rating Scales. (Chapter 3)

C. Administration of specific procedures by the experimenters.

    1. Instances. (Chapter 2)
    2. Free Descriptions of Stick Figures. (Chapter 5)
    3. Thematic Integration. (Chapter 4)
    4. Equivalence Range. (Chapter 4)
    5. Pattern Meanings. (Chapter 2)
    6. Alternate Uses. (Chapter 2)
    7. Emotive Connotations of Abstract Patterns. (Chapter 5)
    8. Bizarre Emotive Attributions for Stick Figures. (Chapter 5)
    9. Similarities. (Chapter 2)
    10. Line Meanings. (Chapter 2)
    11. Free Descriptions of Paths. (Chapter 5)
    12. Band Width. (Chapter 4)
    13. Self-report Measures. (Chapter 6)
    14. WISC Picture Arrangement Subtest. (Chapter 2)
    15. WISC Vocabulary Subtest. (Chapter 2)
    16. WISC Block Design Subtest. (Chapter 2)
    17. Fantasy Measure. (Chapter 6)

References ⫷

ADLER, A. *Study of organ inferiority and its psychical compensation.* New York: Nervous and Mental Diseases Publishing Co., 1917.

ALPERT, R., & HABER, R. N. Anxiety in academic achievement situations. *J. abnorm. soc. Psychol.*, 1960, *61*, 207–215.

ARNHEIM, R. The Gestalt theory of expression. *Psychol. Rev.*, 1949, *56*, 156–171.

ASCH, S. E. *Social psychology.* Englewood Cliffs, N. J.: Prentice-Hall, 1952.

ATKINSON, J. W. Motivational determinants of risk-taking behavior. In J. W. Atkinson (Ed.), *Motives in fantasy, action, and society.* Princeton, N. J.: Van Nostrand, 1958. Pp. 322–339.

BARNHART, C. L. (Ed.) *The American college dictionary.* New York: Random House, 1949.

BARRON, F. The disposition toward originality. *J. abnorm. soc. Psychol.*, 1955, *51*, 478–485.

BARRON, F. *Creativity and psychological health.* Princeton, N. J.: Van Nostrand, 1963.

BARTLETT, F. *Thinking: An experimental and social study.* New York: Basic Books, 1958.

BARTLETT, M. S. Properties of sufficiency and statistical tests. *Proc. Roy. Soc. (London)*, 1937, *160*, 268–282.

BELDOCH, M. Sensitivity to expression of emotional meaning in three modes of communication. In J. Davitz (Ed.), *The communication of emotional meaning.* New York: McGraw-Hill, 1964. Pp. 31–42.

BERLYNE, D. E. *Conflict, arousal, and curiosity.* New York: McGraw-Hill, 1960.

BESTOR, A. Education and its proper relationship to the forces of American society. *Daedalus*, 1959, *88*, 75–90.

336 | References

BONEAU, C. A.   The effects of violations of assumptions underlying the *t* test. *Psychol. Bull.*, 1960, *57*, 49–64.

BOUSFIELD, W. A., & SEDGEWICK, C. H. W.   An analysis of sequences of restricted associative responses. *J. gen. Psychol.*, 1944, *30*, 149–165.

BOX, G. E. P.   Non-normality and tests on variances. *Biometrika*, 1953, *40*, 318–335.

BOX, G. E. P.   Some theorems on quadratic forms applied in the study of analysis of variance problems: I. Effect of inequality of variance in the one-way classification. *Ann. of math. Statist.*, 1954, *25*, 290–302. (a)

BOX, G. E. P.   Some theorems on quadratic forms applied in the study of analysis of variance problems: II. Effects of inequality of variance and of correlation between errors in the two-way classification. *Ann. of math. Statist.*, 1954, *25*, 484–498. (b)

BRIM, O. G., JR., GLASS, D. C., LAVIN, D. E., & GOODMAN, N.   *Personality and decision processes.* Stanford, Cal.: Stanford Univer. Press, 1962.

BROWN, R.   How shall a thing be called? *Psychol. Rev.*, 1958, *65*, 14–21.

BRUNER, J. S.   On going beyond the information given. In *Contemporary approaches to cognition.* Cambridge, Mass.: Harvard Univer. Press, 1957. Pp. 41–69.

BRUNER, J. S.   *The process of education.* Cambridge, Mass.: Harvard Univer. Press, 1960.

BRUNER, J. S., GOODNOW, JACQUELINE J., & AUSTIN, G. A.   *A study of thinking.* New York: Wiley, 1956.

BRUNER, J. S., & OLVER, ROSE R.   Development of equivalence transformations in children. In J. C. Wright & J. Kagan (Eds.), Basic cognitive processes in children. *Monogr. Soc. Res. Child Develpm.*, 1963, *28*, No. 2 (Serial No. 86), pp. 125–141.

BRUNER, J. S., & TAJFEL, H.   Cognitive risk and environmental change. *J. abnorm. soc. Psychol.*, 1961, *62*, 231–241.

BURKS, B. S., JENSEN, D. W., & TERMAN, L. M.   *Genetic studies of genius*: Vol. III. *The promise of youth; follow-up studies of a thousand gifted children.* Stanford, Cal.: Stanford Univer. Press, 1930.

CAMPBELL, D. T., & FISKE, D. W.   Convergent and discriminant validation by the multitrait-multimethod matrix. *Psychol. Bull.*, 1959, *56*, 81–105.

CASTANEDA, A., McCANDLESS, B. R., & PALERMO, D. S.   The children's form of the Manifest Anxiety Scale. *Child Develpm.*, 1956, *27*, 317–326.

CHRISTENSEN, P. R., GUILFORD, J. P., & WILSON, R. C.   Relations of creative responses to working time and instructions. *J. exp. Psychol.*, 1957, *53*, 82–88.

CLAYTON, MARTHA B., & JACKSON, D. N.   Equivalence range, acquiescence, and overgeneralization. *Educ. psychol. Measmt*, 1961, *21*, 371–382.

CLINE, V. B., RICHARDS, J. M., JR., & ABE, C.   The validity of a battery of creativity tests in a high school sample. *Educ. psychol. Measmt*, 1962, *22*, 781–784.

CLINE, V. B., RICHARDS, J. M., JR., & NEEDHAM, W. E.   Creativity tests and achievement in high school science. *J. appl. Psychol.*, 1963, *47*, 184–189.

COOPERATIVE TEST DIVISION.   *Cooperative school and college ability tests: Technical report.* Princeton, N. J.: Educational Testing Service, 1957. (a)

COOPERATIVE TEST DIVISION.   *SCAT: Directions for administering and scoring.* Princeton, N. J.: Educational Testing Service, 1957. (b)

COOPERATIVE TEST DIVISION.   *Cooperative sequential tests of educational progress: Technical report.* Princeton, N. J.: Educational Testing Service, 1957. (c)

COOPERATIVE TEST DIVISION.   *STEP: Directions for administering and scoring.* Princeton, N. J.: Educational Testing Service, 1957. (d)

COOPERATIVE TEST DIVISION.   *Cooperative sequential tests of educational progress: Teacher's guide.* Princeton, N. J.: Educational Testing Service, 1959.

COUCH, A., & KENISTON, K.   Yea-sayers and nay-sayers: Agreeing response set as a personality variable. *J. abnorm. soc. Psychol.*, 1960, *60*, 151–174.

COX, F. N.   Educational streaming and general and test anxiety. *Child Develpm.*, 1962, *33*, 381–390.

COX, F. N., & LEAPER, P. M.   General and test anxiety scales for children. *Australian J. Psychol.*, 1959, *11*, 70–80.

CROWNE, D. P., & MARLOWE, D.   A new scale of social desirability independent of psychopathology. *J. consult. Psychol.*, 1960, *24*, 349–354.

CROWNE, D. P., & MARLOWE, D.   *The approval motive.* New York: Wiley, 1964.

CRUTCHFIELD, R. S.   Conformity and creative thinking. In H. E. Gruber, G. Terrell, & M. Wertheimer (Eds.), *Contemporary approaches to creative thinking.* New York: Atherton, 1962. Pp. 120–140.

CRUTCHFIELD, R. S.   Instructing children in creative thinking. Address delivered at the annual convention of the American Psychological Association, Los Angeles, Cal., September 1964.

CRUTCHFIELD, R. S., & COVINGTON, M. V. Facilitation of creative thinking and problem solving in school children. Paper presented in a symposium on Learning Research Pertinent to Educational Improvement, American Association for the Advancement of Science, Cleveland, Ohio, December 1963.

DAVID, F. N., & JOHNSON, N. L. The effect of non-normality on the power function of the *F*-test in the analysis of variance. *Biometrika*, 1951, *38*, 43–57.

DAVIDSON, K. S. Interviews of parents of high-anxious and low-anxious children. *Child Develpm.*, 1959, *30*, 341–351.

DAVIDSON, K. S., & SARASON, S. B. Test anxiety and classroom observations. *Child Develpm.*, 1961, *32*, 199–210.

DAVITZ, J. Personality, perceptual, and cognitive correlates of emotional sensitivity. In J. Davitz (Ed.), *The communication of emotional meaning*. New York: McGraw-Hill, 1964. Pp. 57–68.

DENTLER, R. A., & MACKLER, B. Originality: Some social and personal determinants. *Behav. Sci.*, 1964, *9*, 1–7.

DEXTER, L. A. *The tyranny of schooling*. New York: Basic Books, 1964.

DUNCKER, K. On problem-solving. *Psychol. Monogr.*, 1945, *58*, No. 5 (Whole No. 270).

EASTERBROOK, J. A. The effect of emotion on cue utilization and the organization of behavior. *Psychol. Rev.*, 1959, *66*, 183–201.

ENGEN, T., LEVY, N., & SCHLOSBERG, H. A new series of facial expressions. *Amer. Psychologist*, 1957, *12*, 264–266.

ENGEN, T., LEVY, N., & SCHLOSBERG, H. The dimensional analysis of a new series of facial expressions. *J. exp. Psychol.*, 1958, *55*, 454–458.

ERIKSON, E. H. *Childhood and society*. New York: Norton, 1950.

EVANS, CATHERINE, & McCONNELL, T. R. *Minnesota T-S-E inventory* (Rev. ed.). Princeton, N. J.: Educational Testing Service, 1957.

FELDHUSEN, J. F., DENNY, T., & CONDON, C. F. Anxiety, divergent thinking, and achievement. *J. educ. Psychol.*, 1965, *56*, 40–45.

FILLENBAUM, S. Some stylistic aspects of categorizing behavior. *J. Pers.*, 1959, *27*, 187–195.

FISKE, D. W., & MADDI, S. R. (Eds.) *Functions of varied experience*. Homewood, Ill.: Dorsey, 1961.

FLAVELL, J. *The developmental psychology of Jean Piaget*. Princeton, N. J.: Van Nostrand, 1963.

FLESCHER, I. Anxiety and achievement of intellectually gifted and creatively gifted children. *J. Psychol.*, 1963, *56*, 251–268.

FREDERIKSEN, N., & MESSICK, S. Response set as a measure of personality. *Educ. psychol. Measmt*, 1959, *19*, 137–157.

FREEDMAN, J. L.   Increasing creativity by free-association training. *J. exp. Psychol.*, 1965, *69*, 89–91.

FRENCH, J. W.   The description of aptitude and achievement tests in terms of rotated factors. *Psychometric Monogr.*, No. 5. Chicago: Univer. Chicago Press, 1951.

FREUD, ANNA.   *The ego and the mechanisms of defense.* New York: International Universities, 1946.

FREUD, S.   The unconscious. In: *Collected papers*, Vol. IV. London: Hogarth, 1925. Pp. 98–136.

FREUD, S.   *Inhibitions, symptoms, and anxiety.* London: Hogarth, 1936.

FRICK, J. W., GUILFORD, J. P., CHRISTENSEN, P. R., & MERRIFIELD, P. R.   A factor-analytic study of flexibility in thinking. *Educ. psychol. Measmt*, 1959, *19*, 469–496.

GARDNER, R. W.   Cognitive styles in categorizing behavior. *J. Pers.*, 1953, *22*, 214–233.

GARDNER, R. W., HOLZMAN, P. S., KLEIN, G. S., LINTON, HARRIET, & SPENCE, D. P.   Cognitive control: A study of individual consistencies in cognitive behavior. *Psychol. Issues*, 1959, *1*, No. 4 (Monogr. 4).

GARDNER, R. W., JACKSON, D. N., & MESSICK, S.   Personality organization in cognitive controls and intellectual abilities. *Psychol. Issues*, 1960, *2*, No. 4 (Monogr. 8).

GARDNER, R. W., & LONG, R. I.   The stability of cognitive controls. *J. abnorm. soc. Psychol.*, 1960, *61*, 485–487.

GARDNER, R. W., & SCHOEN, R. A.   Differentiation and abstraction in concept formation. *Psychol. Monogr.*, 1962, *76*, No. 41 (Whole No. 560).

GARWOOD, DOROTHY S.   Personality factors related to creativity in young scientists. *J. abnorm. soc. Psychol.*, 1964, *68*, 413–419.

GETZELS, J. W., & JACKSON, P. W.   *Creativity and intelligence.* New York: Wiley, 1962.

GHISELIN, B. (Ed.)   *The creative process.* New York: Mentor, 1955.

GOLANN, S. E.   Psychological study of creativity. *Psychol. Bull.*, 1963, *60*, 548–565.

GOLDSTEIN, K., & SCHEERER, M.   Abstract and concrete behavior: An experimental study with special tests. *Psychol. Monogr.*, 1941, *53*, No. 2 (Whole No. 239).

GOMBRICH, E. H.   On physiognomic perception. *Daedalus*, 1960, *89*, 228–241.

GOUGH, H. G.   *California psychological inventory manual.* Palo Alto, Cal.: Consulting Psychologists Press, 1957.

GRONLUND, N. E.   *Sociometry in the classroom.* New York: Harper, 1959.

GUILFORD, J. P. The structure of intellect. *Psychol. Bull.*, 1956, *53*, 267–293.

GUILFORD, J. P. Three faces of intellect. *Amer. Psychologist*, 1959, *14*, 469–479. (a)

GUILFORD, J. P. *Personality*. New York: McGraw-Hill, 1959. (b)

GUILFORD, J. P. Traits of creativity. In H. H. Anderson (Ed.), *Creativity and its cultivation*. New York: Harper, 1959. Pp. 142–161. (c)

GUILFORD, J. P. Potentiality for creativity and its measurement. In: *Proceedings of the 1962 invitational conference on testing problems*. Princeton, N. J.: Educational Testing Service, 1963. Pp. 31–39.

GUILFORD, J. P. Some new looks at the nature of creative processes. In N. Frederiksen & H. Gulliksen (Eds.), *Contributions to mathematical psychology*. New York: Holt, Rinehart and Winston, 1964. Pp. 161–176.

GUILFORD, J. P., & CHRISTENSEN, P. R. A factor-analytic study of verbal fluency. *Rep. psychol. Lab.*, No. 17. Los Angeles: Univer. of Southern California, 1956.

HAGGARD, E. A. *Intra-class correlation and the analysis of variance*. New York: Holt, Rinehart and Winston, 1958.

HALL, K. R. L., & OLDFIELD, R. G. An experimental study on the fitness of signs to words. *Quart. J. exp. Psychol.*, 1950, *2*, 60–70.

HARTMANN, H. *Ego psychology and the problem of adaptation*. New York: International Universities, 1958.

HATHAWAY, S. R., & McKINLEY, J. C. *The Minnesota multiphasic personality inventory* (Rev. ed.). Minneapolis: Univer. Minnesota Press, 1943.

HENLE, MARY. The birth and death of ideas. In H. E. Gruber, G. Terrell, & M. Wertheimer (Eds.), *Contemporary approaches to creative thinking*. New York: Atherton, 1962. Pp. 31–62.

HOLLAND, J. L. Some limitations of teacher ratings as predictors of creativity. *J. educ. Psychol.*, 1959, *50*, 219–223.

HOLT, R. R., & HAVEL, JOAN. A method for assessing primary and secondary process in the Rorschach. In Maria A. Rickers-Ovsiankina (Ed.), *Rorschach psychology*. New York: Wiley, 1960. Pp. 263–315.

HONKAVAARA, SYLVIA. The psychology of expression. *Brit. J. Psychol. Monogr. Suppl.*, No. 32. London: Cambridge Univer. Press, 1961.

HORSNELL, G. The effect of unequal group variances on the F-test for the homogeneity of group means. *Biometrika*, 1953, *40*, 128–136.

HOUSTON, J. P., & MEDNICK, S. A. Creativity and the need for novelty. *J. abnorm. soc. Psychol.*, 1963, *66*, 137–141.

HUMPHREYS, L. G. The organization of human abilities. *Amer. Psychologist*, 1962, *17*, 475–483.

INHELDER, BÄRBEL, & PIAGET, J. *The growth of logical thinking from childhood to adolescence.* New York: Basic Books, 1958.

JACKSON, D. N., & MESSICK, S. Content and style in personality assessment. *Psychol. Bull.*, 1958, *55*, 243–252.

JERSILD, A. T., & HOLMES, FRANCES B. *Children's fears.* New York: Bureau of Publications, Teachers Coll., Columbia Univer., 1935.

JOHNSON, D. M. *The psychology of thought and judgment.* New York: Harper, 1955.

KAGAN, J., & MOSS, H. A. The availability of conflictful ideas: A neglected parameter in assessing projective test responses. *J. Pers.*, 1961, *29*, 217–234.

KAGAN, J., MOSS, H. A., & SIGEL, I. E. Conceptual style and the use of affect labels. *Merrill-Palmer Quart.*, 1960, *6*, 261–278.

KAGAN, J., MOSS, H. A., & SIGEL, I. E. Psychological significance of styles of conceptualization. In J. C. Wright & J. Kagan (Eds.), Basic cognitive processes in children. *Monogr. Soc. Res. Child Develpm.*, 1963, *28*, No. 2 (Serial No. 86), pp. 73–112.

KENNEDY, K., & KATES, S. L. Conceptual sorting and personality adjustment in children. *J. abnorm. soc. Psychol.*, 1964, *68*, 211–214.

KLEIN, G. S. Cognitive control and motivation. In G. Lindzey (Ed.), *Assessment of motives.* New York: Holt, Rinehart and Winston, 1958. Pp. 87–118.

KOESTLER, A. *The act of creation.* New York: Macmillan, 1964.

KOGAN, N., & WALLACH, M. A. *Risk taking: A study in cognition and personality.* New York: Holt, Rinehart and Winston, 1964.

KÖHLER, W. Psychological remarks on some questions of anthropology. *Amer. J. Psychol.*, 1937, *50*, 271–288.

KORCHIN, S. J. Anxiety and cognition. In Constance Scheerer (Ed.), *Cognition: Theory, research, promise.* New York: Harper, 1964. Pp. 58–78.

KRAUSS, R. Über graphischen Ausdruck. *Zsch. f. angew. Psychol.*, 1930, *48*, 1–141.

KRIS, E. *Psychoanalytic explorations in art.* New York: International Universities, 1952.

KRIS, E. Psychoanalysis and the study of creative imagination. *Bull. New York Acad. Med.*, 1953, *29*, 334–351.

KUBIE, L. S. *Neurotic distortion of the creative process.* Lawrence, Kansas: Univer. Kansas Press, 1958.

LEARY, T. *Interpersonal diagnosis of personality.* New York: Ronald, 1957.

LEVY, PHYLLIS K. The ability to express and perceive vocal communications of feeling. In J. Davitz (Ed.), *The communication of emotional meaning.* New York: McGraw-Hill, 1964. Pp. 43–55.

LIGHTHALL, F., RUEBUSH, B., SARASON, S., & ZWEIBELSON, I. Change in mental ability as a function of test anxiety and type of mental test. *J. consult. Psychol.*, 1959, *23*, 34–38.

LUNDHOLM, H. The affective tone of lines. *Psychol. Rev.*, 1921, *28*, 43–60.

McGAUGHRAN, L. S., & MORAN, L. J. "Conceptual level" vs. "conceptual area" analysis of object-sorting behavior of schizophrenic and nonpsychiatric groups. *J. abnorm. soc. Psychol.*, 1956, *52*, 43–50.

McGAUGHRAN, L. S., & MORAN, L. J. Differences between schizophrenic and brain-damaged groups in conceptual aspects of object sorting. *J. abnorm. soc. Psychol.*, 1957, *54*, 44–49.

McGEE, R. K. The relationship between response styles and personality variables: I. The measurement of response acquiescence. *J. abnorm. soc. Psychol.*, 1962, *64*, 229–233. (a)

McGEE, R. K. Response style as a personality variable: By what criterion? *Psychol. Bull.*, 1962, *59*, 284–295. (b)

MacKINNON, D. W. The personality correlates of creativity: A study of American architects. In G. S. Nielsen (Ed.), *Proceedings of the XIV International Congress of Applied Psychology, Copenhagen 1961.* Vol. II. Copenhagen: Munksgaard, 1962. Pp. 11–39.

McNEMAR, Q. Lost: Our intelligence? Why? *Amer. Psychologist*, 1964, *19*, 871–882.

MADDI, S. R., CHARLENS, A. M., MADDI, DOROTHY-ANNE, & SMITH, ADRIENNE J. Effects of monotony and novelty on imaginative productions. *J. Pers.*, 1962, *30*, 513–527.

MALTZMAN, I. On the training of originality. *Psychol. Rev.*, 1960, *67*, 229–242.

MALTZMAN, I., BELLONI, MARIGOLD, & FISHBEIN, M. Experimental studies of associative variables in originality. *Psychol. Monogr.*, 1964, *78*, No. 3 (Whole No. 580).

MANDLER, G., & SARASON, S. B. A study of anxiety and learning. *J. abnorm. soc. Psychol.*, 1952, *47*, 166–173.

MARSH, R. W. A statistical re-analysis of Getzels and Jackson's data. *Brit. J. educ. Psychol.*, 1964, *34*, 91–93.

MASLOW, A. H. Creativity in self-actualizing people. In H. H. Anderson (Ed.), *Creativity and its cultivation.* New York: Harper, 1959. Pp. 83–95.

MAYER, M. *The schools.* New York: Harper, 1961.

MEDNICK, MARTHA T., MEDNICK, S. A., & JUNG, C. C. Continual association as a function of level of creativity and type of verbal stimulus. *J. abnorm. soc. Psychol.*, 1964, *69*, 511–515.

MEDNICK, MARTHA T., MEDNICK, S. A., & MEDNICK, E. V. Incubation of creative performance and specific associative priming. *J. abnorm. soc. Psychol.*, 1964, *69*, 84–88.

MEDNICK, S. A. The associative basis of the creative process. *Psychol. Rev.*, 1962, *69*, 220–232.

MESSICK, S., & FREDERIKSEN, N. Ability, acquiescence, and "authoritarianism." *Psychol. Rep.*, 1958, *4*, 687–697.

MESSICK, S., & KOGAN, N. Differentiation and compartmentalization in object-sorting measures of categorizing style. *Percept. mot. Skills*, 1963, *16*, 47–51.

MESSICK, S., & KOGAN, N. Category width and quantitative aptitude. *Percept. mot. Skills*, 1965, *20*, 493–497.

MILLER, D. R., & SWANSON, G. E. *Inner conflict and defense.* New York: Holt, Rinehart and Winston, 1960.

MORGAN, C. T. *Student's workbook to accompany introduction to psychology.* New York: McGraw-Hill, 1956.

MURPHY, G., & HOCHBERG, J. Perceptual development: Some tentative hypotheses. *Psychol. Rev.*, 1951, *58*, 332–349.

MYDEN, W. Interpretation and evaluation of certain personality characteristics involved in creative production. *Percept. mot. Skills*, 1959, *9*, 139–158.

NEWELL, A., SHAW, J. C., & SIMON, H. A. The processes of creative thinking. In H. E. Gruber, G. Terrell, & M. Wertheimer (Eds.), *Contemporary approaches to creative thinking.* New York: Atherton, 1962. Pp. 63–119.

OSGOOD, C. E. The cross-cultural generality of visual-verbal synesthetic tendencies. *Behav. Sci.*, 1960, *5*, 146–169.

PANEL ON EDUCATIONAL RESEARCH AND DEVELOPMENT. *Innovation and experiment in education.* Washington, D.C.: U. S. Government Printing Office, 1964.

PETERS, G. A., & MERRIFIELD, P. R. Graphic representation of emotional feelings. *J. clin. Psychol.*, 1958, *14*, 375–378.

PETTIGREW, T. F. The measurement and correlates of category width as a cognitive variable. *J. Pers.*, 1958, *26*, 532–544.

PIERS, ELLEN V., DANIELS, JACQUELINE M., & QUACKENBUSH, J. F. The identification of creativity in adolescents. *J. educ. Psychol.*, 1960, *51*, 346–351.

PINE, F. Thematic drive content and creativity. *J. Pers.*, 1959, *27*, 136–151.

PINE, F., & HOLT, R. R. Creativity and primary process: A study of adaptive regression. *J. abnorm. soc. Psychol.*, 1960, *61*, 370–379.

POFFENBERGER, A. T., & BARROWS, B. E. The feeling value of lines. *J. appl. Psychol.*, 1924, *8*, 187–205.

PORTEUS, S. D. *The maze test and clinical psychology.* Palo Alto, Cal.: Pacific Books, 1959.

PROPST, BARBARA. Openness to experience and originality of productions. Unpublished M.A. thesis, Univer. Chicago, 1962.

RAPAPORT, D., GILL, M., & SCHAFER, R. *Diagnostic psychological testing,* Vol. I. Chicago: Yearbook Publishers, 1945.

REID, J. B., KING, F. J., & WICKWIRE, PAT. Cognitive and other personality characteristics of creative children. *Psychol. Rep.,* 1959, *5,* 729–738.

ROGERS, C. R. A theory of therapy, personality, and interpersonal relationships as developed in the client-centered framework. In S. Koch (Ed.), *Psychology: A study of a science:* Vol. III. *Formulations of the person and the social context.* New York: McGraw-Hill, 1959. Pp. 184–256. (a)

ROGERS, C. R. Toward a theory of creativity. In H. H. Anderson (Ed.), *Creativity and its cultivation.* New York: Harper, 1959. Pp. 69–82. (b)

ROGERS, C. R. Actualizing tendency in relation to "motives" and to consciousness. In M. R. Jones (Ed.), *Nebraska symposium on motivation, 1963.* Lincoln: Univer. Nebraska Press, 1963. Pp. 1–24.

ROSENWALD, G. C. The assessment of anxiety in psychological experimentation: A theoretical reformulation and test. *J. abnorm. soc. Psychol.,* 1961, *62,* 666–673.

RUEBUSH, B. K. Interfering and facilitating effects of test anxiety. *J. abnorm. soc. Psychol.,* 1960, *60,* 205–212.

RUEBUSH, B. K. Anxiety. In H. W. Stevenson (Ed.), *Child psychology: The sixty-second yearbook of the National Society for the Study of Education,* Part I. Chicago: Univer. Chicago Press, 1963. Pp. 460–516.

RUEBUSH, B. K., BYRUM, MILDRED, & FARNHAM, LOUISE J. Problem-solving as a function of children's defensiveness and parental behavior. *J. abnorm. soc. Psychol.,* 1963, *67,* 355–362.

RUEBUSH, B. K., & WAITE, R. R. Oral dependency in anxious and defensive children. *Merrill-Palmer Quart.,* 1961, *7,* 181–190.

RUGG, H. *Imagination.* New York: Harper, 1963.

SARASON, S. B., DAVIDSON, K. S., LIGHTHALL, F. F., WAITE, R. R., & RUEBUSH, B. K. *Anxiety in elementary school children.* New York: Wiley, 1960.

SARASON, S. B., HILL, K. T., & ZIMBARDO, P. G. A longitudinal study of the relation of test anxiety to performance on intelligence and achievement tests. *Monogr. Soc. Res. Child Develpm.,* 1964, *29,* No. 7 (Serial No. 98).

SARBIN, T. R. Role theory. In G. Lindzey (Ed.), *Handbook of social psychology*, Vol. I. Reading, Mass.: Addison-Wesley, 1954. Pp. 223–258.

SARBIN, T. R., & HARDYCK, C. D. Conformance in role perception as a personality variable. *J. consult. Psychol.*, 1955, *19*, 109–111.

SCHAFER, R. Regression in the service of the ego: The relevance of a psychoanalytic concept for personality assessment. In G. Lindzey (Ed.), *Assessment of human motives.* New York: Holt, Rinehart and Winston, 1958. Pp. 119–148.

SCHEERER, M., & LYONS, J. Line drawings and matching responses to words. *J. Pers.*, 1957, *25*, 251–273.

SINGER, J. L. Imagination and waiting ability in young children. *J. Pers.*, 1961, *29*, 396–413.

SLOANE, H. N., GORLOW, L., & JACKSON, D. N. Cognitive styles in equivalence range. *Percept. mot. Skills*, 1963, *16*, 389–404.

SNEDECOR, G. W. *Statistical methods.* (ed. 4) Ames, Iowa: Iowa State Coll. Press, 1946.

SPENCE, K. W. A theory of emotionally based drive (D) and its relation to performance in simple learning situations. *Amer. Psychologist*, 1958, *13*, 131–141.

SPENGLER, J. J. Creativity versus cultural drift. *South Atlantic Quart.*, 1964, *63*, 275–294.

STEIN, M. I., & HEINZE, SHIRLEY J. *Creativity and the individual: Summaries of selected literature in psychology and psychiatry.* New York: Free Press, 1960.

STEINBERG, S. *The labyrinth.* New York: Harper, 1960.

STROOP, J. R. Studies in interference in serial verbal reaction. *J. exp. Psychol.*, 1935, *18*, 643–661.

TAGIURI, R. Movement as a cue in person perception. In H. P. David & J. C. Brengelmann (Eds.), *Perspectives in personality research.* New York: Springer, 1960. Pp. 175–195.

TAJFEL, H., RICHARDSON, A., & EVERSTINE, L. Individual consistencies in categorizing: A study of judgmental behavior. *J. Pers.*, 1964, *32*, 90–108.

TAYLOR, C. W. (Ed.) *Creativity: Progress and potential.* New York: McGraw-Hill, 1964.

TAYLOR, C. W., & BARRON, F. (Eds.) *Scientific creativity: Its recognition and development.* New York: Wiley, 1963.

TAYLOR, D. W. Thinking. In M. H. Marx (Ed.), *Psychological theory: Contemporary readings.* New York: Macmillan, 1963. Pp. 475–493.

TAYLOR, JANET A. A personality scale of manifest anxiety. *J. abnorm. soc. Psychol.*, 1953, *48*, 285–290.

TERMAN, L. M. *Concept mastery test.* New York: Psychol. Corp., 1956.

TERMAN, L. M., & ASSOCIATES. *Genetic studies of genius*: Vol. I. *Mental and physical traits of a thousand gifted children.* Stanford, Cal.: Stanford Univer. Press, 1925.

TERMAN, L. M., & ODEN, M. H. *The gifted child grows up: Twenty-five years' follow-up of a superior group.* Stanford, Cal.: Stanford Univer. Press, 1947.

THOMSON, R. *The psychology of thinking.* Baltimore: Penguin, 1959.

THORNDIKE, R. L. Some methodological issues in the study of creativity. In: *Proceedings of the 1962 invitational conference on testing problems.* Princeton, N. J.: Educational Testing Service, 1963. Pp. 40–54.

THURSTONE, L. L. The factorial isolation of primary abilities. *Psychometrika,* 1936, *1,* 175–182.

THURSTONE, L. L. Primary mental abilities. *Psychometric Monogr.,* No. 1. Chicago: Univer. Chicago Press, 1938.

THURSTONE, L. L. Creative talent. In L. L. Thurstone (Ed.), *Applications of psychology.* New York: Harper, 1952. Pp. 18–37.

TORRANCE, E. P. Educational achievement of the highly intelligent and the highly creative: Eight partial replications of the Getzels-Jackson study. (Research Memorandum BER-60-18.) Minneapolis: Bureau of Educational Research, Univer. Minnesota, 1960.

TORRANCE, E. P. *Guiding creative talent.* Englewood Cliffs, N. J.: Prentice-Hall, 1962.

TORRANCE, E. P. *Education and the creative potential.* Minneapolis: Univer. Minnesota Press, 1963.

TORRANCE, E. P., & GOWAN, J. C. The reliability of the Minnesota tests of creative thinking. (Research Memorandum BER-63-4.) Minneapolis: Bureau of Educational Research, Univer. Minnesota, 1963.

VINACKE, W. E. *The psychology of thinking.* New York: McGraw-Hill, 1952.

VYGOTSKY, L. S. *Thought and language.* New York: Wiley, 1962.

WAITE, R. R. Test performance as a function of anxiety and type of task. Unpublished doctoral dissertation, Yale Univer., 1959.

WAITE, R. R., SARASON, S. B., LIGHTHALL, F. F., & DAVIDSON, K. S. A study of anxiety and learning in children. *J. abnorm. soc. Psychol.,* 1958, *57,* 267–270.

WALLACH, M. A. Commentary: Active-analytical vs. passive-global cognitive functioning. In S. Messick & J. Ross (Eds.), *Measurement in personality and cognition.* New York: Wiley, 1962. Pp. 199–215.

WALLACH, M. A. Research on children's thinking. In H. W. Stevenson (Ed.), *Child psychology: The sixty-second yearbook of the National Society for the Study of Education,* Part I. Chicago: Univer. Chicago Press, 1963. Pp. 236–276.

WALLACH, M. A., & CARON, A. J.   Attribute criteriality and sex-linked conservatism as determinants of psychological similarity. *J. abnorm. soc. Psychol.*, 1959, *59*, 43–50.

WALLACH, M. A., GREEN, L. R., LIPSITT, P. D., & MINEHART, JEAN B. Contradiction between overt and projective personality indicators as a function of defensiveness. *Psychol. Monogr.*, 1962, *76*, No. 1 (Whole No. 520).

WAPNER, S., & WERNER, H.   *Perceptual development.* Worcester, Mass.: Clark Univer. Press, 1957.

WECHSLER, D.   *The measurement of adult intelligence.* Baltimore: Williams and Wilkins, 1944.

WECHSLER, D.   *Wechsler intelligence scale for children: Manual.* New York: Psychol. Corp., 1949.

WERNER, H.   *Comparative psychology of mental development.* Chicago: Follett, 1948.

WERNER, H., & KAPLAN, B.   *Symbol formation.* New York: Wiley, 1963.

WERTHEIMER, M.   *Productive thinking.* New York: Harper, 1959.

WHITE, R. W.   *The abnormal personality.* New York: Ronald, 1956.

WILSON, R. C., GUILFORD, J. P., CHRISTENSEN, P. R., & LEWIS, D. J. A factor-analytic study of creative-thinking abilities. *Psychometrika*, 1954, *19*, 297–311.

WITKIN, H. A., DYK, R. B., FATERSON, H. F., GOODENOUGH, D. R., & KARP, S. A.   *Psychological differentiation.* New York: Wiley, 1962.

WITKIN, H. A., LEWIS, HELEN B., HERTZMAN, M., MACHOVER, KAREN, MEISSNER, PEARL B., & WAPNER, S.   *Personality through perception.* New York: Harper, 1954.

YAMAMOTO, K.   Role of creative thinking and intelligence in high school achievement. *Psychol. Rep.*, 1964, *14*, 783–789. (a)

YAMAMOTO, K.   Threshold of intelligence in academic achievement of highly creative students. *J. exp. Education*, 1964, *32*, 401–405. (b)

YAMAMOTO, K.   A further analysis of the role of creative thinking in high-school achievement. *J. Psychol.*, 1964, *58*, 277–283. (c)

ZIMBARDO, P. G., BARNARD, J. W., & BERKOWITZ, L.   The role of anxiety and defensiveness in children's verbal behavior. *J. Pers.*, 1963, *31*, 79–96.

ZWEIBELSON, I.   Test anxiety and intelligence test performance. *J. consult. Psychol.*, 1956, *20*, 479–481.

≫≫ Index of Names

Abe, C., 5, 9, 22, 288
Adler, A., 263
Alpert, R., 193
Arnheim, R., 146
Asch, S. E., 19, 146, 148
Atkinson, J. W., 270
Austin, G. A., 95, 108, 304

Barnard, J. W., 198, 199
Barnhart, C. L., 30
Barron, F., 2, 69, 70, 201, 202, 203, 288
Barrows, B. E., 148
Bartlett, F., 307
Bartlett, M. S., 62
Beldoch, M., 145, 312
Belloni, Marigold, 309
Berkowitz, L., 198, 199
Berlyne, D. E., 76
Bestor, A., 332
Binet, A., 9
Boneau, C. A., 61, 62
Bousfield, W. A., 18
Box, G. E. P., 60, 61, 62
Brim, O. G., Jr., 304
Brown, R., 104
Brown, W., 41, 44, 124, 166, 216
Bruner, J. S., 90, 95, 96, 98, 99, 108,
    110, 135, 139, 237, 298, 304, 316,
    323, 325, 331
Burks, B. S., 308
Byrum, Mildred, 198, 199

Campbell, D. T., 304
Caron, A. J., 96, 112, 124
Castaneda, A., 190, 191, 197
Charlens, A. M., 76
Christensen, P. R., 11, 12, 18, 101, 288
Clayton, Martha B., 97, 116
Cline, V. B., 4, 5, 9, 22, 288
Condon, C. F., 191
Cooperative Test Division, 38, 39, 40,
    44, 292
Couch, A., 170

Covington, M. V., 321
Cox, F. N., 216, 218
Crowne, D. P., 202, 232
Crutchfield, R. S., 69, 201, 307, 309,
    310, 313, 314, 321

Daniels, Jacqueline M., 67
David, F. N., 61
Davidson, K. S., 190, 193, 198, 206,
    207, 221, 226, 300
Davis, A., 192, 193
Davitz, J., 310, 311
Denny, T., 191
Dentler, R. A., 19
Dexter, L. A., 331
Dodson, J. D., 225, 300, 301, 315
Dryden, J., 13
Duncker, K., 304
Dyk, R. B., 106

Easterbrook, J. A., 202, 236, 237
Edwards, A. L., 311
Eells, K., 192, 193
Einstein, A., 13, 18, 289
Engen, T., 161
Erikson, E. H., 190
Evans, Catherine, 208
Everstine, L., 96, 98

Farnham, Louise J., 198, 199
Faterson, H. F., 106
Feldhusen, J. F., 191
Fillenbaum, S., 96
Fishbein, M., 309
Fiske, D. W., 76, 304
Flavell, J., 313
Flescher, I., 5, 6, 7, 9, 22, 191, 288
Frederiksen, N., 98, 99
Freedman, J. L., 309
French, J. W., 101
Freud, Anna, 196
Freud, S., 190, 196, 204
Frick, J. W., 101

Gardner, R. W., 95, 97, 99, 100, 103, 104, 117, 126, 140
Garwood, Dorothy S., 203, 204
Getzels, J. W., 2, 3, 4, 5, 9, 21, 69, 92, 287, 288, 296
Ghiselin, B., 13, 14
Gill, M., 103, 110
Glass, D. C., 304
Golann, S. E., 2
Goldstein, K., 104
Gombrich, E. H., 147
Goodenough, D. R., 106
Goodman, N., 304
Goodnow, Jacqueline J., 95, 108, 304
Gorlow, L., 97, 100, 117
Gough, H. G., 203
Gowan, J. C., 7, 288
Green, L. R., 197
Gronlund, N. E., 67
Guilford, J. P., 7, 9, 10, 11, 12, 15, 18, 22, 23, 29, 101, 203, 205, 288, 291, 292, 304, 309, 311

Haber, R. N., 193
Haggard, E. A., 73
Hall, K. R. L., 149
Hardyck, C. D., 154
Hartmann, H., 153
Hathaway, S. R., 197
Havel, Joan, 204
Heinze, Shirley J., 2, 189
Henle, Mary, 307, 314
Hertzman, M., 106
Hill, K. T., 192
Hochberg, J., 145
Holland, J. L., 67
Holmes, Frances B., 190
Holt, R. R., 204, 205, 312
Holzman, P. S., 97
Honkavaara, Sylvia, 150, 151
Horsnell, G., 61
Housman, A. E., 13, 18
Houston, J. P., 17
Humphreys, L. G., 305

Inhelder, Bärbel, 110, 313

Jackson, D. N., 97, 99, 100, 103, 116, 117, 170
Jackson, P. W., 2, 3, 4, 5, 9, 21, 69, 92, 287, 288, 296
Jensen, D. W., 308

Jersild, A. T., 190
Johnson, D. M., 303, 307
Johnson, N. L., 61
Jung, C. C., 308, 309

Kagan, J., 105, 106, 107, 108, 109, 110, 117, 124, 135, 140, 141, 198, 226, 296, 316
Kaplan, B., 143, 144, 145, 147, 148
Karp, S. A., 106
Kates, S. L., 104
Keniston, K., 170
Kennedy, K., 104
King, F. J., 67, 191
Klein, G. S., 95, 97, 237
Koestler, A., 308
Kogan, N., 98, 100, 101, 104, 124, 126, 206, 219, 229, 237, 304
Köhler, W., 146
Korchin, S. J., 202, 236
Krauss, R., 148, 149
Kris, E., 153, 202, 204
Kubie, L. S., 202
Kuder, G. F., 44

Lavin, D. E., 304
Leaper, P. M., 216, 218
Leary, T., 204
Levy, N., 161
Levy, Phyllis K., 310, 311
Lewis, D. J., 12, 288
Lewis, Helen B., 106
Lightfoot, Marjorie, 161
Lighthall, F. F., 190, 192, 193, 300
Linton, Harriet, 97
Lipsitt, P. D., 197
Long, R. I., 97
Lorge, I., 199
Lundholm, H., 148, 149
Lyons, J., 148, 149

McCandless, B. R., 190, 191
McConnell, T. R., 208
McGaughran, L. S., 104
McGee, R. K., 98
Machover, Karen, 106
McKinley, J. C., 197
MacKinnon, D. W., 68, 201, 203
Mackler, B., 19
McNemar, Q., 305
Maddi, Dorothy-Anne, 76
Maddi, S. R., 76

Maltzman, I., 304, 309
Mandler, G., 190, 193
Marlowe, D., 202, 232
Marsh, R. W., 4
Maslow, A. H., 202
Mayer, M., 331
Mednick, E. V., 321
Mednick, Martha T., 308, 309, 321
Mednick, S. A., 13, 14, 16, 17, 20, 289, 304, 308, 309, 321
Meissner, Pearl B., 106
Merrifield, P. R., 101, 148
Messick, S., 97, 98, 99, 100, 101, 103, 104, 126, 170
Miller, D. R., 26, 198, 211
Minehart, Jean B., 197
Moran, L. J., 104
Morgan, C. T., 161
Moss, H. A., 105, 106, 107, 110, 117, 124, 198, 296
Mozart, W. A., 13
Murphy, G., 145
Myden, W., 205

Needham, W. E., 4, 5, 9, 22, 288
Newell, A., 307

Occam, W., of, 288
Oden, M. H., 308
Oldfield, R. G., 149
Olver, Rose R., 110, 139, 298
Osgood, C. E., 149, 151
Otis, A. S., 192, 193

Palermo, D. S., 190, 191
Panel on Educational Research and Development, 323
Peters, G. A., 148
Pettigrew, T. F., 96, 97, 98, 99, 112, 124, 140, 141, 246
Piaget, J., 110, 312, 313
Piers, Ellen V., 67
Pine, F., 204, 205, 312
Poffenberger, A. T., 148
Poincaré, H., 13, 18
Porteus, S. D., 194, 199
Preston, J. H., 14
Propst, Barbara S., 78

Quackenbush, J. F., 67

Rapaport, D., 103, 104, 110
Reid, J. B., 67, 68, 191

Richards, J. M., Jr., 4, 5, 9, 22, 288
Richardson, A., 96, 98
Richardson, M. W., 44
Rogers, C. R., 19, 196, 197, 202
Rorschach, H., 203, 204, 205, 312
Rosenwald, G. C., 198, 199, 202, 237
Ruebush, B. K., 189, 190, 192, 194, 196, 197, 198, 199, 300
Rugg, H., 19, 290

Sarason, S. B., 190, 192, 193, 194, 195, 197, 198, 201, 206, 207, 216, 218, 221, 225, 226, 229, 234, 235, 247, 248, 249, 300
Sarbin, T. R., 154, 155
Schafer, R., 103, 110, 153, 202
Scheerer, M., 104, 148, 149
Schlosberg, H., 161
Schoen, R. A., 97, 100, 103, 104, 126
Sedgewick, C. H. W., 18
Shaw, J. C., 307
Sigel, I. E., 105, 106, 107, 110, 117, 124, 296
Simon, H. A., 307
Singer, J. L., 84
Sloane, H. N., 97, 100, 117
Smith, Adrienne J., 76
Snedecor, G. W., 60, 230
Spearman, C., 2, 41, 44, 76, 124, 166, 216
Spence, D. P., 97
Spence, K. W., 190
Spengler, J. J., 332
Stein, Gertrude, 14
Stein, M. I., 2, 189
Steinberg, S., 161
Stroop, J. R., 194
Swanson, G. E., 26, 198, 211

Tagiuri, R., 35, 150, 158
Tajfel, H., 96, 98, 99, 237
Taylor, C. W., 2
Taylor, D. W., 304
Taylor, Janet A., 190
Terman, L. M., 203, 308
Thomson, R., 303
Thorndike, R. L., 4, 10, 11, 12, 68, 199, 288
Thurstone, L. L., 2, 202, 305
Torrance, E. P., 7, 8, 9, 20, 22, 68, 69, 288

Vinacke, W. E., 303
Vygotsky, L. S., 110

Waite, R. R., 190, 193, 194, 198, 300
Wallach, M. A., 96, 98, 106, 112, 124, 197, 198, 206, 219, 229, 237, 304, 313
Wapner, S., 106, 145
Wechsler, D., 7, 10, 20, 28, 38, 39, 44, 103, 199, 213, 264, 292
Werner, H., 143, 144, 145, 146, 147, 148
Wertheimer, M., 307, 314

White, R. W., 196
Wickwire, Pat, 67, 191
Wilson, R. C., 12, 18, 288
Witkin, H. A., 106, 124, 194, 226, 316
Wolfe, T., 13, 18

Yamamoto, K., 7, 8
Yerkes, R. M., 225, 300, 301, 315

Zimbardo, P. G., 192, 198, 199, 200
Zimmerman, W. S., 311
Zweibelson, I., 192

➤➤➤ Index of Subjects

Abstraction in conceptualizing, *see* Conceptualizing, abstraction in

Accuracy–inaccuracy in conceptualizing, *see* Conceptualizing, accuracy–inaccuracy in

Acquiescence response style, 98, 170–171, 180–181, 299–300

Age of subjects, 26–27, 62–63

Alternate uses task, 31–32, 333

Analysis of variance technique, 60–62

Analytic-descriptive concepts, *see* Descriptive-analytic concepts

Anxiety, and defensiveness, 189–252, 300–303
  measure of, 208
  other studies on, 189–196, 206–207
  see also Self-report measures

Applications, for education, *see* Education, implications and applications for

Associates, number and uniqueness of, 13–20, 24–25, 28–37, 41–65, 289–293, 308–310

Associational conception of creativity, *see* Associates, number and uniqueness of

"Associative play," 13, 18, 289

Band width, measure of, 112–116, 333
  see also Categorizing

Behavior ratings, 66–94, 293–296
  and modes of thinking, 76–94, 138, 140, 182–183, 185, 293–296
  and other personality indicators, 220–222
  other studies on, 66–70
  procedure for, *see* Procedure, for behavior ratings
  results and interpretation for, *see* Results and interpretation, for behavior ratings
  scales used for, 71–72, 333

Behavioral observations, *see* Behavior ratings

"Bisociation," 308

Bizarre emotive attributions for stick figures task, 164–166, 333

Breadth of categorizing, *see* Categorizing

California Psychological Inventory, 203

California Test of Mental Maturity, 4–6, 107

Case reports, *see* Clinical reports

Categorical-inferential concepts, *see* Inferential-categorical concepts

Categorizing, and conceptualizing, 95–142, 296–299
  and modes of thinking, 128–132, 138–142, 298–299
  other studies on, 96–102
  procedure for, *see* Procedure, for categorizing tasks
  results and interpretation for, *see* Results and interpretation, for categorizing and conceptualizing tasks
  and self-report measures, 236–239

Category Width Test, 96–99
  see also Band width, measure of

Children's Manifest Anxiety Scale, 190–191, 197

Children's thinking, implications for the study of, *see* Thinking, implications for the study of

Clinical reports, 253–285, 303
  boys, 254–270
  girls, 270–285

Cognitive styles, *see* Categorizing, and conceptualizing

"Combinatory play," 13, 18, 289

Compartmentalization, *see* Categorizing

Composition of creativity and intelligence groups, 58–61

Concept Mastery Test, 70, 203

Conceptual differentiation, *see* Categorizing

Conceptualizing, abstraction in, 103–105, 110
accuracy–inaccuracy in, 104–105
and categorizing, *see* Categorizing, and conceptualizing
and modes of thinking, 132–142, 182, 296–298
other studies on, 102–111
procedure for, *see* Procedure, for conceptualizing tasks
results and interpretation for, *see* Results and interpretation, for categorizing and conceptualizing tasks
and self-report measures, 239–241

Context of task, *see* Task context

Convergent thinking, 15, 77, 80, 89, 223, 241–242, 244, 306, 309–310, 312
in relation to divergent thinking, *see* Creativity, in relation to intelligence

Creativity, instruments for assessing, *see* Procedure, for creativity tasks
in relation to intelligence, 1–65, 287–293
results and interpretation for, *see* Results and interpretation, for creativity and intelligence tasks

Criticalness response style, 98–99

Davis-Eells task, 192–193

Defensiveness, and anxiety, *see* Anxiety, and defensiveness
measure of, 209–210
other studies on, 196–207
see also Self-report measures

Defensiveness Scale for Children, 197–198, 218
see also Procedure, for self-report measures

Denial, *see* Defensiveness

Descriptive-analytic concepts, 105–110, 117–119

Dimensionality within the creativity domain, *see* Generality within the creativity and intelligence domains

"Discovery method," 323, 330

Divergent thinking, 9–12, 15, 77, 80, 89, 223–224, 241, 309–310, 312

Divergent thinking (*continued*)
in relation to convergent thinking, *see* Creativity, in relation to intelligence

Education, implications and applications for, 319–332

Edwards Personal Preference Schedule, 311

Ego-centered orientation, 19, 64
see also Task context

Embedded Figures Test, 194

Emotive connotations of abstract patterns task, 160–164, 333

Equivalence range, measure of, 116–117, 333
see also Categorizing

Evaluative task context, *see* Task context

Expressive properties, *see* Physiognomic sensitivity

Fantasy measure, and behavior ratings, 222
and modes of thinking, 226–229, 251–252
procedure for, *see* Procedure, for fantasy measure
results and interpretation for, *see* Results and interpretation, for self-report and fantasy measures

"Formal operations," 312–313

Free descriptions of paths task, 158–160, 333

Free descriptions of stick figures task, 154–158, 333

G concept, 2–3, 6, 20, 305

Gamelike task context, *see* Task context

General Anxiety Scale for Children, 190, 197–198
see also Procedure, for self-report measures

Generality within the creativity and intelligence domains, 2–13, 45–56, 287–293

Gradients of associative response strength, 15–18

Guessing game, *see* Band width, measure of

Guilford-Zimmerman Temperament Survey, 311

"Halo-effect" in rating, 66–68, 76, 86, 94

Implications, for education, *see* Education, implications and applications for
for the study of children's thinking, *see* Thinking, implications for the study of
Individual children, studies of, *see* Clinical reports
"Inductive teaching," *see* "Discovery method"
Inferential-categorical concepts, 105–110, 117–119
Instances task, 29–31, 333
Intelligence, instruments for assessing, *see* Procedure, for intelligence tasks
in relation to creativity, *see* Creativity, in relation to intelligence
results and interpretation for, *see* Results and interpretation, for creativity and intelligence tasks
IQ, in relation to creativity, *see* Creativity, in relation to intelligence

Leary Interpersonal Check List, 204
Lie scale, 197–198
Lightfoot series, 161
Line meanings task, 35–36, 158, 333
Lorge-Thorndike Intelligence Test, 199

Manifest Anxiety Scale, 190
Matching game, *see* Emotive connotations of abstract patterns task
Maturity of story endings, *see* Fantasy measure
Minnesota Multiphasic Personality Inventory (MMPI), 202–203, 311
Minnesota T-S-E Inventory, 208

Number of associates, *see* Associates, number and uniqueness of

Object-Sorting Test, 97
see also Equivalence range, measure of
Observations of behavior, *see* Behavior ratings
Otis tests, 192–193
Overview of findings, 287–303

Paths task, *see* Free descriptions of paths task
Pattern meanings task, 33–35, 333
Permissive task context, *see* Task context
Physiognomic sensitivity, 143–188, 299–300, 310–312
definition of, 144–145
and modes of thinking, 152–153, 171–188, 299–300
other studies on, 147–152
procedure for, *see* Procedure, for physiognomic sensitivity tasks
results and interpretation for, *see* Results and interpretation, for physiognomic sensitivity tasks
and self-report measures, 241–247
views on etiology of, 145–147
Picture game, *see* Equivalence range, measure of
Playful task context, *see* Task context
Porteus mazes, 194, 199
Procedure, for behavior ratings, 71–74
for categorizing tasks, 112–117
for conceptualizing tasks, 117–124
for creativity tasks, 28–37
for fantasy measure, 211–216, 333
general characteristics of, 26–28
for intelligence tasks, 38–40
for physiognomic sensitivity tasks, 153–167
for self-report measures, 207–211, 333
Productivity of associates, *see* Associates, number and uniqueness of

Ratings of observed behavior, *see* Behavior ratings
Reasons for object sortings, 117–119
Relational-thematic concepts, 105–111, 117–119
Reliability, of band-width task, 116
of behavior ratings, 73–74
of bizarre emotive attributions for stick figures task, 166–167
of creativity instruments, 41–44
of emotive connotations of abstract patterns task, 166–167
of equivalence range task, 117
of fantasy measure, 216
of free descriptions of paths task, 159, 166–167

Reliability (*continued*)
of free descriptions of stick figures task, 157, 166–167
of intelligence instruments, 44
of reasons for object sortings, 118
of self-report measures, 208
of thematic integration task, 123–124
Remote Associates Test, 14, 308–309
Repression, *see* Defensiveness
Results and interpretation, for behavior ratings, 74–94, 182–183, 185, 293–296
for categorizing and conceptualizing tasks, 124–142, 182, 296–299
for creativity and intelligence tasks, 41–65, 291–293
for physiognomic sensitivity tasks, 167–188, 299–300, 302
for self-report and fantasy measures, 216–252, 300–302
Rorschach test, 203–205, 312

Sample, description of, *see* Procedure, general characteristics of
School and College Ability Tests, 28, 38–40, 292, 306, 333
Self-report measures, and behavior ratings, 220–222
and categorizing and conceptualizing, 236–241
and modes of thinking, 222–226, 229–236, 247–252, 300–302
and physiognomic sensitivity, 241–247, 302
procedure for, *see* Procedure, for self-report measures
results and interpretation for, *see* Results and interpretation, for self-report and fantasy measures
Sensitivity to physiognomic properties, *see* Physiognomic sensitivity
Sequential Tests of Educational Progress, 28, 38, 40, 292, 306, 333
Setting, general characterization of, *see* Procedure, general characteristics of
Sex differences, on behavior ratings, 74–76, 84, 92–94
on categorizing and conceptualizing tasks, 124–126
on creativity and intelligence instruments, 56–59

Sex differences (*continued*)
on physiognomic sensitivity tasks, 167–168
on self-report and fantasy measures, 216–218
Similarities task, 32–33, 333
Social extraversion, measure of, 210–211
Social psychology of testing situation, 17–24, 289
see also Task context
Socio-economic status of subjects, 26–27
Stick figure game, *see* Free descriptions of stick figures task
see also Bizarre emotive attributions for stick figures task
Story endings, *see* Fantasy measure
Story tasks, *see* Fantasy measure
see also Thematic integration task
Stroop Color-Word Test, 194
Subjects, description of, *see* Procedure, general characteristics of

Task-centered orientation, 19, 64
see also Task context
Task context, 2, 11–12, 17–24, 27–30, 37, 56, 64, 80, 101, 112, 155, 165–166, 192–196, 199–200, 204, 213–214, 235–236, 244, 246, 248–249, 289–292, 304–310, 313–315, 317–332
Telling stories task, *see* Thematic integration task
Temporal constraint and flexibility, 17–24, 30, 37, 56, 64, 101, 192, 194–195, 289–292, 304
see also Task context
Temporal flexibility, *see* Temporal constraint and flexibility
Test anxiety, measure of, 209
Test Anxiety Scale for Children, 190, 192, 197–198
see also Procedure, for self-report measures
Test defensiveness, measure of, 210
Testing context, *see* Task context
Testlike context, *see* Task context
Thematic Apperception Test (TAT), 100, 204–205
Thematic concepts, *see* Relational-thematic concepts

Thematic integration task, 120–124, 333
Thinking, implications for the study of, 303–319
Time pressure, *see* Temporal constraint and flexibility

Uniqueness of associates, *see* Associates, number and uniqueness of

Verbal vs. visual indices of creativity, 7–8, 19–20, 37, 45, 50, 290–291

Visual vs. verbal indices of creativity, *see* Verbal vs. visual indices of creativity

Wechsler Adult Intelligence Scale, 199
Wechsler Intelligence Scale for Children, 7, 10, 28, 38–39, 213, 264, 266, 292, 306, 333
"What I am like" task, *see* Procedure, for self-report measures

Yerkes-Dodson law, 225, 300–301, 315